Do Y
in Roc

MW01283700

Do You Believe in Rock and Roll?

Essays on Don McLean's "American Pie"

Edited by
RAYMOND I. SCHUCK *and*
RAY SCHUCK

McFarland & Company, Inc., Publishers
Jefferson, North Carolina, and London

LIBRARY OF CONGRESS CATALOGUING-IN-PUBLICATION DATA

Do you believe in rock and roll? : essays on Don McLean's "American pie" / edited by Raymond I. Schuck and Ray Schuck.
      p.   cm.
     Includes bibliographical references and index.
    ISBN 978-0-7864-7105-8
    softcover : acid free paper ∞

    1. McLean, Don, 1945– American pie (Song) 2. Rock music — United States — History and criticism. I. Schuck, Raymond I., 1972–   II. Schuck, Ray, 1950–
ML420.M34183D6 2012
781.66092 — dc23
[B]   2012031706

BRITISH LIBRARY CATALOGUING DATA ARE AVAILABLE

On the cover: Don McLean, 1973 (Photofest)

Manufactured in the United States of America

McFarland & Company, Inc., Publishers
  Box 611, Jefferson, North Carolina 28640
   www.mcfarlandpub.com

For Mary Ann Schuck (1946–2010), who left us in body during this project, but whose spirit watches over these pages and without whom this project never would have happened.

Table of Contents

"American Pie" ix

Preface 1

Introduction: Far from Dry, Far from Gone
 RAYMOND I. SCHUCK *and* RAY SCHUCK 9

1. A Long, Long Time Ago: A Lyrical Interpretation
 JOSEPH E. BURNS 15

2. A Line by Line Analysis of a Classic Song
 RAY SCHUCK 49

3. The Perception of Race in Rock and Roll
 RICHARD J. MCGOWAN 76

4. Lyrical History: There Is More to Music Than Making
 the People Dance?!
 RUSS CRAWFORD 87

5. Eight-and-a-Half Minutes Is a Long, Long Time
 WILLIAM B. ROBISON 100

6. Rock and Roll Grows Up
 HARRY EDWIN EISS 135

7. A Generation Lost in Space
 ROBERT MCPARLAND 150

8. A Tale of Two Sagas
 RAYMOND I. SCHUCK 157

Bibliography 173

About the Contributors 195

Index 197

"American Pie"

A long, long time ago,
I can still remember
How that music used to make me smile.
And I knew if I had my chance
That I could make those people dance
And maybe they'd be happy for a while.
But February made me shiver
With every paper I'd deliver.
Bad news on the doorstep,
I couldn't take one more step.
I can't remember if I cried
When I read about his widowed bride,
But something touched me deep inside
The day the music died.

So, bye, bye, Miss American Pie.
Drove my Chevy to the levee,
But the levee was dry,
And them good old boys were drinkin' whiskey in Rye,
Singin', "This'll be the day that I die."
"This'll be the day that I die."

Did you write the book of love,
And do you have faith in God above,
If the Bible tells you so?
Do you believe in rock and roll,
Can music save your mortal soul,
And can you teach me how to dance real slow?
Well, I know that you're in love with him
'Cause I saw you dancin' in the gym.
You both kicked off your shoes.
Man, I dig those rhythm and blues.

I was a lonely teenage broncin' buck
With a pink carnation and a pickup truck,
But I knew I was out of luck
The day the music died.
I started singin',

Bye, bye, Miss American Pie.
Drove my Chevy to the levee,
But the levee was dry.
Them good old boys were drinkin' whiskey in Rye,
Singin', "This'll be the day that I die."
"This'll be the day that I die."

Now for ten years we've been on our own,
And moss grows fat on a rollin' stone,
But that's not how it used to be
When the jester sang for the king and queen
In a coat he borrowed from James Dean
And a voice that came from you and me.
Oh, and while the king was looking down,
The jester stole his thorny crown.
The courtroom was adjourned.
No verdict was returned.
And while Lenin [Lennon] read a book of Marx,
The quartet practiced in the park,
And we sang dirges in the dark
The day the music died.
We were singing...

Bye, bye, Miss American Pie.
Drove my Chevy to the levee,
But the levee was dry.
Them good old boys were drinkin' whiskey in Rye,
Singin', "This'll be the day that I die."
"This'll be the day that I die."

Helter Skelter in a summer swelter.
The birds flew off with a fallout shelter,
Eight miles high and falling fast.
It landed foul on the grass.
The players tried for a forward pass,
With the jester on the sidelines in a cast.
Now the halftime air was sweet perfume
While the sergeants played a marching tune.
We all got up to dance,

Oh, but we never got the chance!
'Cause the players tried to take the field.
The marching band refused to yield.
Do you recall what was revealed
The day the music died?
We started singing...

Bye, bye, Miss American Pie.
Drove my Chevy to the levee,
But the levee was dry.
Them good old boys were drinkin' whiskey in Rye,
Singin', "This'll be the day that I die."
"This'll be the day that I die."

Oh, and there we were all in one place,
A generation lost in space
With no time left to start again.
So come on, Jack be nimble, Jack be quick!
Jack Flash sat on a candlestick
'Cause fire is the devil's only friend.
Oh, and as I watched him on the stage
My hands were clenched in fists of rage.
No angel born in hell
Could break that Satan's spell.
And as the flames climbed high into the night
To light the sacrificial rite,
I saw Satan laughing with delight
The day the music died.
He was singing,

Bye, bye, Miss American Pie.
Drove my Chevy to the levee,
But the levee was dry.
Them good old boys were drinkin' whiskey in Rye,
Singin', "This'll be the day that I die."
"This'll be the day that I die."

I met a girl who sang the blues
And I asked her for some happy news,
But she just smiled and turned away.
I went down to the sacred store
Where I'd heard the music years before,
But the man there said the music wouldn't play.
And in the streets the children screamed,
The lovers cried, and the poets dreamed.

But not a word was spoken.
The church bells all were broken.
And the three men I admire most,
The Father, Son, and the Holy Ghost,
They caught the last train for the coast
The day the music died.
And they were singing,

Bye, bye, Miss American Pie.
Drove my Chevy to the levee,
But the levee was dry,
And them good old boys were drinkin' whiskey in Rye,
Singin', "This'll be the day that I die."
"This'll be the day that I die."

They were singing,
Bye, bye, Miss American Pie.
Drove my Chevy to the levee,
But the levee was dry.
Them good old boys were drinkin' whiskey in Rye,
Singin', "This'll be the day that I die."

Preface

As university professors and instructors, the individuals who have contributed to this book engage in both teaching and research as two of the three pillars (the other being service) upon which academic careers are traditionally based. Typically, a scholar's teaching assignments and research projects go hand in hand. One teaches what one studies, and one studies what one teaches. In the process, what begins as a research project often finds its way into one's teaching practices and assignments, while what one teaches often leads to new ideas for research. Fittingly, then, this book began not as a research project, but as a classroom activity — specifically as one of the editors, Ray Schuck (hereafter through most of this Preface known as "Ray," as opposed to Raymond I. Schuck, who will hereafter be designated as "Raymond"), began to incorporate Don McLean's "American Pie" into history courses that he taught at Ohio Northern University in Ada, Ohio.

At times in his history courses, Ray has sought to demonstrate how music is an important part of most, if not all, cultures. It can range from forms of simple communication to forms of large-scale celebration. Individually and collectively, it can inspire, strengthen, sadden, and provide a host of other attitudes and emotions that serve to define both the music and the society in which it is produced. From the simple tapping of fingers on a table to the melodious raucous cries of military charges, music infects the human spirit and psyche in a way many other forms of external sensory stimuli cannot. This cultural influence of music has led Ray to perform music in some form in his courses, specifically in his public history course. He chooses music to help identify specific time periods, showing how lifestyles and events of specific eras were both reflected in and influenced by the music. As an example, Ray often refers to the music of the 1960s. Playing his twelve-string guitar, he performs several songs of the period and talks about what was happening in American society at the time. Along with the music, Ray and his students engage in discussions about the lyrics of the particular song and what was occurring in America, and even around the world, at the time.

1

After Ray started to utilize music in this way, invariably students began to ask if he knew the song "American Pie" and asked him to perform it — the first time in 1998, almost thirty years after the song's release! As he performed the song, many of the students sang along. After the song was finished, questions followed. What did this mean? What did that mean? As his classes took up these questions, Ray realized that, while he knew the song, he really didn't "know," fully understand, or even fully appreciate it. Wanting to understand the song more fully for his performance, Ray started a search for the meaning to the lyrics of "American Pie."

Ray's search was slow, methodical, and scientific. He studied and thought about the song as a whole, then took it apart word by word. He mulled it over for weeks, months, and even years, tossing out probabilities and sometimes retrieving those same probabilities. He mixed possibilities and looked at their presence in the song, along with the rhyme and meter of the song, in an attempt to find some "new" discovery. He researched every aspect of the song from what others had conceived and thought the meaning to be. He worked it in the abstract and the concrete, and he sought to leave no stone unturned in his investigation. And, with each year that he performed the song in class and received the same request for its performance (after a few years he simply added it to his repertoire), he added to what he had found. Students would inquire about his interpretation or make suggestions that the class would discuss as possibilities.

After ten years of research, study, discussion, and reflection, Ray decided to write the interpretations down and call it quits — not because his mind couldn't handle any more thought of the song and its meanings, but because the song "felt" and appeared correct or as correct as any interpretation could be without definitive documentation. That written interpretation became the basis for Ray's essay that appears in this book.

Soon after writing this interpretation, as Ray started looking into possibilities for trying to publish his essay, Ray happened to mention what he was considering to his son, Raymond. As the two talked about Ray's interpretation and some thoughts on what Ray might do to proceed, they raised the possibility of putting together a book of essays. As Ray mentioned to Raymond, while "American Pie" had been treated to a host of interpretations by various folks, amazingly enough, despite its popularity and apparent cultural significance, it had not been the subject of much scholarly work. Given that, it would stand to reason, they agreed, that such scholarly attention was long past due, and a book of essays that treated the subject seemed like a proper way to do it.

They already knew that they likely had one person whom they could ask. Richard J. McGowan, a long-time family friend who teaches at Butler

University, had already talked to Ray about an interpretation he held of the song that connected it to the deaths of three civil rights movement workers in Mississippi in 1964, which made national news. Meanwhile, given his enjoyment of both *Star Wars* and "Weird Al" Yankovic, the Generation X member Raymond figured he could write something on Yankovic's parody of the song in "The Saga Begins." Surely, they figured, they could find others who would agree on the need for more scholarship on "American Pie" and want to add to a volume of essays about the song. So, in the spring of 2009, Ray and Raymond began to solicit manuscripts for a volume on "American Pie." They sought both contributions that would offer interpretations of the song and contributions that would offer discussion of the cultural significance of the song, both within its time period in the early 1970s and in the four decades since.

Calls for contributions furthered Ray and Raymond's resolve that this project warranted development, as a number of individuals responded to the calls by indicating that while they did not have essays to contribute, they would definitely be interested in purchasing the book should it become available. These folks related stories to Ray and Raymond of memories of "American Pie," places in which they had seen references to "American Pie," and ways that they had used "American Pie" in their lives and even in their own classrooms. Meanwhile, Joseph E. Burns of Southeastern Louisiana University and Robert McParland of Felician College each sent Ray and Raymond an abstract for an essay for the volume that fit very well within the project as Ray and Raymond had conceived it. Burns' abstract, which he accompanied with a CD of a lecture he gave detailing the many references contained in "American Pie" as he had come to see them, offered an interpretation of the song that would make a nice complement to Ray's essay. McParland's abstract offered something very important for the cultural significance part of the book, as he proposed to discuss the generational memory inscribed within the song. Both seemed like excellent additions to the project, and Ray and Raymond happily welcomed them aboard.

At the same time, Ray, Raymond, and McGowan had begun discussing the project with another longtime friend, Harry Edwin Eiss of Eastern Michigan University, as the group of four talked about reviving their old practice of attending the Popular Culture Association/American Culture Association Annual Meeting together by meeting in St. Louis, Missouri, for the conference that was scheduled for April 2010. Ray, Raymond, and McGowan were thinking of proposing a panel or two based on the papers Ray and Raymond received for the "American Pie" project, and Eiss expressed an interest in writing a piece connecting "American Pie" to experimentation in art in the 1960s and early 1970s. Ray and Raymond welcomed Harry aboard for the project, and they began plans for panels on "American Pie" for St. Louis. Those plans materialized into a four-paper panel featuring Burns, Ray, McGowan, and Raymond titled "The Interpretation and Significance of Don McLean's 'American Pie.'"

The panel was a tremendous success. Meanwhile, as Ray and Raymond continued to put the volume together, they also found two more contributors for it in a couple of historians. Burns put Ray and Raymond in touch with his colleague at Southeastern Louisiana, William B. Robison, who expressed interest in writing a piece for the project that would situate "American Pie" within experimental trends in rock and popular music at the time of the song's release. Meanwhile, Ray's colleague at Ohio Northern University, Russ Crawford, proposed an essay that would also situate the song historically, but in this case within the tradition of songs that narrate conditions of musical production. Ray and Raymond gladly accepted both pieces, in the process producing the octet of essays that comprise the volume that lies ahead.

These eight authors represent four disciplines, with Ray, Crawford, and Robison representing history; Raymond and Burns representing communication; McParland and Eiss representing English; and McGowan representing philosophy. This disciplinary spread allows this book to have the kind of interdisciplinary scope and appeal that Ray and Raymond originally hoped it would have. That interdisciplinary scope demonstrates that, as Ray and Raymond suspected, the song warrants further discussion from various perspectives and angles, emanating from various fields of study. This volume of essays seeks to address that exigency, and it does so by proceeding through two interrelated themes for analysis that provide an overall structure for the book.

First, the book's initial three essays offer interpretations of the song. The first two offer interpretations of the song's lyrics that are at once competing and complementary. In the initial essay, Burns provides an extensive analysis of the many intertextual references that occur throughout "American Pie," with an eye on how these references relate to one another to construct an overall story for the song. Burns situates his interpretation within his extensive knowledge of music history and the music industry, which informs his reading of passages throughout the song that offer textual clues toward the cohesive narrative that "American Pie" offers. Then, Ray Schuck turns his historian's gaze toward the song to offer a different interpretation of the song's references. Schuck frames his interpretation through historical inference, whereby he acknowledges the intentional vagueness of the song and suggests that the use of concurrent, similar, or implied evidence from both the song itself as a text and the song's historical context provides a firm basis for determining the meaning of the narrative. Both Burns and Schuck seek to contextualize the lyrics of "American Pie" using very similar yet slightly different methodologies and coming to some very similar yet at times quite different interpretations.

In the third essay, Richard J. McGowan provides a third interpretation of the song, with this one focusing specifically on the song's refrain, which McGowan argues situates the song as a narrative about the three civil rights movement workers who were killed on August 6, 1964, in Neshoba County, Mississippi. McGowan suggests that as "American Pie" recounts the news of the workers' murders and McLean's reaction to the news, it articulates a sentiment of universal human community based in the experience of growing old. Engaging the philosophical claims from an essay by Michael Baur that analyzes the song, McGowan contends that "American Pie" transcends cultural limitation and provides a sense of hope that working together can overcome the kinds of disillusioning experiences that have included not only rock 'n' roll in the 1960s, but also events like bigoted and violent responses to the civil rights movement that occurred in situations such as the August 1964 murders.

While McGowan's piece offers an interpretation of the song and suggests a transcendent theme to the song, it also begins the movement of this book toward its second overarching theme, which takes more precedence in the five remaining essays: contextualization of the song and its meaning, particularly as that meaning demonstrates the song's cultural significance. McGowan situates the song within the context of the 1964 murders of the three civil rights movement workers. Similarly, in essay number 4, Russ Crawford offers both interpretation and contextualization. Crawford suggests that "American Pie," more than just offering the story of the development of rock 'n' roll, provides a historical account of the history of the music industry. This places the song into the genre of texts that document the development of music — a genre with a long tradition dating at least to 800 B.C. and continuing through to recent years, as evidenced in Nickelback's 2006-2007 hit song "Rockstar." Crawford's essay thus offers an alternative way of interpreting the meaning of "American Pie" by suggesting that it can be read most fully as a history of the music industry. Yet, Crawford more heavily addresses the context of engaging in such an interpretation by examining how "American Pie" correlates with other songs that have represented the genre of historical-account songs throughout the history of popular music.

Essays numbered 5 and 6 also offer further contextualization of the song, situating "American Pie" within the period of experimentation in art, music, and culture that was occurring in the United States and the world at the time that the song was written and released. In the fifth essay, William B. Robison, like Crawford, specifically examines "American Pie" within the context of the music industry. Robison, though, focuses on the music-cultural trends that were occurring within the industry that influenced the production of McLean's song. Robison argues that trends in experimentation within the music industry made possible the success of "American Pie" and that "American Pie" provides a useful and significant representative example of the development of these trends at that time period.

In essay number 6, Harry Edwin Eiss also contextualizes "American Pie" within trends of experimentation; however, Eiss broadens the scope of analysis to look at how trends in creative experimentation were occurring beyond just the music industry. More specifically, Eiss shows how experimentation in the music world mirrored experimentation during the same time period in the world of art in general, including painting, performance art, Pop Art, and more. Eiss also demonstrates how these two fields collided during the 1960s as artists and musicians collaborated to produce multiple forms of creative expressions and experiences. Ultimately, in a counterpoint to the other essays in this volume, Eiss suggests that perhaps "American Pie" is not particularly significant, given all of the cross-pollination and experimentation that occurred in music and art at the time.

In the seventh essay, Robert McParland also acknowledges the time period of the song as well as the practice of experimentation that was occurring at the time; however, McParland focuses on how the song serves as a form of cultural memory based in generational identity. Like McGowan, McParland suggests that "American Pie" offers a message about community, and like Crawford and Robison, McParland contextualizes "American Pie" within the musical styles from which it draws. McParland, though, situates his analysis much more fully within the experiences of the generation who, like McLean, grew up alongside the development of rock 'n' roll and experienced national and world events that influenced the narrative presented in McLean's song.

Generational memory also plays a significant role in the final essay of this volume — Raymond I. Schuck's analysis in number 8, which argues that the nostalgic narrative offered to a generational community in "American Pie" serves as a template for telling similar kinds of stories. Schuck illustrates the effectiveness of McLean's song as such a template by showing how "Weird Al" Yankovic's parody of "American Pie" in his 1999 song "The Saga Begins" tells the story of *Star Wars Episode I: The Phantom Menace* by relying on similar patterns of nostalgia and intertextuality as "American Pie." In the case of Yankovic's song, the audience consists largely of a generational community built around growing up with *Star Wars*, not the beginnings of rock 'n' roll, as the dominant narrative of its youth. Schuck contends that Yankovic's parody works successfully because it remains true as a narrative to *Star Wars*, to Yankovic's previous work, and to "American Pie" as a template for telling a saga tale.

These eight essays came together through some of the very same kinds of interpersonal relationships and social resonances that provide the basis for the cultural significance of music that Ray Schuck uses as his theme in the classroom activities that inspired the development of this book in its beginning. Those interpersonal relationships and social resonances brought eight individuals together to produce this book. Meanwhile, this book could not have taken shape without a number of individuals who contributed in ways other than the writing of essays — individuals whom the editors would also like to thank for the roles they played in helping this book come to life.

Among such individuals, the editors would like to thank a number of individuals who have contributed to the development of the journey that has just been described. First, thanks to the students in Ray Schuck's public history courses, whose questions and comments helped stir Ray's interest in researching "American Pie" more formally. Also, thanks to individuals who responded to the initial call for papers for this project by indicating that while they would not have written pieces to contribute, they certainly would look forward to reading the book should it attain publication. Of particular note, Karen Taylor of the University of Alaska and Rebecca A. Weldon of Savannah College of Art & Design each offered particularly enthusiastic sentiments about the song, about memories involving the song, and about the prospect of reading this book some day. Thanks also to a few individuals whose support especially helped make this volume possible. First, thanks to Tom Kitts, who accepted the aforementioned conference panel for the Popular Culture Association/American Culture Association Annual Meeting in 2010, allowing the editors to have the grand experience of delivering their papers to a very warm reception in St. Louis. Second, thanks to Julie McDowell, the permissions manager at Hal Leonard, Inc., for patient assistance in securing the rights to quote lyrics from Don McLean's "American Pie" and "Weird Al" Yankovic's "The Saga Begins" in this volume. Third, thanks to Rich Schuck (Ray's brother, Raymond's uncle), for his ongoing support in general but also in particular for his conversation with Raymond that helped guide the structure of the introduction to this volume.

In addition to those who helped in particular ways along the journey toward the completion of this work, many others offered support in less formal and/or more everyday ways. These individuals include a number of colleagues at our respective institutions, including though not limited to John Lomax and Ellen Wilson at Ohio Northern University, and Mike Butterworth, Lynda Dixon, Ellen Gorsevski, and Lara Martin Lengel at Bowling Green State University, whose encouragement helped make this project possible. Additionally, Raymond would like to thank deeply his wife, Monica Weir, both for her willingness to listen to him prattle on in his usual way as he talked about this project during its various stages and for consistently pushing him to seek more ambitious results from the work that he does. Meanwhile, Ray and Raymond most of all want to express a very bittersweet thank you to Ray's wife and Raymond's mother, Mary Ann Schuck, to whom this book is dedicated. Mary Ann passed away after a battle with cancer in May of 2010, right in the middle of the development of this book, less than a year after she and Ray celebrated their fortieth wedding anniversary, and less than four months away from celebrating her sixty-fourth birthday. Yet her undyingly positive support for all of the projects that both Ray and Raymond have undertaken continues to play a very important role in setting the environment that produced this book.

At the party for Ray and Mary Ann's fortieth anniversary, Raymond wrote the story of their lives together set to the tune of "American Pie." In the last line of the refrain, Raymond wrote that Ray, Mary Ann, their three boys, and all of the other folks who had gathered for the party were "making memories that are not gonna die." If there was ever a theme that seems to permeate all of the steps and stages of this project, the inspirations for this project, the reactions to the project, and the interpretation and significance of "American Pie" itself, that might very well be it. The journey of the creation of this book has created deeply meaningful memories that once again show, just as Ray Schuck meant to show over a decade ago when he first started playing "American Pie" in his courses, how important the relationships and connections built through music are.

Introduction:
Far from Dry, Far from Gone

Raymond I. Schuck and *Ray Schuck*

On the surface, 2005's Hurricane Katrina and 1971's "American Pie" would not necessarily seem to have anything in common. Yet, in the aftermath of Hurricane Katrina, as large sections of New Orleans lie in ruin, a connection would arise — a connection that demonstrates specifically just how culturally significant Don McLean's song is in U.S. culture. The aftermath of Hurricane Katrina has been the subject of much analysis from a large multitude of fields since the time of the hurricane's occurrence.[1] Like so many other significant cultural events in recent U.S. history, part of the afterward resonance of Hurricane Katrina included slogans, often presented on T-shirts, that poked fun at various aspects of the event in ways that voiced frustrations about what happened. For instance, one T-shirt read, "FEMA Fix Everything My Ass," picking up a comment that had begun to circulate as a means of articulating the extreme dissatisfaction that many residents of the Gulf Coast, and New Orleans in particular, felt with the lack of effective response to the situation by government at the federal, state, and local levels.[2]

One other response to Katrina that appeared on a number of T-shirts read, "Drove my Chevy to the levee, but the levee was gone."[3] Like "FEMA Fix Everything My Ass," this line also potentially voiced dissatisfaction with both the situation in New Orleans that caused the flooding and the lack of effective response to the flooding, while also potentially conveying a sense of playful revelry amid the dissatisfaction. Such sentiments were picked up in some online responses to the hurricane that utilized the phrase as well.[4] Meanwhile, the line could not make sense without the reference that it evoked. A person might wonder what would possess people to put this particular sentence together as a way of voicing their feelings about the levees; that is, unless one knew the similarity of this line to a line that by that time had become quite famous: "Drove my Chevy to the levee, but the levee was dry" from Don McLean's song "American Pie."

By the time of Hurricane Katrina, McLean's song had been in the U.S. (and to some extent the global) popular consciousness for more than three decades. Released as a single in the fall of 1971, "American Pie"—or, technically, as it appeared on the charts, "American Pie — Parts I & II"—rose to the number one spot on *Billboard*'s Hot 100 chart during the week ending January 15, 1972. It would remain at the top of the chart for four weeks, through the week ending February 5, 1972, and it would spend a total of 19 weeks on the chart.[5] In the time between its release and initial success and the occurrence of Hurricane Katrina, "American Pie" had become an indelible part of U.S. culture on a number of levels.

In part its popularity had grown through countless conversations about the various references contained within the song. Around the country, since 1971, people have debated the meanings of the many intertextual allusions throughout the song, as exemplified in James M. Fann's "Understanding American Pie" Web site, which is dedicated to exactly that interpretive task.[6] People have also commemorated the song as a chronicle of American life from the late 1950s through the early 1970s. As George Lipsitz suggests, recognition of the demise of the hippie counter-culture "spread most powerfully through a popular song that placed hippie aspirations within the historical context of 1950s rock and roll — Don McLean's 'American Pie.' The nation's best-selling song during the winter of 1971-1972, 'American Pie' located the death of the counter-culture within a historical cycle of death and rebirth, beginning with the plane crash that killed Buddy Holly and Ritchie Valens and ending with the death of Janis Joplin."[7]

The song has even become an iconic part of American life itself as it has been remade, parodied, and referenced within numerous texts and forums. Perhaps most famously, at least in recent years, in 1999 "Weird Al" Yankovic parodied the song by recounting the story of *Star Wars Episode I: The Phantom Menace* in "The Saga Begins," and in 2000 Madonna remade the song to accompany a new generational context. Meanwhile, the song has also been referenced in a number of television shows, like *The Office*, *That '70s Show*, and *Futurama*. In 2003, during the "The Why of Fry" episode of FOX television program *Futurama*, when several characters are trapped in a parallel universe, The Big Brain states, "Here we are. Trapped for eternity," to which Giant Brain #1 responds, "We could sing 'American Pie,'" seemingly suggesting that the extensive length of the song would make singing it an appropriate way to pass the time.[8] Also in 2003, during the "Celebration Day" episode of the FOX television program *That '70s Show*, the character Michael Kelso rewrites part of "American Pie" to tell a fictional tale of reuniting with his ex-girlfriend, Jackie Burkhart, after her current boyfriend, Steven Hyde, passes away.[9] Here, "American Pie" functions as a frame through which one might tell a story of romance amid tragedy.

Similarly, a few years after Hurricane Katrina, in 2008, at the end of the "The Chair Model" episode of the NBC television program *The Office*, branch manager Michael Scott rewrites a verse of "American Pie" to tell his feelings of loss while standing at the grave of a chair model on whom he had developed a crush after seeing her in an office supplies catalog.[10] Michael and salesman Dwight Schrute then proceed to sing the real "American Pie," though stumbling over some of the lyrics. Here again, "American Pie" serves as a frame through which a character tells a story of romance amid tragedy — a theme that directly connects with the original song itself, as Don McLean, like Michael Scott, feels loss over that with which he fell in love. For Don McLean it's the rock 'n' roll on which he grew up, while for Michael Scott it's the woman he never knew. Additionally, like use of the song following Hurricane Katrina, Michael and Dwight singing the song conveys a sense of revelry amid the loss. It's as if, having resolved himself to his loss, Michael must sing to celebrate the hope that once was and the possibilities that could have been. Again, it's a theme that could be culled from "American Pie," as McLean commemorates the loss of the music he loved by singing.

These various examples convey some of the prominent ways in which Don McLean's "American Pie" can signify meaning through its usage in U.S. culture. Meanwhile, they also demonstrate that "American Pie" has been a significant cultural phenomenon since its appearance on the music charts four decades ago. Accordingly, some work has sought to address some of these aspects of the song as a cultural phenomenon. Web sites like Fann's "Understanding American Pie" and Saul Levitt's "The Ultimate American Pie Website" have dedicated their space to explication of the meaning of the song, its historical context, and its significance.[11] Works like Lipsitz's book have alluded to the significance and meaning of "American Pie" amid discussions of popular culture, popular music, and public memory that have focused their attention elsewhere.[12] Most extensively, Michael Baur's essay "'American Pie' and the Self-critique of Rock 'n' Roll" has examined the sentiments offered in the song. In this essay, Baur acknowledges that the song has long been the subject of discussions regarding interpretation and that the song appears to have been created with the intention of containing multiple meanings for individuals to guess and debate. Baur builds out of the work René Descartes, Archimedes, and Aristotle to examine the message of the song, suggesting that "American Pie" attempts to critique the development of rock 'n' roll from the early days of the likes of Buddy Holly, who made the song's narrator smile, to events of the late 1960s that have led the narrator to declare music dead. Baur suggests that the critique offered in "American Pie" must be contextualized by the lim-

itations that result from being inside the culture that one seeks to critique —
in this case, the culture of rock 'n' roll.[13]

Baur's piece hints at the need for cultural contextualization of "American
Pie" to understand the song's meaning and significance. That Baur's piece
stands fairly alone amid academic analysis of "American Pie" shows another
need — namely, the need for more work that looks at the cultural meaning
and significance of the song. As the works that appear in the following eight
essays demonstrate, this volume seeks to address that need by providing an
interdisciplinary examination of "American Pie" that illuminates some of the
significant ways in which the song has had and continues to have meaning in
people's lives. Meanwhile, this volume also recognizes that no collection of
essays offers a complete account of the song's meaning and significance.
Indeed, that the song remains open to new interpretations and personal and
cultural meanings seems both very much in line with the vagueness that
McLean himself encourages in regard to the song's lyrics and very much in
line with the roles of popular music and popular culture in general. As such,
we offer these essays not as definitive treatises on the meaning and significance
of "American Pie," but as a series of perspectives, separate yet interconnected,
at times conflicting and at times overlapping, that provide a diversity of readings of the song as both text and context. Perhaps these essays will reconfirm
thoughts that you already have regarding the song. Perhaps these essays will
challenge other thoughts that you have. Regardless of the degree to which
either of those possibilities occurs, we hope these essays will help you keep
thinking about the song, its meaning, and its significance, because unlike the
levees after Hurricane Katrina, the chair model in *The Office*, and the rock 'n'
roll on which Don McLean grew up, questions over interpretation and meaning of "American Pie" are anything but dry and anything but gone.

Notes

1. As an indication of the breadth of analysis of "Hurricane Katrina" and its aftermath,
an EBSCO search conducted on February 8, 2012, for journal articles containing "Hurricane
Katrina" between 2005 and 2012 turned up 2,215 results. Of particular note, given the rest of
the opening paragraph of this introduction, see Kris Macomber, Christine Mallinson, and Elizabeth Seale, "'Katrina That Bitch!' Hegemonic Representations of Women's Sexuality on Hurricane Katrina Souvenir T-Shirts," *Journal of Popular Culture* 44 (June 2011): 525–44. doi:
10.1111/j.1540-5931.2011.00847.x.
2. For an example of the comment appearing on a T-shirt, see Candy Chang, "Fix Everything My Ass," *CandyChang.com*, accessed February 8, 2012, http://candychang.com/fix-every-
thing-my-ass/. This Web site also contextualizes the phrase and the T-shirt with some
photographs of damage from Hurricane Katrina taken in 2006.
3. See, for instance, "Drove My Chevy to the Levee T Shirt," *Zazzle*, accessed February
8, 2012, http://www.zazzle.com/drove_my_chevy_to_the_levee_tshirt-235959397535378182,

which situates the comment "Drove my Chevy to the levee but the levee was gone" within an outline of the state of Louisiana.

4. For example, see "Drove My Chevy to the Levee but the Levee Was Gone," *The Irreverent Buddhist*, accessed February 8, 2012, http://freedomforall.net/drove-my-chevy-to-the-levee-but-the-levee-was-gone/ and Jim Chen, "Drove My Chevy to the Levee but the Levee Was Gone," *Jurisdynamics*, accessed February 8, 2012, http://jurisdynamics.blogspot.com/2007/11/drove-my-chevy-to-levee-but-levee-was.html. Also, thanks to Karen Taylor of the University of Alaska, who brought the use of the phrase in connection with Hurricane Katrina to our attention in personal correspondence in March 2009.

5. Joel Whitburn, *Joel Whitburn's Top Pop Singles 1955–1990* (Menomonee Falls, WI: Record Research, 1991), 383, 821.

6. James M. Fann, *Understanding "American Pie,"* accessed March 1, 2011, http://understandingamericanpie.com/.

7. George Lipsitz, *Time Passages: Collective Memory and American Popular Culture* (Minneapolis, University of Minnesota Press, 1990), 130.

8. David X. Cohen, "The Why of Fry," *Futurama*, season 5, episode 8, directed by Wesley Archer and Rich Moore, aired April 6, 2003 (20th Century–Fox).

9. Gregg Mettler, "Celebration Day," *That '70s Show*, season 5, episode 25, directed by David Trainer, aired May 14, 2003 (Casey-Werner Productions).

10. B. J. Novak, "The Chair Model," *The Office*, season 4, episode 10, directed by Jeffrey Blitz, aired April 17, 2008 (Universal).

11. See Fann. Also see Saul Levitt, *The Ultimate American Pie Website*, accessed March 1, 2011, http://www.missamericanpie.co.uk/index.html.

12. In addition to Lipsitz, see the following: In *To the Limit: The Untold Story of the Eagles*, Marc Eliot writes, "Besides the Eagles' three hits, the hottest singles of 1972 included such great tunes as Roberta Flack's 'The First Time Ever I Saw Your Face,' Don McLean's classic 'American Pie,' Harry Nilsson's 'Without You'.... With the exception of Harry Nilsson and the Hollies, noticeably missing from the list was any remnant of the British invasion, or music that preached the social lessons that dominated American white protest folk-rock in the first half of the sixties, or psyched-out drug construction, the spine of the second. Don McLean's 'American Pie' was a uniquely nostalgic recap of the history of rock and roll overloaded with melancholy and utterly lacking in irony, the former eliminating the drama, the latter the relevance" (Boston: Little, Brown, and Company, 1998), 80. In *Tomorrow Never Knows: Rock and Psychedelics in the 1960s*, Nick Bromell writes, "As I've tried to show, rock of the '60s was deeply concerned with memory and history — and with how it would be remembered itself. Most famously, Don McLean's 'American Pie,' which was the #1 song for many weeks in 1972, offered its audience an extended meditation on the meaning of '60s rock and in particular on what McLean saw as the victory of the satanic vision over prepsychedelic innocence" (Chicago: The University of Chicago Press, 2000), 160–161. In *It Seemed like Nothing Happened: America in the 1970s*, Peter N. Carroll writes, "By 1972, the only hopeful vision of the American future seemed to exist in the past. The breakup of the Beatles two years earlier had symbolized the end of an era, and the big hit of 1971, Don McLean's 'American Pie,' forecast the death of rock 'n' roll" (New Brunswick, NJ: Rutgers University Press, 2000), 71. In *American Popular Music: From Minstrelsy to MTV*, Larry Starr and Christopher Waterman write, "Some popular songs — for example, Frank Sinatra's version of 'It Was a Very Good Year,' Dolly Parton's 'Coat of Many Colors,' and Don McLean's 'American Pie' — are really about memory and the mixed feelings of warmth and loss that accompany a retrospective view of our own lives" (New York: Oxford University Press, 2003), 5.

13. Michael Baur, "'American Pie' and the Self-Critique of rock 'n' roll," in *Philosophy and the Interpretation of Literature*, ed. William Irwin and Jorge J. E. Garcia (Lanham, MD: Rowan and Littlefield, 2007), 255–73.

1

A Long, Long Time Ago:
A Lyrical Interpretation

Joseph E. Burns

In October of 1971, United Artists (UA) released the album *American Pie*.[1] The eight and a half minute single of the same name followed in December. Such a long song would never fit one side of a 45 so UA released it by breaking the song in half. Side one contained the first 4:11 and side two held the final 4:31 using a fade down and a fade up to separate the two sides.[2] Soon it became apparent to radio stations that simply playing the A side of the single would not satisfy the listening audience and stations began playing the entire album version. *American Pie* was a success and sat at the number one position on the Billboard Pop chart for four weeks in early 1972.[3]

The single began a discussion that continues today. What do the lyrics to "American Pie" mean? Don McLean freely admits he wrote the song in metaphor.[4] It's all open to the listener's interpretation yet the song is so well crafted that when it's played in full, the text seems to deliver a cohesive story line. If the listener could simply decipher key terminology that appears again and again, "The Jester," "The Marching Band," "The King" or the ever present "The Day the Music Died," the song would somehow deliver a Lewis Carroll–style solvable riddle.

For his part, Don McLean claims he has never, and will never, offer any additional clues. When directly questioned about the song's meaning, McLean simply replies, "It means I don't ever have to work again if I don't want to."[5]

THE DAY THE MUSIC DIED

"The Day the Music Died" is generally agreed upon to mean the death of Buddy Holly, Ritchie Valens, and J. P. Richardson, also known as the Big

Bopper, in a Beechcraft Bonanza light aircraft February 3, 1959.[6] In order to attempt to understand the lyrics of the song "American Pie," it would be helpful to understand the events that led to the death of these three rock 'n' roll stars, specifically Buddy Holly. Buddy Holly was a tremendous influence on Don McLean and the album *American Pie* is dedicated to him.[7] Once the lyrics are examined, this crash will play heavily into their meaning.

The Winter Dance Party was a small 24-stop tour that was to cover the upper Midwest including Wisconsin, Minnesota, Iowa, Illinois, and Ohio during January and February of 1959. The headliners at the beginning of the tour were Buddy Holly, Ritchie Valens, The Big Bopper and Dion and the Belmonts. The tour had completed almost the first half of the run of cities playing the Riverside Ballroom in Green Bay, Wisconsin, on February 1 and was on their way to a date at The Armory in Moorhead, Minnesota, February 3. February 2 was to be a night off. However, as tours are often known to do, nights off do not bring in any money so if there is a venue between the last and the next show and a date can be set up, it's often done. This is the case with the show at the Surf Ballroom in Clear Lake, Iowa, February 2, 1959.[8]

By all accounts the show at the Surf Ballroom was a success and the tour bus was to be loaded and driven to the next venue in Moorhead, Minnesota. By this point in the tour problems had begun to arise. First, it was February in Iowa. It was very cold and the bus was running with a broken heater. The drummer for the Crickets, Carl Bunch, had already been sent to the hospital to be treated for frostbite.[9] The Big Bopper had the flu. Because of the large amount of travel, the band members were not given adequate personal time and Buddy Holly had run out of clean clothes.

Holly decided to use these reasons as an excuse to hire a private plane to take him and his two remaining band mates, Tommy Allsup and now country legend Waylon Jennings, ahead to Moorhead so they would have time before the next show. Holly contacted a local company, the Dwyer Flying Service, and contracted a Beechcraft Bonanza four-seat aircraft.[10]

Once word got out that an airplane was available, J. P. Richardson, the Big Bopper, approached Waylon Jennings and pleaded with him to give up his seat. Apparently after much cajoling, Jennings gave in and the Big Bopper was on the airplane. Jennings later told the story that as the group was leaving for the airport Richardson joked to him, "I hope your ol' bus freezes." Jennings states that he joked back, "I hope your ol' plane crashes." He claimed it was a contributing factor to his alcoholism throughout his life.[11]

Although given a chance to have a seat on the plane Dion DiMucci stated in an NPR interview that he could not bring himself to pay the $36 fee for the seat. He had grown up poor and that amount of money was equal to a month's rent.[12]

Ritchie Valens, who had never flown in a small plane before, asked for Tommy Allsup's seat and Allsup said he would flip him for it. A coin flip took place at the Surf Ballroom, not on the tarmac as is portrayed in the film *La Bamba*. Valens won the toss and the three men who would die in the crash departed for the airport.[13]

The pilot for the flight from Mason City Municipal Airport to Moorhead, Minnesota, was a 21-year-old employee for the Dwyer Flying Service named Roger Peterson. Peterson and his three passengers rolled down the runway at 1:05 A.M. February 3, 1959. Jerry Dwyer, the owner of the flying service, stated he saw the lights of the plane rise into the air and fall back to the ground. When attempts to raise the plane on the radio failed, Dwyer reported a downed aircraft to the authorities. The next morning Dwyer himself flew Peterson's route and spotted the aircraft in a cornfield less than five miles from the end of the runway. All three rock stars had been ejected from the aircraft. Peterson was still trapped inside.[14] The coroner reports stated that each surely died upon impact.[15]

The cause of the crash was most likely pilot error as Peterson was not yet instrument nor night-flight rated and would have needed to rely on his instruments to make this flight rather than his eyesight. Furthermore, Peterson was not rated for winter flight.[16]

As is the entertainment creed, the show must go on. Despite the plane crash, The Winter Dance Party met its obligation on the evening of February 3. Bobby Vee and the Shadows were brought in to perform. Dion DiMucci continued to the end of the tour on February 15 at the Illinois State Armory in Springfield. Jimmy Clanton, Fabian, and Frankie Avalon were brought in to be the new headliners. Even the Crickets finished their contractual obligation with Ronnie Smith as lead vocalist.[17]

DECONSTRUCTING THE LYRICS

The following interpretation of the lyrics of "American Pie" is either completely right, completely wrong, or somewhere in between. The only person who would be able to say for sure is Don McLean himself and he has already suggested he won't.

As this section begins the deconstruction of "American Pie," it would be good to lay out two items. What do we know is true? What do we know isn't true? They are both rather short lists.

The following we know is true:

Don McLean wrote the song in 1970. The song was recorded shortly after and released in late 1971.[18] Thus, no reference after those dates can be within the song.

The song is semi-autobiographical. The lyrics suggest this specifically. Many of them are written in first person.

Don McLean was a fan of Buddy Holly. We know this because the album *American Pie* is dedicated to Buddy Holly.[19]

Don McLean is a fan of The Weavers. They were influential in the music he wrote for his first album, *Tapestry*, and a version of The Weaver's song "Psalm 137," re-titled as "Babylon," arranged by McLean and Lee Hanes of The Weavers, appears on the album *American Pie*.[20]

Don McLean was a paperboy.[21]

Don McLean grew up in New Rochelle, New York.[22]

Don McLean was born October 2, 1945.[23]

The following might be true:

Although Don McLean states he has never let the meanings of any clues slip, the newspaper column *The Straight Dope* states that in a 1972 American Top 40 radio show with Casey Kasem episode, Don McLean stated that The Jester was Bob Dylan and the lines "As I watched him on the stage my hands were clenched in fists of rage. No angel born in Hell could break that Satan's spell" meant the Altamont Motor Speedway Free Concert in 1969. McLean himself responded to the column stating that he never made those statements.[24]

The following is not true:

American Pie is not the name of the airplane that crashed carrying Buddy Holly, Ritchie Valens and the Big Bopper. That aircraft was only known by its tail number, N3794N.[25]

American Pie is not the jumbling of the letters in the names Buddy Holly, Ritchie Valens and the Big Bopper or J. P. Richardson. One could make the words but there would be many letters left over. That defeats the concept of an anagram.

American Pie is not the name or nickname of a beauty queen McLean used to date, know, or worship from afar. There is no support for this other than "American Pie" deconstruction Web sites.

Finally, American Pie is not the name of a pizza McLean used to eat growing up. Again, there may be such a pie available now but there is no support for this theory other than "American Pie" deconstruction websites.

Past those items denoted above, what follows constitutes the author's best guess supported by research including and predating 1971.

VERSE ONE

A long, long time ago...
I can still remember

How that music used to make me smile.
And I knew if I had my chance
That I could make those people dance
And, maybe, they'd be happy for a while.
But February made me shiver
With every paper I'd deliver.
Bad news on the doorstep;
I couldn't take one more step.
I can't remember if I cried
When I read about his widowed bride,
But something touched me deep inside
The day the music died.

Verse one stands alone as a real-time recounting of a boy finding out that his musical hero has passed away in a sudden, horrific fashion. It's a well constructed verse in that, compared to the remainder of the lyrics, it is fairly easy to understand and deconstruct; however, it does offer some classic McLean writing with strong double meanings. The verse also offers the first line that can be specifically researched.

A long, long time ago...

This opening line starts a pattern of McLean using the first line of each verse to set a timeline, letting the listener know *when* in the world of music and history he is discussing throughout the verse. Taking a bit of latitude here knowing the remainder of the verse recounts someone, most likely McLean, learning of the plane crash on the day the music died, that would mean the listener is more than a decade in the past.

The song was written in 1970. The crash occurred in 1959. Don McLean was born October 2, 1945. That would make him 13 at the time of the crash.

I can still remember
How that music used to make me smile.

These lines stand out as showing that McLean is writing from an autobiographical standpoint. Note it is written in first person. Furthermore, he is remembering as the man he is today. It is not being written from the standpoint of a 13-year-old boy.

And I knew if I had my chance
That I could make those people dance
And, maybe, they'd be happy for a while.

This is a nice series of double meanings. The word "dance" shows a young man wanting to be a singer/songwriter but it also harkens back to the Winter Dance Party. The fact that the people would be happy for a while also carries a double meaning. The party would allow people to be happy for a while and McLean was happy for a while before the death of his idol.

But February made me shiver

Here again, a well written double meaning. One would shiver at the cold of February and one would shiver at the bad news.

With every paper I'd deliver.
Bad news on the doorstep;
I couldn't take one more step.

This small stanza again lends credence to the thought that the song is autobiographical in that we know that Don McLean was a paperboy growing up New Rochelle, New York.

I can't remember if I cried
When I read about his widowed bride,

Now we arrive at the first line that requires research past a simple interpretation of the lyrical content. Whose widowed bride? This line is referring to Buddy Holly's widowed bride. Buddy Holly married Maria Elena Santiago in Lubbock, Texas, on August 15, 1958. Stories about their relationship suggested that he proposed to her on their first date. Maria Elena accompanied Holly on many smaller tours and gigs after their marriage but was not with him on the Winter Dance Party.[26] She would later comment that had she been on that particular tour, Holly would have never gotten on that plane.[27]

The marriage was kept a secret for professional and personal reasons. First, it would have been bad business for a rock star to have been married. Young girls want to believe they can grow up and marry Buddy Holly. Second, the marriage was interracial. Maria Elena was from Puerto Rico and in 1958 it was a much different time than today.

Furthermore, at the time of the crash, Maria Elena was six months pregnant and lost the baby soon after.[28]

But something touched me deep inside
The day the music died.

Here McLean coins what has become the most famous phrase from the song, "The Day the Music Died." This is generally agreed upon to mean the death of Holly, Valens and The Big Bopper, February 3, 1959, during the Winter Dance Party.

The song then leads into a slow version of the chorus.

THE CHORUS

So, bye-bye, Miss American Pie

To begin with, the idea that "American Pie" is a specific "thing" should be dispelled. As stated before, it is not the name of the airplane that crashed carrying Holly, Valens and Richardson, nor is it a nickname for a girlfriend, nor was it a pizza he ate growing up in New Rochelle, New York. American Pie is an ideal. As we move through the song, it will become apparent that Don McLean is not discussing the death of his idol Buddy Holly. In fact, the song will seldom reference Holly. The song is rather making a statement about how rock 'n' roll music, and society for that matter, is moving in the wrong direction after the death of Holly.

When McLean sings, "bye-bye Miss American Pie," he is lamenting a time when, in his mind at least, it was better, and rock music was pure. It is a farewell to an idea rather than to a specific thing.[30]

Drove my Chevy to the Levee

If written correctly, the word "Levee" should be capitalized because it's a proper noun. The visual of the lyric is an American car sitting on a large earthen dam overlooking water. However, remember that Don McLean is from New Rochelle, New York. There are no major water levees as there would be in, say, New Orleans. There is, however, a Levee bar, a nickname for the Beechmont Tavern.[30] It was located at 750 North Avenue. Furthermore, the term "levee," how the bar was granted its nickname, is slang for a party. The term comes from Europe meaning an afternoon gathering of men as in a royal court.[31] It's slang in the northeast that is often lost on the rest of the country. Knowing this, the line was certainly written using "Chevy" to rhyme with "Levee" rather than the other way around, which is good as well, Chevy being the all–American Car. McLean drove his American car to a bar. That's the meaning of the line.

But the Levee was dry

This is another strong use of double meaning word play, which is found throughout the song. Those that see "levee" in the previous line meaning an earthen structure that holds back water use this line to bolster their point. However, the timeline of both the plane crash and Don McLean's life don't bear it out. The day the music died occurred in 1959. Don McLean was 13 years old at the time of the crash. The Levee, a bar, was dry to him. He was too young to drink.

And them good old boys were drinkin' whiskey in Rye

This line is often misquoted. The final words are "in Rye," not "and rye." By stating the line as "whisky and rye," rye is relegated to be just another drink. Remember that Don McLean is from New Rochelle, New York, less than 10 miles south of Rye, New York. The line is stating that the good old boys are drinking whiskey in Rye, New York, in honor of the three fallen rock stars.

Rye is a place, not a drink.

Singin' this'll be the day that I die
This'll be the day that I die

Those that are drinking whiskey in Rye, New York, are singing a Buddy Holly lyric from the song "That'll Be the Day."[32] It's a wake. Because of the people drinking whiskey, you could go as far as stating it's an Irish wake. This is, in fact, the closest reference to Buddy Holly there will be throughout the remainder of the song.

So the chorus generally reads that an ideal died along with McLean's musical icon. Looking back at what has happened since 1959, McLean is saying bye, bye to a time when he felt America and the music she produced was better. He made his way to the local bar but he was unable to drown his sorrows. Those that were older and truly understood what Holly was to the world, them good old boys in Rye, New York, were good enough to send him off with a wake singing his songs and raising a drink in his honor.

VERSE TWO

Did you write the book of love,
And do you have faith in God above,
If the Bible tells you so?
Do you believe in rock and roll,
Can music save your mortal soul,
And can you teach me how to dance real slow?
Well, I know that you're in love with him
'Cause I saw you dancin' in the gym.
You both kicked off your shoes.
Man, I dig those rhythm and blues.
I was a lonely teenage broncin' buck
With a pink carnation and a pickup truck,
But I knew I was out of luck
The day the music died.
I started singin',

The overriding concept of this second verse is that rock 'n' roll is now under attack from societal forces. What was once fun and seemingly pure is now the focus of people who are self-appointed do-gooders in McLean's eyes. The music is starting to become feared by many and used by many for purposes that it was never intended for in the first place.

Did you write the book of love,

As stated above, the first line of the verses sets a timeline. This line is lifted almost verbatim from the Monotones' song "Book of Love."[33] The song was recorded in September 1957 and became a hit for the group in early 1958, peaking in February.[34] This would put the listener in the same general time frame as the Winter Dance Party and the Day the Music Died.

And do you have faith in God above,
If the Bible tells you so?
Do you believe in rock and roll,
Can music save your mortal soul,

These four lines appear to go together and all play off of "If the Bible tells you so?" That line is probably taken from the 1955 song by Don Cornell, "The Bible Tells Me So."[35]

The reason the "American Pie" stanza appears to hinge on the line "If the Bible tells you so" is that they all talk about religion and music, specifically rock 'n' roll having an effect in order to save your soul. The lines are probably a jab at those people who are starting to talk down rock 'n' roll music as being ungodly. McLean saw rock 'n' roll music as pure and simple fun, a way "to be happy for a while." It certainly wasn't going to alter anyone's moral fiber.

The lines are probably his way of firing back at those who saw rock 'n' roll music as yet another opportunity to advance a religious cause by attacking the popular music of the day. There will always be those that will proclaim what is popular as being against God and for the Devil. Blues, jazz, big band, and now rock 'n' roll have all been the subject of attacks by such people. This is simply McLean's way of asking if what they are preaching is actually truthful.

And can you teach me how to dance real slow?

Times may have changed but in 1958, slow dancing was seen as a very sexual thing to do. This line probably furthers the jabs McLean is making at those who wish to talk down rock 'n' roll music.

Well, I know that you're in love with him
'cause I saw you dancin' in the gym.

This also denotes the importance of slow dancing and how it was used to signal who was going steady with whom. Also, where did most school dances take place? They were in the gym. It was normally well decorated for the event but still a gym.

You both kicked off your shoes.

This line harkens back to a specific kind of dance, a high school sock hop.

Man, I dig those rhythm and blues.

Often, this line is glossed over as a simple appreciation for the rhythm and blues music that was starting the take hold in the late 1950s, but there must certainly be more to the line that that. Why else would McLean go out of his way to specifically state "rhythm and blues" music?

Remember that this verse seems to be about people that are starting to stick their noses into the music that McLean loved so much. They are becoming the answers to questions no one asked. If that is what's prevalent throughout the verse, then this line must have a stronger meaning.

The time line puts this verse in late 1957 or early 1958 and at that time rhythm and blues was code word in the music and radio industry for African American music. It was the time of what were termed "race records."[36]

Radio and the music industry had a belief that black artists such as Little Richard, the Ike Turner Band and Big Joe Turner would have a detrimental effect on the young white culture so much so that squeaky clean white artists were found to cover popular rhythm and blues songs and radio stations were told to only play those white cover versions.

For example, Bill Haley and the Comets covered Ike Turner's "Rocket 88" and Big Joe Turner's "Shake Rattle and Roll" with greatly altered lyrics. Pat Boone had bigger hits with some of Little Richard's songs than Richard did simply because of Richard's lack of airplay. Boone also covered songs by the Flamingos and Fats Domino.[37]

It was a time in music when blatant racism was allowed and McLean is probably stating that he did not go along with the white cover trend. He liked the original rhythm and blues.

However, to this point in the song, past the grouping of lines that discuss religion, the verse discusses dancing. Now, the verse may simply be talking about McLean and his high school days but the timeline and McLean's reference to rhythm and blues suggest he may be talking about a specific dancing incident.

At WJW in Cleveland, Ohio, in the mid–1950s was a disc jockey named Alan Freed. He went by the moniker "The King of the Moondoggies." Many believe him to be the person who coined the term "rock and roll," although that title is probably not deserved. Freed is credited with creating and putting on the what is widely believed to be the first rock 'n' roll concert, The Moondog Coronation Ball. His influence in early rock 'n' roll went a long way to putting the Rock and Roll Hall of Fame in Cleveland, Ohio.[38]

Alan Freed was known for bucking the radio trends of playing the white cover songs and simply spinning the original hits by the African American artists. It made him very popular and gave him the chance to move up to WABC in New York City where he was so popular that he was also given a television show on ABC television titled *The Big Beat*.[39]

The show was popular even though it did feature many African American artists. On July 19, 1957, a young group on the up and come called Frankie

Lymon and the Teenagers performed their hit song "Why Do Fools Fall in Love."[40]

Lymon, who was only 15 at the time, kicked off his shoes, pulled a white girl out of the audience and danced with her. There was such uproar from the television audience, especially from southern states, that the show was cancelled that evening.[41]

The timeline, the tone of the verse, the references to dancing and the reference to rhythm and blues all point to this single dancing incident possibly being what Don McLean is referencing through this small grouping of lines.

I was a lonely teenage broncin' buck
With a pink carnation and a pickup truck,

These two lines, as has been done twice before within the verse, have taken text almost directly from another song, Marty Robbins' "White Sports Coat."[42]

This is rather clever on the part of McLean in that he used the lyrics of another song to make his point in wrapping up this second verse. Robbins discusses dancing in "White Sports Coat" but now the dance is a prom.

The protagonist is a little older. McLean is now a "teenage broncin' buck."

The text of the Robbins song is in a down mood. It is tipping that the next verse, and the rest of the song for that matter, will be in a blue mood.

McLean is again using an automobile to return the listener's attention to Americana, a pickup truck, but using the term "pink carnation" to reference the Marty Robbins song to set the mood. It's very clever.

But I knew I was out of luck
The day the music died.
I started singin',

McLean now returns to writing in first person suggesting that the forces he is referencing are winning and that he is personally out of luck now that the music he loved is gone and the world is changing. Now he is personally singing the chorus.

VERSE THREE

Now for ten years we've been on our own
And moss grows fat on a rollin' stone,
But that's not how it used to be.
When the jester sang for the king and queen,
In a coat he borrowed from James Dean
And a voice that came from you and me,
Oh, and while the king was looking down,

The jester stole his thorny crown.
The courtroom was adjourned;
No verdict was returned.
And while Lenin read a book of Marx,
The quartet practiced in the park,
And we sang dirges in the dark
The day the music died.
We were singing...

Now for ten years we've been on our own

The first line of a verse sets a timeline. The Day the Music Died occurred in 1959. The listener must be in 1969.

And moss grows fat on a rollin' stone

This line probably has to do with the group The Rolling Stones. In 1969, the group did move to France to avoid paying the higher taxes levied in the United Kingdom, but the line states that moss grows fat.[43] That would suggest that the Stones had become complacent. It's quite the opposite. The Rolling Stones put out the albums *Beggar's Banquet* in December of 1968 and *Let It Bleed* in December of 1969, two of their most popular and recognizable albums.[44]

How McLean tips off the meaning of this line is by his stating, "moss grows fat on 'a' Rollin' Stone." He's talking about the death of Brian Jones, July 3, 1969.

Jones left the Stones for good in June of 1969 and went into a sort of self-imposed seclusion at Cotchford Farm in East Sussex, a place he had purchased in 1968.[45]

Jones died by drowning in a swimming pool after an evening of heavy drinking. He was found by his then-girlfriend Anna Wohlin who claims that Jones was alive when he was pulled from the pool but by the time help had arrived, he had passed away.

There are theories of his death being a suicide, a murder and an accident.[46] Whichever it is, McLean seems to be most concerned with the fact that drugs and alcohol were so involved in the death. In fact, Jones' autopsy proved that he was quite an abuser, which is probably the reason McLean used him specifically to make his point. Many more times throughout the remainder of the song, McLean will decry the use of drugs in rock 'n' roll. This reference to Jones is only the first. The next line helps to further strengthen the point.

But that's not how it used to be.

"Moss grows fat on a Rollin' Stone but that's not how it used to be." It's as if Don McLean is stating, "My musical heroes didn't drug themselves to death."

When the jester sang for the king and queen,

As stated earlier, Don McLean may have let it slip that the jester is Bob Dylan. He personally claims he did not but even if he didn't, it's fairly easy using the many times the jester is denoted throughout the song that it's probably Bob Dylan. The jester clue later in lyrics that cements the fact that the jester is Bob Dylan is "The jester on the sideline in a cast." The reference is probably suggesting Dylan's Triumph motorcycle accident, July 29, 1966, his broken leg in a cast and subsequent two-year seclusion.[47]

The nickname "jester" probably comes from the fact that Dylan was a folk singer, a type of music known to call for societal change and to point out where society was being pushed in the wrong direction by its leaders, calling them to task. Dylan spoke truth to power much like the jesters of the time of kings and queens. It was only the jester who had the ability to speak the truth to those in charge and McLean points out Dylan's ability to quickly cut to the truth in his lyrics by giving him the nickname.

The question here is when would the jester, Dylan, have sung for the king and queen? This is another well-crafted lyric with a double meaning. Many people would take the term "king" in a literal sense and remember back to Dylan singing at the Martin Luther King civil rights march in Washington, D.C., the time of the famous "I Have a Dream" speech.[48] That would make sense for the king. The question then would be "Who is the queen?" It could be Coretta Scott King, the King and his queen.

Another theory states that it could be Joan Baez. She sang with Dylan at the same civil rights march.[49] One could conceivably call her the queen of the folk movement. Now we have the king and the queen.

There is yet another theory that President Kennedy and first lady Jacqueline watched Dylan perform on television. Their presidency was often called Camelot.[50] That would suggest royalty even though they were president and first lady. That would also fulfill the moniker of king and queen.

In each of these scenarios, the "queen" portion doesn't fit. It takes the next line to help set the timeline to another year to give what is more logically the correct answer to who the king and queen might be.

In a coat he borrowed from James Dean

The coat worn by James Dean is easy to figure out. McLean is almost certainly talking about the famous red jacket from the 1955 movie *Rebel Without a Cause*.[51] Bob Dylan is pictured wearing almost the exact same jacket on the cover of his 1963 album *The Freewheelin' Bob Dylan*.[52] This was the album that began to set Dylan apart as a true master singer/songwriter. It contained the classic songs "Blowin' in the Wind," "Masters of War" and "A Hard Rain's a-Gonna Fall."

Furthermore, this was the album that allowed Dylan to tour England. He made his English debut at a pub named The Pinder of Wakefield.[53]

Now we have the answer to the question, "Who are the king and queen?" In the year 1963, Bob Dylan performed for Martin Luther King, a literal King, and he performed in the United Kingdom, a place ruled by a literal Queen, Queen Elizabeth II.

And a voice that came from you and me,

Following the 1963 album *The Freewheelin' Bob Dylan,* Dylan was beginning to become the voice of his generation speaking for the masses. People were so enamored with him that even something as simple as Dylan switching from acoustic to electric instruments at the Newport Jazz Festival in 1965 brought a hail of boos from the crowd.[54]

Oh, and while the king was looking down,
The jester stole his thorny crown.

Here we return to the use of the word "king" but it's probably not meant to mean Martin Luther King. In this case the king is probably the king of rock 'n' roll, Elvis Presley.

The line seems to say pretty plainly that McLean believes that Elvis has stumbled and was no longer keeping his eye on the music. He was looking down and while he was looking down, the jester, Dylan, came along and took the crown from his head. Be it thorny or not, it seems that McLean is crowning Bob Dylan the new king of rock 'n' roll.

There's also a question of what year the listener is in. The verse started with 1969. That was clearly stated but after the commentary regarding Brian Jones, the timeline quickly changed to 1963. However, it may not matter to this statement of Dylan becoming the new king of rock 'n' roll surpassing Elvis Presley. The years 1963 through 1969 were, relative to his previous years, not good to Elvis Presley in terms of music. This was the time of the Beatles and through those years Elvis only placed six songs into the top ten. "Suspicious Minds" was his only number one single. He seemed to be focused more on movies early in the 60s, even staging a well-received 1968 comeback special to announce he was ready to focus solely on music once again. He would only reach the top ten three more times and never again see number one before his death.[55]

The courtroom was adjourned;
No verdict was returned.

To this point, the song "American Pie" has focused solely on musical references, but here, it seems, the lyrics begin to make reference to historical events. Later references in the lyrics will also be outside of music. This is simply the first.

These two lines can be interpreted as having a single meaning taken together or having two meanings individually. If they carry a single meaning then they are probably referencing the Chicago Seven: Tom Hayden, Jerry Rubin, Abbie Hoffman, David Dellinger, Rennie Davis, John Froines, and Lee Weiner. Originally the Chicago Eight, including Black Panther Bobby Seale, the men were charged with crossing state borders in order to incite a riot at the 1968 Democratic National Convention in Chicago. Once the trial was underway, the Chicago Eight became the Chicago Seven when activist Seal was taken from the courtroom and sentenced to four years on contempt charges after hurling insults at the judge.

The trial was at times a grand affair with large demonstrations both inside and outside the courtroom and counterculture figures including the Rev. Jesse Jackson, Timothy Leary, Judy Collins, and Arlo Guthrie being called to testify.

When the verdict was read, all seven men were found not guilty of conspiracy. Tom Hayden, Jerry Rubin, Abbie Hoffman, David Dellinger and Rennie Davis were convicted of crossing state lines with the intent to incite a riot, fined $5000 and sentenced to five years in prison. John Froines and Lee Weiner were acquitted completely.

However, on November 21, 1972, the United States Court of Appeals for the Seventh Circuit reversed and dropped all charges on the basis that the judge refused to allow the defense to properly screen the jurors for racial bias. The prosecution refused to retry the case.[56]

The courtroom was adjourned.

If there is a double meaning, then we need to look at the two sets of years the verse is referencing, 1969 and 1963. The Chicago Seven has already referenced the event that would have taken place in 1969. The event that would have taken place in 1963 could be the Warren Commission established November 29, 1963, by President Lyndon Johnson.

The commission released its finding in an 888-page report to President Johnson on September 24, 1964, making it public three days later, stating that Lee Harvey Oswald acted alone in the assassination of President Kennedy.[57]

Both of those events would fit in both topic and timeline.

And while Lenin read a book of Marx,
The quartet practiced in the park,

This is another line that is often misquoted. The line should read as written above with "Lenin" spelled as in Vladimir Ilyich Lenin. However, lyrics pages will often print the line as *"And while Lennon read a book of Marx"* to suggest John Lennon. The reason is probably because the next line states that a quartet practiced in the park. The thinking is that the quartet must obviously be The Beatles.

The problem is that historically there isn't much, if any, partnership between Communism and The Beatles. John Lennon may have read books by Marx but such propaganda doesn't show up in their music nor are there news stories linking The Beatles with any pro–Communism activism. Besides, later in the song, The Beatles are referenced in a far more blatant fashion.

In this case, the quartet is The Weavers. Remember that Don McLean is a fan of The Weavers and The Weavers' song "Psalm 137," reworked and retitled "Babylon," arranged by McLean and Lee Hanes, appears on the album *American Pie*.[58] Moreover, The Weavers fit better with the first line being concerned with Communism.

The Weavers were formed in the late 1950s and were made up of Ms. Ronnie Gilbert, Lee Hays, Fred Hellerman and Pete Seeger. They were the mold for future folk groups setting down the architecture of melody lines, instrumentation, harmonies and song standards including "Kisses Sweeter Than Wine," "On Top of Old Smokey" and "The Sloop John B" known then as "The Wreck of the John B."[59]

The Weavers sang protest songs and songs that were pro-union during the McCarthy era and were placed under FBI surveillance. As was the case at the time, the governmental pressures cost the group their radio airplay and ultimately their recording contract and career. They broke up first in 1952.

Pete Seeger pursued a solo career, was brought before the House Un-American Activities Committee in 1955 and pled the fifth. The Weavers reunited off and on through the 1960s folk revival finally disbanding for good in 1964.[60]

And we sang dirges in the dark
The day the music died.
We were singing...

Of all the lines in "American Pie" this is one of the more difficult to specifically interpret because of its placement and because of this verse having changes in its timeline. To begin with, a dirge is a funeral song, so sad music is playing. That much is certain. The question is "Who is singing the funeral dirge?" McLean writes, "we." Is that an-all inclusive term to mean all music listeners? If so, then this line could simply be harkening back to the Day the Music Died as is suggested by the next line but that seems too easy an answer in such a complex song.

Could that "we" mean he and The Weavers? If so, that could mean he was lamenting the end of their career cut short by the evils of government. It could also mean McLean and other folk music lovers who are lamenting the death of the music of The Weavers. After The Weavers broke up in the

1950s, they started making money singing cigarette commercials seemingly walking away from their "purpose."[61]

This verse also stepped outside of the musical realm and began discussing events that were happening in the world. Allowing for that and staying within the bounds of the 1963 to 1969 timeline there is an event that plunged many people into darkness.

On November 9, 1965, over 25 million people were left without power in what was up until that time the largest power outage in the United States, covering Ontario, Canada, and seven U.S. states including Don McLean's home state of New York.[62]

That explains the concept of darkness but it doesn't account for why someone would be singing a dirge in the dark. The best guess is that the line is a conglomeration of all of these meanings, and probably many more, and McLean saw the blackout as a culmination of all that was going wrong in the world up until that point in time. There was a lot of bad news, and then the lights went out.

Note now that "we were singing."

VERSE FOUR

Helter Skelter in a summer swelter.
The birds flew off with a fallout shelter,
Eight miles high and falling fast.
It landed foul on the grass.
The players tried for a forward pass,
With the Jester on the sidelines in a cast.
Now the half-time air was sweet perfume
While the Sergeants played a marching tune.
We all got up to dance,
Oh, but we never got the chance!
'cause the players tried to take the field;
The marching band refused to yield.
Do you recall what was revealed?
The day the music died?
We started singing...

Helter Skelter in a summer swelter.

As before, the first line of the verse will set the time line. Helter Skelter is a fairly straightforward clue. Don McLean is probably referencing the Tate-LaBianca killings by the followers of Charles Manson, which took place August 9 and August 10 in 1969.[63]

The probable reason for the reference is that Charles Manson believed that The Beatles' "White Album" held clues to the coming apocalypse and that the members of the band were speaking to him through the songs. Manson believed the song "Helter Skelter" to be the predictor of a coming race war.

The Tate-LaBianca killings were meant to help to start this race war. It was the "Helter Skelter" called for within the song.[64]

Manson believed himself to be a Jesus Christ on earth. He thought that the race war would mean the end of the white race at the hands of the African American race. Manson and his followers would hide out in a cavern in the desert until the war had finished and then emerge and be the new rulers of the African American race on earth.[65]

The actual meaning of the song "Helter Skelter" is much less nefarious. Paul McCartney readily admits he was attempting to write a song that matched the power of the band The Who. Helter Skelter is also not a thought process or a warning. It's a carnival ride. A Helter Skelter is normally a very tall tube that has a slide corkscrewing around it. The rider either climbs a ladder or is carried to the top and then rides down to the bottom.[66]

Returning to the line in the song, the lyric ends talking about a summer swelter. The killings occurred in August so it would have been one of the hotter times of the year. The text was probably also used to help with the rhyme in the next line.

The Byrds flew off with a fallout shelter,
Eight miles high and falling fast.

This is yet another line that is often written incorrectly on lyrics pages. One will often see the first line written as "The birds flew off to a fallout shelter." In reality the spelling of "birds" should be "Byrds" because the second line in the stanza pretty clearly suggests that Don McLean is talking about the Roger McGuinn/David Crosby Byrds. The song "Eight Miles High" was one of the Byrds biggest hits in 1965 and 1966.[67]

There are a couple of reasons why McLean might be referencing the Byrds. First off, the reference is not flattering. The drug culture terminology of the time suggests that what he is saying in the first line is that the band is going off to a rehab clinic, a fallout shelter, to get off of drugs. The second line reinforces that thought using the title of their song "Eight Miles High."

This is McLean once again suggesting his dislike for the drug culture, most likely David Crosby as he had a well-known affinity for drugs.[68] The reference for "Eight Miles High" is misused however. The song, written by McGuinn, is not a drug culture tune. The song was written after the Byrds toured Europe for the first time and McGuinn had to fly. He disliked it so much that he wrote a song about it. The song is about just that and was never meant to imply drugs. Why "eight" miles high? It simply sounded better than any other number.[69] However, using it as a drug reference works for what McLean is attempting to say in this case.

There is probably another reason why McLean chose to call out The Byrds specifically. The Byrds were the leaders of what was known as the Folk Rock movement. It was a movement that was attempting to combine the folk music that McLean loved so much with the rock movement, and apparently many of the poor life choices that come with it, that he clearly disdained.

It landed foul on the grass.
The players tried for a forward pass,
With the jester on the sidelines in a cast.

The first line of this grouping seems to have no specific meaning but rather to only start the sports metaphor McLean is going to use throughout the rest of the verse bringing in a marching band and a halftime show.

The next two lines must be taken together to be understood. Earlier it was pointed out that Bob Dylan is most likely the jester and this line is probably referencing his motorcycle crash July 29, 1966, and subsequent two-year seclusion. Note again the sports analogy having him on the sidelines.

So the jester is obviously out of the game. The McLean-crowned king of rock 'n' roll is not there. This makes the previous line easier to understand. The players tried for a forward pass. This is probably a reference to other people in the music industry attempting to capitalize on the fact that the major player, Dylan, is no longer there and because of it, an opening has been created.

Now the half-time air was sweet perfume

This is yet another drug reference using the terminology of the day. If you smelled marijuana smoke, you might refer to it as "perfume." Note the sports metaphor suggesting it is now half time and the marching band can now take the field.

While the Sergeants played a marching tune.

Here is the blatant reference to The Beatles mentioned within the discussion of the last verse. The Sergeants probably mean Sergeant Pepper's Lonely Hearts Club Band. However, this is yet again another nice line with a double meaning. As the song progresses, McLean will make more references to war and this line allowed him to not only reference The Beatles but also suggest sergeants in the literal sense and people starting to beat the drums toward war.

We all got up to dance,
Oh, but we never got the chance!
'cause the players tried to take the field;
The marching band refused to yield.

These four lines taken together seem to make a single statement about the music industry in regards to The Beatles. There had never been a band like The Beatles before. They were, at the time the verse suggests, so powerful and so dominating that the companies that put out music were completely taken by them. There was no room for other forms of music. The players, as suggested before, those attempting to get their music out, are not being given the chance. Why? McLean is suggesting it is because the marching band, The Beatles, is too dominant. Record companies are not interested in anything new. Folk music is falling by the wayside. Bands must sound like The Beatles. They must have twin guitars, bass, drums, and double harmonies and write catchy little ditties that can be sold in nice, neat packages.

Music is moving out of the hands of the musicians and into the hands of the companies that produce music and those companies are now creating product, not music. Sound like The Beatles or tough luck.

Do you recall what was revealed
The day the music died?
We started singing...

This is probably a continuation of the last grouping of lines. What was revealed? Music had become corporate. Now the last line of the verse might have taken on a new meaning. Here McLean may no longer be talking about the death of Buddy Holly, Ritchie Valens and The Big Bopper but rather his cherished Folk or music in general.

Note now that the final line reads that "we started" singing the chorus.

VERSE FIVE

Oh, and there we were all in one place,
A generation lost in space
With no time left to start again.
So come on: Jack be nimble, Jack be quick!
Jack Flash sat on a candlestick
'Cause fire is the Devil's only friend.
Oh, and as I watched him on the stage
My hands were clenched in fists of rage.
No angel born in hell
Could break that Satan's spell.
And as the flames climbed high into the night
To light the sacrificial rite,
I saw Satan laughing with delight
The day the music died
He was singing,

Oh, and there we were all in one place,

This is most likely the Woodstock Music and Art Fair held August 15 to August 18, 1969. It certainly is where "we were all in one place." Some estimates put the total number of people at close to a half million.[70] It is also important to remember that Don McLean starts this verse with Woodstock in the Summer of Love. It will become integral to how he ends the verse.

A generation lost in space
With no time left to start again.

This is yet again another example of McLean's use of lines with double meanings. This line includes the title of the television show *Lost in Space*, which ran from 1965 through 1968.[71] That allows the listener to set a time frame but moreover it allows the listener to remember the Apollo rockets and the space race of the time as well.[72]

There is probably a third meaning as suggested by the following line, "With no time left to start again." It's a jab at those who did not listen nor pay attention to the warnings that the folk singers were offering. To say someone is lost in space is to say that they are in their own little world and are immune to any warning the folk singers were putting out and now, as McLean may be suggesting, there is no time left to start again and those who did not listen will have to live with the results of their actions.

So come on: Jack be nimble, Jack be quick!
Jack Flash sat on a candlestick

McLean is clever here incorporating a Mother Goose rhyme to make a point. The lines are probably playing off of the two before it and are referencing the space race that culminated in the United States putting the first man on the moon in July of 1969. Jack probably refers to President John "Jack" Kennedy calling for putting a man on the moon by the end of the decade and then NASA achieving the goal early.[73] It has also been said that the line could refer to President Kennedy quelling the Cuban Missile Crisis. That's possible but the timeline seems off. The Cuban Missile crisis was in 1962.[74]

The second line further reinforces the thought that this refers to the space race and landing a man on the moon. Jack Flash could be a nickname for an astronaut. "Candlestick" was a nickname for a rocket during the Apollo missions.

The beginning of the second line, however, is a nice use of language that tips off the next run of lyrics and their meaning. "Jack Flash sat on a Candlestick." The use of "Jack Flash" is what's important. There's a song that uses that lyric. The Rolling Stones sing about Jumpin' Jack Flash.[75]

'Cause fire is the Devil's only friend.
Oh, and as I watched him on the stage
My hands were clenched in fists of rage.
No angel born in hell
Could break that Satan's spell.

This is the second set of lyrics that it is alleged that Don McLean let slip although he, again, denies it. It is suggested that this grouping of lyrics means the Altamont Speedway Free Festival.[76] Even if that fact wasn't known, these lines along with those that follow do lead the listener to that conclusion. McLean is talking about a specific person. The Devil and Satan references are simply name calling. It's blatantly a concert. The person is on a stage. Something terrible happened. McLean's hands are clenched with rage. He obviously dislikes the person on stage.

It's the line "No angel born in hell" that sets it off though. An angel born in hell would be a Hells Angel. Putting the clues together for a concert, near the time of Woodstock, and the moon shots, where the Hells Angels played a major part, you can only come up with the Rolling Stones' Altamont Speedway Free Festival held Saturday, December 6, 1969.[77]

The story of the Altamont Speedway Free Festival, herein known only as "Altamont," was that the Rolling Stones, easily one of the most popular bands in America at the time, wanted to have a Woodstock of their own except now on the west coast. After deals with Golden Gate Park and Sears Point raceway fell through, promoters of this west coast Woodstock settled on a the defunct motor speedway, Altamont.[78]

From the beginning of the concert's planning, there were concerns. There was no power to the speedway and none would be permitted so the entire festival would need to be run off of generators. The staging was built only four feet high so it was difficult for people farther back in the crowd to see. There wasn't an ample public address system for the musical acts. The bands played their concerts from the stage much like bar bands would play. There wasn't enough food. There weren't enough toilets. It wasn't as if these concerns weren't known; promoters simply allowed the concerns to go with the decisions that were made stating that it was only for one day. Patrons could deal with the problems for one day.

The lineup for the concert included Santana, Jefferson Airplane, The Flying Burrito Brothers, Crosby, Stills, Nash, & Young and the headliners, The Rolling Stones. The Grateful Dead were scheduled to play but pulled out of the concert.[79]

There is a question as to how the Hells Angels came to be so involved in the concert. There's a series of stories that the Grateful Dead suggested to the Rolling Stones that they hire the Hells Angels as security. The Grateful

Dead had done this in the past and were happy with the results. All three parties deny that this is the case. The stories vary slightly but it is for certain that the San Francisco chapter of the Hells Angels led by Ralph "Sonny" Barger was at Altamont very early on the day of the concert and had ringed themselves around the stage. Barger states the Angels were not summoned to the concert. They came to enjoy the music and were approached once they were already there.

The Rolling Stones' road manager Sam Cutler said that a deal was struck between him and Sonny Barger that the Hells Angels would make sure that no one tampered with the generators. Barger remembers that the only deal that was struck was that the Angels would help people by giving directions. They were not hired to be a security force of any kind. Whatever the agreement was, it is generally believed that in exchange for their services the Hells Angels received $500.00 and most if not all of the backstage beer.[80]

Whether they were hired to be security or not, the Hells Angels acted as if they were, harassing the crowds that pushed closer and closer to see the bands on stage. There were reports of fans being pushed, punched and struck with pool cues. The second band to play, Jefferson Airplane, began to comment on the Angels' actions after a fan knocked over one of the Angels' motorcycles, and the gang began to become aggressive towards the musicians. Airplane guitarist Marty Balin was knocked unconscious when a Hells Angel punched him.[81] This, it's said, was the incident that caused the Grateful Dead to pull out of the concert.[82] They were to be the second to last band of the evening playing just before the Rolling Stones.

The Flying Burrito Brothers and Crosby, Stills, Nash & Young finished their sets among ever-growing anger and violence. The Rolling Stones, instead of taking the stage immediately, let the crowd wait until sundown.[83]

And as the flames climbed high into the night
To light the sacrificial rite,
I saw Satan laughing with delight

The Rolling Stones opened their set with "Jumping Jack Flash," which is possibly another clue from Don McLean earlier in the verse. They finished "Carol" and began "Sympathy for the Devil" when the fighting became so bad that the concert had to be stopped. McLean is name-calling in this verse; however, the name calling may have a purpose. The Rolling Stones' song "Sympathy for the Devil" is sung in first person as if the Devil is speaking and it was the first song that had to be stopped at the concert. It's entirely possible the names are not just anger but clues in and of themselves.[85]

The documentary *Gimme Shelter*, which was filmed partly at Altamont, shows a clearly nervous Jagger asking for the crowd to be calm and to "be cool." The crowd does calm and the song is finished.[85]

The Rolling Stones complete "The Sun Is Shining," "Stray Cat Blues" and the Robert Johnson classic "Love in Vain" when there is a scuffle in the front of the crowd. Jagger, now seemingly more confident, continues into "Under My Thumb."[86]

The scuffle involved 18-year-old Meredith Hunter. Apparently Hunter's girlfriend Patty Bredahoff had made statements about how attractive she thought Mick Jagger was and this enraged a very high Hunter. He, with Bredahoff in tow begging him to stop, made his way to the front of the crowd. Dressed in a light green to white suit and hat Hunter is clearly visible in the documentary *Gimme Shelter* pulling a chrome-plated, long-barreled pistol from inside of his jacket. The Hells Angels see him immediately and surround him but not before the film shows something near the front of the pistol. If Hunter gets off a shot then it's fire coming from the gun. If not, then the flash is just light glinting off the chrome of the barrel. If it is fire, then he was shooting at Jagger.[87]

The Hells Angels converged on Hunter and killed him. Angel Alan Passaro was caught on film stabbing Hunter five times. Many other members stomped Hunter on the ground. The gun was taken but later turned over to police.

Charges were filed against those Angels involved, specifically Passaro, but he was found not guilty by reason of self defense as the film clearly showed Hunter was brandishing a gun and most likely shot it.[88]

When Don McLean writes, "And as the flames climbed high into the night," he is surely talking about the escalating violence of the day and evening between the Hells Angels and the crowd at the concert.

The line "To light the sacrificial rite" must mean the death of Meredith Hunter. It's the line "I saw Satan laughing with delight" that sets off the entire section. There are many ways to take the lyric. McLean could be saying that Jagger is responsible for the terrible concert and in turn the death of Hunter. There are also reports that Jagger was performing and smiling at the beginning of the song "Under My Thumb" when Hunter was killed. That would make the line literal. Whichever is correct, or if all of them are correct, it's for sure McLean is making a strong commentary against Mick Jagger, The Rolling Stones and The Altamont Concert.

The day the music died

Remember that at the beginning of this verse Don McLean stated that we were all in one place, probably meaning Woodstock. It's important the verse opened with Woodstock and closed with Altamont.

Rolling Stone magazine wrote a review of the Altamont concert published February 7, 1970, and titled "Rock & Roll's Worst Day: The Aftermath of

Altamont."[90] The story stated that someone tried to buy another Woodstock but it couldn't be done. It was bad. Woodstock was good intentions. Altamont was bad from the beginning.

What McLean was probably saying by using one to start the verse and another to finish it was that if Woodstock opened the Summer of Love, Altamont closed it.

He was singing...

Now the chorus belongs to someone else, someone who has done something terrible. It belongs to Mick Jagger.

VERSE SIX

I met a girl who sang the blues
And I asked her for some happy news,
But she just smiled and turned away.
I went down to the sacred store
Where I'd heard the music years before,
But the man there said the music wouldn't play.
And in the streets: the children screamed,
The lovers cried, and the poets dreamed.
But not a word was spoken;
The church bells all were broken.
And the three men I admire most:
The Father, Son, and the Holy Ghost,
They caught the last train for the coast
The day the music died.
And they were singing,

I met a girl who sang the blues
And I asked her for some happy news,
But she just smiled and turned away.

As before, the first line of the verse sets the timeline; however, verse six tells a short story right at the beginning so the timeline is told in more narrative than a single, short lyric. This is the last and latest, in terms of time, of the verses. The girl who sang the blues who is now unable to offer happy news is probably Janis Joplin.

Joplin had just recorded "Mercedes Benz" on October 1, 1970, as a birthday greeting to John Lennon and was set to record the lead vocal tracks for the song "Buried Alive in the Blues" on October 4. When she failed to show up to the Sunset Sound Studios, her road manager John Cooke went to visit her at what was then called the Landmark Hotel in Los Angeles. He found Joplin dead of what was later determined to be a heroin overdose compounded by alcohol.[91]

I went down to the sacred store
Where I'd heard the music years before,

This lyric has caused some controversy in terms of meaning due to the timeline. Many believe the lyric is simply referencing a record store as being sacred. This is Don McLean lamenting the beginning of the end for the independently owned record stores and the beginning of the large conglomerate stores making their way into the major cities.

There is also a theory that McLean is referencing the closing of Bill Graham's Fillmore East, a popular concert hall located at Second Avenue and East Sixth Street in New York's East Village.[92] The Fillmore was very popular and known to people outside of New York for famous live albums including Frank Zappa's *Fillmore East—June 1971*, The Allman Brothers Band's *At Fillmore East* and Jimi Hendrix's Band of Gypsys' *Live at the Fillmore East*. Miles Davis, The Grateful Dead and Jefferson Airplane also put out live albums of their performances at the Fillmore.[93]

The concern over the lyric meaning the Fillmore East is that the timeline of the song itself may disallow it. The Fillmore closed on June 27, 1971.[94] The album *American Pie* was recorded during the months of May and June in 1971.[95] If the lyric means the Fillmore, then it was a lyric written right at the last moment of recording and that last minute writing doesn't appear anywhere else throughout the song. It's possible but it isn't probable.

The lyric more than likely is naming a record store a sacred store.

But the man there said the music wouldn't play.

Those who hold to the previous lines meaning the Fillmore state that this must be Bill Graham. Again, it's possible.

More likely the lyric is talking about the oncoming demise of the independent record store and the new influx of the corporate record stores. That thought process would also fit with the rest of the song.

What McLean may be specifically talking about is that there is no more music of that wonderful bygone era. There is no more Crickets music. He may also be talking about the end of a specific business practice, the listening booth.

In the 1950s, record stores would have what were known as listening booths where customers could come to a record store, request a listening copy of a new single and then take that to a turntable with headphones and actually listen to the song.[96] That practice was now being phased out in a new corporate world. Buy the music before you listen to it. It was now profit before enjoyment. Music was corporate.

And in the streets: the children screamed,

If we are in 1970 then the nation is mired in the Vietnam War, known as the living room war for the media's ability to bring the horror of the conflict right into the nation's living room through television. This is probably a commentary against the war using the images of children screaming in the streets.

Often people will make reference to the famous photo of a naked Phan Thị Kim Phúc and other children running down a Trang Bang road following a South Vietnamese napalm attack. Although the photo fits the scenario, it was not taken until June 8, 1972, and thus could not have been the inspiration for the lyric.[97]

The lovers cried, and the poets dreamed.

This is probably more imagery against the war. The lovers are wives, girlfriends and the like who are at home to receive the flag draped coffins that are coming back from overseas.

The "poets dreamed" is probably a generalized encompassment of all those artists that were creating works of peace in a time of war.

But not a word was spoken;
The church bells all were broken.

The line is harkening back to the section about the sergeants and how the Beatles were so dominant and how because of that dominance the music industry has become such a corporate machine.

The "church bells" are probably persons that would sing out against the war, those that would write protest songs and cry out that something is wrong. It's no mistake that they are specifically called "church" bells.

The reason that not a word was spoken was probably not because no one wanted to speak; it was probably because they couldn't speak. The music industry simply wouldn't allow it. Music was to be hit-oriented and protest music was not what was selling. It wasn't what was good for the country at a time of war. Thus, not a word was spoken. The church bells all were broken.

And the three men I admire most:
The Father, Son, and the Holy Ghost,
They caught the last train for the coast
The day the music died.

If there is a lyric in "American Pie" that has received more discussion than any other, this is probably it. Who exactly are the Father, Son and the Holy Ghost? Two groupings immediately come to mind, but they are both probably incorrect.

The first is the literal translation that McLean means the Holy Trinity. Things have become so bad that God has left us. That's probably overstating the impact McLean wanted to have, and why at the very end would he become so literal?

The second grouping to come to mind is Buddy Holly, Ritchie Valens, and J. P. Richardson, The Big Bopper. That seems to fit but it doesn't make any logical sense as each of the lines before it seem to do. To begin with, which person is which character? Which of the three is the Holy Ghost? Furthermore, why do they need a train to the coast and to which coast are they traveling? Buddy Holly is from and is buried in Lubbock, Texas.[98] Ritchie Valens is from and buried in Los Angeles, California.[99] The Big Bopper was born in Sabine Pass, Texas, and is buried in Beaumont, Texas.[100] That's two different coasts, the west and the gulf.

Moreover, Buddy Holly is the only member of the three that's even referenced in the song. Why go out of your way to reference them all now at the end in 1970? This grouping doesn't work.

Other groupings that have been suggested for various reasons are:

John F. Kennedy, Robert Kennedy, and Martin Luther King. This grouping doesn't work because there is a set of brothers in the group.

Martin Luther King, John F. Kennedy and Malcolm X. This one is more logical. King is a father, a pastor. Kennedy is famously the son of Joe Kennedy but why Malcolm X? That's too far of a stretch since he is never denoted throughout the first part of the song.

Chuck Berry, Ricky Nelson and Pat Boone. This grouping has the same concern as the one above. Berry and Nelson are being mentioned for the first time.

John F. Kennedy, Richard Nixon and Billy Graham. This grouping has the same problem as noted above. Two members are being mentioned for the first time.

Pete Seeger, Bob Dylan, Buddy Holly. This grouping has a logical chance of being correct. Pete Seeger is the father of the music, Bob Dylan the son and Buddy Holly, being dead, is the Holy Ghost. The problem is that it's out of order. Holly came before Dylan and there's still no satisfactory explanation of the train and the coast.

If there's not a logical explanation for the entire lyric, as there seemingly has been throughout the past five and a half verses, then the grouping cannot be correct. Logically the three people McLean is talking about would be alive because they caught a train. They would not be the actual Father, Son and Holy Ghost Trinity so that must be a metaphor and since only one coast is mentioned they must have all gone to the same coast.

The three people are probably drummer Jerry Allison, bassist Joe B. Mauldin, and rhythm guitarist Niki Sullivan, Buddy Holly's Crickets. Although they specifically have not been mentioned in the song, the Crickets certainly have been. The song "That'll Be the Day" has been referenced every time the chorus played. Moreover, the names logically fit being three men who were alive in 1970, people that McLean admires, and all traveling to the same coast, Los Angeles.

Jerry Allison retained the name of The Crickets and toured with many different musicians before moving to Los Angeles and working as a session musician with the likes of The Everly Brothers, Bobby Vee and Eddie Cochran.[101]

Joe B. Mauldin moved to Los Angeles and became a recording engineer for Phil Spector's Gold Star Studios.[102]

Niki Sullivan left the music business altogether and took a job at Sony in Los Angeles.[103]

The three men Don McLean admired most caught the last train for the coast the Day the Music Died. *And THEY were singing,*

> *Bye-bye, Miss American Pie.*
> *Drove my Chevy to the Levee,*
> *But the Levee was dry.*
> *And them good old boys were drinkin' whiskey in Rye*
> *Singin', "this'll be the day that I die."*
> *"This'll be the day that I die."*
>
> *They were singing...*
> *"Bye-bye, Miss American Pie."*
> *Drove my Chevy to the Levee,*
> *But the Levee was dry.*
> *Them good old boys were drinkin' whiskey in Rye*
> *Singin', "this'll be the day that I die."*

McLean ends his epic, eight and a half minute commentary on the world and the world of music just as he started it, slowly. The song finishes with two complete movements through the chorus further reinforcing that the lyrics are to be a wake for his musical idol. The recording has more and more people joining in, often coming in late and off beat as if the song is being sung at a bar in Rye, New York, February 3, 1959, and everyone has a small glass of whiskey raised say goodbye to Ritchie Valens, The Big Bopper, and Buddy Holly singing, "This'll be the day that I die."

IS THAT IT?

After all of the research and all of the study into the life and times of Buddy Holly, Ritchie Valens, The Big Bopper and Don McLean, this essay creates one large lingering question, "Is anything you've just read correct?" Is the jester really Bob Dylan? Are the king and queen correctly identified? Is Altamont really the flames climbing higher into the night and are the names of the three men Don McLean admired most the three noted just above?

Maybe. Maybe not.

What you have is one interpretation built from over a decade in the radio industry and as many years as an academic bringing together my own thoughts and those of others. Only one man can say for certain and we already know his answer. "American Pie" means he simply does not have to work again if he doesn't want to. Listen for yourself. Become part of the discussion. Agree. Disagree. Enjoy.

Don McLean would probably have wanted it just that way.

Notes

1. Don McLean, *American Pie* (United Artists, 1971).

2. Don McLean, "American Pie," 1971, *American Pie* (United Artists, 1971).

3. Joel Whitburn, *The Billboard Book of Top 40 Hits* (New York: Billboard Books, 2000), 418.

4. Don McLean, "Don McLean's American Pie," http://www.don-mclean.com/?p=68.

5. Don McLean "About Don McLean" http://www.don-mclean.com/aboutdon.asp.

6. Larry Lehmer, *The Day the Music Died: The Last Tour of Buddy Holly, the Big Bopper and Ritchie Valens* (New York: Music Sales Corporation, 2003).

7. McLean, "American Pie."

8. Martin Huxley and Quinton Skinner, *Behind the Music: The Day the Music Died* (New York: MTV, 2000), 69–77.

9. R. Gary Patterson, *Take a Walk on the Dark Side: Rock and Roll Myths, Legends, and Curses* (New York: Fireside, 2004), 22.

10. Lehmer, *The Day The Music Died*, 95.

11. *Behind the Music*, "The Day the Music Died" season 2, episode 19, February 3, 1999.

12. Terry Gross, "Dion the Wanderer, Back 'In Blue,'" http://www.npr.org/templates/story/story.php?storyId=5132750.

13. *Behind the Music*, "The Day the Music Died."

14. NTSB, "Civil Aeronautics Board: Aircraft Accident Report; Beech Bonanza N3794N," http://www.ntsb.gov/Publictn/1959/CAB_2-3-1959.pdf.

15. Ralph E. Smiley, "The Coroner's Report," http://www.fiftiesweb.com/coroner.htm.

16. NTSB, "Civil Aeronautics Board."

17. Shawn Nagy, "Winter Dance Party," http://www.buddyhollyonline.com/mainwdp.html.

18. Keith Zimmerman and Kent Zimmerman, *Sing My Way Home: Voices of the New American Roots Rock* (San Francisco: Backbeat, 2004), 57–64.

119. Lisa Waite, "Rock and Roll! Using Classic Rock as a Guide to Fantasy-Theme Analysis," *Communication Teacher* 22 (January 2008): 10–3.

20. Answers.com, "Don McLean," http://www.answers.com/topic/don-mclean.

21. Super Seventies, "Don McLean in His Own Words," http://www.superseventies.com/ssdonmclean.html.

22. Don McLean, "About Don," http://www.don-mclean.com/?p=106.

23. Ibid.

24. Cecil Adams, "What Is Don McLean's Song 'American Pie' All About?" http://www.straightdope.com/columns/read/908/what-is-don-mcleans-song-american-pie-all-about.

25. NTSB, "Civil Aeronautics Board."

26. William Kerns, "Buddy and Maria Elena Holly Married 50 Years Ago," http://www.lubbockonline.com/stories/081508/loc_318846994.shtml.

27. Patterson, *Take a Walk on the Dark Side*, 13–36.

28. Kerns, "Buddy and Maria Elena Holly Married 50 Years Ago."

29. This concept is mentioned in multiple books including Larry Starr and Christopher Waterman, *American Popular Music: From Minstrel Shows to MTV* (New York: Oxford, 2003), 5–7; Zimmerman and Zimmerman, *Sing My Way Home.* McLean himself makes the reference on his own Web site when discussing the song: Don McLean, "Don McLean's American Pie."

30. Mr. Talk, "Levee Goes Dry as 'American Pie' Tavern Loses Liquor License," http://www.newrochelletalk.com/node/93, and DJ Allyn, "American Pie ~ Don McLean," http://djallyn.org/archives/133.

31. *The New Lexicon Webster's Encyclopedic Dictionary of the English Language* (New York: Lexicon, 1990), 569.

32. Buddy Holly and the Crickets, "That'll Be the Day," 1957, *The "Chirping" Crickets* (Brunswick, 1957).

33. The Monotones, "Book of Love," (Mascot, 1958).

34. Joel Whitburn, *The Billboard Book of Top 40 Hits* (New York: Billboard Books, 2000), 437.

35. Don Cornell, "The Bible Tells Me So" (Coral, 1955).

36. The concept of race records is discussed in both David Brackett, *The Pop, Rock and Soul Reader: Histories and Debates* (New York: Oxford University Press, 2008), 17–19, and Nelson George, *The Death of Rhythm & Blues* (Middlesex, UK: Plume, 2003), 8–11.

37. Kerry Segrave, *Payola in the Music Industry: A History, 1880–1991* (Jefferson, NC: McFarland, 1994), 18–9.

38. The information in this paragraph is from the following sources: Marc Fisher, *Something in the Air: Radio, Rock, and the Revolution That Shaped a Generation* (New York: Random House, 2007), 51–8, and "The Official Alan Freed Website," http://www.alanfreed.com.

39. John Jackson, *American Bandstand: Dick Clark and the Making of a Rock 'n' Roll Empire* (New York: Oxford University Press, 1999), 55.

40. Frankie Lymon and the Teenagers, "Why Do Fools Fall in Love" (Gee, 1956).

41. Thomas Hine, *The Rise and Fall of the American Teenager* (New York: Harper Perennial, 2000), 247.

42. Marty Robbins, "A White Sport Coat (and a Pink Carnation)" (Columbia, 1957).

43. Sean Egan, *The Rough Guide to The Rolling Stones 1 (Rough Guide Reference)* (London: Rough Guides, 2006), 150.

44. The Rolling Stones, *Beggars Banquet* (Decca, 1968), and The Rolling Stones, *Let It Bleed* (Decca, 1969).

45. Gloria Sheppard, *Brian Jones Straight from the Heart: The Rolling Stones Murder* (Johnstown, CO: High Seas, 2007), 261–71.

46. The preceding paragraph and this sentence are referenced from multiple sections of the book Anna Wohlin, *The Wild and Wycked World of Brian Jones: The True Story of My Love Affair with the Rolling Stone* (London: Blake, 2005).

47. Howard Sounes, *Down the Highway: The Life of Bob Dylan* (New York: Grove, 2011), 334.

48. Ibid.

49. Rolling Stone, "Bob Dylan Biography," http://www.rollingstone.com/artists/bobdylan/biography.

50. Noam Chomsky, *Rethinking Camelot: JFK, the Vietnam War, and U.S. Political Culture* (Cambridge, MA: South End, 1999).

51. *Rebel Without a Cause,* dir. Nicholas Ray, Warner Bros., 1955.

52. Bob Dylan, *The Freewheelin' Bob Dylan* (Columbia, 1963).

53. Jude Rogers, "Josh Ritter: Monto Water Rats, London," http://www.guardian.co.uk/music/2007/sep/17/popandrock.folk, and Enoch Kent, "Reviews" http://www.enochkent.ca/reviews.htm.

54. Nigel Williamson, *The Rough Guide to Bob Dylan 2 (Rough Guide Reference)* (London: Rough Guides, 2006), 49.

55. Joel Whitburn, *The Billboard Book of Top 40 Hits* (New York: Billboard Books, 2000), 500–4.

56. Information for the preceding four paragraphs was taken from the following sources: James Tracy, *Direct Action: Radical Pacifism from the Union Eight to the Chicago Seven* (Chicago: The University of Chicago Press, 1996); Jules Feiffer, Tom Hayden and Jon Wiener, *Conspiracy in the Streets: The Extraordinary Trial of the Chicago Eight* (New York: The New Press, 2006); Douglas O. Linder, "The Chicago Seven Conspiracy Trial," http://www.law.umkc.edu/faculty/projects/ftrials/Chicago7/Chicago7.html.

57. "Report of the President's Commission on the Assassination of President Kennedy," http://www.archives.gov/research/jfk/warren-commission-report.

58. See Don McLean, http://www.answers.com/topic/don-mclean and "About Don McLean," http://www.don-mclean.com/aboutdon.asp.

59. Folk Music Archives, "The Weavers," http://folkmusicarchives.org/weavers.htm.

60. For Weavers and Pete Seeger references see The Vocal Group Hall of Fame Foundation, "The Weavers," http://www.vocalhalloffame.com/inductees/the_weavers.html, and "House Unamerican Activities Committee, August 18, 1955, Pete Seeger," http://www.peteseeger.net/HUAC.htm.

61. David King Dunaway, *How Can I Keep from Singing?: The Ballad of Pete Seeger* (New York: Villard, 2008), 237–9.

62. Blackout History Project, "Archive (1965 Blackout)," http://www.blackout.gmu.edu/archive/a_1965.html.

63. Vincent Bugliosi and Curt Gentry, *Helter Skelter: The True Story of the Manson Murders* (New York: Norton, 2001).

64. All references pertaining to Charles Manson and his interpretation of the Beatles song "Helter Skelter" come from the following three sources: Bugliosi and Gentry, *Helter Skelter*, "Testimony of Paul Watkins in the Charles Manson Trial," http://www.law.umkc.edu/faculty/projects/ftrials/manson/mansontestimony-w.html, and "The Influence of the Beatles on Charles Manson," http://www.law.umkc.edu/faculty/projects/ftrials/manson/mansonbeatles.html.

65. "The Prosecution's Closing Argument," http://www.2violent.com/closing_argument4.html, and "Testimony of Paul Watkins in the Charles Manson Trial," http://www.law.umkc.edu/faculty/projects/ftrials/manson/mansontestimony-w.html.

66. "Helter Skelter (Ride)," http://dic.academic.ru/dic.nsf/enwiki/312526. A photo of a Helter Skelter can be found here: "Helter Skelter, South Shields Fairground," http://www.southshields-sanddancers.co.uk/your_photos/kurly_med5.htm.

67. Joel Whitburn, *The Billboard Book of Top 40 Hits* (New York: Billboard Books, 2000), 99.

68. Margaret Moser and Bill Crawford, *Rock Stars Do the Dumbest Things* (New York: Renaissance, 1998), 51–3.

69. Johnny Rogan, *The Byrds: Timeless Flight Revisited: The Sequel*, 4th ed. (London: Rogan House, 1998).

70. Pete Fornatale, *Back to the Garden: The Story of Woodstock* (New York: Touchstone, 2009).

71. IMDB, "Lost in Space," http://www.imdb.com/title/tt0058824/.

72. Jim Lebans and Bob McDonald, *The Quirks & Quarks Guide to Space: 42 Questions (and Answers) About Life, the Universe, and Everything* (Toronto: McClelland & Stewart, 2008), 18–9.

73. John F. Kennedy, "We Choose to Go to the Moon Speech," http://www.historyplace.com/speeches/jfk-space.htm.

74. John F. Kennedy Presidential Library and Museum, "Cuban Missile Crisis," http://www.jfklibrary.org/JFK/JFK-in-History/Cuban-Missile-Crisis.aspx.

75. The Rolling Stones, "Jumpin' Jack Flash" (Decca, 1968). This record is being listed as a single as it was not released as part of any album in 1968. It was released as a single alone.

76. "What Is Don McLean's Song 'American Pie' All About?" http://www.straightdope.com/columns/read/908/what-is-don-mcleans-song-american-pie-all-about.

77. Eric R. Danton, "Ill-Fated Altamont Is a Far More Fitting Symbol of the '60s Than Glorified Woodstock," http://www.courant.com/entertainment/hc-altamont.artaug09,0,5403034.story.

78. Deeha, "The 1969 Altamont Free Concert: The End of the Hippie CounterCulture," http://www.associatedcontent.com/article/1236057/the_1969_altamont_free_concert_the.html?cat=33.

79. "Altamont Music Festival," http://www.absoluteastronomy.com/topics/Altamont_Music_Festival.

80. Support for this paragraph came from the following sources: Ralph J. Gleason, "Aquarius Wept," http://www.esquire.com/features/altamont-1969-aquarius-wept-0870, Mike D. Goldenberg, "Altamont," http://www.mikegoldenberg.com/index.php?SCREEN=altamont.php, and Peter Murphy, "Altamont: The Killing Field," http://www.hotpress.com/archive/392017.html.

81. Unremitting Failure: Pointless Expostulations on the Utter Futility of Everything, "Punch Marty Balin in the Face Day," http://futility.typepad.com/futility/2007/12/punch-marty-bal.html.

82. David Dalton, "Altamont: End of the Sixties: Or Big Mix-Up in the Middle of Nowhere?" http://www.gadflyonline.com/archive/NovDec99/archive-altamont.html.

83. Ibid.

84. Collector's Music Reviews, "Rolling Stones: Altamont Speedway Free Festival," http://www.collectorsmusicreviews.com/rolling-stones/rolling-stones-altamont-speedway-free-festival-tarkl-tcd-001-12.

85. *Gimme Shelter*, dir. Albert Maysles and David Maysles, Maysles Films, 1970.

86. "The Rolling Stones: Altamont Speedway Free Festival," http://www.collectorsmusicreviews.com/rolling-stones/rolling-stones-altamont-speedway-free-festival-tarkl-tcd-001-12.

87. References used for this paragraph are: *Gimme Shelter* (Maysles Films, 1970), Al Barger, "The Rolling Stones' Altamont Music Festival, December 6, 1969: The Anti-Woodstock — Page 4," http://blogcritics.org/video/article/the-rolling-stones-altamont-music-festival/page-4/, and "Rolling Stones Photo Galleries: Hells Angels at Altamont, December 6, 1969," http://www.morethings.com/music/rolling_stones/images/hells_angels/index.html.

88. Associated Press, "Investigators Close Decades Old Altamont Killing Case," http://www.usatoday.com/news/nation/2005-05-26-altamont_x.htm.

89. The Rolling Stones, "Sympathy for the Devil," 1968, *Beggars Banquet* (ABKCO, 1968).

90. John Burks, "Rock & Roll's Worst Day: The Aftermath of Altamont," http://www.rollingstone.com/news/story/5934386/rock__rolls_worst_day.

91. Alice Echols, *Scars of Sweet Paradise: The Life and Times of Janis Joplin* (New York: Holt, 2000), and "Janis Joplin Biography," http://www.rollingstone.com/artists/janisjoplin/biography.

92. Bill Graham, "Bill Graham's Fillmore East," http://subrealities.waiting-forthe-sun.net/Pages/BeIn/HaightAshbury/Fillmore/fillmore_east_history.html.

93. "Discography," http://www.fillmore-east.com/discography.htm.

94. Bill Graham's Fillmore East, http://subrealities.waiting-forthe-sun.net/Pages/BeIn/HaightAshbury/Fillmore/fillmore_east_history.html.

95. Zimmerman and Zimmerman, *Sing My Way Home*.

96. In the following reference the son of a record story owner discusses the bygone practice of listening booths in his father's record store and how patrons come to the store even today to reminisce about the booths and their being part of a bygone era: Phil Cutler, "Cutler's History," http://www.cutlers.com/history.html. In this reference HMV Music Stores proclaim to have been the first to offer patron's listening booths in 1921: "HMV Group plc," http://www.fundinguniverse.com/company-histories/HMV-Group-plc-Company-History.html.

97. World Press Photo, "World Press Photo of the Year: 1972," http://www.worldpressphoto.org/index.php?option=com_photogallery&task=view&id=177&Itemid=115&bandwidth=high.

98. Find a Grave, "Buddy Holly," http://www.findagrave.com/cgi-bin/fg.cgi?page=gr&GRid=492.

99. Find a Grave, "Ritchie Valens," http://www.findagrave.com/cgi-bin/fg.cgi?page=gr&GRid=1363.

100. Find a Grave, "J. P. 'Big Bopper' Richardson, Jr.," http://www.findagrave.com/cgi-bin/fg.cgi?page=gr&GRid=1705.

101. JamBase, "Not Fading Away: Jerry Allison," http://www.jambase.com/Articles/57 03/NOT-FADING-AWAY-JERRY-ALLISON, and "Jerry Allison," http://www.ask.com/music/artist/Jerry-Allison/51382.

102. BBC, "Joe B. Mauldin," http://www.bbc.co.uk/music/artists/019209c4-4f28-474b-80d8-ca2fc52b10d0, and Utopia Artists, "The Crickets," http://www.utopiaartists.com/bio_crickets.htm.

103. The Music's Over, "On This Date (April 6, 2004) Niki Sullivan / Buddy Holly & the Crickets," http://themusicsover.wordpress.com/2009/04/06/niki-sullivan, and "Niki Sullivan," http://www.buddyhollyandthecrickets.com/related/sullivan.html.

2

A Line by Line Analysis of a Classic Song

Ray Schuck

The song, "American Pie," by Don McLean has been an enigma since its release in 1971. Listeners immediately wondered about and discussed the meaning of the lyrics. This bewildering song seemed riddled with subtle meaning and led to many intense and in-depth analyses. The search for meaning has been confounded by the artist's relative lack of definition regarding the lyrics or the music (tempo, pitch, structure, etc.). In a BBC Radio 2 interview, conducted on November 4, 1993, he does mention that the initial stanza deals with the tragic death of Buddy Holly but gives no further clues.[1] While this was, no doubt, exciting for those still pondering the meaning of the lyrics after twenty years, it still left huge gaps in the interpretation. Yet, despite these gaps, the popularity of the song didn't dwindle. It clearly had, and still has, listening power.

In another interview held in December 2005, he relates that his religious philosophy is that of pantheism: "I am not a devoted Christian. I do believe in God. I would say I'm some sort of a pantheist. I live in the forest and I think I'm living in church; that's my God."[2] Pantheism is a belief that God is everything and everything is God; thus, all life is of God and God is inherent in all life. Practitioners of pantheism live personal, conscientious lives, each as a separate entity within the biosphere, yet co-joined with that same biosphere. Consequently, pantheists recognize a certain equality among all living beings, and through social and civic action and interaction and "socialistic" discourse they find meaning, justification, and self-satisfaction in their lives. This brings to mind the transcendentalist movement and their small but significant influence in America in the mid–1800s. McLean's remark leads to thoughts of Henry David Thoreau and his life and writings in a cabin at Walden Pond and publishing a book by the same name in 1854 of his experiences there. It is interesting to note that the complexity of meaning and discussion that exists in Thoreau's work is mirrored in McLean's work, "American Pie."

In 1972 McLean wrote and released the song "Vincent," a tribute to Vincent Van Gogh and his painting *The Starry Night* (painted by Van Gogh in Saint Remy, France, in 1889). In an interview for the *Washington Post* in 1998, Charles Moffett, the director of the Phillips Collection (an art museum founded in 1921 by Duncan Phillips at the Phillips Memorial Gallery located in the DuPont Circle neighborhood of Washington, D.C., and considered America's first museum of Modern Art) relates that "Van Gogh spends a lot of time focusing on the cycle of birth, death and regeneration. The whole idea of the wheat field, a recurrent theme, reflects that: You see it at its ripest moment; you see the sower, and you see the reaper.... We're dealing, in effect, with a pantheist."[3] The association is evident. McLean's "religious" belief, along with other religious analogies, allegories, and metaphors, especially associated with the Judeo-Christian tradition, plays an important part in understanding the lyrics of "American Pie." It can be argued — with little difficulty and considerable reliability — that McLean retains and practices the transcendentalist ideals and values, albeit in a more modern fashion.

Because of its limitations, to extract as much information as possible from "American Pie," the method of historical inference must be used. When direct or tangible evidence is lacking, historical inference is a tool historians will use to decipher and explain events utilizing evidence based on concurrent, similar or implied circumstances that emulate the lacking evidence and substantially support the inference. It is akin to circumstantial evidence or indirect evidence, used by practitioners of law, which implies that something occurred but does not bear direct witness or cannot be directly proven. Most importantly, however, is that the analysis be convincing. There must be "weight" to the analysis, either based on scholarship and/or reliable sources, so that it will successfully pass close scrutiny. The strength of any meaningful examination or discussion of a specific incident, event or topic is based on it being not only convincing but accurate, or as accurate as can be based on available information and the use of available documentation. To "rewrite" history is not necessarily a nefarious activity; it is often a valuable means of improving and clarifying a prior interpretation because of the availability of additional information and documentation. This article is a good case in point. Herein lies the beauty of interpreting the lyrics to "American Pie." McLean ingeniously leaves the meaning vague, perhaps in the hope that people will study and discuss it, thus heightening social awareness to the social, cultural, and even musicological difficulties and dynamics of the time that the song was written — and, no doubt, leading to the popularity and longevity of the song. That the song can be anything a person wants it to be, based on the person's personal perspectives and experiences, is a tribute to the songwriter and, often, the true test of an artist. McLean passes this test.

First and foremost, it must be acknowledged and recognized that this is a song about music, especially rock 'n' roll music from the 1950s to 1970, just prior to the song's release in 1971. There is a loose chronological sequence to the stanzas, starting with the tragic plane crash in Iowa in 1959, and ending with another tragedy in California in December 1969. Each stanza is itself a story, yet part of a larger unfolding tale. Most, if not all, of the inferences pertain to music in some manner or another. In addition, beneath the surface of this musical interpretation of the period there is a strong undercurrent of association to and with the events transpiring in the social and cultural milieu of the time, especially in the last stanza. To understand and grasp the full meanings of the verses, both elements must be considered.

This interpretation, while focusing on the manifest meaning, as indicated through the musical interpretation, will also discuss the latent meaning, as indicated by the activities and events occurring in America at the time. There is little, if no, doubt that the twenty-year period covered in "American Pie" was tumultuous and revolutionary. While America experienced enormous economic growth following World War II, it also experienced considerable social and cultural uncertainty. Racial and gender prejudices did not disappear, nor did the demands of many blue-collar workers who sought a greater, and fairer, share of the economic prosperity. By the 1950s, the social issues and concerns went from being latent to a clear manifestation of importance. The roots of the civil rights movements of the 1960s were planted during this period. The "separate but equal" doctrine, established in 1896 with the U.S. Supreme Court ruling in the case of *Plessy v. Ferguson,* is repeatedly refuted by the Court starting in 1950, culminating in the Court's 1954 decision to end the practice in the case of *Brown v. Board of Education of Topeka, Kansas.* In August, 1955 Emmett Till, a black teenager from Chicago, Illinois, is murdered in Mississippi, leading to nationwide condemnation of the incident. In December of that year Rosa Parks, in direct defiance and violation of a local segregation law, refuses to give up her seat on a municipal bus. Her action leads to a bus boycott in Montgomery, Alabama, ending a year later in the desegregation of buses in that city. The refusal to allow black students to attend high school in Little Rock, Arkansas, in 1957 — the incident now known as The Little Rock Nine — brought significant attention to the plight of young people of African descent to acquire a fair and equal education in public schools. Even music changed as a new genre of music, rock 'n' roll, made its appearance. On the surface life in general appeared calm and full of certainty, but beneath the surface uncertainty roiled and eventually boiled over into a full-fledged re-examination of "American" values.

The next decade revealed the strength of this discontent, as America exploded with issues and events that incited the populace and made headlines on a daily basis. The nation was not only embroiled in a variety of divisive domestic issues, but involved in a war overseas that literally tore it apart. The activities of the 1960s forced America to face the dividing issues and somehow find solutions. This divisiveness was not lost on the popular music industry as it sought music expressing this discontent and produced music that seemed to feed the same discontent — an ever-expanding cycle of growth. By the time "American Pie" appeared on the music scene America had gone through the throes of social awareness that has shaped its domestic and international policies and attitudes to the present.

This period is of particular importance in the song "American Pie." The "noise" of this period infects the narrator's prior and almost naïve view of rock 'n' roll music. The introduction of so many adverse and diverse views and practices in American life and culture, especially its popular music, seems to have the narrator churning with dissatisfaction, which, by the end of the narration, has the narrator exhausted. This dissatisfaction and exhaustion is reflected and noted in the last two stanzas of the song and cements its foremost intent as a song about music, especially rock 'n' roll music.

Until Don McLean, himself, relates exactly what the lyrics mean, all interpretations remain suspect. There have been numerous interpretations,[4] mostly based on opinion and guesswork that have appeared over the years. People who weren't even born when the song appeared are enamored with it and still discuss its meaning and place in American popular culture. All the interpretations and discussions, whether accurate or not, add to the mystique of this ever-popular piece of music.

VERSE ONE

A long, long time ago, I can still remember how that music used to make me smile.

Speaking of the past, the narrator refers to rock 'n' roll music of the 1950s and early 1960s — especially music that spoke of teenage "innocence" and romance, and the joy it brought. There was a heart-warming quality about the music. It spoke to the rites and rituals of growing up and experiencing life in America. There was happiness and hope in the music, despite the uncertainties America faced.

And I knew if I had my chance, that I could make those people dance, and maybe they'd be happy for awhile.

Given the opportunity, the narrator, as a singer/songwriter, would compose music with similar themes and hopefully have people put aside, for a while, the burdens of life experienced off the dance floor. Music that makes people dance is usually associated with happiness and contentment. It is a unique social force that binds a people, and even a society, together. Dancing is seen as a universal form of speaking without words. Both the informal and formal, movements express, individually and collectively, some latent meaning in a manifest manner.

But February made me shiver, with every paper I'd deliver. Bad news on the doorstep. I couldn't take one more step.

With an allegorical twist, the narrator relates his feelings as a young newspaper delivery boy following the news of a tragic airplane crash, not necessarily the cold weather associated with the month of February. The "bad news" is the tragic airplane crash on February 3, 1959, and consequent deaths of Buddy Holly, Ritchie Valens, J. P. Richardson (the Big Bopper), and the pilot, Roger Peterson, shortly after takeoff from the municipal airport at Mason City, Iowa.

Having just finished a performance at the Surf Ballroom in Clear Lake, Iowa, as part of the Winter Dance Party Tour, the three performers were on their way to a concert in Fargo, North Dakota, scheduled for the next day. Rather than take the bus, which had no heat, they opted to fly, at $36 apiece — a goodly sum of money at the time — to their next venue. Waylon Jennings was initially to fly with the group, but gave up his seat to J. P. Richardson. Richardson, at the time, was sick and, because of his body size, found the bus seats uncomfortable. It is related that when Buddy Holly learned that Waylon Jennings wasn't going to join them he jokingly said, "Well, I hope your old bus freezes up," to which Jennings wryly responded, "Well, I hope your old plane crashes." These were words, no doubt, that would haunt Jennings for the remainder of his life. Tommy Allsup also agreed to fly, but lost his seat to Ritchie Valens in a coin toss after the concert at the Ballroom.[5] As a result of this incident, the narrator is stopped "cold" in his tracks, both in life and music.

And I can't remember if I cried when I read about his widowed bride, but something touched me deep inside the day the music died.

A reference to Buddy Holly's wife of five months, Maria Elena Santiago (married August 15, 1958). Maria was pregnant at the time of the airplane crash. She would experience a miscarriage shortly afterward.

The narrator reveals an emotional, and perhaps physical, transformation after learning of and coping with the tragic incident involving the musicians: a time he refers to as the initial "day the music died" or ceased to be relevant and meaningful. The tragic accident would bring sorrow and questions of how and why for people, especially fans, to experience and ponder this incident. These were musicians on the rise in rock 'n' roll music.

So,

Therefore, with regard to the circumstances indicated:

REFRAIN

Bye, bye Miss American Pie. Drove my Chevy to the levee but the levee was dry.

A farewell tribute to the loss of "innocence" or musical and cultural traditions in America, expressed as "Miss American Pie." It is a metaphorical use of the phrase "as American as apple pie." A further metaphorical rendition could include the advertising slogan used by an American car manufacturer through the 1970s: "I love baseball, hot dogs, apple pie, and Chevrolet." This seems evident with the driving of a Chevy to the levee.

It was not uncommon for the youth of America in the 1950s and early 1960s, especially in the suburbs and rural areas, to escape their surroundings and drive to a secluded place where they could express themselves freely without adult supervision or interference. Such a place might be a levee or river embankment, an inlet or possibly a secluded rural area. Seclusion was the objective. That the levee or meeting place was "dry" indicates that no liquor was present, suggesting, instead, the presence by now (the 1960s) of marijuana and, with it, a different type of people gathering there — certainly not good ol' boys.

It seems, too, that the narrator could be speaking of a lost love: a woman. This elusive loss appears periodically throughout the song. Losing a loved one is often a monumental event in a person's life. It transforms the person's attitude toward life in general and the specifics that make up that life. In the narrator's sense, music is of prime importance. It would not be unusual to lose interest in music that once meant something. This loss is reflected in the next stanza, when he casually casts aside his feelings of loss and mentions that, at least, he still digs those rhythm and blues. By referring to her as "Miss American Pie" he gives her the qualities of innocence and associates her with the virtues of youth and beauty. It could also be a mocking reference to the woman he loved and lost — that she was too good for him. This would be enough motive to drive his car to a place where he could drink away his misery in private or with his friends. A place where bonds of friendship were formed and cemented.

Them good ol' boys were drinkin' whiskey in Rye; and singin' this'll be the day that I die. This'll be the day that I die.

In juxtaposition to the youth of the counterculture (whose values and behavior run counter to the accepted, traditional values and behavior of the social mainstream), who bought into the psychedelic musical changes of the period (1960s) and to whom marijuana and drugs were the mediums of choice for getting "high" or intoxicated, the "good ol' boys" represented the traditional, hard-working, hard-fighting, hard-drinking, mainly rural dwellers of American society. Finding the levee "dry," the boys would have to go elsewhere to drink. With rye — the grain of choice of America's earliest distillers — being a type of whiskey (in America there are a variety of whiskies, including blended, bourbon, rye, Tennessee, and wheat whiskies) it is apparent that the boys probably would not be drinking whiskey and rye, as rye was a form of whiskey, but drinking whiskey somewhere in Rye, New York. The narrator, himself, would have personal experience of this, having lived in New Rochelle, New York, a community several miles southwest of Rye: communities outside New York City, but close enough to be exposed to the influences of "the city." Both communities, Rye and New Rochelle, are close to the Long Island Sound, which, with its myriad inlets, marshes, and vacant spaces, would make levee-finding quite easy. The Long Island Sound has been a significant part of the history of New York, from the early Dutch merchants through the spy activities and smuggling activities during the American Revolution and industrial growth afterward.

Singing "this'll be the day that I die" indicates that they are not about to give up their rural "mainstream" values and lifestyle, especially for the "new" values and lifestyles of the counterculture. The good ol' boys would rather die than do so. There is a hint of association with Buddy Holly's song "That'll Be the Day," released in 1957. Here, too, the association with his lost love is subtly noted.

In referring to "them good ol' boys" the narrator is mentioning others he observes. There is no reason to assume or believe that the narrator is referring to himself in this instance; although, later in the song he will. While each stanza of the refrain has a binding all-encompassing meaning, it also holds specific meaning with the passing of the years in the chronological order of the song.

VERSE TWO

Did you write the book of love, and do you have faith in God above? If the Bible tells you so.

The initial wording appears to reference the Monotones song "The Book of Love," released in 1958. The song contains four chapters outlining the substance of this Book of Love and how to deal with a relationship. These chapters have meaning in this verse and appear to resonate throughout the various verses of the song "American Pie." The question being posed is somewhat rhetorical, even allegorical, asking if you, the audience or listeners, wrote this book of love as witnessed by the way you live and act, following the instructions of the four chapters outlined in the song, and not deviating from them in light of the "new" concept of free love and thought. It is a poignant indictment to America and the developing social adjustments.

He asks that if you, the audience and listeners, did write it, do you have faith that God will keep the traditional and pure way of love and life alive? But, you are a fickle audience and uncertain of the free-thought, and somewhat transcendental, revival gathering sway in America, and you must rely on the Bible to make the decisions for you. He seems to imply that the reason people have faith in God is because the Bible calls for it and not as a result of their personal understanding and association with God — a pantheist belief. There could be hints of references to music with similar themes and associations: for example, Don Cornell's 1955 song "The Bible Tells Me So."

It must be noted that associations in some form or manner with various songs of the time occur frequently throughout "American Pie." This aspect helps identify with what period each stanza is associated.

Now do you believe in Rock and Roll, can music save your mortal soul, and can you teach me how to dance real slow?

This is a rather straightforward question, asking if you, the audience, believe in the staying power and the "magic" of rock 'n' roll at a time when music passing itself off as rock 'n' roll is starting to gain attention and prominence. There appears to be a very strong association with the song "Do You Believe In Magic," released in 1965 by the Lovin' Spoonful, who identify, in their lyrics, the magic of rock 'n' roll. This song could easily be the mantra for traditional rock 'n' roll music as identified by the narrator. It encompasses all the virtues the narrator holds dear in this genre. Do you, the audience, believe that music is so powerful that it can affect your being? That it can consume you entirely — heart, body, and soul. The narrator, believing that it can and does, asks to learn to dance slow — something essential for a successful evening of dance and perhaps a wee romance. This would make his being complete, and necessary to experience the "magic" as pronounced by the Lovin' Spoonful, where the music is all encompassing both spiritually and physically.

There could be a vaguely disguised reference to the song "Heart and Soul," made popular in 1961 by the Cleftones, a group from Queens, New York. This would segue nicely into the verses comprising the remainder of this stanza, albeit with a disappointing outcome.

Well I know that you're in love with him, 'cause I saw you dancing in the gym.

Watching the body language at a dance in a gymnasium reveals to the narrator a relationship he, perhaps, is envious of and ruefully acknowledges.

Dances held in gymnasiums, especially high school gymnasiums, were common in the late 1950s and throughout the 1960s. The phenomenon is identified in the popular song, released in 1957, by Danny and the Juniors, "At the Hop." In addition, having a live band — and not a deejay, disc jockey or record spinner, as they were aptly referred to — was preferred. Hops were kept alive through the medium of radio, especially in the New York City area on stations WABC, WINS, WMCA, and WMGM. Numerous disc jockeys had shows dedicated to promoting rock 'n' roll music — the term coined, perhaps as early as 1951, by Alan Freed when he was at radio station WJW in Cleveland, Ohio, in referring to rhythm and blues music. Not least among these disc jockeys in New York City was WINS jockey Murray the K (Murray Kaufman) and his Swingin' Soiree. Forty years after the release of "American Pie" Cousin Brucie (Bruce Morrow), a disc jockey on WABC in the 1960s, is still popular on radio.

You both kicked off your shoes. Well I dig those rhythm and blues.

By kicking off their shoes, the dancers were getting serious about their activity. Also, because shoes might scuff the hardwood floor, dancers were often "required" to remove them. The inference here, too, is to the sock hops of the 1950s, as told in the song by Danny and the Juniors, and one released in 1956 by Little Richard: "She's Got It." The narrator, as if shrugging, comments that, despite the activity of the two people he is particularly watching and paying attention to and his inability to participate in it, he still enjoys rhythm and blues music nonetheless — music which, by the late 1950s and early 1960s, was entering the rock 'n' roll genre more expressively and expansively. The roots of rhythm and blues originate in the 1930s, with a following from Swing Music, especially that of Louis Jordan. In the 1940s, Sonny Boy Williamson and others emerged to bring a "new" style to rhythm and blues, leading to different "sounds" emanating from different parts of the country. It also led to the recording and distribution under "black" labels. In 1959, the period under review in "American Pie," Motown was established as the distributor of many black artists and their music. Numerous rock 'n' roll artists and musicians attribute their styles and success to early rhythm and blues artists.

I was a lonely teenage bronkin' buck, with a pink carnation and a pickup truck.

The narrator doesn't fit in at the dances, and perhaps at other youth activities, suggesting a loose tie to the Beat Generation. He has energy to burn, with the implication of a rebel without a cause or a cause immersed in music seeming to slip away from his personal standards and beliefs. Yet he wants desperately to fit in, and he is still lamenting his loss at the dance, as noted and exemplified by the release in 1957 of the song by Marty Robbins

"A White Sport Coat and a Pink Carnation." The song reflects his loneliness and despair. There is no reason to associate the 1960 song "Lonely Teenager" by Dion in this verse. The narrator's loneliness, as inferred, is completely different than that expressed in Dion's song.

Having a pickup truck, instead of a sedan or expensive automobile, suggests an association with the good ol' boys and their lifestyle, and someone who has the means to "escape." It is clear the narrator is aging and experiencing a more adult view of the world.

But I knew that I was out of luck, the day the music died.

For the narrator life is changing, but in some respects it is not — the girl is lost, his luck has run out, and the music is going to pot, literally. For him it would be a "day the music died." The music to dance to and the heady music of romance are fading away.

And I was singin'

Thus, the narrator, himself, is singing and, at this time, includes himself as one of those good ol' boys.

Refrain...

Repeat interpretation....

VERSE THREE

Now for ten years we've been on our own, and moss grows fat on a rolling stone, but that's not how it used to be.

There are two ten-year periods at work in the song. The initial ten-year period — the one indicated in this verse — refers to the period from the inception of rock 'n' roll music, as coined by Alan Freed, to the arrival of musicians from overseas, who would dramatically influence rock 'n' roll music. By the mid–1950s, rock 'n' roll was an established genre in the American popular music industry and in American culture, seemingly reinforced by Danny and the Juniors with the release in 1958 of their song "Rock and Roll Is Here to Stay." But, in July, 1963, the Beatles released their first album or LP [long-playing record] in America: *Introducing the Beatles: England's No. 1 Vocal Group.*[6] This was preceded by single releases of three 45s [records played at 45 rpm or revolutions per minute on record turntables], with their first "hit" coming in February 1963, with the release of the single "Please, Please Me/Ask Me Why." A year later, on February 7, 1964, the Beatles arrived in the United States, leading what would become known as the "British Invasion." Prior to their arrival, only a handful of European musicians achieved success on the

American rock 'n' roll scene. Thus, American rock 'n' roll had been on its own for the ten years prior to the British Invasion.

By 1969/70, the end of the musical story the narrator is relating in "American Pie," it has been ten years from the tragic deaths of February 1959, the arrival of the Beatles and their music and the consequent British Invasion, to the concert by the Rolling Stones referred to later in the song. This is the second ten-year period constructed in the song, and it would lead to the final death knell for music as the narrator is explaining it and experiencing it.

Thus, American rock 'n' roll had been on its own for approximately ten years, only to be frustrated, and influenced, by strong competition from overseas — an influence from which it would never recover.

There is a slight association with the song released in 1965 by Bob Dylan titled "Like a Rolling Stone." Playing on Dylan's question and description of a rolling stone, and with the clever use of metaphor, the narrator utilizes the adage "A rolling stone gathers no moss" to interpret the infusion and popularity of rock 'n' roll music at the time by the British Invasion groups onto the American music scene. As the adage goes, a rolling stone, because of its movement, can gather no moss. Stone is another word for rock, as in a stone or rock garden or fence. Thus, moss is growing fat on a rolling rock or rock rolling or rock 'n' roll! This happens because the British groups, and the "sound" they brought with them, had virtually captured and ruled the music charts and consequent marketing. Traditional American artists for the most part were not keeping pace, thereby gathering moss, and, in some instances, stopping or dying, with the moss growing heavy. Yet, rock 'n' roll, as expressed in myriad other genres — Psychedelic, Acid, Space, etc. — is still rolling along and prospering. This is a superb play on words by the narrator, akin to "having your cake and eating it, too." The narrator clearly sees the death of traditional rock 'n' roll.

When the jester sang for the king and queen, in a coat he borrowed from James Dean, and a voice that came from you and me.

This verse along with the previous verse, when configured as a complete sentence, firmly establishes the ten-year period mentioned in this stanza: from the inception Freed's pronouncement of rock 'n' roll music (ca. 1951–52) to the appearance of Bob Dylan in England (1962).

The allusion is to Bob Dylan[7] as the jester — a jester being the only person who could speak candidly and with impunity to a person or persons in positions of power. The reference is an apt one, as Dylan had become, by the early 1960s, a balladeer akin to Woody Guthrie and Pete Seeger. His songs were thorns in the sides of those in power in America, and Dylan sang them with impunity. In 1962, Bob Dylan sang in the King & Queen Pub behind

Goodge Street Station in London.[8] To sing "for" something or someone signifies a greater sense of fulfillment in music, as opposed to singing "at" some place. Thus, singing for the crowd at the King & Queen Pub heralded the beginning of Dylan's acceptance in the United Kingdom.

The coat Dylan borrows from James Dean has a dual meaning — literally and figuratively. In the literal interpretation, Dylan is pictured on the cover of his *The Freewheelin' Bob Dylan* album (released in 1963) in a similar coat worn by James Dean in the 1955 film *Rebel Without a Cause*. In the figurative meaning, Dylan adopted and adapted to or "wore" the lifestyle of the Beat Generation in his poetry/music, mannerisms, and persona. Whether he actually wore such a coat at the King & Queen Pub is moot.

In one regard, Dylan's voice is not that of a trained vocalist; it is a common voice, albeit a wee raspy. In another regard, his lyrics and manner of singing reflect the dilemmas and plight of the common person — "you and me." He is singing our life's song for us, as many would come to acknowledge. His music captured the realities of American social and cultural discontent and gave a voice to that discontent.

While the "king" may seem an obvious reference to Elvis Presley, who was dubbed by the media as such after a fan inference, there is no reason to surmise that the "king" is Elvis or anyone comparable, nor the queen anyone of similar note of either sex. If anything, Big Joe Turner (whose song "Shake, Rattle, and Roll" Elvis borrowed in 1954) or Chuck Berry could be considered the king of rock 'n' roll, with Elvis as the jester or, seen in the domain of "Colonel" Tom Parker and his soon-to-be-realized merchandizing empire,[9] as the court clown — another meaning to the word "jester." A more persuasive argument along these lines could be made that the "king" is B.B. King, and the "queen" is Aretha Franklin, the "Queen of Soul," who had several musical hits in about an 18 month span between early 1967 and late 1968 — an amazing feat by popular music standards. Dylan — if we recognize him as the jester — could have sang for, sang with or, at least, appeared on the same stage with either or both these musicians during his appearances at the various blues, jazz, and folk festivals and other venues held across America throughout the 1960s.

Oh and while the king was looking down, the jester stole his thorny crown.

The king referred to here is Woody Guthrie, who died October 3, 1967, of Huntington's disease. The narrator is adding an "aside" that plays on one of the words — "king" — as mentioned. Guthrie is looking down from heaven, a reference to the biblical belief of heaven being above the earth and hell below or within the earth. In the Christian belief God resides in heaven, a place above the earth. The narrator has already indicated this earlier in the song. The concept of heaven above is immortalized in the hymn by Martin Luther, written in 1523, "Our Father, Thou in Heaven Above." Heaven stands in juxtaposition to hell, which is below the earth. The concept of hell, as noted, is depicted in Chapter 24 of the New Testament book of Matthew, where the cursed will be cast into "the everlasting fire prepared for the devil and his angels." This concept plays out later in the song, when the narrator introduces Mick Jagger and his music. This place is epitomized in "The Inferno" by Dante Alighieri, ca. early 1300s, as part of his book *The Divine Comedy*. The concept of hell is especially poignant in Pieter Bruegel the Elder's painting *Dulle Griet* or *Mad Meg*, painted ca. 1562.

The thorny crown is a reference to the crown of thorns put on the head of Jesus the Christ, the self-proclaimed King of the Jews according to rabbinical claims of the time. The crown signifies not only a "kingly" station, but in this instance — with thorns — one that is full of adversity and suffering, often at the hands of others, aspects of life Guthrie knew well.

The jester is still Bob Dylan, who, as revealed and outlined in the next verse, appears to "steal" the crown from Guthrie.

The courtroom was adjourned. No verdict was returned.

In the court of public opinion of the time, there is no decision yet whether Dylan has indeed replaced Guthrie, whom he admired and emulated, as the spokesperson for the common folk of America, and, in 1962, Dylan wrote a tribute to Guthrie in "A Song for Woody." Dylan himself proclaimed that he was "A Woody Guthrie jukebox." On the cover of his album *The Times They Are A-Changin*,' released in 1964, Dylan appears to mimic Guthrie.[10] But, by the time of Guthrie's death, Dylan had "electrified" his music — initially at the Newport Folk Festival in 1965 [where, by the way, McLean had his guitar stolen] — leaving doubt as to whether he had indeed inherited the crown. While there were others who could have claimed Guthrie's mantel — not the least being Pete Seeger, who helped establish and fund the organization, People's Songs, a progressive organization dedicated to creating, promoting, and distributing songs relating to the struggles of the labor movement and other social issues — it was Dylan who gained the attention, notoriety, and popularity for expressing the issues and people affected by them at the time.

And while Lennon read a book on Marx,

In the late 1960s John Lennon was associated with the International Marxist Group and contributed to their publication, "Red Mole," edited by Tariq Ali and Robin Blackburn.[11] He later joined protest marches in London organized by the Troops Out movement, a group whose aim was to end British involvement in Northern Ireland, and is photographed in 1971 marching in a demonstration carrying a sign reading, "Red Mole/For the IRA/Against British Imperialism." He is depicted here as spending his time with revolutionary ideas and with social activism, and not necessarily his music career. He has often been associated with revolutionary ideas and ideals. In 1968 the Beatles would release a song written by Lennon titled "Revolution."

The quartet practiced in the park

This appears to be a reference to the free concert the Rolling Stones performed at Hyde Park, England, on July 5, 1969 — the "park" referred to in the song. The concert included the songs "Jumpin' Jack Flash" and "Sympathy for the Devil." Both songs are referred to in a later stanza. By playing free, at Hyde Park, it allegorically implies the band was "practicing" for another concert. This concert would come in December of the same year at Altamont Raceway Park in Alameda County in Northern California, which is also referenced in a later stanza.

While it could be argued that the Beatles did play in a park — they played at Shea Stadium in New York and later at Candlestick Park in San Francisco, California — thus establishing them as the probable quartet playing there, the evidence does not support this. The Beatles performing at Candlestick Park does not follow the chronological sequence; although, the Shea Stadium concert does. However, with — "while," as noted in the previous verse — Lennon reading a book on Marx, it is unlikely this reference to the quartet pertains to the Beatles, as they'd be a trio with Lennon not with them, and not a foursome or quartet. Additionally, the Beatles retired from touring in the summer of 1966 following their concert in San Francisco, thus officially eliminating any performances in public as a group [when Paul McCartney was supposed to have died — as discussed further on].

And we sang dirges in the dark, the day the music died.

With the growing popularity of the Rolling Stones and their "expressive" lyrics that run counter to the mainstream ideology of the period, perhaps the narrator is referring to the dirge-like quality of folk music and some of its musical mourning. Groups like the Weavers, the Kingston Trio, and others are now relegated to the background or "dark" area of music. The narrator is suggesting that "We," he and others, the folk singers and the standard-bearers of traditional rock 'n' roll music at the time, are in the background singing these forgotten ballads and songs. Here, too, the implication is that "American" rock 'n' roll, growing moss, is ebbing away. He appears to be strongly implying that he, too, and his music, is transforming into another genre — folk.

Thus, with the cultural move toward a non-traditional, counterculture lifestyle, and the music reflecting and even generating and contributing to this move, it would be another "day the music died."

And we were singin'

"We," the folk artists and the standard-bearers of traditional rock 'n' roll music, are singing.

Refrain...

Repeat interpretation....

Verse Four

Helter skelter in the summer swelter, the birds flew off with the fallout shelter, eight miles high and fallin' fast.

In 1969, the Beatles released the song "Helter Skelter" on their "White Album," as it was commonly referred. Charles Manson believed the song reflected an apocalyptic war that would unfold across America, with resultant racial tensions between blacks and whites. From 1964 through the remainder of the 1960s, there would be public race riots and other civil disturbances in various cities throughout America. One of the most notable and costly was the Watts Riots in the suburbs outside Los Angeles, California, in 1965. Thus, in August 1969, Manson declared, "Now is the time for Helter Skelter," and instructed his followers to carry out the Tate-LaBianca murders just north of Los Angeles. Manson found numerous references in songs appearing on the "White Album" to back up his fanatical contentions.[12]

The music of the Byrds, who for a brief period of time challenged the Beatles commercially and covered many songs written and played by Bob Dylan, could be seen as protection and safety from such fanatical interpretations [consider the "Paul is Dead" mania — which will be discussed further on] and a fragile link to traditional rock 'n' roll music. But in 1969 the Byrds released a song "Eight Miles High," which plummeted — along with their stellar popularity — in its rise on the music charts when radio stations refused to continue playing it on the airwaves. With this, they would have relinquished that safety net.

It landed foul on the grass, the players tried for a forward pass, with the jester on the sidelines in a cast.

As mentioned, after its release, many radio stations banned the song "Eight Miles High" for what were believed to be references to drug use. This could be a reference to the popularity of the Byrds landing foul or out-of-bounds upon the grass — an allusion to a foul ball in baseball and to marijuana, which is called, colloquially, "grass." This could also be a reference to the 1967 release by Buffalo Springfield of the songs "Expecting to Fly" and "Flying on the Ground Is Wrong." Both would tie in perfectly with the lyrics of the second stanza, indicating lingering thoughts about a broken romantic relationship. Such lingering resentments, spiked with remorse and self-pity, would not be unusual.

The "players" refers to the rock 'n' roll bands attempting to move some of the traditional rhythm and blues aspects of rock 'n' roll music ahead, away from, and even over, the predominating psychedelic influences, and the Acid Rock and Space Rock genres that were proliferating at the time, especially with the demise of the Byrds. Perhaps, they were even attempting to move ahead of the popularity and resurgence of folk music that Bob Dylan and others were bringing back. This occurred while Bob Dylan, a.k.a. "the jester," briefly quit touring and literally disappeared from the music scene following a motorcycle accident (July 29, 1966), and devoted his time to "electrifying" his music with a group or "cast" of players/musicians from Canada. There is considerable doubt about the severity of Dylan's accident, and it is further doubted he wore a protective plaster bandage or cast of any sort. The narrator is merely utilizing an allegorical reference here. Dylan would reappear in public almost eighteen months later at a benefit concert for the, then, late Woody Guthrie to help raise money to fight the disease from which Guthrie died. Their relationship is discussed and noted in a previous stanza.[13]

Now the halftime air was sweet perfume, while the sergeants played a marching tune.

The narrator suggests the presence of marijuana wafting through the air at a football game, a popular high school and college sport, where the crowd is treated to musical performances by marching bands at halftime — or the halfway point of the game/match.

In June 1967, the Beatles released *Sgt. Pepper's Lonely Hearts Club Band*, an album, along with *Magical Mystery Tour* album (December 1967), that significantly changed the "sound" of the Beatles. It was a composition of vibrant music meant to be listened to, rather than danced to. This appears to be the reference to the "sergeants." The releases occur at a time when marijuana and drug use were alluded to in music and becoming more pronounced with America's youth.

We all got up to dance. But we never got the chance.

Believing that this "new" Beatles sound would resurrect the past, the crowd was disappointed as the music from *Sgt. Pepper's Lonely Hearts Club Band* was composed in such a way that you could not dance to it!

However, in an interview with Barry Melton, cofounder and lead guitarist of Country Joe [McDonald] and the Fish, he mentions, "we were playing a show in Vancouver, Canada, and we were told there was no dancing on Sundays. During the concert, people got up to dance, and I remember the promoter looking at me desperately. 'What are you doing? The RCMP [Royal

Canadian Mounted Police] will be all over the place.' He had to stop them from dancing."[14] Perhaps this verse is referring to that event?

'Cause the players tried to take the field, but the marching band refused to yield.

The "players," as noted above, would attempt a return to the fore of rock 'n' roll music, but the Beatles refused to "yield" or depart from the compositional road they were on, and in some ways established. They never would go back. Following the Country Joe and the Fish incident, then, "the players" would be the band or even the concert-goers and "the marching band" the RCMP.

Do you recall what was revealed, the day the music died.

What may well have been revealed was that rock 'n' roll bands would never successfully go back to the traditional musical styles — thus, the day the music died ... again.

Continuing along with the Country Joe and the Fish analysis, the revelation could well be the death of innocence and "respectability" in music indicated by the popularity of the Fish Cheer: F-U-C-K. The Rolling Stones concert at Altamont in December 1969, could be added to this interpretation, thus officially closing the musical day the music died.

Perhaps, too, this verse is a reference to the fact that Paul McCartney of the Beatles is alive, as featured in a *Life* magazine story on November 7, 1969. The rumor that McCartney was dead started only a month earlier that year and led to a "Paul is Dead" mania, including a fan magazine that appeared at the same time relating all the details of his death. In addition, McCartney himself in the article appearing in *Life* mentions that "The Beatle thing is over."[15] It is possible that this revelation could be what the narrator is suggesting as part of "the day the music died."

And we were singin'

"We," being the traditionalists, were singing.

Refrain...

Repeat interpretation....

VERSE FIVE

And there we were all in one place, a generation lost in space, with no time left to start again.

The reference appears to be to the Woodstock Music and Arts Fair, commonly called "Woodstock" or the "Woodstock Music Festival" held near Bethel, New York, in August 1969, when an estimated 500,000 people gathered at a venue prepared to accommodate about half that many. The media attention focused on the Hippies attending the music concert, sleeping in tents, partying, using drugs, etc.— seemingly surviving with no care for what the next day might or could bring. The reference used at the time for people practicing such a lifestyle was that they were "lost in space." To be such was to be living a care-free existence, without serious regard for the future. Thus, the reference in the song. The music of choice for such a population was known as "psychedelic music" or music that both enhanced drug use and sounded more vibrant and relevant when using drugs. With the popularity of this music, there would be no going back to the more traditional days of rock 'n' roll music — no starting over again.

So come on Jack be nimble, Jack be quick, Jack Flash sat on a candlestick because fire is the devil's only friend.

Another play on lyrics, the narrator is using the title of the song by the Rolling Stones, "Jumpin' Jack Flash," to refer to Mick Jagger, whose antics on stage make the title appropriate. The narrator is encouraging Jagger to get on with it — it being the final knell or death blow to traditional rock 'n' roll music.

Again, there are religious overtones with regard to the betrayal of Jesus by Judas the Iscariot. Jagger and the band do get on with it when they perform at Altamont Raceway Park — commonly called "Altamont."[16] The concert was originally planned to be performed in San Francisco's large urban Golden Gate Park, but was moved to Altamont only twenty-four hours before the performance was scheduled to accommodate the expected large number of spectators. This change of venue did not allow the promoters sufficient time to make the necessary arrangements to handle such a large crowd, estimated to be over 300,000 people. As a result, chaos often prevailed at the concert. It surely was not the mirror image of Woodstock.

As noted earlier, the last public performance by the Beatles was at Candlestick Park, the colloquial term for Monster Park, which name itself has metaphorical meaning. By not performing there, the Rolling Stones were essentially quashing the remnants of the Beatles legacy, insinuating that they could do better, and, at the same time, determinedly maintaining their place as the top act. It is like pouring fire or damnation and torment on an already ruined situation. Thus, Jagger himself is identified with the devil, as he displays the traits associated with that entity: deception, arrogance, a tempter and sower of discord, and a purveyor of false doctrine — all borne out in his music.

Oh and as I watched him on the stage, my hands were clenched in fists of rage.

Here the "watching" is both literal — referring to Jagger's performance on the stage at Altamont — and figurative — borrowing a phrase from Shakespeare, "All the world's a stage," relating to Jagger's activities and actions off the performance stage as he precariously lived his life. The narrator displays extreme displeasure, disgust, and hatred with the clenching of his hands. Could this distaste and rage be severe enough to have the narrator, himself, turn away from rock 'n' roll music and the path it is now on? It appears so.

No angel born in hell could break that Satan's spell.

For the Altamont concert, Hells Angels, a motorcycle club, provided stage security for the band. A chapter of this group had also provided security at the Hyde Park concert. Authorities designate this club an OMG or Outlaw Motorcycle Gang. Their exploits are notorious and tend to be violent. This violence was displayed at the Altamont concert when members of the group attacked Meredith Hunter, who was wielding a gun in front of the stage, and stabbed, kicked, and beat him to death. There were several instances of violence during the concert, but none as pronounced as this.

In Chapter 28 of the Old Testament book of Ezekiel, it is revealed that Satan was once anointed as a guardian cherub and driven from the Holy Mount because of his evil ways. The motorcycle club is depicted as Satan's helpers/angels [see notation in stanza 3] or as their name indicates: Hells Angels. Thus, the narrator plays off the group's moniker with the lyrics, "no angel born in hell."

Further observation reveals that even with all this violence taking place, Jagger, with his attire, actions on stage, and music, appears to be under Satan's spell as he continues to perform. This is reinforced by the lyrics of the band's 1968 release of "Sympathy for the Devil." This song was sung both at the Hyde Park[17] and the Altamont concerts.

And as the flames climbed high into the night, to light the sacrificial rite, I saw Satan laughing with delight, the day the music died.

The "flames" refers to the vitriolic lyrics of the music, which, being amplified from the stage to reach the large audience, would have to be projected far into the night. The surrealism of the concert is not lost on the narrator, as he recognizes it as a "sacrificial rite" or the killing of traditional rock 'n' roll. All this is to the pleasure of Satan, the evil adversary of God or all that is good. This is yet another unhappy ending as the day the music died.

And he was singin'

"He": a delighted Satan, mockingly singing.

Refrain...

Repeat interpretation....

VERSE SIX

I met a girl who sang the blues, and I asked her for some happy news. She just smiled and turned away.

The reference here seems to be about Janis Joplin, who, along with Big Brother and the Holding Company, brought popularity to blues arrangements and singing in the traditional blues rock 'n' roll genre. Perhaps she might have some promising news about this breakthrough. But, she does not. Smiling, as she always seemed to be, she turns away or dies, her death occurring in 1970.

Of course, asking a blues musician or singer for happy news is almost certainly to be met with a negative response. This seems to set the tone for this stanza: one of sadness and loss.

So I went down to the sacred store, where I'd heard the music played before, but the man there said the music wouldn't play.

The narrator travels to and enters a notable record store — a place where traditional rock 'n' roll was frequently played. But the desired music is no longer popular and, consequently, not being played in the store. As a marketing strategy it is common to play the popular music of the day as people shop in the store to enhance their shopping and purchasing appetite. Not having it played would indicate its demise.

And in the streets the children screamed.

This verse suggests a reference to numerous protests by the youth of America in the streets of America for a variety of causes, most notably, perhaps, the riot at Sunset Strip, California, in 1966, which inspired the immensely popular song "For What It's Worth" by Buffalo Springfield released the following year. It could also refer to the hysterical, screaming fans at concerts or accompanying many of the bands at the time. This, however, seems unlikely considering the change in tempo of the song, unless, of course, the narrator is bemoaning the fact that it is occurring.

The lovers cried and the poets dreamed.

The lovers of traditional rock 'n' roll, those who kept the spirit of the music alive in a variety of ways, would be saddened, along with the narrator. Tears could, and according to the narrator would, be shed for this passing — tears similar to those shed at a funeral, where the passing hurts emotionally, with the good deeds and personal and social accomplishments remembered. Here, too, the narrator could be revealing his emotional attachment and sadness over his lost love.

Yet, with each passing comes hope. Hope that the next day, and every day thereafter, will bring joy and the promise of something better. Thus, "the poets" or folk musicians, for whom music was fluid poetry, are looking toward the future, toward a day when that joy will return and that promise will be fulfilled. Such "dreams" would be a part of the narrator's disposition and transformation, as well, as he laments both the day the music died and his love lost.

But not a word was spoken. The church bells all were broken.

It is tempting to read in these words the termination of the work done with American folk, jazz, and blues musicians by John Lomax, the musicologist who spent decades recording and documenting the music and lifestyles of the world's folk music and the people who made it. His interviews and work with Bill Broonzy, Woody Guthrie, Vera Hall, Lead Belly Ledbetter, Jelly Roll Morton, Pete Seeger, Memphis Slim, Muddy Waters, and many other musicians helped bring national attention to the lives and accomplishments of these artists. By 1970, Lomax would move on to the interpretation and the teaching of his work on cantometrics and choreometrics, and no longer be as actively involved as he was in conducting oral documentation projects.[18] Thus, there would be no more words spoken to preserve for posterity the work of American musicians in these genres — all of which would have been seen as significant by the narrator. But, the narrator appears to be speaking of the deathly silence, both commercially and popularly, regarding public concern for the new trends in music — not as a social catharsis, which was quite loud, but as a musical one.

Church bells serve a variety of purposes: they keep time and alert people to the time of day; they announce joyous occasions, like weddings, etc.; they call people to prayer for a variety of purposes; they toll for the dead — one chime for each year of the person's life; they serve as a solemn notice of excommunication in the Roman Catholic Church; they play music on holidays, such as Christmas, and for special occasions. To have them broken is to deprive a community of an important part of its meaning and heritage. That they were broken implies that no one was able to or wanted to fix them. In this instance it is a silent death knell to traditional rock 'n' roll music.

Perhaps, though, this verse, along with the mention of the lovers crying in the previous verse, is a reference, and a closing statement, to the second stanza, where the girl so sought after to dance with is gone. There would be no "I dos" or words, as such, spoken, nor the joyous ringing of the church bells to announce the happy event. It would, then, close this chapter of the underlying story being told in this song — and, to an extent, in The Book of Love — although there would be no reconciliation.

And the three men I admire the most—The Father, Son, and Holy Ghost—

This verse, perhaps more than any of the others, has been, and still remains, the most problematic. Who could these three people be? What could this trinity represent? While difficult to pinpoint, the evidence is there to make a safe and fair analysis and prediction.

There is an outside chance that the narrator is referring to Buddy Holly, Ritchie Valens, and J. P. Richardson, as this would bring the song full circle and neatly close it. But, this interpretation lacks credibility: in historical perspective (for example, these entertainers, as well as their music, were heading into the interior of the country, not either coast, when they passed away), in grammatical tense (the narrator is speaking in the present tense, not the past tense), and in the manner in which the song comes to a climax, among other reasons.

To suddenly insert popular persons of the time — John F. Kennedy, Robert Kennedy, and Martin Luther King, Jr., all of whom met untimely deaths by assassination — does not fit the overall storyline of the song. Certainly their deaths would be mourned, but the narrator gives no hint of his admiration for these figures as the song unfolds; thus, inserting them here seems a wee awkward.

Here, in this verse, there is a religious analogy at work. While there are three persons, they are as if one — as in the Christian doctrine of three persons in one entity. It is not necessary to attempt to fetter out which of the three actual people is the father, the son or the holy ghost, but that the three are as if one in being. What must be considered to properly ascertain the meaning of the verse and identity of the three persons is to determine what three people — identified as men — had an influence on the narrator's musical background and career, as these people would be the ones worthy of his admiration, respect, and even gratitude. Whoever "they" are, they served as the narrator's inspiration; they influenced his music; they shared common convictions about life; and they were all balladeers who dealt with music in a way that heightened awareness to social and cultural issues. They were contemporaries.

Thus, the only fit appears to be Ramblin' Jack Elliott, Pete Seeger, and Woody Guthrie — who, in this order, could also respectively represent the individual entities as the "father," the "son," and the "holy ghost" or spirit, as Guthrie's death no longer makes him a physical presence in this trinity. Perhaps, had Bob Dylan not "electrified" his music, he, too, would find a way into this list, as well as Woody's son, Arlo, who was quickly gaining stature as a folk singer. But Arlo is tied closely to the "new" forms of folk music, not the traditional one of his father and others — consider the 1969 song "Comin' into Los Angeles."

Bob Dylan and Arlo Guthrie, like the narrator, are new kids on the block. They have yet to fulfill their status as legends of their genre or music in general. Although, a good argument could be made that Dylan, in his short career as a folk musician and balladeer, had attained such lofty status; after all he was often referred to as Jack Elliott's son — the two were inseparable for a period of time in the early 1960s. Thus, with just one more person — who could easily be Woody Guthrie, whom Elliott mimicked and copied — they could form this musical, non-competitive triumvirate. But, the narrator is not looking this way; the reference is loftier than mere human association — almost pantheistic.

Ramblin' Jack Elliott (Elliott Adnopoz) is represented as one of the figures in this verse.[19] Born in Brooklyn, New York, he aspired to be a "singing cowboy." He attained that status and, by the mid–1950s, was appearing with Woody Guthrie on the New York folk scene, and mimicking him in his performances. The two traveled together sporadically throughout the early 1950s. The influence of Guthrie on Elliott's early musical career is profound. When Elliott went to Europe in 1955, he not only performed Guthrie's songs, but related stories about him. Elliott's first solo album of music was titled *Woody Guthrie's Blues*, which he recorded and released in England in January 1957. Guthrie, himself, has been quoted as saying, "He [Elliott] sounds more like me than I do."[20]

When Elliott returned to America in 1961 he met and befriended Bob Dylan — who was initially introduced to him during a visit with Guthrie at the Greystone Park Memorial Hospital in New Jersey, where Guthrie was being treated for Huntington's Disease, as mentioned earlier. Guthrie would pass away in 1967, and Elliott would move on, leaving his Guthrie impersonation behind, and singing and establishing himself in a different genre — a genre fast developing and called, at the time, Cowboy and Western music [it should be noted that in the song's album release of the same name *American Pie* in 1971, a tribute to William Boyd, a.k.a. Hopalong Cassidy, initially appears inside the cover. Cassidy often sang in his role as cowboy hero, a style epitomized by other singing cowboys like Gene Autry and Roy Rogers]. The nickname "Ramblin'" fit Elliott well, as the absentee father traveled America performing, and never giving up the folk tradition.

In 1969, the narrator accompanied Pete Seeger aboard Seeger's sloop, *Clearwater*, on a singing tour of the Hudson Valley, New York, to bring attention to issues of pollution on the river and elsewhere [the sloop still travels the river teaching ecological and environmental safety and awareness, and was added to the National Register of Historic Places in 2004].[21] By this time, Seeger[22] had reached the level of popularity that his deceased friend and cohort, Woody Guthrie, had reached earlier. The two had shared music, the stage, and their lives together since the early 1940s — they met at a migrant worker's concert in March 1940, and both were members of the folk groups The Almanac Singers and The Weavers. Seeger would be influenced by, and in turn influence, the elder Guthrie.

Both musicians, however, would acknowledge their debt to Huddie "Lead Belly" Ledbetter, whose apartment in New York City was a gathering spot for many musicians in the 1940s. The narrator would not have met Lead Belly, who died in 1949, but no doubt would have heard about him from Seeger and others[23] — one of whom would be Ramblin' Jack Elliot, who accompanied them on the *Clearwater*. Elliott would influence and inspire Seeger with his stories and tales of sailing vessels, and now share in that inspiration. After Woody's death, Seeger continued the folk music traditions the two shared, including persistent activism in environmental issues. Thus, Seeger is represented as another of the three people referred to in this verse.

The final person, but no less significant, is Woodrow Wilson "Woody" Guthrie. By the time of his death, he had steadfastly established himself as the legend — even "king" — of folk music in America.[24] His life and accomplishments are legendary, encompassing the entire timeline of "American Pie" — even after his death. His music was copied and sung by many aspiring folk singers, and many musicians working in other genres. Not only the lyrics, but the mannerisms of his style were being studied and utilized by musicians everywhere. Guthrie's entire life was devoted to political and social activism, and his music was almost solely given to themes associated with this activity. He also wrote numerous songs in an effort to teach and bring music to the children of America and around the world. His most famous song, "This Land Is Your Land," written in 1940, has attained international recognition, has been re-recorded by many musicians since, and is sung at numerous schools throughout America — although, without the final two stanzas, which contain political and social diatribes against the American way of life.

Well they took the last train for the coast, the day the music died.

Obviously, the three — Elliott, Seeger, and Guthrie — could not literally take a train anywhere, unless Guthrie accompanied Elliott and Seeger in spirit. This verse, then, is full of metaphor. The music and ideals of the three are headed to the West Coast of America, perhaps to save rock 'n' roll and its folk ally from the rise of such genres as Hard Rock, Heavy Metal, Shock Rock, and Glam Rock proliferating at the end of the 1960s by such artists as Led Zeppelin, Frank Zappa, the Grateful Dead, Steppenwolf, Alice Cooper, and David Bowie, among many others — some popular nationally, and some popular in local venues.

It is quite possible the three are heading toward the setting sun, thus indicating the finality of the music — with not only the "day" coming to an end or dying, but the "music" along with it. That they were taking a train indicates that the movement westward is a slow one, even as the steam locomotive met a similar demise, and, by so doing, tacitly acknowledges that the trip would be, perhaps, a wasted effort or a slow death march. Thus, the final "day the music died."

And they were singin'

"They" are Elliott, Seeger, and Guthrie, and perhaps the narrator, himself, who by this time had all but surrendered his idealism associated with rock 'n' roll and had put himself in tune and line with the "folkies." If you close your eyes, you can almost see them riding off into the sunset.

Refrain...

Repeat interpretation, but with a sense of finality to it.

It has been over forty years now since the release of the song, and its rise to prominence in popularity — "American Pie" reached the top of the Billboard charts in 1972, only two months after it release. It has embedded itself into both the individual and public consciousnesses in a way that appears to have outlasted its initial rise as another song on the hit parade. Yet, the song casts a long shadow. The narration just presented stands within that shadow. The interpretation just presented contains some firm and irrefutable evidence and some loose associations. This interpretation, along with others, especially those in this volume, attempts to identify the breadth of the song and reveal the complexities of interpretation. The effort is not futile as it brings to light a message or messages contained in a popular song that still retains life in popular music. Only Don McLean himself can extinguish that shadow.

Notes

1. Saul Levitt, "American Pie by Don McLean." n.d. http://www.missamericanpie.co.uk/pie.pdf.

2. Taken from "Questions posed by fans of Don McLean" at the Don McLean Official Web site, http://www.don-mclean.com/articles/faninterview.asp.

3. Jo Ann Lewis, "Everybody Loves van Gogh." *Washington Post*, 14 January 1998. http://www.washingtonpost.com/wp-srv/style/museums/features/98vangogh/ 980114vangogh.htm.

4. Internet FAQ Archives. This site is contains a lengthy analysis of the lyrics to the song "American Pie" as well as a considerable resource listing: http://www.faqs.org/faqs/music/american-pie/. The Fifties Web, July, 2005. This site contains a brief historical outline of the performers Buddy Holly, Ritchie Valens, and J. P. Richardson, and an account of the tragic plane crash that took their lives. It includes the coroner's report of the crash, Buddy Holly's death certificate, and the Official Civil Aeronautics Board Report. A link is provided for "The Annotated American Pie," which interprets the song: http://www.fifiesweb.com/crash.htm.

5. Kevin Baskins, "Buddy Holly 'The Legend.'" (Mason City, Iowa: The Globe Gazette), Web site. 2000–2007. This site contains information, photographs, documents, and memorabilia concerning Buddy Holly, his death, and contemporary Winter Dance Party revivals. It offers a "Related Links" link to several related Web sites: http://www.globegazette.com/northiowatoday/buddyholly/pages/memories.php. Internet Accuracy Project. "Buddy Holly." 2005–2007. This site contains a considerable amount of factual information pertaining to Buddy Holly: http://www.accuracyproject.org/cbe-Holly,Buddy.html. *Lubbock Avalanche-Journal.* Web site

containing the Buddy Holly Archive. 2004. A significant archival resource of articles related to Buddy Holly appearing in the *Lubbock Avalanche-Journal* and *The Lubbock Evening-Journal* newspapers: http://www.buddyhollyarchives.com/index.shtml. Scott Michaels, "Buddy Holly, Ritchie Valens, and J. P. Richardson." Web page. (Hollywood: California), n.d. A comprehensive ongoing discussion, with selected photographs, of the activities pertaining to the deaths of Buddy Holly, Ritchie Valens, and J. P. Richardson, http://www.findadeath.com/Deceased/h/ Buddy%20Holly/buddy_holly.htm. "The Winter Dance Party," n.d. Brief history of The Winter Dance Party schedule, including a synopsis of the airplane crash the killed Buddy Holly, Ritchie Valens, and J. P. Richardson. Contains a link to the Iowa Rock 'n' Roll Music Association, where further related information can be found: http://www.history-of-rock.com/winter_dance_party. htm.

6. There are numerous Web sites, books, and articles dealing with the history of the Beatles and their music. An extensive, and nearly comprehensive, source is a Web site maintained by Mario Giannella, "The Beatles," at http://beatlesong.info/. See also: http://www.beatles-dis cography.com/appendicies/.

7. For comprehensive information regarding the life and music of Bob Dylan see: http: //www.schoneveld.com/bd/.

8. Dave Brazier, "A Conversation with Martin Carthy" (September, 26, 1991), *The Telegraph* 42 (Summer 1992): 88–91, 94–6. Martin Carthy discusses his meetings with Bob Dylan in the King & Queen Pub in England and elsewhere: http://www.bobdylanroots.com.

9. See Dirk Vellenga and Mick Farren, *Elvis and the Colonel* (New York: Delacorte, 1988).

10. Steve Lescure, "The Dylan Commentaries: A Guide to the Works of Bob Dylan." *Judas!* n.d. This includes a discussion of Bob Dylan's earliest record, *Bob Dylan*, and contains references to Dylan's relationship to and with Woody Guthrie. http://www.judasmagazine.com/ pages.asp/net7.asp.

11. Robert Blackburn and Tariq Ali, "Power to the People." Web site interview with John Lennon and Yoko Ono. 1971. http://homepage.ntlworld.com/carousel/pob12.html.

12. Anonymous. "The Influence of the Beatles on Charles Manson." This Web site contains the original Beatles lyrics with interpretations by Manson, along with comments, and a direct link to the Manson Trial Homepage: http://www.law.umkc.edu/faculty/projects/ftrials/manson/mansonbeatles.html. See also: Vincent Bugliosi's book *Helter Skelter: The True Story of the Manson Murders* (New York: Norton, 2001), 238–45.

13. Anonymous. Web site dedicated to Woody Guthrie and his music: http://www.bobdy lanroots.com/guthrie.html.

14. Jeff Kisseloff, *Generation on Fire: Voices of Protest from the 1960s, an Oral History* (Lexington: The University Press of Kentucky, 2007), 204–5.

15. John Neary, "The Magical McCartney Mystery," *Life*, 7 November 1969, 103–6. The particular quote by McCartney appears on page 105.

16. Alan Barger, "The Rolling Stones' Altamont Music Festival, December 6, 1969: The Anti-Woodstock." Web site. *BC Blogcritics Magazine*. 2006. This offers comprehensive discussion of the Rolling Stones performance at Altamont Raceway Park, December 6, 1969: http://blog critics.org/archives/2006/08/27/171008.php.

17. For a list of songs played at Hyde Park See: http://www.geetarz.org/reviews/stones/ hyde-park-69.htm.

18. Folkstreams.net. Web site. 2000–2005. Biographical information about Alan Lomax, American musicologist, anthropologist, and folklorist. http://www.folkstreams.net/filmmaker, 121. For additional information on the Alan Lomax Collection see also: http://www.loc.gov/folk life/lomax/.

19. Randy Poe, "Ramblin' Jack Elliott: An American Minstrel," *Sing Out!*, 22 September 2001. An in-depth review of the life of Jack Elliott and an extensive biography and other information regarding Elliott appear at http://www.ramblinjack.com/.

20. See: Rob Patterson's article "Reason to Roam Brooklyn-Born Ramblin' Jack Elliott Moseys Through Houston with Some Friends," *Houston Press*, 9 April 1998, at: http://ramblin jack.com/sk_060498.html.

21. Hudson River Sloop "Clearwater." Web site. A site devoted to the project started by Pete Seeger in 1969, when he sailed his sloop, "Clearwater," down the Hudson River promoting environmental awareness: http://www.clearwater.org/index.html.

22. For a brief biography regarding Pete Seeger see: http://www.harvardsquarelibrary.org/unitarians/seeger.html.

23. See the article by Richard Albero and Fred Styles, "There's More to the Man Than American Pie," *Guitar Player*, July/August 1972, 19; wherein McLean mentions his interest in "people like Bessie Smith, and Leroy Carr, and Scrapper Blackwell, and Mississippi John Hart, and people like that."

24. For information concerning Guthrie's life and music see the official Woody Guthrie website at: http://www.woodyguthrie.org/. Information regarding Guthrie's music and life can also be found at: http://www.woodyguthrie.de/links.html.

3

The Perception of Race in Rock and Roll

Richard J. McGowan

Since its release in 1971, Don McLean's "American Pie" has been a source of joy and delight not only to its listeners, but also to those who would unravel its "highly nuanced and sophisticated ... multiple allusions and layers of meaning."[1] The song's acclaim, for instance, being voted into the Grammy Hall of Fame in 2002, heightens the adventure for interpreters of the song.

The fact that Don McLean himself has been considerably less than complete in providing explanation for the song's lyrics also adds to the adventure in "deciphering" "American Pie."

As a consequence, debate about specific verses and their possible meanings is rife. Yet, explanations of the song's refrain have been relatively absent. This essay attempts to fill the lacuna. First, I offer general remarks about interpreting the song. I suggest that the refrain explicates the song's overall arc. Second, I show what other commentaries have said about the refrain. Third, I provide information about the event corresponding to the refrain as I show how knowledge of the refrain may affect the interpretation of other lyrics in "American Pie." Then I show how variations in the refrain, both in terms of lyrics and delivery, show the coherence of "American Pie" and impact the meaning of other lines.

GENERAL REMARKS

A long, long time ago, I can still remember talking with my friends about "American Pie" and the meaning of its lyrics. We were not certain about many of the allusions but on one point we were certainly agreed: the "Chevy at the levee" referred to civil rights activists Michael Schwerner, Andrew Goodman, and James Chaney.

Yet, what my friends and I took to be common knowledge has been relatively unexamined and largely ignored by those who would seek to penetrate "American Pie." Most people who would unravel the song's "highly nuanced and sophisticated ... multiple allusions and layers of meaning"[2] focus on the lyrics of the verses and look to "real world" correlates from within the music scene and from national news events.

For instance, when the song says "the three men I admire most — the Father, Son, and the Holy Ghost ... took the last train to the coast," whom does McLean have in mind? Perhaps the question's answer returns listeners to the original trio from the opening stanza, namely Ritchie Valens, J. P. Richardson, and Buddy Holly. But it might be, as Schuck suggests in this volume, Ramblin' Jack Elliott, Pete Seeger, and Woody Guthrie, folk singers who inspired and taught Don McLean a little something about music. Conjecture has it that the trio is John F. Kennedy, Robert Kennedy, and Martin Luther King, Jr., though current analysis suggests that few clues in the song point to them.

Baur warns against looking for correspondence to real world events and figures. He states that "it would be a mistake to conclude that the critical, philosophical meaning of 'American Pie' is to be found primarily in such one-to-one correspondences."[3] However, the song is rife with correspondence and "multiple allusions and layers of meaning." It would be a bigger mistake to think that the coherence of "American Pie" is not found in some central correspondence.

An analysis of the song's refrain and the correspondence, rather unremarked in various analyses, reveals the arc of "American Pie." Such an analysis also blunts the force of Baur's hermeneutical question: "Doesn't the very idea of self-critique imply that the 'tools of critique' are derived from — and thus virtually useless with respect to — the culture or tradition being scrutinized?"[4] Baur seems to think that standing inside a culture, which everyone including McLean does, limits critical capacity. Baur theorizes that McLean is aware of the limitation and, thus, cannot properly justify his critique of American rock 'n' roll.[5]

Again, I think Baur's claims are mistaken and for several reasons, not the least of which is the implicit assumption that cultural experience is necessarily unique and limits the tools of thought. Instead, it could be that culture is the start of thought which produces some understanding of universal human experience. The result is a cultural transcendence built on the notion of a shared humanity. An examination of the refrain from "American Pie," both in the refrain's correspondence with an important event in American history and its delivery in the song, suggests as much. In fact, the central narrative of "American Pie" is precisely that internal, critical thought, the self-critique

Baur speaks of, can be very useful indeed as a step toward communion with others.

The song begins with the unrealized fantasies of youth and is, to that extent, self-centered; it becomes a song about the lost idealism of youth, and concludes with a chorus of voices singing together, representing commitment, maturity, and through it all, the cardinal virtue of hope. Hence, the song may be embedded in a culture, but the universal experience of finding awareness of a self with others is the more salient feature of "American Pie." An analysis of the song's refrain, upon which the song itself hinges, will show as much.

What Others Say About the Refrain

It might be worthwhile even if obvious to point out that the refrain is where the title, "American Pie," is found. It appears as though McLean thinks that the central narrative of the song is found there. That refrain and its corresponding event represent the turning point for Don McLean and for rock 'n' roll. They mark the transformation of Don McLean into an older, more circumspect person; at the same time, the joie de vivre of rock 'n' roll becomes somber and serious commentary about civic affairs. It is as though rock 'n' rollers forgot the fun of their music and instead "sang dirges in the dark." However, most commentaries on "American Pie" do little with the refrain even though the refrain is delivered six times during the course of the song and no two presentations of the refrain are the same.

Here is how the master commentator, Saul Levitt, explains the refrain:

"The levee" refers to the man made banks that hold back a river. Or as described by Don himself "A levee is a pile of dirt." Apparently going to the levee is common practice among teenagers then & now as a place to drink and hang out with friends. (Ref: Doug L) Don even mentions this in a radio interview. The music of the area, such as country and rhythm & blues, were the source of rock & roll. McLean may also be hinting at the source of the music having dried up for him.

But is McLean either using double meaning or trying to mislead us here? Rye is whiskey distilled from Rye, though this makes for a good play on words, there is another explanation that seems to work better. Rye is a place in New York. Don McLean's home town was nearby New Rochelle. "The Levee" was a music playing bar in New Rochelle that closed, so Don & his rock & roll music loving buddies had to drive across the river to drink & listen to music in Rye.

There are also a number of other references to "the levee" neither of which resonate for me as well as the above. The Grateful Dead's song, Friend of the Devil, written & released in 1970 on the American Beauty album contains the lyrics "I ran down to the levee, but the Devil caught me there!" (Ref: Ed Chapin) Another reference comes from an old chevy TV ad though this has not been confirmed: "On a holly on a road or on a levee...performance is sweeter, nothing can beat her, life is completer in a chevy" [(Ref: Miya)].[6]

Knowing the song has very specific references to people and events throughout, a person might expect that the refrain, the central piece of the song, would also point very specifically to an important event or person. Is it possible that the whole refrain comes to a personal comment about bars in the nearby vicinity of where McLean grew up?

Given the multiple allusions of the song's lyrics, e.g., who might the "three men I admire most" be, Levitt's suggestions have merit.

In fact, in Levitt's entire ten or so pages of interpretation, the only particular remarks about McLean as a person growing up occur when Levitt speaks of McLean's job as a paperboy and of the bar, "The Levee." No other reference to any detail of McLean's life on the streets of New Rochelle is found in Levitt's interpretation.

Here is how another interpreter, Jim Fann, accounts for the levee:

"Drove my Chevy to the levee" alludes to a "drive along a levee" mentioned in a series of popular 1950s television commercials sung by Dinah Shore:

> Drive your Chevrolet through the USA,
> America's the greatest land of them all
> On a highway or a road along a levee...
> ...life is completer in a Chevy
> So make a date today to see the USA
> And see it in your Chevrolet

and which serves as a signpost to that era — just as the Chevrolet itself is a familiar icon of 1950s America. Also, given that a drive to a levee carries the suggestion of romance in a car, we can almost see him on a date here. But the date is over, the levee is dry — someone he once loved has betrayed him; something that once gave him sustenance has evaporated.[7]

While this interpretation of the chorus has some appeal for its notion of betrayal, as symbolized by a dry levee, the interpretation does not capture the gravitas in the warp and woof of "American Pie." Neither Levitt's nor Fann's explanation of the refrain account for the number of times the refrain appears and the changes that occur in the refrain during "American Pie." A person could legitimately ask why the first delivery of the refrain begins abruptly whereas all other renditions of the refrain involve pronouns, namely, "I," "we," and "he." How do the changes in the refrain work?

Bob Dearborn's famous interpretation, one of the earliest, public, and respected commentaries, says of the refrain: "McLean conveys the idea that he was typical of his generation. Their idea of a wild 'high,' was drinking whiskey and rye, and dancing 'real slow' at the dance in the high school gymnasium."[8] Dearborn leaves the refrain largely unexamined and unattended.

Another interpretation, Cecil Adams' "What Is Don McLean's Song 'American Pie' All About?," does even less with the refrain than Dearborn's interpretation: "*Them good old boys were ... singing 'This'll be the day that I die*': Holly's hit 'That'll Be the Day' had a similar line."[9] By Adams' account, the refrain, where the title of the song originates and which is repeated six times with six different deliveries, is simply a reference to a Buddy Holly song.

O'Brien's commentary has the event correct, but it neither examines the import of the event in question nor is historically accurate. O'Brien says,

> Driving the Chevy to the levee almost certainly refers to the three college students whose murder was the subject of the film "Mississippi Burning." The students were attempting to register black voters, and after being killed by bigoted thugs their bodies were buried in a levee. Them good old boys being: Holly, Valens, and the Big Bopper. They were singing about their death on February 3.[10]

O'Brien's account leaves a lot to be desired. For one thing, not all the slain civil rights workers were students. Schwerner was 24; he and his wife were hired on by CORE to do field work in Mississippi, primarily registering black voters. Chaney, 21, was not enrolled in college and had long since left high school by the time of his death. As to the claim that "them good old boys" refers to Holly, Valens, and the Big Bopper, no evidence, either in other commentaries or in the song itself, supports the interpretation. Finally, O'Brien's saying that the "Chevy to the levee" "almost certainly" refers to the slain civil rights workers is too weak a claim. There is no "almost" about it.

THE REFRAIN'S CENTRAL EVENT AND ITS PLACE IN "AMERICAN PIE"

"American Pie," by all accounts, "is a song about music, especially rock 'n' roll music from the 1950s to 1970," as Schuck puts the matter in this volume. It is also a song about the events in Don McLean's life and his feelings and experiences growing up in New Rochelle, New York, as he himself said in a BBC interview.[11]

Thus, the song alludes to specific figures in the musical landscape of the late 1950s and 1960s as it refers to the events of the day. For instance, interpretation regarding "Jack be nimble, Jack be quick" suggests that Jack is Mick Jagger or Jack Kennedy, nimbly handling the Cuban missile crisis. In other words, the lyrics could point to newsworthy events standing on their own or, alternatively, could point independently to people in rock 'n' roll. Often, the lyrics point to the news where rock 'n' roll music coincides with the events of the day.

Certainly that is the case with Buddy Holly's death in an Iowa plane crash. As everyone knows, the Big Bopper (J.P. Richardson) and Ritchie Valens died with Holly and as McLean admitted in one of the rare interviews when he did explain a piece of the "Pie," the plane crash was the "day the music died."[12] The unintended, accidental deaths of the three musical performers on February 3, 1959, made the headlines. Music and news blurred in print but also on television sets, which, by 1959, were in most American living rooms.

Another case in point about music and news coinciding is the Rolling Stones' December 6, 1969, performance at the Altamont Speedway Free Festival. Thought of as sort of a "Woodstock West" and organized by the Rolling Stones, the concert became increasingly violent. In fact, the Grateful Dead refused to play before the Stones did because of the crowd behavior. When the Stones performed as the last act of the "free" festival, Hells Angels, whom the Stones hired for security, killed Meredith Hunter. The death was an intended, homicidal act occurring in a musical context.

That homicide, which made a lot of people shiver, was the news on December 7, 1969, and appears in the next-to-last verse, before the elegiac coda, of "American Pie."

So, the song begins with the plane crash and Don McLean's personal and private sense of loss — he couldn't remember if he cried, but the song concludes with a very public homicide. McLean, whose "hands were clenched in fists of rage," expresses publicly a sense of betrayal and clear anger. He has an understanding of what it is to get older and see the world as it is; he also understands better what it is to be a person in a community.

Between the two events of 1959 and 1969, at the dead center of the timeline, stands the event that pushed McLean from boyhood to manhood, from "being touched deep inside" though apparently not crying and not giving his feelings away in public, to clenching his fists in public. The event stands at the center of "American Pie," too. Here is how *Time* magazine described the "Grim Discovery in Mississippi":

> In 101° heat, FBI agents swarmed over an earthen dam on Olen Barrage's Old Jolly Farm, six miles southwest of Philadelphia, Miss. Through the scrub pines and bitterweed, the FBI bulldozed a path to the dam, then brought up a lumbering dragline whose huge bucket shovel began chewing a V-shaped wedge out of the 25-ft.-high levee. Twenty feet down, the shovel uncovered the fully clothed, badly decomposed bodies of three young men ... they had been dumped there while the dam was still being built.[13]

The *Neshoba Democrat*'s headline for August 6, 1964, declared: "Bodies of missing trio found buried in levee."[14]

Michael Schwerner, Andrew Goodman, and James Chaney, young civil rights workers who used their energy to help register "negroes" for the vote, had been murdered by the Ku Klux Klan in Neshoba County. The *Daily Mis-*

sissippian reported in a commemorative piece that "their bodies were found in an earthen levee."[15] Edgar Ray Killen and other Klansmen never faced murder charges at that time; when "American Pie" was written, "no verdict was returned" in the case of the murders of the three young men.

Newsday, a widely circulated New York newspaper, blared the news of their deaths across Long Island, where I lived in 1964. Though the word "levee" never appeared in the August 5 and 6 editions of the *New York Times*, I recall the word "levee" appearing often in the news articles from *Newsday*.[16] I wondered what this unusual word meant. The New York media coverage of the discovery of the bodies was thorough and understandably so: Michael Schwerner was from Pelham, New York, and Andrew Goodman was from New York City.

The young Don McLean could not have missed the story. Michael Schwerner, at 24, the oldest and the leader of the three young men, grew up in Pelham, two miles from McLean's hometown of New Rochelle.

Not only was the discovery of the slain civil rights workers a national event, it had the proximity to McLean of being a personal event.

As such, the refrain of "American Pie" appears to capture a central narrative of the 1960s and a galvanizing event from the civil rights movement. The event could turn innocence into maturity and sweetness into rage.

So a person might think "Bye, bye Miss American Pie." To get to the levee on the Old Jolly Farm, in the incredible "summer swelter" of 101 degree heat and through the scrub pines and bitterweed, a person would need something sturdy and maybe "drove a Chevy to the levee." However, the levee was being constructed and did not yet hold back any water. In short, "the levee was dry." The rural, redneck Klan members who shot Schwerner and Goodman but savagely beat Chaney before killing him probably had to get drunk first. "Them good ol' boys were drinkin' whiskey and rye," (and perhaps were too ignorant and stupid to know that rye is a whiskey), possibly for courage and possibly for celebrating the death of "a n____, a Jew, and a white man," as Judge Cox said. They probably thought that the day "negroes" could vote fair and square in an election as the end of days. They might have been thinking that "this'll be the day that I die," for their world would have to change completely for an event of that magnitude to occur. And they would fight that day to their death and the death of others.

Yet, for Don McLean, the discovery of the bodies meant a day "that I die," too. His identity, thinking happy rock 'n' roll thoughts of innocence and youth, where the worse trauma is to have a "pink carnation and a pickup truck" but no date for the dance, have been given over to an adult knowledge of a grim world. Music might have saved his mortal soul but for the fact that he grew up and, anyway, rock 'n' roll followed the path of the real world, culminating in Altamont and the death of a black man, Meredith Hunter. It appears that "American Pie" is a narrative about race and racial consciousness both for McLean and the country.

ANALYSIS OF THE REFRAIN

The refrain is presented first as a statement of fact, even if the refrain is a conclusion, objective and distant. It begins, "so, bye-bye, Miss American pie." There appears to be no ownership of the refrain, no one who is singing it. It is presented as a truth that the rest of the song will explain. The next refrain begins a shift and the start of an explanation of why McLean has reached his conclusion: "I started singin' bye-bye Miss American pie." Here McLean moves toward introspection of and hints at consciousness about the event. The refrain suggests that he has neither integrated the event nor resolved the challenge the event puts to his youthful identity. However, he is aware of the event and working toward co-opting its impact. He initiates action, "I started singing."

It might be wise, here, to observe that "American pie," as a phrase, portends something wholesome and good about the United States. The phrase captures a bit of security and trust, possibly connoting a degree of naïveté and innocence. The song is about the loss of innocence, if its interpreters are correct. In light of the event involving the slain civil rights workers, McLean could be speaking in fragments. That is, he could be saying good bye to his youth and the word, "miss," is not only a title but a verb as well. It is a statement of what McLean misses in his life. The refrain continues with fragments. "Drove my Chevy to the levee" is a fragment. There is no subject. If the refrain is consistent, then "drive" and "miss" are verbs. As such, the refrain announces that McLean misses the wholesome, winsome, sweet American youth he has had. The refrain's evolution also points the listener in that direction.

The third appearance of the refrain brings other people into the song: "we were singin' bye, bye, Miss American pie." The phrasing captures an observation. People sang the verse though without complete volition. It was similar to a person humming throughout the day the last song on the morning radio. Yet, the next appearance of the refrain mimics the second appearance: "We started singin'." If the logic is the same, refrain four presents people initiating thought and may imply that many people were attempting to integrate the event into their consciousness and to determine an appropriate response to the events on the levee.

Not everyone would resolve the events on the levee in the way that Don McLean would, though. Some would delight in the killing, laughing in a cynical manner. Or they might be opportunistic and uncaring, which produces in McLean a personal and public response of clenched fists. Besides the murder at Altamont, what else might the Stones have done to make McLean angry? In a song whose central narrative event is the murder of civil rights workers, the fact that the Stones co-opted so many songs with "black" roots without much attribution might produce rage. And, as noted earlier, Meredith Hunter, killed by the Hells Angels, was a black man. Instead of rock and roll furthering integration, the Stones used rock 'n' roll to further their own ends.

A look at the various commentaries suggests as much, too. For instance, in their interpretations of verse one, Levitt and Schuck identify white and black singers as corresponding to the lyrics in the verse. The day the music died was an integrated event involving white and black performers. Verse two is consciously about race, if Levitt is correct: "R & B had been purely for black audiences, originally known as 'race music.'"[17] Schuck's analysis mentions Danny and the Juniors, the Cleftones, and Marty Robbins. Levitt and Schuck offer integrated allusions for verse three, too, mentioning the Beatles, Bob Dylan, B.B. King, Jimi Hendrix, and Muddy Waters among others.

However, Levitt's and Schuck's interpretations mention only white performers in their explanations of verse four: the Beatles, Byrds, Buffalo Springfield, Country Joe, Bob Dylan, and Barry Sadler. Verse four also has the lyric that might allude to race riots in L.A.: "helter skelter in a summer swelter." That line might also be a reference to the "White Album" by the Beatles, or Loving Spoonful's "Summer in the City," but it could also put the listener squarely in Mississippi: "In 101° heat, FBI agents swarmed over an earthen dam on Olen Barrage's Old Jolly Farm, six miles southwest of Philadelphia, Miss." Of course, the phrase, "helter skelter," would refer to the mayhem and nihilism of three murders. So, verse four appears to be about race and, if Levitt and Schuck are correct, the verse involves only white performers.

Verse five continues in the latter trend, if Levitt and Schuck are correct. Their explanations of the verse mention the Stones, the Beatles, the Grateful Dead, and Don McLean himself.

Verse six breaks the trend of segregation. Levitt's and Schuck's explanations mention a plethora of performers, white and black. Among those identified are Janis Joplin, Holly, Valens, and the Big Bopper, Jelly Roll Morton, and Memphis Slim. Verse six also has the famous "Father, Son, and the Holy Ghost" line. Levitt considers it might be Abraham Lincoln, Martin Luther King, Junior, and John F. Kennedy.[18] If so, the verse returns the song to the central narrative, at least as suggested by the refrain, of race. If that verse puts the listener back onto the narrative of race in the 1960s, another trio which must be considered, as alluded to by McLean, is Schwerner, Goodman, and Chaney.

CONCLUSION

From the first delivery of the refrain as "objective news," McLean moves the refrain through a process of thought, concluding, as I note below, with a chorus. Along the way, the jester gave up singing folk songs and opted for electronic help with his performances. Songs of youthful insouciance, ebullience, and innocence were replaced by measured social protest, guitar-smashing rants, and anger. What might have been music to bring a person toward happiness morphed into lamentation, and if a person were asked for happy news, the person would only turn away. Music was no longer the vehicle to make people smile.

Instead, the world beyond music might be the best hope for a more pleasant world. But then, the harbingers of hope, "the Father, Son, and the Holy Ghost," were murdered, and in that way, hope died. So, Baur is correct: culture, especially American culture of the 1960s, can limit thought, hopes, and dreams.

And yet, all is not lost. We all grow old. The universal experience of growing old, losing fantastic dreams — imagine a kid who thinks his playing music can make the world happy for a while — has been replaced by a wiser, more mature person. That older person, having seen and understood suffering and pain, nonetheless, believes that there is something more than cultural limitation, remains committed to doing good, and has faith that a better world is possible.

McLean understands the limit of thinking but does not despair.

By the last delivery of the refrain, the question has been posed: which way will the world turn? What direction will society take? The last delivery of the refrain begins, "And they were singing bye-bye Miss American pie." The pronoun, "they," refers to the "three men I admire most, the Father, Son, and the Holy Ghost" of the previous stanza. However, this refrain's delivery is not exclusive to those three men. In fact, while the refrain begins with only McLean's solitary voice and no musical accompaniment, it shifts into a voice with guitar accompaniment and then repeats itself in a groundswell of voices. The chorus of the last refrain paints a picture of McLean standing with many others, firm in their opposition to the events on the levee and in their commitment to a better world.

So "American Pie" starts its final refrain with a slow tempo, intimating a resigned, tired manner; on the other hand, its rousing, communal delivery suggests people joining together to make a better world and "shouting down" the savages of Philadelphia, Mississippi, through song. It is as though Don McLean recaptured the days of his youth, when music was enough to "be happy for a while." He might think that it will take more than him and music to solve the world's problems, but he knows, as the chorus shows, we are in the world together.

And that's a happy thought.

Notes

1. Michael Baur, "'American Pie' and the Self-critique of rock 'n' roll," in *Philosophy and the Interpretation of Literature*, ed. William Irwin and Jorge J. E. Garcia (Lanham, MD: Rowan and Littlefield, 2007), 255.

2. Ibid., 255.

3. Ibid., 257.

4. Ibid., 263.

5. Ibid., 265–6.

6. Saul Levitt, "American Pie by Don McLean Verse 1," *The Ultimate American Pie Website*, accessed March 15, 2009, http://www.missamericanpie.co.uk/v1.html.

7. James M. Fann, "Chorus," *Understanding "American Pie,"* accessed March 15, 2009, http://understandingamericanpie.com/chorus.htm.

8. Bob Dearborn, "Bob Dearborn's Original Analysis of Don McLean's 1971 Classic 'American Pie,'" originally published August 10, 2002, accessed June 29, 2009, http://user.pa.net/~ejjeff/pie.html.

9. Cecil Adams, "What is Don McLean's Song 'American Pie' All About?" The Straight Dope, Chicago Reader, Inc., originally published May 15, 1993, accessed June 29, 2009, http://www.straightdope.com/columns/read/908/what-is-don-mcleans-song-american-pie-all-about.

10. Paul O'Brien, "American Pie — The Analysis and Interpretation of Don McLean's Song Lyrics," *The Rare Exception: Music Rumors, Legends, and Fictions*, accessed June 29, 2009, http://www.rareexception.com/?p=140.

11. Saul Leavitt, "American Pie by Don McLean," accessed May 31, 2011, http://www.missamericanpie.co.uk/pie.pdf.

12. Ibid.

13. "Grim Discovery in Mississippi," *Time*, 14 August 1964, available at http://www.time.com/time/magazine/article/0,9171,897227-1,00.html.

14. "Bodies of Missing Trio Found Buried in Levee," *Neshoba Democrat*, 6 August 1964, accessed June 6, 2009, http://neshobademocrat.com/main.asp?TypeID=1&ArticleID=8154&SectionID=17&SubSectionID=326&Page=2.

15. Michael Newsom, "UM Remembers Slain Civil Rights Workers," *Daily Mississippian*, 18 June 2004, accessed June 10, 2009, www.thedmonline.com/2.2838/um-remembers-slain-civil-rights-workers-1.123056.

16. *New York Times*, 5 August 1964; *New York Times* 6 August 1964.

17. Saul Levitt, "American Pie by Don McLean Verse 2," *The Ultimate American Pie Website*, accessed March 15, 2009, http://www.missamericanpie.co.uk/v2.html.

18. Saul Levitt, "American Pie by Don McLean Verse 6," *The Ultimate American Pie Website*, accessed March 15, 2009, http://www.missamericanpie.co.uk/v6.html.

4

Lyrical History: There Is More to Music Than Making the People Dance?!

Russ Crawford

Since the first court musician sang the praises of the first lucky warrior, music has provided a record of human history. However, until Lawrence Levine, in *Black Culture and Black Consciousness*, used slave songs to help recover their culture, the recognition of songs as historical documents was largely overlooked, but since then, historians have taken a closer look at what songs can tell us about our history.[1] Don McLean's "American Pie" is one such historical document that fits neatly into the category of songs that can tell us about how we were, and it is especially useful in exploring the history of the music business and artists' feelings about their place in it.

Since around 800 B.C., when Chinese emperors sent their minions to collect folk songs, later collected into the *Shi Jing* (*Book of Songs*), from the provinces to "inspect the popular will,"[2] musicians have been placed under scrutiny for their art. One would not expect Shi Huangdi, the first emperor of a unified Chinese state, who climbed to the throne over the bodies of whoever stood in his way, to hear of a folk song from one of his provinces that criticized life under his rule and allow the songwriter to live for long.

In addition to inspecting the popular will, rulers have also sought to shape it; to present a positive image of their rule or to make sure their martial exploits were remembered, wealthy and powerful patrons have supported songwriters and performers creating messages that massaged their vanity and controlled their public image. The court minstrels of the Middle Ages, as well as traveling performers, were dependent on their audiences, whether royal or popular, for their living, as were musicians such as Wolfgang Mozart, Ludwig van Beethoven and others since then. Music, therefore, has been a business for millennia.

Not until the nineteenth century, when French philosophers argued that art had intrinsic value above and beyond its commercial appeal, did singers and songwriters begin to dream of art for art's sake. The children of the baby boom (1946–1960) perhaps took that slogan too much to heart, and "American Pie" represents the leading edge of an exploration and often a critique of the music business that found its voice in the 1970s.

The song as a historical document in the United States predates the creation of the republic. During the seventeenth century, songs such as "The Bold Soldier" told the story of one of the many traveling soldiers such as Miles Standish or Captain John Smith spawned by English wars against the Portuguese, French, and Spanish, who then sought their fortunes in the new world.[3] Songs such as this were popular in the colonies and each of the various immigrant groups who populated the British Americas brought their own traditions with them. One such song, "Whiskey in the Jar," originated in Ireland in the 1650s and traveled with immigrants to their new homes. This particular song continued to enjoy popularity in the United States through the twentieth century, and was later recorded by Thin Lizzy (1972) and Metallica (1998).

The Scots-Irish and West-African musical traditions were particularly influential in the later history of the country. The Scots-Irish, with their tradition of sad and sweet ballads later produced the sound that would become known as country music. African slaves, involuntary immigrants, also contributed their musical traditions, which formed the basis for the jazz, rhythm and blues, and rock 'n' roll genres. From wherever they came, immigrants to the Thirteen Colonies, and later the United States, would bring along their musical story-telling tradition and would use that to begin telling their own stories of life here. For those, like the African slaves who left precious little written record behind, music was a powerful tool in recovering their history.

As the immigrants became acclimated to their new environment, they also began thinking of themselves as being Americans rather than British, Irish, or the like. They also began creating their own songs to describe the lives they created here. Songs such as "Yankee Doodle Dandy," which possibly was written to mock colonial troops in the French and Indian war, nevertheless was embraced by the soldiers who would later defeat the British Empire in the Revolutionary War (1776–1781). In adopting the song, the colonials changed the lyrics, in some instances to make fun of their officers, including George Washington himself. In contrast to his later reputation as "Father of the Nation," common soldiers sung verses such as:

> There came Gen'ral Washington
> Upon a snow-white charger
> He looked as big as all outdoors
> And thought that he was larger.[4]

Other songs included "The Liberty Song," written by John Dickenson in 1768, seven years before the outbreak of hostilities at Lexington and Concord. Dickenson would go on to play an important role in the revolution, writing the popular *Letters from a Pennsylvania Farmer* that helped unite the colonies in opposition to the Townshend Acts, serving as a militia officer, a Continental Congressman, and a delegate to the Constitutional Convention in 1787. Dickenson would echo the sentiment of Benjamin Franklin's political cartoon calling for colonial unity that depicted a snake cut in segments labeled with the abbreviations of the colonies on the sections. Though the idea originated earlier, Dickenson's use of the phrase "By uniting we stand, by dividing we fall," would become an oft-used motto in U.S. history.

> Then join hand in hand, brave Americans all,
>   By uniting we stand, by dividing we fall;
>   In so righteous a cause let us hope to succeed,
> For heaven approves of each generous deed.[5]

After the Revolution, songs such as "The Defence of Fort McHenry" (1814), the poem written by Francis Scott Key, which would later be set to music as "The Star-Spangled Banner" and would become the national anthem of the United States in 1931, and "America" (1832), told of the effort to build patriotic sentiments in the new republic. Lyrics such as "the land of the brave and the home of the free" or "sweet land of liberty" told of the project to instill a nationalistic pride in the nation that has continued, if perhaps more aggressively, to modern times in lyrics such as the words to the song "Courtesy of the Red, White, and Blue" (2002) that country music artist Toby Keith released after the September 11, 2001, terrorist attacks.

Wars were particularly fruitful for finding song lyrics that inspect the popular will, and the American Civil War (1861–1865) was no exception. Songs such as Daniel Decatur Emmett's "Dixie" (1859), though it was written by a Northerner for a minstrel act, told of Southerners' love for their region, later their country, and Julia Ward Howe's "The Battle Hymn of the Republic" (1861) told of the need to destroy that country in a holy crusade. Songs like the "Bonnie Blue Flag" (1861) by Harry McCarthy kept Confederate soldiers marching to defend their "property," and "When Johnny Comes Marching Home" (1863) by Louis Lambert told soldiers of what awaited them when the war was over.

After the war, songs such as "The Mulligan Guard" (1873) by Ned Harrigan and David Braham told of old soldiers who longed for their glory days in the army and held on to their memories by donning ornate uniforms and marching in parades, then retiring to a pub to tell war stories. Songs such as "Oh! Susanna" (1848) by Stephen Foster told of the excitement of the gold rush to California that started that year. "Cowboy Jack" by G. Malcom Laws told of the lonely life of the cowboy on the Great Plains. "I've Been Working on the Railroad" (1894) described connecting the nation with rails, and "Eight Hours" by I.G. Blanchard told of the struggle by workers to earn an eight hour day. Interestingly enough, by this time, the rich and powerful had dropped off the charts, so to speak. Wealthy industrialists such as J.P. Morgan, Andrew Carnegie, and others no longer supported artists to sing their praises, which may be one reason why they came to be described as "robber barons." Rather, they built opera houses adorned with their names, but those operas only provided entertainment for a small elite and could not compete with the growing popular music business.

Prior to the twentieth century, the music industry was haphazard, with many songs published for patriotic or folk purposes rather than profit. New York's Tin Pan Alley, a section of the city where many music publishers set up shop, became the center of the industry between the 1880s and the 1930s. The focus was on selling sheet music that formal and informal groups could play on their own. Live performances by groups in the employ of a publishing house during this time were often merely advertising to sell sheet music. Intellectual property rights were not regulated and writers were typically exploited, often being paid to allow more famous composers' names to appear in their place. The industry was fluid enough, however, so that successful composers could break away and start their own companies.

The ability to record and broadcast music over the airwaves was provided by Thomas Edison, who patented the phonograph in 1877, and by Reginald Fessenden, who played the first recorded music using a radio transmitter (George F. Handel's "Ombra mai fu") on Christmas Eve 1906. In the 1920s, broadcasting corporations such as the National Broadcasting System (NBC) and the Columbia Broadcasting System (CBS) were established to exploit the new medium. A surprise to the scientists who developed radio, by the 1920s, listeners could tune in to hear their favorite music, or to learn what their favorites should be, as well as listening to their favorite serials, soap operas, or comedies. The music was supported by advertising and provided to the public free of any direct charge.

During that decade radio sales swept the nation, and by the 1930s, there were millions of sets in use. Singers such as Bing Crosby became recording stars and programs such as the Grand Ole Opry (1925) continually brought new artists and songs (country and western) to the nation. Fueled by popular music that included jazz and swing, the music industry targeted a new youth culture that began to worry their parents. Although this new culture was put on hold for the Great Depression (1929–1941) and World War II (1941–1945), it came roaring back in the forties and fifties with a new music style; rock 'n' roll. With "Rock Around the Clock" (1954) by Bill Haley and the Comets, music added a new genre that spawned stars such as The Big Bopper (Jiles P Richardson), Ritchie Valens, Elvis Presley, and Buddy Holly. And so we come, finally, to Don McLean and the day the music died.

Among the many analyses of the meaning of the lyrics to McLean's epic is one by Craig Sanders that argues the artist was writing about the demise of what the author calls the "first wave of rock and roll."[6] This era saw upbeat songs about love, or maybe maudlin songs about loss, but whether happy or sad, these works spoke to the individual human condition or were just entertaining songs that could "make the people dance."[7] After lamenting the passing of the era with the death of Richardson, Valens, and Holly, and the induction of Presley into the U.S. Army, McLean proceeded to bemoan the new politically charged songs of the sixties and to tell listeners of his despair about the personalities who were writing and performing them.

Sanders asserted that Bob Dylan was the jester who sang (during the 1963 Civil Rights March on Washington) to the king and queen (the Kennedys). He also later added lines about (John) Lennon reading a book on Marx, Satan (Mick Jagger) laughing with delight, and angels born in hell, which reference the tragedy that occurred at the Altamont Free Concert in 1969, when Hells Angel working security stabbed a man to death.[8] Sanders places "American Pie" in the genre, then, of songs about the music business and the history of rock 'n' roll, and the 1970s proved to be a fruitful decade for songs about that subject.

By the 1970s, the chaos of the early decades of the twentieth century was being rationalized by corporate consolidation. The environment that saw record companies come and go with alarming frequency was replaced by one in which the so-called "Big 6," which included corporations such as the Electrical & Music Industries Ltd. (EMI), the Bertelsman Music Group (BMG), and MCA Records, among others, dominated the industry. The rationalization of the industry opened floodgates of money, a share of which found its way to the artist, but it also hardened the control of the "label" over their contracted performers. Billy Joel, in "The Entertainer" (1975), referenced the oppressive, in the artist's mind, control that labels and their Artists and Repertoire (A & R) Men exercised over their creative process. When he sang about how he poured his soul into his masterpiece, only to have the callous "suits" force him to cut the length to fit radio requirements, he was echoing what many artists felt when they first became aware of the commercial realities of the business.[9]

This angst over the compromises that singers and bands were forced to make was no doubt as old as the music business itself, but in the sixties and seventies, this suppressed rage boiled onto the airwaves. The first song that would foreshadow the rage and despair of the seventies was "So You Want to Be a Rock 'n' Roll Star" recorded by The Byrds in 1967. The song was a reaction to the tawdry reality that Roger McGuinn and Chris Hillman, who had middle-class childhoods that included music lessons, concert attendance, and parental support, found when they started to achieve fame. Written as a primer for future musicians, the band told those who wanted to be (wannabe) rock stars that they should focus as much on getting their "look" (tight pants, hair in the latest style, etc.) right as on their art. This might require selling one's soul, but the results would be fame, fortune, and girls.[10]

The first mild indication of a non-satirical complaint about what the music industry could do to the artist, and his or her art, came in 1970, with the New Seekers' release of the hit single "Look What They've Done to My Song Ma" by Melanie Safka. In this work, the singer wails about the changes heartless corporate drones forced upon what no doubt could have made people forget Mozart.[11] This is a fairly innocuous complaint that lacks the specific grievances of the later Joel song, and the New Seekers' upbeat arrangement turned the complaint into a feel-good crowd pleaser, but that specificity would increase as the decade progressed.

In 1972, David Gates and Bread released "The Guitar Man," which told the story of the career arc of a star performer, moving from being the man who only cared for his guitar and what he could make it do, through fame and adulation, and finally to a rather sad and obsessed figure who finds that when his fame begins to fade, he is left with only his music. What was once the focus of his life is now only a means for maintaining the life he had come to need. This song speaks to the often fleeting nature of the fame that music could bring a person or group. The term "one hit wonder" was coined to describe those for whom fame was all too brief, and once their short time in the spotlight ended, they were relegated to performing in any venue they could find, no matter how seedy.

Ricky Nelson, who parlayed childhood stardom on *The Adventures of Ozzie & Harriet* into a music career as an adult, sang about the fickleness of his fans in "Garden Party" (1972). Nelson wrote the song after a Madison Square Garden crowd booed his attempts to sing new material, including covering "Honky Tonk Women" (1969) by the Rolling Stones. They seemed to want the clean-cut teen heartthrob who sang rockabilly songs like his hit "Travelin' Man" (1961) that belonged, in spirit, to Sanders' first wave of rock 'n' roll rather than the long-haired budding rock star who took the stage that night. Nelson wrote his bitterness into music bemoaning how his fans no longer recognized him as he tried to remain current in the music business.[12]

In the same vein as "American Pie," which debuted the year before, Nelson also referenced many famous rock personalities in his song, making references to John Lennon and Yoko Ono, George Harrison, and Chuck Berry, among others. He contrasted his wish to remain current with other artists like Berry who had made a career out of providing the audience exactly what they expected, and who looked like he "should." Some of the song's references were arcane, such as his mention of Harrison traveling incognito and planning to cover the Rolling Stones on an album. In contrast to those who decided to sell out and remain fixed forever in the form that made them famous, "Garden Party" was Nelson's memo to his fans that he would rather drive a truck than become a slave to nostalgia. In the end, Nelson told his disappointed fans, he must please himself, since he could no longer please them.[13]

The Southern rock band Lynyrd Skynyrd, in a parody of earlier labor songs, released "Workin' for the MCA" (1974), which told of the band's exploitation by label executives who signed them to a contract. The promises of big money were not met, however, and the band sings of how they were pursued and pressured by the label representative, but did not see the promised riches.

The theme of describing oily practices of the label and signing naïve artists to exploitative contracts continued with Pink Floyd's "Have a Cigar" (1975) that told, presumably, of the tactics and promises used to sign them to a contract. Like Jesus in the wilderness, the band was tempted by offers of fame and fortune laid out before them. The label man told them that the record label and the band would work together as a team to produce a hit record that could make all their dreams come true. But while he maintained that he always had a deep respect for them, the song revealed that he was so ignorant that he thought that the name Pink Floyd referred to the first names of the singers.[14]

The trials of a band to arrive at the point where they could be exploited by an A&R Man were documented by groups such as Sugarloaf, who sang about the struggles of a band to find someone to give them a break in "Don't Call Us, We'll Call You" (1975). The song was in the form of stanzas detailing a series of short phone calls in which the A&R Man brushes off the band, telling them, among other things, that they had nothing new to offer, that he had heard it all before. In this case, the band finally made it, despite the obtuseness of the A&R Man.[15] The man who continually brushed them off then attempted to get the band to sign a new contract with him, but the band could now return the insult, using the same title phrase that they had heard so often.

Even when a band finally grabbed the brass ring of a recording contract, cynicism often set in, as the artist realizes that he or she is being sucked dry and will eventually be discarded. AC/DC sang about this in "It's a Long Way to the Top" (1975). Many of the previous songs seemed to be sung by bewildered young people learning hard truths, but AC/DC added a bit more cyn-

icism to that bewilderment, singing about how the luster disappears from the
dream over time as their albums began to appear in the second-hand bins at
record stores.

Though the seventies was a watershed decade for songs about the struggles of the music business, the same issues continued to occupy singers, though
not in such large numbers, into the next decades and beyond. The lower frequency of songs exploring the dark side of making hit records likely indicated
that after listening to the seventies songs protesting the commercialization of
music, the newer generation of artists went into the void with their eyes open.

Warren Zevon, still one of the baby boom generation (1946–1960), took
another crack at the subject in 1987 with "Even a Dog Can Shake Hands,"
but by the eighties, the song's lyrics seems to be more of a satire of the typical
A&R Man than the authentic loss-of innocence that the seventies songs indicated. Zevon opened with a description of the prototypical music executive,
and in an almost anthropological manner, went on to explore their natural
habitat of Mulholland Drive, the restaurant Le Dome, and the Valley, which
was taboo territory. Zevon described the denizens of the record companies as
"worms" and "gnomes" who fattened themselves off of the work of others
then met to celebrate themselves in trendy restaurants where those not in the
business could not hope to get a table. Once the singer's value dropped, however, those same executives who once promised riches would leave only the
picked-over bones of the artist to rot in the valley.[16]

One final example is warranted. Todd Snider wrote "Talkin' Seattle
Grunge Rock Blues" (1994), a parody of a label's search for an "authentic"
sound, even if they had to manufacture the authenticity. Snider, an alternative
country singer and humorist, along the lines of Ray Stevens, sang about a
country band's effort to cash in on the grunge rock scene emanating from
Seattle, Washington, in the 1990s. In it he describes a band that wore the
flannel shirt uniform of the day and exhibited the ennui attitude of the "serious" artists that made up the grunge scene. Eventually they would become so
avant-garde that they would record songs with no music at all that would be
snapped up by the idiots at record labels and celebrated on MTV.[17]

This fanciful song turned the genre on its head, and it spoke of the gulli-
bility of A&R Men who would jump at the chance to sign any band who
claimed to be from Seattle, even if they didn't even play a song. Much like
the story "The Emperor's New Clothes," the band hoodwinked everyone,
including MTV and the Grammy Awards. The song also made reference to
the seeming stock story that was typically presented on VH1's *Behind the
Music*, which profiled famous acts and singers. The program, and the fictitious
band, seemed to follow a monotonous pattern of hard work, success, drug/
alcohol/sex addiction, eventually hitting rock bottom, and then, if they didn't

die, staging a comeback, often-times clean and sober. This same theme was followed by Kevin Gilbert's album *The Shaming of the True*, which followed the career of the fictional Johnny Vigil, who found fame and then fell to sex, drugs, and, of course, rock 'n' roll.

All the musical hand-wringing indicated that this generation was indeed "lost in space."[18] For the most part, the singers and bands had enjoyed sheltered middle-class upbringings, and the reality that the music industry was just that, an industry, obviously came as a rude awakening to many. There was more to being a rock star than "making the people dance."[19] Rather, the artists of the seventies found themselves being shaped and molded, often out of all recognition, instead of merely playing the music into which they had poured their souls. The hard and gritty reality of the industry and the demands place on its workers also formed a sub-genre of songs that described the life of the rockstar, and while some embraced that lifestyle, others spoke of the ordeals that they faced.

Released in 1970, the Grateful Dead's "Truckin'," was an autobiographical look at the trials and tribulations of life on the road as a touring act that was one of the first to address that life. The Dead sang of all the cities appearing the same, which was parodied by *This Is Spinal Tap* (1984), and gave their take on various cities. One verse told of one of the hazards of the drug use to which many bands and singers succumbed and referred to a police raid of their motel room that year where several people were arrested for drug possession, which was one of the downsides of the lifestyle.[20]

Another song in the same vein was Bob Seger's "Turn the Page" (1973), which also spoke to the rigors of the road, of the long road trips, the hostile people in small towns who mock the long hair of many performers, and the anonymous sexual encounters. Seger also mentioned the possible physical effects of the amplified music, in the last verse, singing about how long it took to get the echoes of the amplifier out of his head after the concert was over.[21]

A less self referential and more satirical look at the life was "The Cover of the *Rolling Stone*," by Dr. Hook and the Medicine Show (1973), which told of the band's efforts to get their photo on the cover of the magazine dedicated to rock music. The song, written by Shel Silverstein, the famous children book's author, foreshadowed songs like "Even a Dog Can Shake Hands" and "Talkin' Seattle Grunge Rock Blues" in that it skewered some of the rock star lifestyle's stereotypical behaviors such as maintaining that as rock stars they had access to all of the perks of the lifestyle, including drugs, limousines, and constant adulation. They were so successful at their craft that they could even hire their parents, who presumably taught them to work hard and keep their noses to the grindstone, to drive them around. Later, the song referenced the sexual opportunities available to the rock star, satirized the Beatles' famous trip to India to study with the Maharishi Mahesh Yogi, and previewed the "entourage," or "posse" (for rap or hip hop), that would become central to the rock 'n' roll lifestyle. However, despite all the trappings of the rock star lifestyle, the ultimate recognition of being featured on the cover of *Rolling Stone*, eluded them, and therefore their lives were not complete.[22]

As with most of the complaints in these songs, Dr. Hook's illustrated the central dilemma of the rock star: that their fate is always in the hands of others. To become famous took more than writing and performing good art; it also required that the performer or band catch the attention of a ruthless industry that most often forced the artists to compromise their craft. Their continued access to the "gravy train" depended on the fickle nature of their fans, and when tastes changed, they faced the awful fall from fame, with its subsequent return to obscurity. It may have started with the music, but fame and all of its trappings had come to have a life of its own, and that life was in the hands of others.

Grand Funk Railroad also explored the topic of "groupies," or sexually available and often aggressive women who attached themselves to rock bands, in their "We're an American Band" (1973). They told of a group of girls who stalked the band in a motel in Omaha and who caused a significant amount of property damage in the process. The band seemed to relish the experience, however, and such easy and casual access to the opposite sex was, along with the piles of money that bands made, the reason that many people began to pick up instruments in the first place, as well as emblematic of the sexual revolution of the sixties and seventies.[23]

The effect of the easy sex, drugs, and general all-around debauchery often had disastrous consequences, including, according to Joe Walsh, the loss, or surrender, of one's own sanity, and descent into paranoia. In "Life's Been Good" (1978), Walsh told listeners of his lifestyle, which included mansions, fast cars, all-night parties, and devoted fans. But along with the upside, there existed a concurrent downside that included legal troubles from driving too fast, life lived on the road away from the palatial mansion, and the loss of privacy that fame brought with it. The result of all the abuses and mayhem that were part of the rock star lifestyle was the fictional singer's descent into madness, which he didn't really mind, but rather embraced. So no problems really; as long as one has a mansion, has a limo, can make all the parties, and has others pay for it all, everything was cool.[24]

Despite all of the pitfalls that so many artists sang about, young boys and girls still dream of being a rock star. Aided by computer technology, now anyone can play, virtually, the music using the wildly popular Rock Band game debuted by Electronic Arts Studios in 2007. But many continued to want the real deal, as evidenced by Foreigner's "Juke Box Hero" (1981) that describes a young man who was inspired by a performance he heard as a boy. There was no mention of venal A & R Men, drug problems, money problems, or any of the other baggage that by then was common knowledge to anyone who actually listened to the lyrics. There was only the instrument and the art.[25]

The road to that top may be a long one, littered with moral compromise, artistic and financial exploitation, trips to drug rehab, STDs, and other assorted problems, but the wannabes continue to call the A & R Man, hoping that their call will be returned, and that they too can make the people dance. Some of the new generation of singers and bands seemingly embrace the chance to make the compromises necessary for stardom. In 2005, the Canadian rock band Nickelback released "Rockstar" catalogued the supposed benefits of the rock star lifestyle, which included the *de rigueur* mansions with giant bathrooms, all the better to have group sex in, along with access to the "Mile High Club," or sex in an airplane, and invitations to the Playboy Mansion.

The sung verses are interspersed with spoken lines provided by Billy Gibbons of ZZ Top, questioning and encouraging the neophyte. After the line about joining the Mile High Club, Gibbons lets the wannabe know, somewhat like Satan tempting Christ in the wilderness, that all this is possible. In contrast to Joel and others like him who felt that they were being forced to become something they weren't to sell records, this singer was well aware of the compromises necessary and didn't mind at all. Does the company want appearance changes? No problem, for the compromises give the rock star access to bodyguards, free meals, and dates with centerfold models. There is not even a pretense that the art is important now, with the singer telling of hiring has-beens to write the songs and lip-synching them on stage.[26]

From the simple desire to make the people dance expressed by Don McLean in 1971 to the necessity of having a drug dealer on speed dial, as imagined by Nickelback in 2005, songs about the music industry and its history have provided us with a record of youthful idealism that was crushed by the hard realities of corporatization, and finally a cynical embrace of taking the steps necessary to achieve the status of rock star, if not rock god.

Unlike Lawrence Levine, we are not bereft of documentary sources to write the history of the rock star. The songs discussed above give us considerable information that is useful in understanding what artists and bands felt about their lives and their place in the music business. Their complaints or celebrations of the music business, and the artist's place in it, provide historians with a treasure trove of documents from which we may recreate the creation of the rock star and the lifestyle that grew around that institution.

"American Pie," though open to interpretation in many of its lyrics, did help capture an era in American history. McLean's song told us of an industry that was changing in the styles of music that sold records and attracted labels. He also told us of the loss of innocence, at least for the sheltered children who were entering it during those years. These were young men and women who began their careers with the idealistic desire to make people smile and dance, but who then encountered a corporate juggernaut designed to mass produce an entertainment form, and who dangled the lifestyle that went along with it to entrap the neophytes. Behind the glitter and allure of the rock star lifestyle lay the assembly line grind of turning out fodder for the masses, a lesson those aspirants had to learn the hard way.

If some apocalyptic event took place and these songs were all that were left to future historians, they could reconstruct a somewhat balanced and accurate record of what the life of a rock star was like from the 1970s to 2005. Those historians could document the positive features of the rock 'n' roll lifestyle and could also explore the perils. In short, they could with some accuracy inspect the common will of the people who made up the talent side of the music industry in the late twentieth and early twenty-first centuries in their own words. That is a tune that we as historians can dance to.

Notes

1. Lawrence W. Levine, *Black Culture and Black Consciousness: Afro-American Folk Thought from Slavery to Freedom* (New York: Oxford University Press, 1978).

2. Music. of China, accessed on June 22, 2010, http://www.chinesemusic.eu/.

3. Burl. Ives, *The Burl Ives Songbook* (New York: Ballantine, 1953); accessed on June 22, 2010, http://www.contemplator.com/america/boldsold.html.

4. Lesley Nelson-Burns, "Yankee Doodle," Popular Songs in American History, accessed on June 22, 2010, http://www.contemplator.com/america/ydoodle.html.

5. Nelson-Burns, "The Liberty Song," Popular Songs in American History, accessed on June 22, 2010, http://www.contemplator.com/america/liberty.html.

6. Craig Sanders, "The True Story of American Pie: History in McLean's Lyrics," Suite 101.com, April 22, 2010, accessed on June 28, 2010, http://folkmusic.suite101.com/article.cfm/the-true-story-of-american-pie-history-in-mcleans-lyrics.

7. Don McLean, "American Pie," *American Pie*, sound recording, New York: United Artists, 1971.

8. Sanders, "The True Story of American Pie."

9. Billy Joel, "The Entertainer," *Streetlife Serenade*, sound recording, New York: Columbia, 1975.

10. The Byrds, "So You Want to Be a Rock 'n' Roll Star," *Younger Than Yesterday*, sound recording, New York: Columbia, 1967; help with the lyrics was obtained from online sites such as lyricsfreak.com and other similar.

11. The New Seekers, "What Have They Done to My Song Ma," *Keith Potger and the New Seekers*, sound recording, London: Phillips, 1970.

12. Ricky Nelson, "Garden Party," *Garden Party*, sound recording, Santa Monica: Geffen, 1990.

13. "In Ricky Nelson's 'Garden Party,' who is Mr. Hughes?" *The Straight Dope*, August

10, 2004, accessed on June 29, 2010, http://www.straightdope.com/columns/read/2173/in-ricky-nelsons-garden-party-who-is-mr-hughes.

14. Pink Floyd, "Have a Cigar," *Wish You Were Here*, sound recording, Harvest/EMI, 1975.

15. Ibid.

16 Warren Zevon, "Even a Dog Can Shake Hands," *Sentimental Hygiene*, sound recording, Virgin, 1987.

17. Todd Snider, "Talkin' Seattle Grunge Rock Blues," *Songs for the Daily Planet*, sound recording, Haw River, NC: Yep Roc, 1994.

18. McLean, "American Pie."

19. Ibid.

20 Grateful Dead, "Truckin," *American Beauty*, sound recording, Burbank: Warner Bros., 1970.

21. Bob Seger, "Turn the Page," *Back in '72*, sound recording, Tijuana, OK: Paradise, 1973.

22. Dr. Hook and the Medicine Show, "The Cover of the Rolling Stone," *Sloppy Seconds*, sound recording, New York: Columbia, 1973.

23. Grand Funk Railroad, "We're an American Band," *We're an American Band*, sound recording, Hollywood: Capitol, 1973.

24. Joe Walsh, "Life's Been Good," *But Seriously Folks*, sound recording, Burbank: Asylum, 1978.

25. Foreigner, "Jukebox Hero," *4*, sound recording, New York: Atlantic, 1981.

26. Nickelback, "Rockstar," *All the Right Reasons*, sound recording, Burbank: Roadrunner, 2005.

5

Eight-and-a-Half Minutes
Is a Long, Long Time[1]
William B. Robison

The title track of Don McLean's 1971 album *America Pie* is an unusual piece of music for a number of reasons, including its subject matter, humorous but oblique lyrics, mixture of folk and rock idioms, and extended format. At a time when the typical pop song was less than three minutes long and Top 40 radio forbade any record longer than 3:30, it ran to eight minutes and thirty-three seconds. When United Artists Records released the song as a single, it did not edit it down to a more "acceptable" length; rather, it split the song in two, releasing the first half as the "A" side and the second half as the "B" side. Radio stations initially played only the livelier "B" side, but the song became so popular — staying at number one for four weeks in 1972 — and audience demand was so great that eventually DJs began playing the whole song, even on AM stations.[2] Just as this would have been impossible a few years earlier, it is inconceivable that it could happen today. Commercial radio (AM and FM) is now tightly formatted and genre driven, and syndicated programs largely have replaced local DJs. Extended-format remixes of popular songs for dance clubs and raves may occasionally be heard on alternative radio stations, but these are altogether different from the longer-form, experimental songs that appeared on albums in the late 1960s and early 1970s and found their way onto commercial radio playlists.[3]

So how did Don McLean get an eight-and-a-half minute pop song on the radio? First and foremost, it is a great song — musically flawless with intelligent lyrics and extremely well recorded, especially given the technology available at the time.[4] Were that not the case, the scholars contributing to this volume would not be writing about it nearly forty years after its release. The Songs of the Century project sponsored in 2001 by the National Endowment for the Arts, the Recording Industry Association of America, and Scholastic

Inc. ranked it number five among the top 365 songs of the twentieth century, though of course such rankings are eminently subjective.[5] When re-released in 1992, it reached number 12 in the United Kingdom. It remains a staple of McLean's concerts, and numerous artists have covered it, notably Madonna in 2000.[6]

Beyond that, McLean recorded and United Artists released "American Pie" in the midst of one of the most creative and artistically daring periods in the history of popular music. Though post-punk revisionism downplays all but a handful of artists from the late 1960s and early 1970s and is openly disdainful toward some of the most ambitious, no reasonably objective observer can deny their openness and inventiveness.[7] Anyone who bothers to go back and listen with "unbiased ears" to the songs that lie outside the limited, repetitive repertoire of "classic rock" radio stations will find that the music of the period remains incredibly compelling, despite its occasional excesses and missteps. This era witnessed extensive blending of musical genres, both in recordings by individual bands and in live concerts, where acts that might now be deemed "incompatible" frequently appeared on the same bill. It was a time in which popular musicians became much more proficient as players and composers, trying out alternate time signatures (other than 3/4 and 4/4), incorporating more complex melodies and harmonic structures, and using more instruments beyond the typical guitar-bass-drums combination. Lyrically, artists moved beyond such adolescent obsessions as cars, surfing, and teen romance to address politics, war, drugs, sexuality, and other adult subjects, to incorporate irreverent humor, and to push the limits of censorship. Particularly relevant to the airplay given to "American Pie" is that the increasing sophistication of music and lyrics led to longer songs on records, as the standard three minutes was often inadequate for the ideas artists sought to express. Simultaneously, increasing prowess allowed musicians to "stretch out" even more onstage, and for many extended improvisation (hitherto the province of jazz) became a regular element of performances.[8]

This essay explores how that period of experimentation made possible a hit like "American Pie" and how the song in turn exemplifies the aforementioned trends. It briefly examines what might be called the "music-cultural" milieu, i.e., how and to what extent cultural phenomena shaped the creation, production, distribution, and reception of music. It also analyzes in greater detail the musicological context, considering McLean's most significant precursors and contemporaries and emphasizing the maturation of rock music as an art form, the emergence of numerous gifted musicians, the short-lived but vibrant free-form eclecticism that characterized the period, the sheer speed at which music evolved, and the link between creativity and the expanded song format. It addresses selected works by many major artists and some minor ones, but limitations on space preclude its being comprehensive — for the same reason, it does not address the role of record labels and producers. A table at the end of the text indicates the number of songs by each artist exceeding five minutes in length for each year from 1966 to 1972, thereby indicating the increasing tendency of artists to resort to a longer format (so many songs exceeded 3:30 that it would be impossible to include them all).[9]

"All I remember is waking up one morning in 1967 and the whole world had changed," writes Steven van Zandt in the foreword to Richard Neer's *FM: The Rise and Fall of Rock Radio*.[10] He is referring to the emergence, almost overnight, of free form radio — a.k.a. "progressive" or "underground" — which temporarily revolutionized music programming before losing ground to more commercial formats in the mid–1970s, not long after the heyday of "American Pie." This occurred largely on FM stations, where unconventional disk jockeys eschewed the tight structure of AM Top 40 and began playing whatever they and their audiences wanted to hear. Though FM technology had existed since 1933, FM stations had little commercial importance prior to 1965, when the Federal Communications Commission ordered broadcasters to provide different programming for their AM and FM stations. For the first few years thereafter, FM largely was limited to classical and "easy listening" music, for which there was a limited and largely adult audience. However, AM Top 40 already had demonstrated the huge commercial potential of rock 'n' roll, at least in the form of 45-rpm singles. All that remained was for a new breed of disk jockeys to move beyond that limited format and build an audience for a broader and looser selection of album cuts.[11]

Though many DJs claim to have invented free-form radio, among the first and most influential were Larry Miller and Tom Donahue at KMPX in San Francisco and William "Rosko" Mercer, Jonathan Schwartz, Scott Muni, and Alison Steele at WNEW in New York ("where rock lives"), who went on the air with the new format (or "non-format") in 1967. Reputedly, what motivated Donahue was listening to the Doors' first album — which includes two lengthy tracks, "Light My Fire" and "The End" — and wondering why such music was not on the radio. Initially station owners were seeking ways to fill air time (especially at night), but free form took off, attracting a large audience of more "hip" listeners and spawning imitators all over the country. One of the most significant was Jim Ladd of KLOS in Los Angeles, who is still on the air today and to whom Tom Petty paid tribute in "The Last DJ."[12] Free form even established a toehold in AM with Clyde Clifford's late night "Beeker Street" program on clear-channel KAAY in Little Rock (a staple of this author's youthful listening).[13]

The essential characteristic of free form was that DJs had complete freedom. There were no playlists. All that mattered was what the DJ wanted to play and — if he chose to pay attention — what his audience requested. Free-form DJs might play whole albums or sides of albums, long sequences of songs by the same artist or with a similar theme, and tapes of live concerts, or they might mix disparate genres, including classical music, jazz, blues, old standards, and even comedy records. They also talked about the music — not the mindless patter of AM DJs but serious discussions about artists, technique, influences, history, instrumentation, and so on. In such a format, longer songs were not only acceptable; they were welcomed with open arms. Not surprisingly, some free-form DJs embraced radical politics, the anti-war movement, the sexual revolution, and drug use (sometimes while on the air), and their programs and audiences reflected that. This, too, encouraged the extended song style, which was more conducive to "message" lyrics and unlikely to wear on listeners whose sense of time was chemically altered.[14]

Still, none of this would have happened if there had not been profound changes in rock music. No matter how much free-form radio may have encouraged and facilitated musical experimentation, the music came first. One of the most convincing accounts of what happened in the 1960s — especially compelling because it emphasizes music rather than making it a function of other social phenomena — is Philip Ennis's *The Seventh Stream: The Emergence of Rocknroll in American Popular Music*. Ennis argues that between 1900 and 1940 six "streams" of popular music developed in America: the three major streams of pop (commercial music), black pop (African American music), and country pop (white Southern music), and the three minor streams of jazz, folk, and gospel. Rock and roll gradually emerged between 1945 and 1965, which saw disc jockeys assuming a prominent role in shaping musical tastes, the alignment of the six streams, and the appearance of "crossover" artists who mingled the styles of multiple streams, most notably Elvis Presley. Finally, according to Ennis, rock matured between 1965 and 1970 as the Beatles and a whole new generation of younger musicians made their mark.[15] Facilitating this last stage were significant changes in technology — four track (and later multi-track) recording, new effects for guitars and other instruments, and electronic instruments, particularly the Mellotron and the Moog synthesizer, all of which the younger generation eagerly embraced.[16]

Almost all historians of popular music identify the Beatles' release of *Sergeant Pepper's Lonely Hearts Club Band* on June 1, 1967, as a pivotal moment. But *Sergeant Pepper* did not emerge in a musical vacuum, and neither — five years later — did "American Pie" (with its many Beatles references, including the line "the sergeants played a marching tune"). Although "music-cultural" influences were important in establishing the context for both songs, much more significant were musicological factors. In fact, at the very time that rock music was becoming more forward-looking or "progressive," many rock musicians also seemed much more aware of music history. *Sergeant Pepper* drew on decades on British musical traditions — for example, "When I'm 64" has a pre-rock dance hall feel (accentuated by the use of clarinets) and "Being for the Benefit of Mr. Kite," which was inspired by a nineteenth century circus poster, includes elements of carnival music.[17] As Joseph E. Burns' essay in this volume demonstrates, there were numerous milestones, lyrically speaking, on the road to "American Pie," not just the plane crash that killed Buddy Holly, the Big Bopper, and Ritchie Valens on February 3, 1958.[18] Musically, there were many as well, and one of the most significant was the emergence of Elvis Presley[19] — Don McLean's favorite artist — who had his first number one album and single in 1956.[20]

The year 1956 is a useful starting point for examining the background to the creative explosion that occurred a decade later, not only because Elvis was the biggest star to hit the charts between Frank Sinatra and the Beatles — another of McLean's major influences — but also because *Billboard Magazine* began tracking LP sales that year. Furthermore, one might argue that it is less useful for historians to think of twentieth-century rock music in terms of decades (the '50s, '60s, '70s, and so on) than from mid-decade to mid-decade: thus, early rock 'n' roll (1956–65), more sophisticated rock (1966–75), punk and new wave vs. disco and commercialized rock (1976–85), and grunge vs. genre-based radio (1986–95). In any case, it is instructive that from 1956, as AM Top 40 boomed, rock 'n' roll increasingly took over the singles charts, but it was not until 1967 that it began to do the same with LPs, which were the vehicle for more musical experimentation c. 1966–1975 and the staple of free-form radio.[21]

The best-selling albums for the decade from 1956 to 1965 were almost all original cast records and soundtracks for stage and screen musicals: after Harry Belafonte's *Calypso* (1956) came the original cast recording for *My Fair Lady* (1957–58), Henry Mancini's *Music from Peter Gunn* (1959), original cast recordings for *The Sound of Music* (1960) and *Camelot* (1961), the soundtrack from the film *West Side Story* (1962–63), the original cast recording for *Hello, Dolly!* (1964), and the soundtrack for *Mary Poppins* (1965). Musicals dominated the rest of the top five, though folk albums began to appear in 1959 — the Kingston Trio had albums at number four and five that year (after debuting in 1958). But Elvis was the only rocker to make the list until the Beatles in 1965. Even in the realm of singles Elvis and later the Beatles, the Rolling Stones, and other rockers shared the charts with a great deal of very bland pop.

Several major folk artists who influenced Don McLean began recording in the early 1960s — Joan Baez in 1960; Judy Collins in 1961; Hoyt Axton,

Bob Dylan, Peter, Paul, and Mary, Tom Paxton, and Tom Rush in 1962; the Holy Modal Rounders, Phil Ochs, and Simon and Garfunkel in 1964; and Richie Havens in 1965.[24] Indeed, folk had a substantial impact on rock music throughout the 1960s and early 70s. Not only did important new folk artists continue to emerge, folk singers — especially Dylan — had a profound influence on the Beatles and their imitators and on a disparate group of American bands ranging from folk rock (e.g., the Byrds) to country rock (e.g., the Eagles) to psychedelic rock (the Grateful Dead, the Jefferson Airplane).[23]

But even more important in changing the musical landscape was the British invasion that began taking over the American charts in 1964 and 1965, propelling to fame many artists destined to play a role in revolutionizing music later in the decade.[25] It began in 1964 with the Beatles, the Rolling Stones, the Animals, Chad & Jeremy, the Dave Clark Five, Freddie and the Dreamers, Wayne Fontana and the Mindbenders, Gerry and the Pacemakers, the Hollies, the Kinks, Manfred Mann, Peter and Gordon, Dusty Springfield, and the Yardbirds, and gained momentum in 1965, which witnessed the advent of Petula Clark, the Spencer Davis Group, Donovan, Herman's Hermits, John Mayall, the Moody Blues, the Pretty Things, the Who, the Zombies, and others.[26] British rock groups, who had drawn heavily upon an earlier generation of U.S. rock 'n' roll, now had a huge influence on their American contemporaries, including Paul Revere and the Raiders, who had debuted as recording artists in 1961; the Beach Boys, who debuted 1962; and the Beau Brummels, bluesman Paul Butterfield, the Byrds, Country Joe and the Fish, the Knickerbockers, the Lovin' Spoonful, and the Turtles in 1965.[27]

The Beatles led the way, both in terms of their phenomenal output and their ever-evolving creativity. They also wrote much of their own material — which their contemporaries emulated — and by the end of 1965 they largely had ceased to record cover songs for their albums. *Rubber Soul*, released near the end of 1965, was a major turn in the road that led from "Love Me Do" to *Sergeant Pepper*. Its main importance was as an album — it was the first Beatles LP released in America that did not produce a number one single; yet, it was clearly their most impressive artistic achievement up to that point. It was the first album that the Beatles made using a four-track recorder, then a major technological innovation, and the first western record to feature the sitar, played by George Harrison on "Norwegian Wood." It also demonstrated increasing lyrical and musical sophistication. Like everything else the Beatles did, it also spawned imitators.

The year 1966 began the transition that was to provide so much music for free-form radio a year later. Atop the album charts there was a shift from soundtracks to fairly innocuous pop music with the Latin-inflected Herb Alpert & the Tijuana Brass's *Whipped Cream & Other Delights* topping the list in 1966, and two other albums by the group at numbers three and five. The movie soundtrack for *The Sound of Music* still managed to finish second. However, *Rubber Soul* was at number four for the year, and it was by no means the only album to signal a new maturity for rock 'n' roll.[28] The brilliant trio of musicians in Cream — Ginger Baker, Jack Bruce, and Eric Clapton — released their first album, *Fresh Cream*, with its signature mixture of avant-garde compositions, traditional blues, fuzz-tone guitar, stunning improvisation, and songs that extended well beyond the traditional length. There were also debuts by fellow Britons, the proto-punk garage band, the Troggs (*From Nowhere ... The Troggs*, released as *Wild Thing* in the U.S.) and the psychedelic folk group Incredible String Band's eponymous LP.[29] Indeed, the very fact that one can use the term "psychedelic folk group" emphasizes that change was afoot.

In America there was a similar outpouring of talent. The Richie Furay–Stephen Stills–Neil Young folk rock collaborative, Buffalo Springfield, released its self-titled first album. The pre–Grace Slick incarnation of Jefferson Airplane issued *Jefferson Airplane Takes Off*— more akin to folk rock than its later politically radical psychedelia. Love — one of the first racially mixed bands in America and fronted by African American multi-instrumentalist Arthur Lee — released its Byrds-influenced self-titled debut. The Mamas and Papas, who had put out singles in 1965, followed with two albums in 1966, the hit-laden *If You Can Believe Your Eyes and Ears* and *The Mamas and the Papas*. Appropriately for a year when folk remained a major influence on the new generation of rockers, several new folk artists appeared on record, including Tim Buckley, Tim Hardin, and Gordon Lightfoot. *The Young Rascals* provided an early example of blue-eyed soul. Finally, a Texas band fronted by the eccentric Doug Sahm released its ironically titled first album, *The Best of the Sir Douglas Quintet.*[30]

Meanwhile, the Beatles released their most innovative album thus far with *Revolver*, routinely ranked as one of the greatest albums of all time. It featured George Harrison's best composition yet in the sarcastically biting "Taxman," as well as his "I Want to Tell You"; Paul McCartney's haunting imagery in "Eleanor Rigby" enhanced by George Martin's "string octet" arrangement, the beautiful "Here, There, and Everywhere" (one of Lennon's favorite McCartney songs), the upbeat "Good Day Sunshine," the touching "For No One" (perhaps McCartney's most underrated song), and the Beatles' first use of a brass section in "Got to Get You into My Life"; John Lennon's languorously humorous "I'm Only Sleeping" (with Harrison's backwards guitar), the spooky "She Said She Said," the employment in "And Your Bird Can Sing" of the harmonizing twin lead guitars soon to become commonplace in rock music, the sly drug references of "Doctor Robert," and the use of special sonic effects (processed vocals, tape loops) to enhance the Indian drone of the psychedelic "Tomorrow Never Knows"; and one of Ringo's most beloved vocals, "Yellow Submarine." The Rolling Stones released *Aftermath*, another artistic milestone and their first with all compositions by Mick Jagger and Keith Richards. They also experimented with different instruments, notably the signature sitar riff on "Paint It Black" and the funky marimba on "Under My Thumb."[31]

Established American artists also began to take new directions. Brian Wilson abandoned the stage and the Beach Boys as a whole left the surf to produce the critically acclaimed and extraordinarily influential *Pet Sounds* and the separate single "Good Vibrations," both of which showed a new level of sophistication and Wilson's willingness to experiment with new instruments, including the cello, flute, harpsichord, and such unconventional additions as bells, whistles, and the Theremin.[32] The previous year Bob Dylan had horrified folk purists by playing with an electric band at the Newport Folk Festival and releasing two albums using electric instruments, *Bringing It All Back Home* and *Highway 61 Revisited*, the latter of which included several extended tracks, including the hit single, "Like a Rolling Stone." In 1966 he followed this with one of rock's first double albums, *Blonde on Blonde*, recorded with the Hawks (later the Band) and featuring more lengthy compositions. Also, Simon and Garfunkel released two important albums, *Sounds of Silence* and *Parsley, Sage, Rosemary, and Thyme*.

Finally, among the 1966 releases, it is hard to top the unmitigatedly audacious creativity of Frank Zappa and the Mothers of Invention's debut, the double album *Freak Out!*, which Paul McCartney cites as a major inspiration for *Sergeant Pepper*. Critics hated the record, which sold poorly in the United States, but it attracted a small but fanatical American following, was popular in Europe, and is now regarded as seminal in the development of progressive rock. There was simply nothing else like it at the time, and outside the Zappa oeuvre there still is not. Zappa later would ask, ironically, with a 1986 album title, "Does humor belong in music?" With this album, he already had answered with a resounding yes — lyrically it is a hilariously sarcastic send-up of American pop music. But that does not mean Zappa was not serious about the music or its message: mixed in with doo-wop (which he loved) and rock are wildly experimental pieces like "Who Are the Brain Police?" "Help, I'm a Rock" (with musical references to Edgard Varèse), and "The Return of the Son of Monster Magnet," an unfinished ballet. Zappa is credited — correctly — as conductor, and the performers included horn players, six cellists, and Jeanne Vassoir as "the voice of Cheese." This was the first (but not last) Zappa record to feature censor-challenging profanity, and the name "Mothers" was controversial (Zappa reluctantly changed it to "Mothers of Invention" to satisfy the Verve record label). After *Freak Out,* no musical boundary was safe.[33]

Not surprisingly, rock continued to explore new territory in 1967. *Sergeant Pepper* was the first Beatles album from which the band released no singles that might hit the AM Top 40 charts. However, it was much more revolutionary than that. It is a concept album, meant to be listened to in its entirety, not merely as a collection of songs (singles, B-sides, and other tunes). Though most of the songs are less than the traditional three-and-a-half minutes in length, several tracks segue into the following song — most notably the opening title track and "With a Little Help from My Friends" (combined 4:43) and the reprise and "A Day in the Life" (combined 6:23) — and George Harrison's Eastern-influenced "Within You Without You" exceeds five minutes. The album employs horns and strings, Indian instruments and motifs, atypical instrumentation (George Martin's use of a mallet on the strings of a mini-piano in "Getting Better All the Time"), key changes and variations in time signature ("Lucy in the Sky with Diamonds"), tempo changes and dissonance ("A Day in the Life"), countermelody ("Lucy," "She's Leaving Home"), circus music ("Mr. Kite"), the dance hall style ("When I'm Sixty-Four") animal noises and kazoo ("Good Morning Good Morning"), and combs covered with toilet paper and blown like harmonicas ("Lovely Rita"). Free-form DJs played the album relentlessly, often an entire side or even the whole thing at once.[34]

Ironically, in the year of the Beatles' most critically acclaimed album, a "manufactured" band of imitators, the Monkees, held the top two spots on the 1967 album charts, followed by soundtracks for *Doctor Zhivago* and *The Sound of Music* and The Temptations' *Greatest Hits.*[35] However, though the Monkees were meant to lure teens to television and record stores, they did produce some good albums, and their success is not without significance. In particular, the sound quality of their records is very good, showing what accomplished engineers and producers could accomplish in the studio by this time.[36] More change was afoot farther down the charts, with an amazing crop of debuts from Britain and America.

From the United Kingdom came several foundational albums in the emerging genre of progressive rock. Perhaps the most acclaimed was Pink Floyd's *Piper at the Gates of Dawn,* which featured the brilliant Syd Barrett's whimsical lyrics set to intensely psychedelic music, as well as the extended collaborative instrumental and concert favorite, "Interstellar Overdrive." Another was *The Thoughts of Emerlist Davjack,* the first album by the Nice, the direct forerunner of Emerson, Lake, and Palmer. Though also heavily psychedelic, it has embryonic elements of ELP, particularly on the lengthy instrumental adaptation of jazz pianist Dave Brubeck's "Rondo." Procol Harum's self-titled album is another ambitious effort, though their mega-hit, the Bach-inspired single "Whiter Shade of Pale," appeared only on the U.S. release. The former David Jones, who adopted the new surname Bowie to avoid confusion with the British member of the Monkees, released his eponymous first album, and despite rather unexceptional songs, one can discern the voice that emerged so powerfully on *Space Oddity* two years later.[37]

Closely related to progressive was the arty and psychedelic debut from Traffic, *Mr. Fantasy*. Along with Steve Winwood's trademark organ and ethereal vocals, it also features heavy doses of Mellotron, sitar, flute, saxophone, and percussion. Significantly, the most memorable track, "Dear Mr. Fantasy," is the longest. Winwood previously had been known for blues and rock with the Spencer Davis Group (and briefly with Eric Clapton in Powerhouse), and two other debuts featured plenty of each: Savoy Brown's *Shake Down* and an eponymous LP by Ten Years After, soon to achieve rock immortality at Woodstock. Van Morrison produced his first solo album since his departure from the R&B group Them, *Blowin' Your Mind*, a mixed bag that includes the hit "Brown Eyed Girl" and a long, bluesy track about a girl dying of tuberculosis, "T.B. Sheets." The Jimi Hendrix Experience — the American Hendrix on guitar and the English musicians Mitch Mitchell on drums and Noel Redding on bass — stunned the world with *Are You Experienced*. It is difficult, if not impossible, to explain to anyone born since 1967 just how incredible it was to hear Hendrix for the first time. This amalgam of blues and psychedelic rock is generally considered to be one of the best guitar albums ever. Hendrix did things with a guitar that no one had heard before, using distortion, feedback, and effects (fuzz box, wah-wah pedal) designed by Roger Mayer. Rock guitar has not been the same since then. Hendrix followed this up later the same year with the equally amazing *Axis: Bold as Love*. Finally, the zany Bonzo Dog Doo-Dah Band released its first album, *Gorilla*.[38]

In America there was an equally stellar batch of releases by new artists. The Doors released their groundbreaking, self-titled debut, which included the classic "Light My Fire," and set the censors buzzing with its sexually charged lyrics and open drug references. Musically different but equally controversial in terms of lyrics was *The Velvet Underground and Nico*, produced by Andy Warhol with Tom Wilson and featuring several lengthy tracks as well. *The Grateful Dead*— the first LP from a band known for mingling folk and psychedelia and extended live jams — soon became a free form radio staple. Among other psychedelic bands, Moby Grape recorded its heralded self-titled debut, which was unusual both because all five members composed and sang and because the band had three lead guitarists; Vanilla Fudge released an album consisting entirely of stretched-out cover songs; and the Electric Prunes issued their first album, which included the previous year's single, "I Had Too Much to Dream (Last Night)." Also dabbling with psychedelic rock, as well as beginning the transition from soul to funk, was the racially mixed band Sly and the Family Stone, fronted by multi-instrumentalist, singer, and genuinely unique character Sylvester Stewart a.k.a. Sly Stone.[39]

There were several important new blues-rock albums: Janis Joplin's debut with *Big Brother and the Holding Company, Canned Heat,* and Electric Flag's film score for *The Trip* (though the latter was less bluesy than subsequent albums by the band). There also were significant folk debuts. The importance of one, Arlo Guthrie's *Alice's Restaurant,* was immediately apparent, and its 18:20 title track became one of the most popular songs in the history of free form radio, as well as one that concert goers continue to demand over four decades later. Another, Cat Stevens' *Matthew and Son,* was successful but rather different from the string of hit albums that he put out in the 1970s. Also in the folk vein were *Songs of Leonard Cohen*; Janis Ian's self-titled album; folk-trio *The Stone Poneys* featuring singer Linda Ronstadt; and the debut from Jesse Colin Young's group, *The Youngbloods,* which was re-released in 1971 as *Get Together.* Very nearly in a class all its own — save for its affinity to Zappa-esque experimentation — was *Safe as Milk* by Captain Beefheart (Don Van Vliet).[40]

Among older bands, the Beatles issued *Magical Mystery Tour,* the soundtrack for an unsuccessful television movie that nonetheless contains some excellent music, including the title track; the Lewis Carroll–inspired "I Am the Walrus"; the hits "Hello, Goodbye," "Strawberry Fields Forever," and "Penny Lane"; and perhaps the first rock song ever to employ the 7/4 time signature, "All You Need Is Love."[41] The Beach Boys released *Smiley Smile* in the aftermath of Brian Wilson's legendary aborted project, *Smile.*[42] Jefferson Airplane released its first two LPs of the Grace Slick era, the fairly commercial *Surrealistic Pillow* and the heavier, more experimental *After Bathing at Baxter's,* which was divided into five suites and featured longer tracks. Zappa and the Mothers' *Absolutely Free* also is divided into suites. Some artists made a significant change of direction. Eric Burdon recruited a new, more psychedelic batch of Animals for *Winds of Change.* The Moody Blues, with new guitarist Justin Hayward and bassist John Lodge, moved from pop to progressive with *Days of Future Passed,* a song cycle featuring the London Festival Orchestra, heavy doses of Michael Pinder's Mellotron (he worked for the manufacturer), and the hit "Nights in White Satin." Other important releases, all featuring extended tracks, included *Buffalo Springfield Again,* the Country Joe and the Fish LPs *Electric Music for the Mind and Body* and *I-Feel-Like-I'm-Fixin'-to-Die,*[43] Cream's superb *Disraeli Gears,* Dylan's *John Wesley Harding,* Love's all-time classic *Forever Changes,* and the Rolling Stones' *Their Satanic Majesties Request.*

In 1968 more experimental music rose to the top, with the first four places on the album charts going to the Jimi Hendrix Experience's *Are You Experienced,* Simon and Garfunkel's soundtrack for the controversial film *The*

Graduate, Cream's *Disraeli Gears,* and the Beatles' soundtrack for *Magical Mystery Tour.*[44] Interestingly, though Hendrix and Cream kept most of the songs on their respective albums under three minutes, in concert they extended many of them into brilliant and lengthy improvisational jams, changing the whole nature of the live rock performance in the process.[45] The mix of rock and pop continued on the singles charts into the late 1960s and early 1970s (and, in fact, that has been the case ever since), but a noteworthy developments was that the Beatles had the number one single for 1968 with "Hey Jude," which clocked in at 7:11. But, generally, AM Top 40 was becoming irrelevant to serious rock music fans, so the LP charts are much more revealing.

There one could find an eclectic batch of debut albums in 1968. The Band released the quirky and unique *Music from Big Pink,* the equally (if differently) eccentric Dr. John (Mac Rebennack), a funky slice of New Orleans called *Gris-Gris,* New Orleanian-turned-Californian Randy Newman's self-titled premier, and Southern-sounding Californians Creedence Clearwater Revival with their own eponymous debut. Several veterans of other bands appeared in new groups or released solo albums, including the star-studded Jeff Beck Group with *Truth,* George Harrison with the electronic *Wonderwall Music,* John Lennon with the controversial *Unfinished Music No. 1: Two Virgins* (with Yoko Ono), and Neil Young's *Neil Young.* Two blues-based but ultimately very different bands that critics initially linked under the label "jazz-rock" were the first of the big horn bands, the American Blood, Sweat, & Tears, which released *Child Is the Father to the Man* before initial leader Al Kooper gave place to David Clayton Thomas, and the English Jethro Tull, whose first album, *This Was,* showcased leader Ian Anderson's flute virtuosity (hence the jazz label) and is the only Tull album not to feature perennial guitarist Martin Barre. Tull soon became part of the progressive rock movement, as did Soft Machine, another English band sometimes given the jazz-fusion label. A genuine blues band that later took a very different path was the English Fleetwood Mac, initially the vehicle for guitarist Peter Green, who at the time blues aficionados mentioned in the same breath with Beck, Clapton, and Page. Another English group that began with psychedelia but later became a blues-based boogie band is Status Quo, whose first album is *Picturesque Matchstickable Messages from the Status Quo* and features the wah-wah pedal-driven hit single, "Pictures of Matchstick Men."[46]

In 1968 the term "heavy metal" was not yet part of the rock lexicon, but one of the early exemplars of what then was called "hard rock" was Steppenwolf, whose self-titled debut included the song "Born to Be Wild" (soon to be made even more famous in the movie *Easy Rider*), which refers to "heavy metal thunder," from whence the name came. Other bands who appeared on the scene that year and who soon would share the label "heavy metal" were the power trio Blue Cheer, whose first album is *Vincebus Eruptum*; Deep Purple, whose first is *Shades of Deep Purple*; and Iron Butterfly, whose debut is — appropriately — called *Heavy*.[47] At the other end of the spectrum were several major folk debuts — eponymous albums from the English groups Fairport Convention, which at the time featured the brilliant singer-songwriter-guitarist Richard Thompson, and Pentangle, which included guitarist John Renbourn, as well as premiers from Americans Melanie Safka, whose first LP was *Born to Be*, and Joni Mitchell, whose initial offering was *Song to a Seagull*. Both the American Quicksilver Messenger Service and the English Tyrannosaurus Rex (later T. Rex) played psychedelic music rooted in earlier folk music. Other debuts of interest were *The Crazy World of Arthur Brown*, which included the single "Fire," and *Nazz* (featuring a young Todd Rundgren), with the single "Hello It's Me."[48]

Returning in 1968 from their sojourn with the Maharishi in India, the Beatles released the "White Album," a decidedly odd assortment of songs and pieces of songs, but brilliant nonetheless. Among other veteran artists, Cream delivered the dazzling double album *Wheels of Fire*, the studio half of which is heavily psychedelic (even the blues standard "Sitting on Top of the World"), employs 5/4 time in portions of the spectacular "White Room," features a spoken piece by Ginger Baker ("Pressed Rat and Warthog"), and makes heavy use of unconventional instrumentation, including bells, brass, calliope, cello, glockenspiel, recorder, and viola. The live half includes what may be the world's most imitated guitar solo in "Crossroads" and a number of other extended improvisations. Jimi Hendrix also released a double album, *Electric Ladyland*, which showcases his versatility as a guitarist, singer, and lyricist, encompassing blues, psychedelic rock, and soul. It is the last Jimi Hendrix Experience album and uses a number of additional musicians — Jack Casady, Al Kooper, Buddy Miles, Dave Mason, Steve Winwood, and Chris Wood. The Kinks began producing more sophisticated music with *Village Green Preservation Society*, a concept album about traditional English society that was ahead of its time — though initially unsuccessful, it has become one of the band's most popular albums.

Several English bands made deeper forays into progressive rock in 1968. The Moody Blues (now heavily influenced by LSD advocate Timothy Leary) produced the concept album *In Search of the Lost Chord*, the Nice (reduced to a trio by the departure of guitarist O'List) released *Ars Longa Vita Brevis*, Pink Floyd (with Syd Barrett increasingly disengaged) put out *A Saucerful of Secrets*, and Procol Harum offered *Shine On Brightly*. Other releases from veteran artists included the Buffalo Springfield's *Last Time Around*, the Byrds' turn from psychedelia (*The Notorious Byrd Brothers*) to country-rock (*Sweetheart of the Rodeo*), Jefferson Airplane's *Crown of Creation*, the Rolling Stones' highly regarded *Beggars Banquet*, Simon and Garfunkel's *Bookends*, Traffic's eponymous second album, and the Mothers' merciless send-up of *Sergeant Pepper*, flower power, and hippies, *We're Only in It for the Money*, plus Zappa's orchestral album, *Lumpy Gravy* (featuring tape loops, *musique concrète*, and considerable atonality) and the Mothers' doo-wop LP, *Cruising with Ruben & The Jets*.[49]

The year 1969 truly was one for long experimental songs. The top-selling album in America was Iron Butterfly's *In-A-Gadda-Da-Vida*, the much-played title track of which covered an entire side at 17:05. Number two was the original cast recording for the musical *Hair*, but numbers three, four, and five — Blood, Sweat, and Tears' eponymous second album, Creedence Clearwater Revival's *Bayou Country*, and the debut from Led Zeppelin, another band of gifted improvisers — all featured numerous extended tracks. That is also true of the rich variety of other debuts farther down the charts. A number of acts, some of which included veterans of earlier successful bands, shared Led Zeppelin's propensity for improvisation, including the blues-based Southern rockers in the Allman Brothers Band, the versatile virtuosos in Blind Faith (with former members of Cream, Family, and Traffic), Joe Cocker's *With a Little Help from My Friends*, Delaney and Bonnie's *Home,* and Humble Pie's *As Safe as Yesterday Is* (with former members of the Herd and the Small Faces) and *It's a Beautiful Day*.[50]

Other heavily blues-based debuts were Michael Bloomfield's *It's Not Killing Me* and Janis Joplin's *I Got Dem Ol' Kozmic Blues Again Mama!* A band joining the jazz-rock field with a powerful horn section was the highly talented and politically radical Chicago Transit Authority, while Santana introduced to rock 'n' roll the Latin American motifs and instrumentation that many other artists soon embraced. There were several major additions to the burgeoning genre of progressive rock: Genesis' *From Genesis to Revelation* (obviously influenced by the Moody Blues and more pop-oriented than the band's subsequent records), Van der Graaf Generator's *The Aerosol Grey Machine* (fronted by the multi-talented Peter Hammill), *Yes,* two more debuts from the subfield of Krautrock — Amon Düül II's *Phallus Dei* and Can's *Monster Movie* — and the most fully-formed prog album yet, King Crimson's *In the Court of the Crimson King*.[51]

There were several straight-ahead rockers: the Zappa protégé Alice Cooper's *Pretties for You*, Grand Funk Railroad's *On Time, Mott the Hoople,* and two new bands that greatly influenced punk rock — the MC5's *Kick Out the Jams* and the Stooges self-titled LP. There were also releases from three new folk rock groups that included former members of the defunct Buffalo Springfield and the Byrds — *Crosby, Stills, & Nash,* the Flying Burrito Brothers' *The Gilded Palace of Sin,* and Poco's *Pickin' Up the Pieces,* as well as the first solo album from a closely allied artist, Linda Ronstadt's *Hand Sown ... Home Grown*. There were several other first releases from folk or folk-influenced artists: Nick Drake's *Five Leaves Left*, Elton John's *Empty Sky* (which gave little clue to the flamboyant persona and stage act to come), and Jamie Brockett's *Remember the Wind and the Rain*, including the very long and hilarious track, "The Legend of the U.S.S. *Titanic*," which became a staple of freeform radio. The first major nostalgia act appeared with Sha Na Na's *Rock and Roll Is Here to Stay* (this band featured many older songs by artists who influenced Don McLean). Finally, a band that owed its style directly to the Beatles was Badfinger, which debuted with *Maybe Tomorrow*.[52]

The year 1969 also brought numerous classic albums from established acts. The Beatles released the soundtrack for the animated film *Yellow Submarine* and the last album that they recorded together (though not the last they released), *Abbey Road*, while John Lennon pursued his anti-war agenda with *Live Peace in Toronto*. The Rolling Stones, in the midst of one of their most creative periods, put out *Let It Bleed*. One of the most ambitious projects to emerge in rock music (much more adventurous at the time than it might seem today) was Pete Townshend's rock opera, *Tommy*, released by the Who and performed live in its entirety. Yet another veteran British rock act, the Kinks, released the concept album, *Arthur*. As Jimmy Page was blazing new trails with Led Zeppelin, other former Yardbirds were busy as well: the Jeff Beck Group released *Beck-Ola*, and Eric Clapton appeared not only on the new release from Blind Faith but also on *Goodbye*, the farewell album from Cream, which remained innovative to the last. Another farewell — premature as it turned out — was *Last Exit* from Traffic, the group fronted by Clapton's new Blind Faith band mate, Steve Winwood.

In America the Grateful Dead continued blending genres and exploring the possibilities of improvisation with *Aoxomoxoa* and *Live/Dead*, while Neil Young also stretched out on his first album with Crazy Horse, *Everybody Knows This Is Nowhere*. The prolific roots rockers Creedence Clearwater Revival released two more excellent albums, *Green River* and *Willy and the Poor Boys*; Dylan recorded the country-flavored *Nashville Skyline*; the Doors continued exploring psychedelia with *Soft Parade*; Jefferson Airplane issued the highly politicized *Bless Its Pointed Little Head* and *Volunteers*; Sly and the Family Stone issued the controversial *Stand*; Johnny Winter released his eponymous debut and *Second Winter*; and Captain Beefheart and his Magic Band released the wonderfully eccentric *Trout Mask Replica*. The year 1969 also witnessed the most famous rock festival in history at Woodstock, which led to a documentary film and a triple album soundtrack.

The same year that brought several important new progressive acts also brought significant albums from older prog bands. David Bowie's pre-glam release *Space Oddity* really belongs in this category — Rick Wakeman, who later joined the most successful version of Yes, played keyboards, including the signature Mellotron riff on the title track. Jethro Tull's *Stand Up* saw flute virtuoso Ian Anderson moving away from the blues-based style of Tull's first album, as well as guitarist Mick Abrahams' replacement by Martin Barre, whose influence on the band's style was second only to Anderson's. Two more albums featuring a great deal of both flute and Mellotron were the Moody Blues' *On the Threshold of a Dream* and *To Our Children's Children's Children*. The Nice continued its classical and jazz-influenced rock with *Everything as Nice as Mother Makes It*. Pink Floyd had a particularly productive year, releasing both the *Soundtrack for the Film More* and the double album *Ummagumma*, with both a studio and a live LP included. Procol Harum issued perhaps its most famous album, *A Salty Dog*. Frank Zappa and the Mothers released another highly experimental double album, *Uncle Meat*, while Zappa on his own put out *Hot Rats*, the first of a trio of jazz-influenced solo albums.

In 1970 — the year that Don McLean released his debut album, *Tapestry* — Simon and Garfunkel owned the top spot on both charts with the LP *Bridge Over Troubled Waters* and the unusually long single of the same name. Second on the album charts was *Led Zeppelin II*; third *Chicago Transit Authority*, a double album full of lengthy tunes; fourth the Beatles' *Abbey Road*, with a medley covering most of side two; and fifth Santana's first album. By this time, the Beatles had split, but they still released two more successful albums, *Hey Jude* and *Let It Be*. The former members all had albums on the charts as well, including two solo debuts, *McCartney* and Ringo Starr's *Sentimental Journey*, plus *John Lennon and the Plastic Ono Band* and George Harrison's incredible triple album *All Things Must Pass*, which helped him to escape from the shadow of Lennon and McCartney.[53]

There were a great many more important debut albums. The highly peripatetic Eric Clapton released his own first solo album and Derek and the Dominos' brilliant double album debut (and only studio release) *Layla and Other Assorted Love Songs*, as well as appearing on *All Things Must Pass*, Stephen Stills' debut (which also featured Hendrix), and Delaney and Bonnie's *On Tour with Eric Clapton* (Harrison also toured with them). Other veterans who debuted with solo albums or in new bands (though none as many as Clapton) were former Zombie Rod Argent's release with his new band *Argent*, the Lovin' Spoonful's John B. Sebastian (solo), Keith Emerson (Nice), Greg Lake (King Crimson), and Carl Palmer (Atomic Rooster) in ELP, Nazz's Todd Rundgren with *Runt*, Eric Burdon with War's *Eric Burdon Declares War*, and Edgar Winter's *Entrance*.[54]

Argent and ELP were both part of a bumper crop of new progressive rock bands that also included eponymous albums from Gentle Giant, Hawkwind, Supertramp, the Dutch band Focus' *In and Out of Focus*, and two more examples of Krautrock, Kraftwerk and Tangerine Dream's *Electronic Meditation*. Albums from established prog acts included David Bowie's *The Man Who Sold the World*, Genesis' first genuinely progressive album *Trespass*, Jethro Tull's *Benefit*, King Crimson's *In the Wake of Poseidon* and *Lizard*, the Moody Blues' *A Question of Balance*, the Nice's *Five Bridges*, Pink Floyd's *Atom Heart Mother*, Procol Harum's *Home*, Van der Graaf Generator's *The Least We Can Do Is Way to Each Other* and *H to He, Who Am the Only One*, Zappa's *Burnt Weeny Sandwich* and *Weasels Ripped My Flesh* (with the Mothers) and *Chunga's Revenge* (without them). With *Vehicle*, Ides of March, another big horn band, joined *Blood, Sweat & Tears 3* and *Chicago* (the band's second) in the jazz-rock category. Although not rock 'n' roll, Miles Davis' jazz-fusion LP, *Bitches Brew*, is also indicative of the boundary-breaking going on in the music world at this time.[55]

It was a big year for hard rock debuts, one of the most significant of which was *Black Sabbath*, followed later in the year by the band's second album, *Paranoid*, one of the foundational albums for the later development of the heavy metal genre. Also important were Mountain's *Climbing!*, built around the core of guitarist Leslie West and former Cream producer Felix Pappalardi on bass, and *Very 'eavy ... Very 'umble* from Uriah Heep, a band with a sound similar to that of Deep Purple with prog overtones. Other rock-heavy debuts included the blues-based J. Geils Band (with harmonica wizard Magic Dick) and the twin-guitar sound of Wishbone Ash. Two important folk band debuts from England were Lindisfarne's *Nicely Out of Tune* and Steeleye Span's *Hark! The Village Wait*, both of which used traditional and electric instruments to add a rock flavor to traditional music. In America James Taylor, one of the most influential folk artists of all time, released *Sweet Baby James*. Finally, there was the eponymous debut release from George Clinton's Funkadelic, which — with its alter ego Parliament — has been in a class all its own ever since; before the year was out it also released *Free Your Mind ... and Your Ass Will Follow*.[56]

Other important releases by older artists included the Allman Brothers' *Idlewild South*, the Band's *Stage Fright*, Joe Cocker's incredible *Mad Dogs and Englishmen*, CCR's *Cosmo's Factory* and *Pendulum*, Crosby, Stills, Nash & Young's masterpiece *Déja Vu*, *Deep Purple in Rock*, the Doors' *Morrison Hotel*, Dylan's *Self Portrait* and *New Morning*, Elton John's self-titled second album and *Tumbleweed Connection*, the Grateful Dead's *Workingman's Dead* and *American Beauty*, Hendrix's *Band of Gypsies*, the Kinks *Lola versus Powerman*, Led Zeppelin's underrated *III*, Melanie's *Candles in the Rain*, Joni Mitchell's *Ladies of the Canyon*, Van Morrison's *Moondance*, Linda Ronstadt's *Silk Purse*, Santana's *Abraxas*, Spirit's concept album *Twelve Dreams of Dr. Sardonicus*,

Cat Stevens' *Mona Bone Jakon* and first huge hit *Tea for the Tillerman*, the Stooges' *Fun House*, Ten Years After's *Cricklewood Green*, Traffic's return with *John Barleycorn Must Die*, a self-titled album from the newly abbreviated T. Rex, and Neil Young's classic *After the Gold Rush*.

In 1971—the year McLean released *American Pie*—the top five albums were the original cast recording for *Jesus Christ Superstar*, Carole King's *Tapestry*, the Carpenters' *Close to You*, Janis Joplin's *Pearl*, and Santana's *Abraxas*. Among new arrivals on the charts were eponymous releases from Southern rockers Black Oak Arkansas, yet another big horn band, Chase, the initially folk-oriented Doobie Brothers, the string-heavy progressive rock of Electric Light Orchestra, the witty folk of John Prine, and sensual folksinger Carly Simon, along with long-established songwriter Carole King's first album, the enormously successful *Tapestry* (not to be confused with McLean's album of the same name), the quartet of virtuosos in Mahavishnu Orchestra with *The Inner Mounting Flame*, McCartney's new band Wings with *Wild Life*, as well as his second solo album *Ram*, and a bow from that little old band from Texas, *ZZ Top's First Album*.[57]

Among the most stellar releases from older artists were Jethro Tull's landmark LP *Aqualung*, Led Zeppelin *IV* (with the legendary "Stairway to Heaven" at 7:55), the Rolling Stones' *Sticky Fingers*, *Who's Next*, and the Allman Brothers' live breakthrough album *At Fillmore East*, which set a standard for improvisation that rarely, if ever, has been equaled. It was a great year for live albums, also including *Chicago at Carnegie Hall*, ELP's *Pictures at an Exhibition*, George Harrison's *The Concert for Bangladesh*, half of Mountain's *Flowers of Evil*, *Live Johnny Winter And*, and Zappa and the Mothers' *Fillmore East*. It was also a banner year for hard rock, with Alice Cooper's *Killer*, the Jeff Beck Group's *Rough and Ready*, Black Sabbath's *Master of Reality*, Deep Purple's *Fireball*, Hendrix's posthumous *Cry of Love* and *Rainbow Bridge*, Mott the Hoople's *Wildlife* and *Brain Capers*, Mountain's *Nantucket Sleighride*, Ten Years After's *A Space in Time*, T. Rex's *Electric Warrior*, and Uriah Heep's *Salisbury* and *Look at Yourself*.

Folk rock continued to be prominent, with the Band's *Cahoots*, the Byrds' *Byrdmaniax* and *Farther Along*, Steeleye Span's *Please to See the King* and *Ten Man Mop*, Cat Stevens' *Teaser and the Firecat*, *Stephen Stills 2*, and James Taylor's *Mud Slide Slim and the Blue Horizon*. Progressive rock maintained its powerful presence with Bowie's *Hunky Dory*, ELP's *Tarkus*, Focus' *Moving Waves*, Genesis' *Nursery Crime*, Gentle Giant's *Acquiring the Taste*, Hawkwind's *In Search of Space*, King Crimson's *Islands*, the Moody Blues' *Every Good Boy Deserves Favor*, the Nice's *Elegy*, Pink Floyd's *Meddle*, Procol Harum's *Broken Barricades*, Supertramp's *Indelibly Stamped*, Tangerine Dream's *Alpha Centauri*, Van der Graaf Generator's *Pawn Hearts*, Yes' *The Yes Album* (the first with Steve Howe) and *Fragile* (the first with Rick Wakeman), Zappa's *200 Motels* (with the Mothers) and *Waka/Jawaka* (without). The premier horn bands remained busy with *Blood, Sweat & Tears 4* and *Chicago III*, and an assortment of other excellent albums included the Doors' *L.A. Woman*, Elton John's *Madman Across the Water*, the double album *Grateful Dead* ("Skull and Roses"), Janis Joplin's *Pearl*, the Kinks' *Muswell Hillbillies*, Joni Mitchell's *Blue*, Van Morrison's *Tupelo Honey*, Funkadelic's *Maggot Brain*, *Santana III* (with the twin-guitar wizardry of Santana and Neal Schon), Sly and the Family Stone's *There's a Riot Going On*, Traffic's *The Low Spark of High Heeled Boys*, and *Edgar Winter's White Trash*.

In 1972 Neil Young's *Harvest* topped the album charts, followed by Carole King's *Tapestry*, McLean's *American Pie*, Cat Stevens' *Teaser and the Firecat*, and the Rolling Stones' *Hot Rocks 1964–71*. *American Pie* was in extremely good company that year, which saw an incredibly rich and eclectic batch of releases. New arrivals to the charts included self-titled debuts from Jackson Browne, the Eagles, Foghat, Manfred Mann's Earth Band, Lou Reed, and Roxy Music, as well as the Incredible Broadside Brass Bed Band's *The Great Grizzly Bear Hunt* (with the hilarious track, "Grizzly Bear," another free form staple and perhaps the only rock song ever to mention former Vice President Spiro T. Agnew), Steely Dan's *Can't Buy a Thrill*, and Richard Thompson's *Henry the Human Fly*.[58] Another rich year from older artists produced Alice Cooper's *School's Out*, the Allman Brothers' *Eat a Peach*, Amon Düül II's *Wolf City*, *Jeff Beck Group*, *Black Sabbath vol. 4*, Bowie's *The Rise and Fall of Ziggy Stardust and the Spiders from Mars*, *Chicago 5*, *Joe Cocker*, Deep Purple's *Machine Head*, the Doobie Brothers' *Toulouse Street*, Nick Drake's *Pink Moon*, Dr. John's *Gumbo*, Elton John's *Honky Chateau*, ELP's *Trilogy*, Fleetwood Mac's *Bare Trees*, *Focus III*, Funkadelic's *America Eats Its Young*, Genesis' *Foxtrot*, Gentle Giant's *Three Friends* and *Octopus*, Hawkwind's *Doremi Fasol Latido*, J. Geils Band's *"Live" Full House*, Jefferson Airplane's *Long John Silver*, Jethro Tull's *Thick as a Brick*, the Kinks' *Everybody's in Show-Biz*, Lennon's *Some Time in New York City*, Joni Mitchell's *For the Roses*, the Moody Blues' *Seventh Sojourn*, Van Morrison's *Saint Dominic's Preview*, Mott the Hoople's *All the Young Dudes*, Pink Floyd's *Obscured by Clouds*, the Rolling Stones' *Exile on Main Street*, Todd Rundgren's *Something/Anything?*, Steeleye Span's *Below the Salt*, Cat Stevens' *Catch Bull at Four*, Stephen Stills' *Manassas*, James Taylor's *One Man Dog*, T. Rex's *The Slider*, Uriah Heep's *Demons and Wizards* and *The Magician's Birthday*, War's *The World Is a Ghetto*, Edgar Winter's *Roadwork* and *They Only Come Out at Night*, Yes' *Close to the Edge*, Zappa's *Just Another Band from LA* (with the Mothers) and *The Grand Wazoo* (without), and ZZ Top's *Rio Grande Mud*. From the soul charts but still very relevant to changes taking place in music were Stevie Wonder's *Music of My Mind* and *Talking Book*.

Thus, the stage was set for a song like "American Pie" to become a hit on FM and even to infiltrate some AM stations. By no means, of course, is the foregoing discussion intended to suggest that Don McLean was influenced by — or even heard — every artist or album mentioned. However, "American Pie" certainly fits into both the "music-cultural" and musicological context described here. It is an extended format song with a sophisticated structure, changes in tempo and dynamics, excellent musicianship, and intelligent lyrics that are a virtual history of rock 'n' roll up to the time. Like the best music of the period, it remains eminently listenable today. Moreover, what the evidence provided here should make clear is that the musical culture of the time — the recording industry, radio (especially FM), and, most importantly, the listening audience — was prepared for an extended, genre-busting song like "American Pie" and for the rest of the varied and excellent LP on which it appeared: the subtle anti-war songs "Till Tomorrow" and "The Grave," the haunting take on Van Gogh in "Vincent," the biblical imagery of "Crossroads," the country-influenced "Winterwood," the ballad "Empty Chairs," the light-hearted "Everybody Loves Me Baby," the satirical "Sister Fatima," and the beautiful traditional round, "Babylon."

Regrettably the moment that gave rise to "American Pie" and the other music described here did not last that much longer. Influential bands dissolved, and talented members died or departed, though other artists from this era continued to perform and record, and brilliant albums were still in the offing. But the later 1970s belonged to punk and new wave in the hearts of discerning fans and to disco on the radio. Regrettably rock journalists at the time (and still) set up punk in opposition to the older music of "dinosaur" bands (a term coined, ironically, by King Crimson's Robert Fripp), though in fact a great many serious music fans found it entirely possible (and still do) to listen to both Pink Floyd and the Sex Pistols (Johnny Rotten's famous tee-shirt notwithstanding). Ironically, many of the best artists — both the old and the new — found it difficult, if not impossible, to get air time anywhere except on college radio in the new era of broadcasting that followed the demise of free form radio. Don McLean himself continued to record excellent new albums, but none matched the commercial success of *American Pie*. Sadly, at least as far as commercial radio was concerned, the music died again.

Songs Over Five Minutes
(Selected Artists)

Artist	1966	1967	1968	1969	1970	1971	1972
Alice Cooper				2		3	2
Allman Brothers Band				3	1	4	3

Artist	1966	1967	1968	1969	1970	1971	1972
Amon Düül II				3			
Animals		3					
Argent					1		
Badfinger				2			
Band			2		1		
Beatles			1	2			
Beck, Jeff			1	1		4	3
Black Oak Arkansas						2	
Black Sabbath					3	6	3
Blind Faith				3		1	
Blood Sweat & Tears			2	3	1		
Bloomfield, Michael				1			
Blue Cheer			3				
Bowie, David				4	2	2	
Brockett, Jamie				6			
Brown, Arthur			3				
Browne, Jackson							1
Buffalo Springfield		2					
Can				3			
Canned Heat		1					
Captain Beefheart				1			
Chase						1	
Chicago				8	6	12	3
Cocker, Joe				2	7		3
Country Joe & the Fish		2					
Cream	2	1	3	3			
Creedence Clearwater Revival			1	5	5		
CSN/CSNY				3	1		
Davis, Miles					6		
Deep Purple			4		4	5	4
Delaney & Bonnie					3		
Derek & the Dominos					8		
Doobie Brothers							1
Doors		2		1		3	
Dr. John			4				
Drake, Nick				1			
Dylan, Bob	10	1			1		
Electric Light Orchestra						4	
Elton John				2	6	5	4
Emerson, Lake & Palmer					4	2	3
Eric Burdon & War					3		
Fairport Convention		0	1				
Fleetwood Mac							2
Focus					2	2	6
Foghat							1
Genesis					5	4	4
Gentle Giant					4	3	1
Grand Funk Railroad				6			
Grateful Dead		3		8	6	6	
Guthrie, Arlo		1					

Artist	1966	1967	1968	1969	1970	1971	1972
Harrison, George					6		
Hawkwind					3	4	4
Hendrix, Jimi		1	3		6	3	
Humble Pie				4			
Ides of March					2		
Incredible Broadside BBB							1
Iron Butterfly			1				
It's A Beautiful Day				4			
Jefferson Airplane		2	1	4			2
Jethro Tull			3		3	3	2
J. Geils Band					1		1
Joplin, Janis				3			
King, Carole						1	
King Crimson				5	6	4	
Kinks				3		1	1
Kraftwerk					4		
Led Zeppelin				4	4	3	
Lennon, John				1	2		3
Love		2					
Mahavishnu Orchestra						7	
Manfred Mann							3
MC5				4			
McCartney, Paul/Wings						5	
McLean, Don					1		
Melanie					1		
Mitchell, Joni			1		1		1
Moody Blues		5	2		2	2	3
Morrison, Van		3			1	3	3
Mott the Hoople				4		4	3
Mountain					1	4	
Nice	2	2		4	4	4	
Parliament/Funkadelic					6	2	8
Pentangle			2				
Pink Floyd		1	3	11	4	4	2
Procol Harum			1	1	1	3	
Quicksilver Messenger Service			2				
Reed, Lou							3
Rolling Stones		2	2	3		4	1
Roxy Music							4
Rundgren, Todd					2		1
Santana				1	2	5	
Simon, Carly						1	
Simon & Garfunkel					1		
Sly & the Family Stone				3		3	
Soft Machine			2				
Spirit					1		
Steeleye Span						4	2
Steely Dan							1
Steppenwolf			5				
Stevens, Cat					1		1

Artist	1966	1967	1968	1969	1970	1971	1972
Stills, Stephen					2	2	1
Stooges				2	3		
Supertramp					4	2	
Tangerine Dream					3		
Taylor, James						1	
Ten Years After					2	2	
Traffic	1		3	3	4	3	
T. Rex			1				
Uriah Heep					4	6	4
Van der Graaf Generator				5	10	3	
Vanilla Fudge		6					
Velvet Underground		4					
War							3
The Who				3		4	
Winter, Edgar					2	3	6
Winter, Johnny				1		3	
Wishbone Ash					4		
Yes				4		4	3
Young, Neil			2	4	1		
Zappa/Mothers	3		1	4	7	6	7
ZZ Top						1	1

Notes

1. The author would like to thank Donna Gay Anderson, Joseph Burns, Charles Chamberlain, Charles Elliott, Daniel McCarthy, Benjamin Price, Elizabeth Robison, Tucker Robison, George Sanchez, and Randall Settoon for reading and commenting on an earlier version of this essay, providing valuable insights, and pointing out various errors. Much gratitude also is due to the Interlibrary Loan section of the Sims Memorial Library at Southeastern Louisiana University for assistance in obtaining hard-to-find books. Since the beginning of the twenty-first century there has been a flood of new scholarship on the artists of the late 1960s and early 1970s. The biographies and critical studies of artists cited here are generally the most authoritative available, but they vary substantially in quality and in many cases represent only a portion of what is in print. All web citations for artist information are to artists' official websites and/or the Rock and Roll Hall of Fame website, though among the former some of are much more useful than others. All citations for U.S. album and singles charts are to *Billboard Magazine*, its ancillary publications, and its website, http://www.billboard.com/. Fred Bronson, *The Billboard Book of Number One Hits* (2003); Craig Rosen, *The Billboard Book of Number One Albums* (1996); Joel Whitburn, *The Billboard Book of Top 40 Hits* (2010), *Billboard's Top 1000 Hits of the Rock Era 1955–2005* (2006), and *Joel Whitburn's Top Pop Singles 1955–2002* (2004).

2. McLean recorded the album *American Pie* at the Record Plant in New York from May through June 1971 with Ed Freeman producing, and United Artists released it in October. McLean performed on guitar, banjo, and vocals; Robbie Rothstein, bass; Roy Markowitz, drums and percussion; Ray Colcord, electric piano; Mike Mainieri, marimba and vibes; Paul Griffin, piano; David Spinoza, electric guitar. Liner notes for the 2003 Capitol Records CD release; Alan Howard, *The Don McLean Story: Killing Us Softly with His Songs* (n.p.: Starry Night Music, Inc., 2007), chapter 5; http://www.don-mclean.com/, accessed 9/5/2010.

3. For a good explanation as to how and why the music business and radio have changed, see Hank Bordowitz, *Dirty Little Secrets of the Record Business: Why So Much Music You Hear Sucks* (Chicago: Chicago Review Press, 2007).

4. Howard, chapter 5; http://www.don-mclean.com/.

5. Ranked ahead of "American Pie" were Judy Garland's "Over the Rainbow," Bing Crosby's "White Christmas," Woody Guthrie's "This Land Is Your Land," and Aretha Franklin's "Respect," http://archives.cnn.com/2001/SHOWBIZ/Music/03/07/list.top.365.songs/index. html, accessed September 5, 2010. Strangely "American Pie" did not make *Rolling Stone's* Top 500 Songs of All Time, but neither did songs by many other stellar artists who recorded in the decade preceding "American Pie" (1963–1972). Rolling Stone updated the list in May 2010, but — not surprisingly — "American Pie" is still not there, *Rolling Stone* (May 2010). "American Pie" ranks 190 on *Billboard's* top 1000 hits for 1955–2005, Joel Whitburn, *Top 1000 Hits of the Rock Era 1955–2005* (Menomonee Falls, WI: Record Research 2006), 30. It was the number one song in 1972 at Chicago's WCFL, Ronald Smith, *WCFL Chicago Top 40 Charts 1965–1976* (New York: iUniverse, Inc., 2007), 220.

6. Howard, chapter 13.

7. Punk was much more effective critiquing 1970s British politics that it was in providing historical analysis of late '60s and early '70s rock music. Journalists frequently exaggerate the sharpness of the break in rock music as a whole before and after the advent of punk.

8. On live performance, see Ben Fong-Torres, *Not Fade Away: A Backstage Pass to 20 Years of Rock & Roll* (San Francisco: Miller Freeman, 1999); John Glatt, *Rage & Roll: Bill Graham and the Selling of Rock* (Secaucus, NJ: Carol, 1993); Robert Greenfield and Bill Graham, *Bill Graham Presents: My Life Inside Rock and Out* (New York: Doubleday, 1992); Brian Hinton, *Message to Love: Isle of Wight Festival 1968, 1969, 1970* (Tampa, FL: Sanctuary, 1996); Gayle Lemke, *The Art of the Fillmore: 1966–1971* (Secaucus, NJ: Carol, 1999); Bob Spitz, *Barefoot in Babylon: The Creation of the Woodstock Music Festival 1969* (New York: W.W. Norton & Co., 1989).

9. On "music-cultural" influences (politics, war, drugs, etc.) and the role of labels, producers, and music magazines, see Hank Bordowitz, *Turning Points in Rock and Roll* (New York: Citadel, 2004); Gary Marmorstein, *The Label: The Story of Columbia Records* (New York: Da Capo, 2007); Robert Matheu, *CREEM: America's Only Rock 'N' Roll Magazine* (New York: Collins Living, 2007); Robert Stephen Spitz, *The Making of Superstars: Artists and Executives of the Rock Music Business* (Garden City, NY: Anchor Press, 1978). A possible fruitful area of investigation — I owe this point to Ben Price — is the question of how British pirate radio related to American free form radio and the musical experimentation of the late 1960s and early 1970s. On pirate radio, see Steve Conway, *ShipRocked: Life on the Waves with Radio Caroline* (Dublin: Liberties, 2009); Adrian Johns, *Death of a Pirate: British Radio and the Making of the Information Age* (New York: W. W. Norton & Co., 2010); Tom Lodge, *The Ship that Rocked the World: How Radio Caroline Defied the Establishment, Launched the British Invasion and Made the Planet Safe for Rock and Roll* (Savage, MD: Bartleby, 2010).

10. Richard Neer, *FM: The Rise and Fall of Rock Radio* (New York: Villard, 2001), vii.

11. Good accounts of the emergence of free form radio can be found in Philip H. Ennis, *The Seventh Stream: The Emergence of Rocknroll in American Popular Music* (Hanover, NH: Wesleyan University Press, 1992); Marc Fisher, *Something in the Air: Radio, Rock, and the Revolution That Shaped a Generation* (New York: Random House, 2007); Jim Ladd, *Radio Waves: Life and Revolution on the FM Dial* (New York: St. Martin's Griffin, 1992); Neer, *FM*; Dave Pierce, *Riding on the Ether Express: A Memoir of 1960s Los Angeles, the Rise of Freeform Underground Radio, and the Legendary KPPC FM* (Lafayette, LA: Center for Louisiana Studies, 2008). For AM Top 40 in this period, Ben Fong-Torres, *The Hits Just Keep on Coming: The History of Top 40 Radio* (San Francisco: Backbeat, 2001).

12. Ibid.; John Leonard's "Nightsounds" on KPFA Berkeley, which went on the air in 1949, was a much earlier prototype for free form radio. The Doors' first album is called simply *The Doors*.

13. Stephen Koch, "KAAY: The Mighty 1090 Gave Arkansas to North America," *Arkansas Business* 20 (2004) online, http://www.arkansasbusiness.com/20/icon_essay.asp?essayID=19, accessed September 5, 2010.

14. Ennis, *The Seventh Stream*, chapters 9–12; Fisher, *Something in the Air*, chapters 5–8;

Neer, *FM*. Politics, anti-war sentiment, sexual liberation, and drugs certainly had an influence on the musical culture of this period, but it is easy to exaggerate the importance all of these with the possible exception of sex. Some artists were overtly political — e.g., the Jefferson Airplane, the MC5, the post–Beatles John Lennon — and it is probably safe to say that most disliked the LBJ and Nixon administrations and the Vietnam War, but much of the lyrical content of this period is apolitical. Drug use certainly was widespread, but it is doubtful that it did much to enhance creativity. Lennon himself denied that drugs had that effect, and two of the most outrageous artists of the period — Ian Anderson of Jethro Tull and Frank Zappa — openly opposed drug use. More likely is that drugs were a symptom rather than a cause of the experimentation of this period — young people were willing to try all sorts of new experiences, musical and otherwise, and drugs were just one of them. As for sex, there was a lot of it. Peter Doggett, *There's a Riot Going On: Revolutionaries, Rock Stars, and the Rise and Fall of the '60s* (Edinburgh: Cannongate, 2009); Harry Shapiro, *Waiting for the Man: The Story of Drugs and Popular Music*, 2d ed. (London: Helter Skelter, 2003); Tom Wolfe, *The Electric Kool-Aid Acid Test*, reprint (New York: Picador, 2008).

15. Ennis, *The Seventh Stream*, *passim*. The mingling of streams produced a variety of interesting hybrids. For blues rock, see Summer McStravick and John Roos, *Blues-Rock Explosion* (Mission Viejo, CA: Old Goat, 2002); for country rock, John Einarson, *Desperadoes: The Roots of Country Rock* (New York: Cooper Square, 2001); for folk rock, Richie Unterberger, *Turn! Turn! Turn!: The '60s Folk-Rock Revolution* (San Francisco: Backbeat, 2002) and *Eight Miles High: Folk-Rock's Flight from Haight-Ashbury to Woodstock*, prologue (San Francisco: Backbeat, 2003); for progressive rock, Kevin Holm-Hudson, ed., *Progressive Rock Reconsidered* (London: Routledge, 2001); Edward Macan, *Rocking the Classics: English Progressive Rock and the Counterculture* (Oxford,: Oxford University Press, 1997); Bill Martin, *Listening to the Future: The Time of Progressive Rock 1968–1978* (Peru, IL: Open Court, 1998); Bradley Smith, *The Billboard Guide to Progressive Music* (New York: Billboard Books, 1998); Charles Snider, *The Strawberry Bricks Guide to Progressive Rock* (Chicago: Strawberry Bricks, 2008); Paul Stump, *The Music's All That Matters: A History of Progressive Rock* (London: Quartet, 1998); Dave Thompson, *Space Daze: The History and Mystery of Electronic Ambient Space Rock* (Los Angeles: Cleopatra Records, 1994).

16. Nick Awde, *Mellotron: The Machine and the Musicians That Revolutionised Rock*, (London: Desert Heart, 2008); Mark Brend, *Strange Sounds: Offbeat Instruments and Sonic Experiments in Pop* (San Francisco: Backbeat, 2005); Dave Hunter, *Guitar Effects Pedals: The Practical Handbook* (San Francisco: Backbeat, 2004) and *Guitar Rigs: Classic Guitar and Amp Combinations* (San Francisco: Backbeat, 2005); Frank Samagai, *The Mellotron Book* (Vallejo, CA: Artistpro, 2002); Steve Waksman, *Instruments of Desire: The Electric Guitar and the Shaping of Musical Experience* (Cambridge, MA: Harvard University Press, 1999).

17. Philip H. Ennis, *The Seventh Stream: The Emergence of Rocknroll in American Popular Music* (Hanover, NH: Wesleyan University Press, 1992).

18. Joe Burns, "A Long, Long Time Ago: An Interpretation of the Lyrics of Don McLean's 'American Pie'"; on the accident, Larry Lehmer, *The Day the Music Died: The Last Tour of Buddy Holly, the Big Bopper, and Ritchie Valens* (New York: Music Sales Corporation, 2003).

19. Among the many studies of Elvis' early career, one of the best is Peter Guralnick, *Last Train to Memphis: The Rise of Elvis Presley* (Boston: Little, Brown, and Company, 1995), the first volume in a two-part biography.

20. Howard, 33.

21. For album and singles charts, see above, note 1.

23. On Baez: Joan Baez, *And a Voice to Sing With: A Memoir* (New York: Simon & Schuster, 2009); David Hajdu, *Positively 4th Street: The Lives and Times of Joan Baez, Bob Dylan, Mimi Baez Fariña, and Richard Fariña* (New York: Picador, 2001); http://www.joanbaez.com/, accessed September 5, 2010. On Collins: Judy Collins, *Singing Lessons: A Memoir of Love, Loss, Hope, and Healing* (New York: Pocket, 2007); http://www.judycollins.com/index1.php, accessed September 5, 2010. On Axton: Frederic P. Miller, Agnes F. Vandome, and John McBrewster, eds., *Hoyt Axton* (Mauritius: Alphascript, 2010). On Dylan: Clinton Heylin, *Bob Dylan: Behind*

the Shades Revisited (New York: HarperCollins, 2003); Brian Hinton, *Bob Dylan Complete Discography* (New York: Universe, 2006); Patrick Humphries and John Bauldie, *Oh No! Not Another Bob Dylan Book* (Brentwood, UK: Square One, 1991); Howard Sounes, *Down the Highway: The Life of Bob Dylan* (New York: Grove, 2002); Bob Spitz, *Dylan: A Biography* (New York: W.W. Norton & Co., Inc., 1991); http://www.bobdylan.com/, accessed September 5, 2010. Sean Wilentz, *Bob Dylan in America* (New York: Doubleday, 2010) appeared too late to be consulted for this essay. On Peter, Paul, and Mary: Unterberger, *Turn! Turn! Turn!*, chapter 1; http://www.peterpaulandmary.com/, accessed September 5, 2010. On Paxton: Tom Paxton, *The Honor of Your Company* (New York: Cherry Lane Music Company, 2000); http://www.tom paxton.com/, accessed September 5, 2010. On Rush: Unterberger, *Eight Miles High*, chapter 3; http://tomrush.com/, accessed September 5, 2010. On the Holy Modal Rounders and Ochs, ibid., chapters 2–3. Not surprisingly, more has been written about Simon than Garfunkel. Useful, though dated, are Chris Charlesworth, *The Complete Guide to the Music of Paul Simon and Simon & Garfunkel* (London: Omnibus, 1997); Patrick Humphries, *Paul Simon* (New York: Doubleday, 1989); Joe Morella and Patricia Barey, *Simon and Garfunkel: Old Friends: A Dual Biography* (Secaucus, NJ: Carol, 1991); http://www.simonandgarfunkel.com/news.html, accessed 9/5/2010. Marc Eliot, *Paul Simon: A Life* (Hoboken, NJ: Wiley, 2010) appeared too late to be consulted for this essay. On Havens: Richie Havens and Steve Davidowitz, *They Can't Hide Us Anymore* (New York: Spike, 1999); http://www.richiehavens.com/official_site/home.html, accessed September 5, 2010.

  24. Einarson; Rich Unterberger, *Turn! Turn! Turn!* and *Eight Miles High*.

  25. Useful studies include Alan Clayson, *Beat Merchants: The Origins, History, Impact, and Rock Legacy of 1960's British Pop Groups* (Worcestershire, UK: Blandford, 1995); James E. Perone, *Mods, Rockers, and the Music of the British Invasion* (Westport, CT: Praeger, 2009); Nicholas Schaffner, *The British Invasion: From the First Wave to the New Wave* (New York: McGraw-Hill, 1982). British bands typically released singles that did not appear on their albums in the UK, whereas their American album releases usually included their current singles and had significantly different song combinations and order. Many were released in both mono and stereo. On sixties music in general, Joe Boyd, *White Bicycles: Making Music in the 1960s* (London: Serpent's Tail, 2007). For a more negative take on the British Invasion, see Kevin Courrier, *Artificial Paradise: The Dark Side of the Beatles' Utopian Dream* (Westport, CT: Praeger, 2008); Elijah Wald, *How the Beatles Destroyed Rock n Roll: An Alternative History of American Popular Music* (Oxford: Oxford University Press, 2009).

  26. The Beatles literature is immense and varies in quality; among the best works are *The Beatles Anthology* (San Francisco: Chronicle, 2000); Peter Brown and Steven Gaines, *The Love You Make: An Insider's Story of the Beatles*, with a new foreword by Anthony DeCurtis (New York: New American Library, 2002); Alan Clayson, *The Beatles Box* (Tampa, FL: Sanctuary, 2003); Peter Doggett, *You Never Give Me Your Money: The Beatles After the Breakup* (New York: Harper, 2010); Geoff Emerick and Howard Massey, *Here, There and Everywhere: My Life Recording the Music of the Beatles* (New York: Gotham, 2007); Jonathan Gould, *Can't Buy Me Love: The Beatles, Britain, and America* (New York: Three Rivers, 2007); Mark Hertsgaard, *A Day in the Life: The Music and Artistry of the Beatles* (New York: Delacorte, 1995); Philip Norman, *Shout! The Beatles in Their Generation*, revised and updated ed. (New York: Fireside, 2003); Nicholas Schaffner, *Beatles Forever* (New York: Fine, 1994); Bob Spitz, *The Beatles: The Biography* (New York: Back Bay, 2006); http://www.thebeatles.com/, accessed September 5, 2010. Peter Doggett and Patrick Humphries, *The Beatles: The Music and the Myth* (London: Omnibus, 2010) appeared too late to be consulted for this essay. Among many books on the Stones, two that deal effectively with the '60s are Stanley Booth, *The True Adventures of the Rolling Stones* (Chicago: Chicago Review Press, 2000) and Alan Clayson, *The Rolling Stones: The Origin of the Species: How, Why, and Where It All Began* (New Malden, UK: Chrome Dreams, 2008); http://www.rollingstones.com, accessed September 5, 2010. On the Animals: Eric Burdon and J. Marshall Craig, *Don't Let Me Be Misunderstood* (New York: Thunder's Mouth, 2001); http://ericburdon.ning.com/, accessed September 5, 2010. On Chad & Jeremy: http://www.chadand jeremy.net/, accessed September 5, 2010. On the Dave Clark Five: Perone, Chapter 5. On the

Hollies: http://www.hollies.co.uk/, accessed September 5, 2010. On the Kinks: Dave Davies, *Kink: An Autobiography* (New York: Hyperion, 1997); Ray Davies, *X-Ray: The Unauthorized Autobiography* (New York: Overlook, 2007); Doug Hinman, *The Kinks: All Day and All of the Night: Day by Day Concerns, Recordings, and Broadcasts, 1961–1996* (San Francisco: Backbeat, 2004) and Jason Brabazon, *You Really Got Me: An Illustrated World Discography of the Kinks* (Rumford, RI: D. Hinman, 1994); Thomas M. Kitts and Michael J. Kraus, eds., *Living on a Thin Line: Crossing Aesthetic Borders with the Kinks* (Rumford, RI: rock 'n' roll Research, 2002); Thomas M. Kitts, *Ray Davies: Not Like Everybody Else* (New York: Routledge, 2007); Andy Miller, *The Kinks Are the Village Green Preservation Society* (New York: Continuum, 2003); Jon Savage, *The Kinks: The Official Biography* (London: Faber & Faber, 1985). On Manfred Mann: Greg Russo, *Mannerisms: The Five Phases of Manfred Mann* (Floral Park, NY: Crossfire, 1995); http://www.manfredmann.co.uk/, accessed September 5, 2010. On Peter and Gordon: http://www.peterandgordon.net/discography.htm, accessed September 5, 2010. On Springfield: Annie J. Randall, *Dusty!: Queen of the Postmods* (Oxford: Oxford University Press, 2008). On the Yardbirds: Annette Carson, *Jeff Beck: Crazy Fingers* (San Francisco: Backbeat, 2001); George Case, *Jimmy Page: Magus, Musician, Man: An Unauthorized Biography* (New York: Hal Leonard, 2007); Eric Clapton, *Clapton: The Autobiography* (New York: Broadway, 2007); Alan Clayson, *The Yardbirds: The Band That Launched Eric Clapton, Jeff Beck and Jimmy Page* (San Francisco: Backbeat, 2002); Christopher Hjort and Doug Hinman, *Jeff's Book: A Chronology of Jeff Beck's Career 1965–1980: From the Yardbirds to Jazz-Rock* (Rumford, RI: rock 'n' roll Research, 2000); Greg Russo, *Yardbirds: The Ultimate Rave-Up* (Floral Park, NY: Crossfire, 2001); Chris Welch, *Power and Glory: Jimmy Page and Robert Plant* (New York: Cherry Lane Music Company, 1986); http://www.theyardbirds.com/, accessed September 5, 2010. On Clark: http://www.petulaclark.net/, accessed September 5, 2010. On the Spencer Davis Group: Alan Clayson, *Back in the High Life: A Biography of Steve Winwood* (London: Sidgwick & Jackson, 1988); Chris Welch, *Steve Winwood: Roll with It* (New York: Perigee, 1990). On Donovan: Donovan Leitch, *The Autobiography of Donovan: The Hurdy Gurdy Man* (New York: St. Martin's Griffin, 2005); http://www.donovan.ie/, accessed September 5, 2010. On Herman's Hermits: http://www.hermanshermits.com/, accessed September 5, 2010. On Mayall: Christopher Hjort, *Strange Brew: Eric Clapton and the British Blues Boom* (London: Jawbone, 2007); less useful is Richard Newman, *John Mayall: Blues Breaker* (Tampa, FL: Sanctuary, 1996); http://www.johnmayall.com/, accessed September 5, 2010. Frederic P. Miller, Agnes F. Vandome, John McBrewster, eds., *John Mayall* (Mauritius: Alphascript, 2010) appeared too late to be consulted for this essay. Mayall was the most prominent of the jazz and bluesmen — also including Long John Baldry, Graham Bond, and Alexis Korner — who influenced the slightly younger musicians like Clapton. On the Moody Blues: http://www.moodybluestoday.com, accessed February 18, 2012. On the Pretty Things: Richie Unterberger, *Urban Spacemen and Wayfaring Strangers: Overlooked Innovators and Eccentric Visionaries of '60s Rock* (San Francisco: Miller Freeman, 2000), 13–16. On the Who: Richard Barnes, *The Who: Maximum R&B*, 5th ed. (Medford, NJ: Plexus, 2004); Chris Charlesworth and Ed Hanel, *The Who: The Complete Guide to Their Music*, 2d ed. (London: Omnibus, 2004); Dave Marsh, *Before I Get Old: The Story of the Who* (Medford, NJ: Plexus, 2003); http://www.thewho.com, accessed September 5, 2010. On the Zombies: Greg Russo, *Time of the Season: The Zombies Collector's Guide*, revised ed. (Floral Park, NY: Crossfire, 2007); Claes Johansen, *The Zombies: Hung Up on a Dream* (London: SAF, 2001); http://thezombies.net/, accessed September 5, 2010.

27. On the Raiders: http://www.paulrevereraiders.com/ and http://www.marklindsay.com, accessed September 5, 2010. On the Beach Boys: Steven Gaines, *Heroes and Villains: The True Story of the Beach Boys* (New York: Da Capo, 1995); Timothy White, *The Nearest Faraway Place: Brian Wilson, the Beach Boys, and the Southern California Experience* (New York: Henry Holt, 1996); http://www.thebeachboys.com, accessed September 5, 2010. On the Beau Brummels: Unterberger, *Urban Spacemen and Wayfaring Strangers*, 174–83; http://www.beaubrummels.com/, accessed September 12, 2010. On Butterfield: Ken Brooks, *The Adventures of Mike Bloomfield and Al Kooper with Paul Butterfield and David Clayton Thomas* (Andover, UK: Agenda, 1999). On the Byrds: John Einarson, *Mr. Tambourine Man: The Life and Legacy of Byrds' Gene*

Clark (San Francisco: Backbeat, 2005); Christopher Hjort, *So You Want to Be a Rock 'n' Roll Star: The Byrds Day-by-Day 1965–1973* (London: Jawbone, 2008); Johnny Rogan, *The Byrds: Timeless Flight Revisited: The Sequel,* 4th ed. (London: Rogan House, 1998), pages; Unterberger, *Turn! Turn! Turn!,* and *Eight Miles High,* prologue; http://www.ibiblio.org/jimmy/mcguinn/, accessed September 5, 2010. On Country Joe: Unterberger, *Eight Miles High,* chapter 1; http://www.countryjoe.com/, accessed September 12, 2010. On the Lovin' Spoonful: http://www.lovinspoonful.com/, accessed September 5, 2010. On the Turtles: http://www.theturtles.com/, accessed September 5, 2010.

28. In 1966 Herb Alpert & the Tijuana Brass *Whipped Cream and Other Delights* (1), *Going Places* (3), and *What Now My Love* (5), the soundtrack for *The Sound of Music* (2) and the Beatles *Rubber Soul* (4).

29. On Cream: Ginger Baker, *Hellraiser: The Autobiography of the World's Greatest Drummer* (London: John Blake, 2010); Clapton, *Clapton: The Autobiography*; Hjort, *Strange Brew*; Harry Shapiro, *Eric Clapton: Lost in the Blues* (New York: Da Capo, 1992) and *Jack Bruce: Composing Himself: The Authorized Biography* (London: Jawbone, 2010); Dave Thompson, *Cream: The World's First Supergroup* (London: Virgin, 2010); Chris Welch, *Cream: Eric Clapton, Jack Bruce, and Ginger Baker—The Legendary 60s Supergroup* (San Francisco: Backbeat, 2000). On the Troggs: Alan Clayson and Jacqueline Ryan, *The Troggs Files: Rock's Wild Things* (London: Helter Skelter, 2001); http://www.my-generation.org.uk/Troggs/, accessed September 5, 2010. On the Incredible String Band: Adrian Whittaker, ed., *An Incredible String Band Compendium* (London: Helter Skelter, 2003).

30. On the Buffalo Springfield: John Einarson, *For What It's Worth: The Story of Buffalo Springfield* (New York: Cooper Square, 2004). On Jefferson Airplane: Craig Fenton, *Take Me to a Circus Tent: The Jefferson Airplane Flight Manual* (West Conshohocken, PA: Infinity, 2006); Jeff Tamarkin, *Got a Revolution! The Turbulent Flight of Jefferson Airplane* (New York: Atria, 2005); http://www.jeffersonairplane.com/, accessed September 5, 2010. On Love: John Einarson, *Forever Changes: Arthur Lee and the Book of Love* (London: Jawbone, 2010); http://www.lovearth urlee.com/, accessed September 5, 2010. On the Mamas and the Papas: Matthew Greenwald, *Go Where You Wanna Go: The Oral History of the Mamas and the Papas* (New York: Cooper Square, 2002); Michelle Phillips, *California Dreamin': The True Story of the Mamas and the Papas: The Music, the Madness, the Magic That Was* (New York: Warner, 1986). On Buckley: Paul Barrera, *Once He Was: The Tim Buckley Story* (Andover, UK: Agenda, 1997); David Browne, *Dream Brother: The Lives and Music of Jeff and Tim Buckley* (New York: Harper, 2001); Lee Underwood, *Blue Melody: Tim Buckley Remembered* (San Francisco: Backbeat, 2002); http://www.timbuckley.net/, accessed September 12, 2010. On Hardin: Unterberger, *Turn! Turn! Turn!,* chapter 5. On Lightfoot: Maynard Collins, *Gordon Lightfoot: If You Could Read His Mind* (Toronto: University of Toronto Press, 1988). On the Young Rascals: http://www.therascalsar chives.com/, accessed September 5, 2010. On Sahm: Jan Reid, *Texas Tornado: The Times and Music of Doug Sahm* (Austin, TX: University of Texas Press, 2010).

31. *Revolver* well might have charted higher in the United States if Capitol Records had released it in the same form as EMI Parlophone did in Britain instead of chopping it up to include portions on the America-only *Yesterday and Today,* though even *Sergeant Pepper* did not make the list of top five albums in the United States in 1967). As with *Revolver,* the U.S. version of *Aftermath* was different—four tracks from the UK album were missing, including "Mother's Little Helper," and the single "Paint It Black" was added.

32. "Good Vibrations" later appeared on the album *Smiley Smile.*

33. "Cheese" was the famous but fictitious Suzy Creamcheese. "Mothers" was short for "motherfuckers," a slang term among jazz aficionados for extremely proficient players. Kevin Courrier, *Dangerous Kitchen: The Subversive World of Zappa* (Toronto: ECW, 2002); Billy James, *Necessity Is: The Early Years of Frank Zappa and the Mothers of Invention,* 2d ed. (London: SAF, 2002); Greg Russo, *Cosmik Debris: The Collected History and Improvisations of Frank Zappa,* 2d ed. (Floral Park, NY: Crossfire, 2003); Neil Slaven, *Electric Don Quixote: The Definitive Story of Frank Zappa,* 2d ed. (London: Omnibus, 2003); Ben Watson, *Frank Zappa: The Complete Guide to his Music* (London: Omnibus, 2005); Ben Watson, *Frank Zappa: The Negative Dialectics*

of Poodle Play (New York: St. Martin's, 1995); Frank Zappa and Peter Occhiogrosso, *Real Frank Zappa Book* (New York: Fireside, 1990); http://www.zappa.com/flash/greasylovesongs/index. html, accessed September 5, 2010.

34. *Sergeant Pepper* was the first Beatles album to have the same tracks on both the British and American versions. "Penny Lane" and "Strawberry Fields Forever," originally intended for the LP, were released as a single but not included. As soon as the album came out, Jimi Hendrix began performing the title track in his live shows.

35. In 1967 *More of the Monkees, The Monkees*, the soundtracks for *Dr. Zhivago* and *The Sound of Music*, and the Temptations *Greatest Hits*.

36. Among the more useful of the many books on the band are Mickey Dolenz and Mark Bego, *I'm a Believer: My Life of Monkees, Music, and Madness*, revised ed. (New York: Cooper Square, 2004); Davy Jones, *Daydream Believin'* (Metairie, LA: Hercules Promotions, 2000); Eric Lefcowitz, *The Monkees Tale*, 2d ed. (Berkeley, CA: Last Gasp of San Francisco, 1989); Randi L. Massingill, *Total Control: The Monkees Michael Nesmith Story* (Carlsbad, CA: FLEXquarters, 2005); Andrew Sandoval, *The Monkees: The Day-By-Day Story of the 60s TV Pop Sensation* (San Diego: Thunder Bay, 2005).

37. On Pink Floyd: Mark Blake, *Comfortably Numb: The Inside Story of Pink Floyd* (New York: Da Capo, 2008); Nick Mason, *Inside Out: A Personal History of Pink Floyd* (San Francisco: Chronicle, 2005); Glenn Povey, *Echoes: The Complete History of Pink Floyd* (Chicago: Chicago Review Press, 2010) and *Pink Floyd: In the Flesh: The Complete Performance History* (New York: St. Martin's Griffin, 1998); Nicholas Schaffner, *Saucerful of Secrets: The Pink Floyd Odyssey*, 2d ed. (London: Helter Skelter, 1992); http://www.pinkfloyd.com/, accessed September 5, 2010. On the Nice: Keith Emerson, *Pictures of an Exhibitionist: From the Nice to the Emerson, Lake and Palmer—The True Story of the Man Who Changed the Sound of Rock* (London: John Blake, 2004); Martyn Hanson, *Hang on to a Dream: The Story of the Nice* (London: Helter Skelter, 2002). On Procol Harum: Claes Johansen, *Procol Harum: Beyond the Pale* (London: SAF, 2000). On Bowie: David Buckley, *Strange Fascination: David Bowie, the Definitive Story*, revised ed. (London: Virgin, 2010); Chris Charlesworth, *David Bowie: Profile* (London: Proteus, 1985) and *David Bowie: The Archive* (London: Omnibus, 1987); Barney Hoskyns, *Glam! Bowie, Bolan and the Glitter Rock Revolution* (London: Faber & Faber, 1998); James Perone, *The Words and Music of David Bowie* (Westport, CT: Praeger, 2007); Marc Spitz, *Bowie: A Biography* (New York: Three Rivers, 2009); Dave Thompson, *David Bowie: Moonage Daydream* (Medford, NJ: Plexus, 1996) and *Your Pretty Face Is Going to Hell: The Dangerous Glitter of David Bowie, Iggy Pop, and Lou Reed* (San Francisco: Backbeat, 2009); Chris Welch, *David Bowie: We Could Be Heroes* (New York: Da Capo, 1999) and *Changes: The Stories Behind Every David Bowie Song 1970–1980* (London: Carlton, 1999); http://www.davidbowie.com/, accessed September 5, 2010.

38. On Traffic: Clayson, *Back in the High Life*; Welch, *Steve Winwood*; http://www.steve winwood.com/, accessed September 5, 2010. On Savoy Brown: http://www.savoybrown.com/, accessed September 5, 2010. On Ten Years After: http://www.ten-years-after.com/, accessed September 5, 2010. On Morrison: Clinton Heylin, *Can You Feel the Silence? Van Morrison: A New Biography* (Chicago: Chicago Review Press, 2004); Brian Hinton, *Celtic Crossroads: The Art of Van Morrison*, 2d ed. (Tampa, FL: Sanctuary, 2000); Greil Marcus: *When That Rough God Goes Riding: Listening to Van Morrison* (New York: Public Affairs, 2010); Peter Mills, *Hymn to the Silence: Inside the Words and Music of Van Morrison* (New York: Continuum, 2010); Johnny Rogan, *Van Morrison: No Surrender* (New York: Random House, 2005); http://www.vanmor rison.com/, accessed September 5, 2010. On Hendrix: Alan Clayson, *Jimi Hendrix: As It Happened* (New Malden, UK: Chrome Dreams, 2002); Charles Cross, *Room Full of Mirrors: A Biography of Jimi Hendrix* (New York: Hyperion, 2006); Peter Doggett, *Jimi Hendrix: The Complete Guide to His Music*, 2d ed. (London: Omnibus, 2004); Sharon Lawrence, *Jimi Hendrix: The Intimate Story of a Betrayed Music Legend* (New York: Harper, 2006); Noel Redding and Carol Appleby, *Are You Experienced? The Inside Story of the Jimi Hendrix Experience* (New York: Da Capo, 1996); Harry Shapiro, *Jimi Hendrix: Electric Gypsy* (New York: St. Martin's, 1991); Richie Unterberger, *The Rough Guide to Jimi Hendrix* (London: Rough Guides, 2009); Chris Welch, *Hendrix: A Biography* (London: Omnibus, 1982); http://www.jimihendrix.com/us/home,

accessed September 5, 2010. Steven Roby and Brad Schreiber, *Becoming Jimi Hendrix: From Southern Crossroads to Psychedelic London, The Untold Story of a Musical Genius* (New York: Da Capo, 2010) appeared too late to be consulted for this essay. On the Bonzo Doo-Dah Dog Band: Unterberger, *Urban Spacemen and Wayfaring Strangers,* 109–21; http://www.neilinnes.org/bonzo.htm, accessed September 5, 2010.

39. On the Doors: Alan Clayson, *Maximum Doors: The Unauthorised Biography of the Doors* (New Malden, UK: Chrome Dreams, 2002); John Densmore, *Riders on the Storm: My Life with Jim Morrison and the Doors* (New York: Dell, 1991); Ben Fong-Torres, *The Doors* (New York: Hyperion, 2006); http://www.thedoors.com/, accessed September 5, 2010. On the Velvet Underground: Peter Doggett, *Lou Reed: Growing Up in Public* (London: Omnibus, 1995); Johan Kugelberg, ed. *The Velvet Underground: New York Art* (New York: Rizzoli, 2009); Thompson, *Your Pretty Face Is Going to Hell*; Richie Unterberger, *White Light/White Heat: The Velvet Underground Day by Day* (London: Jawbone, 2009). On the Dead: Dennis McNally, *A Long Strange Trip: The Inside History of the Grateful Dead* (New York: Broadway, 2003); http://www.dead.net/, accessed September 5, 2010. On Moby Grape: Unterberger, *Eight Miles High,* chapter 2. On the Vanilla Fudge: http://www.vanillafudge.com/, accessed September 12, 2010. On the Electric Prunes: Unterberger, *Urban Spacemen and Wayfaring Strangers,* 52–67; http://www.electric prunes.net/, accessed September 5, 2010. On Sly and the Family Stone: Jeff Kaliss, *I Want to Take You Higher: The Life and Times of Sly and the Family Stone,* revised ed. (San Francisco: Backbeat, 2009); Eddie Santiago, *The Lives of Sylvester Stewart and Sly Stone* (n.p.: Lulu.com, 2008); http://www.slystonemusic.com/, accessed September 5, 2010.

40. On Joplin: Alice Echols, *Scars of Sweet Paradise: The Life and Times of Janis Joplin* (New York: Holt, 2000); Myra Friedman, *Buried Alive: The Biography of Janis Joplin* (New York: Three Rivers, 1992); http://www.bbhc.com/, accessed September 5, 2010. On Canned Heat: Fito de la Parra, with T.W. McGarry and Marlane McGarry, *Living the Blues: Canned Heat's Story of Music, Drugs, Death, Sex, and Survival,* 3rd ed. (n.p.: Canned Heat Music, 2002); http://www.cannedheatmusic.com/, accessed September 5, 2010. On Electric Flag: Brooks, *The Adventures of Mike Bloomfield and Al Kooper with Paul Butterfield and David Clayton Thomas*; Jan Mark Wolkin, *Michael Bloomfield—If You Love These Blues: An Oral History* (San Francisco: Miller Freeman, 2000). On Guthrie: Laura Lee, *Arlo, Alice, and Anglicans: The Lives of a New England Church* (Lee, MA: Berkshire House, 2000); http://www.arlo.net/, accessed September 5, 2010. On Stevens: Chris Charlesworth, *Cat Stevens* (London: Proteus, 1985); http://catstev ens.com/, accessed September 5, 2010. On Cohen: Tim Footman, *Leonard Cohen: Hallelujah: A New Biography* (New Malden, UK: Chrome Dreams, 2009); Ira B. Nadel, *Various Positions: A Life of Leonard Cohen* (Austin, TX: University of Texas Press, 2007); http://www.leonardco-hen.com/, accessed September 12, 2010. Anthony Reynolds, *Leonard Cohen: A Remarkable Life* (London: Omnibus, 2010) appeared too late to be consulted for this essay. On Ian: Janis Ian, *Society's Child: My Autobiography* (New York: Tarcher, 2008); http://www.janisian.com/, accessed September 12, 2010. On Ronstadt: Mark Bego, *Linda Ronstadt: It's So Easy: An Unauthorized Biography* (New York: Eakin, 1990). On Captain Beefheart: Mike Barnes, *Captain Beefheart: A Biography,* revised ed. (London: Omnibus, 2009); Kevin Courrier, *Captain Beefheart's Trout Mask Replica* (New York: Continuum, 2007), pages; Billy James, *Lunar Notes: Zoot Horn Rollo's Captain Beefheart Experience* (London: SAF, 2001). John French, *Beefheart: Through the Eyes of Magic* (London: Omnibus, 2010) appeared too late to be consulted for this essay.

41. The verses are in 7/4 and the chorus in 4/4.

42. Brian Wilson released a re-recorded version of *Smile* in 2004.

43. Free form DJs played "Section 43," "Grace," and "Not So Sweet Martha Lorraine" regularly, often back-to-back.

44. Number five was Diana Ross and the Supremes' *Greatest Hits.*

45. For examples, see the live half of Cream's *Wheels of Fire, Live Cream,* and *Live Cream Volume II,* Hendrix's *Band of Gypsys* and, among the plethora of posthumous live releases, *Experience, Isle of Wight,* and *Hendrix in the West.*

46. On the Band: Levon Helm and Stephen Davis, *This Wheel's on Fire: Levon Helm and the Story of the Band,* 2d ed. (Chicago: Chicago Review Press, 2000); Barney Hoskyns, *Across*

the Great Divide: The Band and America, revised ed. (New York: Hal Leonard, 2006). On Dr. John: Mac Rebennack and Jack Rummel, *Under a Hoodoo Moon: The Life of the Night Tripper* (New York: St. Martin's Griffin, 1995); http://www.drjohn.org/, accessed September 5, 2010. On Newman: Kevin Courrier, *Randy Newman: American Dreams* (Toronto: ECW, 2005); http://randynewman.com/, accessed September 5, 2010. On Creedence Clearwater Revival: Hank Bordowitz, *Bad Moon Rising: The Unauthorized History of Creedence Clearwater Revival* (Chicago: Chicago Review Press, 2007); Craig Werner, *Up Around the Bend: The Oral History of Creedence Clearwater Revival* (New York: Harper Perennial, 1999); http://www.johnfogerty. com/, accessed September 5, 2010. On Beck: Carson, *Jeff Beck*; Hjort and Hinman, *Jeff's Book*; Dave Thompson, *Truth! ... Rod Stewart, Ron Wood, and the Jeff Beck Group* (London: Cherry Red, 2006); http://www.jeffbeck.com/, accessed September 5, 2010. On Harrison: Joshua M. Greene, *Here Comes the Sun: The Spiritual and Musical Journey of George Harrison* (Hoboken, NJ: Wiley, 2007); George Harrison, *I, Me, Mine* (San Francisco: Chronicle, 2002); Simon Leng, *While My Guitar Weeps: The Music of George Harrison* (New York: Hal Leonard, 2006), among others; http://www.georgeharrison.com/, accessed September 5, 2010; the albums is the soundtrack to the film *Wonderwall* and inspiration for the 1995 Oasis song of the same name. On Lennon: Ray Coleman, *Lennon: The Definitive Biography* (New York: Harper, 2002) tends toward hagiography; Albert Harry Goldman, *The Lives of John Lennon* (Chicago: Chicago Review Press, 2001) is more negative; Philip Norman, *John Lennon: The Life* (New York: Ecco, 2009) is more balanced; Johnny Rogan, *The Complete Guide to the Music of John Lennon* (London: Omnibus, 1997) and *John Lennon: The Albums* (London: Music Sales Group, 2008); http://www. johnlennon.com/, accessed September 5, 2010; see additional citations under Beatles above, note 36. John Blaney, *John Lennon: In His Life*, ed. Valeria Manferto De Fabianis (Vercelli, Italy: White Star, 2010) appeared too late to be consulted for this essay. Recorded in one night, the album is mostly tape loops, sound effects, and Yoko Ono's random ad-libs. The controversy stems from the nude photo of the couple on the cover. On Young: Daniel Durchholz and Gary Graff, *Neil Young: Long May You Run: The Illustrated History* (Minneapolis: Voyageur, 2010); Jimmy McDonough, *Shakey: Neil Young's Biography* (New York: Anchor, 2003); Johnny Rogan, *Neil Young: Zero to Sixty: A Critical Biography* (London: Calidore, 2000); http://www.neil young.com/, accessed September 5, 2010. On Blood, Sweat, and Tears: Brooks, *The Adventures of Mike Bloomfield and Al Kooper with Paul Butterfield and David Clayton Thomas*; http://www. bloodsweatandtears.com/, accessed September 5, 2010. On Jethro Tull: Scott Allen Nollen, *Jethro Tull: A History of the Band 1968–2001* (Jefferson, NC: McFarland, 2001); David Rees, *Minstrels in the Gallery: A History of Jethro Tull* (Wembley, UK: Fire Fly, 2001); Greg Russo: *Flying Colours: The Jethro Tull Reference Manual (Remastered Version)* (Floral Park, NY: Crossfire, 2009); http://www.j-tull.com/, accessed September 5, 2010. On Soft Machine: Graham Bennett, *Soft Machine: Out-Bloody-Rageous* (London: SAF, 2005). On Fleetwood Mac: Martin Celmins, *Peter Green—Founder of Fleetwood Mac*, 2d ed. (Tampa, FL: Sanctuary, 1998); Mick Fleetwood, *Fleetwood: My Life and Adventures in Fleetwood Mac* (New York: Avon, 1991); http://www.fleet woodmac.com/, accessed September 5, 2010. On Status Quo: http://www.statusquo.co.uk/, accessed September 5, 2010.

    47. On Steppenwolf: John Kay and John Einarson, *Magic Carpet Ride: The Autobiography of John Kay and Steppenwolf* (Kingston, ON: Quarry, 1994); http://www.steppenwolf.com/, accessed September 5, 2012. On Deep Purple: Jerry Bloom, *Deep Purple: Stormbringers* (n.p.: Angry Penguin, 2008); Chris Charlesworth, *Deep Purple: The Illustrated Biography* (London: Omnibus, 1998); Michael Heatley, *The Complete Deep Purple*, 2d ed. (London: Reynolds & Hearn, 2008); Dave Thompson, *Smoke on the Water: The Deep Purple Story* (Toronto: ECW, 2004); http://www.deeppurple.com/, accessed September 5, 2010. On Iron Butterfly: Peter Buckley, *The Rough Guide to Rock* (London, Rough Guides, 2003); http://www.ironbutterfly. com/, accessed September 5, 2010.

    48. On Fairport Convention: Brian Hinton and Geoff Wall, *Ashley Hutchings: The Guv'nor & The Rise of Folk Rock* (London: Helter Skelter, 2002); Patrick Humphries, *Meet on the Ledge: Fairport Convention—The Classic Years*, 2d ed. (London: Virgin, 1997) and *Richard Thompson: The Biography* (New York: Schirmer, 1997); http://www.fairportconvention.com/, accessed Sep-

tember 5, 2010. On Pentangle: http://www.jacquimcshee.co.uk/, accessed September 5, 2010. On Safka: http://www.melaniesmusic.com/, accessed September 5, 2010. On Mitchell: Brian Hinton, *Joni Mitchell: Both Sides Now—The Biography*, 2d ed. (Tampa, FL: Sanctuary, 2000); Michelle Mercer, *Will You Take Me as I Am: Joni Mitchell's Blue Period* (New York: Free Press, 2009); Sheila Weller, *Girls Like Us: Carole King, Joni Mitchell, Carly Simon—and the Journey of a Generation* (New York: Washington Square, 2009); Lloyd Whitesell, *The Music of Joni Mitchell* (Oxford: Oxford University Press, 2008). On Quicksilver Messenger Service: Unterberger, *Eight Miles High*, Chapter 2. On T. Rex: Hoskyns, *Glam! Bowie, Bolan and the Glitter Rock Revolution*; Mark Paytress, *Bolan: The Rise and Fall of a 20th Century Superstar*, 2d ed. (London: Music Sales, 2007). On Brown: Unterberger, *Urban Spacemen and Wayfaring Strangers*, 39–51; http://www.arthurbrownmusic.com/, accessed September 5, 2010. On Nazz: Billy James, *A Dream Goes on Forever—The Continuing Story of Todd Rundgren: The Utopia Years* (Bentonville, AR: Golden Treasures, 2002), Chapters 3–4.

49. With the Byrds, Gram Parsons helped instigate the move toward country-rock. Ben Fong-Torres, *Hickory Wind: The Life and Times of Gram Parsons* (New York: St. Martin's Griffin, 1998); David Meyer, *Twenty Thousand Roads: The Ballad of Gram Parsons and His Cosmic American Music* (New York: Villard, 2008).

50. On the Allman Brothers Band, Scott Freeman, *Midnight Riders: The Story of the Allman Brothers Band* (Boston: Little, Brown and Company, 1996); Randy Poe, *Skydog: The Duane Allman Story* (San Francisco: Backbeat, 2008); http://www.allmanbrothersband.com/, accessed September 5, 2010. On Blind Faith: Clapton: *Clapton*; Hjort, *Strange Brew*; Shapiro, *Eric Clapton*; http://www.ericclapton.com/, accessed September 5, 2010. On Cocker: Julian P. Bean, *Joe Cocker: The Authorised Biography* (London: Virgin, 2003); http://www.cocker.com/us/home, accessed September 5, 2010. On Delaney and Bonnie: http://www.bonniebramlett.com/. On Humble Pie: Paulo Hewitt and John Hellier, *Steve Marriott—All Too Beautiful* (London: Helter Skelter, 2004).

51. On Bloomfield: Brooks, *The Adventures of Mike Bloomfield and Al Kooper with Paul Butterfield and David Clayton Thomas*; Wolkin, *Michael Bloomfield*; http://www.mikebloomfield.com/, accessed September 5, 2010. On Joplin: Echols, *Scars of Sweet Paradise*; Myra Friedman, *Buried Alive*. On Chicago: http://chicagotheband.com/, accessed September 5, 2010; Danny Seraphine, *Street Player: My Chicago Story* (Hoboken, NJ: Wiley, 2010) appeared too late to be consulted for this essay. On Santana: Norman Weinstein, *Carlos Santana: A Biography* (Santa Barbara, CA: Greenwood, 2009); http://www.santana.com/, accessed September 5, 2010. On Genesis: Tony Banks, Phil Collins, Peter Gabriel, Steve Hackett, and Mike Rutherford, *Genesis: Chapter and Verse* (New York: St. Martin's Griffin, 2007); Armando Gallo, *Genesis: I Know What I Like*, 2d ed. (London: Omnibus, 1987), pages; Dave Thompson, *Turn It on Again: Peter Gabriel, Phil Collins, and Genesis* (San Francisco: Backbeat, 2004); Chris Welch, *Genesis: The Complete Guide to Their Music* (London: Omnibus, 2006); http://www.genesis-music.com/, accessed September 5, 2010. On Van der Graaf Generator: Jim Christopulos and Phil Smart, *Van der Graaf Generator, The Book: A History of the Band Van der Graaf Generator 1967 to 1978* (n.p.: Phil and Jim, 2005); http://www.vandergraafgenerator.co.uk/, accessed September 5, 2010. On Yes: Peter Banks and Billy James, *Beyond & Before: The Formative Years of Yes* (Bentonville, AR: Golden Treasures, 2002); Bill Bruford, *Bill Bruford: The Autobiography* (London: Jawbone, 2009); Alan Farley, *The Extraordinary World of Yes* (New York: iUniverse, 2004); Bill Martin, *Music of Yes: Structure and Vision in Progressive Rock* (Peru, IL: Open Court, 1996); Tim Morse, *Yesstories: Yes in Their Own Words* (New York: St. Martin's Griffin, 1996); Rick Wakeman, *Grumpy Old Rockstar and Other Wondrous Stories* (London: Preface, 2009) and *Further Adventures of a Grumpy Old Rock Star* (London: Preface, 2010); David Watkinson and Rick Wakeman, *Yes: Perpetual Change* (Medford, NJ: Plexus, 2001); http://www.yesworld.com/, accessed September 5, 2010. On Krautrock: Nikos Kotsopoulos, *Krautrock: Cosmic Rock and Its Legacy* (London: Black Dog, 2010); http://www.amonduul.de/, accessed September 5, 2010; Pascal Bussy, *The Can Book* (London: SAF, 1989); http://www.spoonrecords.com/, accessed September 5, 2010. On King Crimson: Sid Smith, *In the Court of King Crimson* (London: Helter Skelter, 2002); http://www.king-crimson.com/, accessed September 5, 2010.

52. On Alice Cooper: Alice Cooper, with Keith Zimmerman and Kent Zimmerman, *Alice Cooper, Golf Monster: A rock 'n' roller's Life and 12 Steps to Becoming a Golf Addict* (New York: Three Rivers, 2007); Dale Sherman, *The Illustrated Collector's Guide to Alice Cooper* (Burlington, ON: Collector's Guide Publishing, 2009); http://www.alicecooper.com/, accessed September 5, 2010. On Grand Funk: Billy James, *An American Band: The Story of Grand Funk Railroad* (London: SAF, 1999); http://www.grandfunkrailroad.com/, accessed September 5, 2010. On Mott the Hoople: Campbell Devine, *All the Young Dudes: Mott the Hoople and Ian Hunter* (London: Cherry Red, 2007). On the MC5: Mathew J. Bartkowiak, *The MC5 and Social Change: A Study in Rock and Revolution* (Jefferson, NC: McFarland, 2009); Brett Callwood, *MC5: Sonically Speaking: A Tale of Revolution and Rock n Roll* (Church Stretton, UK: Independent Music Press, 2007); David Carlson, *Grit, Noise, & Revolution: The Birth of Detroit rock 'n' roll* (Ann Arbor, MI: University of Michigan Press, 2005); John Sinclair, *Guitar Army: Rock and Revolution with the MC5 and the White Panther Party*, 35th anniversary ed. (Port Townsend, WA: Process, 2007); http://www.mc5.org/, accessed September 5, 2010. On the Stooges: Brett Callwood, *The Stooges: A Journey Through the Michigan Underworld* (Church Stretton, UK: Independent Music Press, 2008); Robert Matheu, *The Stooges: The Authorized and Illustrated Story* (New York: Abrams, 2009); http://www.iggypop.com/, accessed September 5, 2010. Mick Rock, *Iggy and the Stooges: Raw Power* (Bath, UK: Palazzo Editions, 2011) appeared too late to be consulted for this essay. On Crosby, Stills, and Nash: Barney Hoskyns, *Hotel California: The True-Life Adventures of Crosby, Stills, Nash, Young, Mitchell, Taylor, Browne, Ronstadt, Geffen, the Eagles, and Their Many Friends* (Hoboken, NJ: Wiley, 2007); Dave Zimmer, *Crosby, Stills & Nash: The Biography*, 3rd ed. (New York: Da Capo, 2008) and *Four Way Street: The Crosby, Stills, Nash, & Young Reader* (New York: Da Capo, 2004); http://www.crosbystillsnash.com/ and http://csny.com/, accessed September 5, 2010. On the Flying Burrito Brothers: John Einarson, *Hot Burritos: The True Story of the Flying Burrito Brothers* (London: Jawbone, 2008). On Poco: Hoskyns, *Hotel California*; http://www.poconut.org/, accessed September 5, 2010. On Drake: Trevor Dann, *Darker Than the Deepest Sea: The Search for Nick Drake* (New York: Da Capo, 2006); Patrick Humphries, *Nick Drake: The Biography* (New York: Bloomsbury, 1998). On Elton John: Mark Bego, *Elton John: The Bitch Is Back* (Beverly Hills, CA: Phoenix, 2009); David Buckley, *Elton: The Biography* (Chicago: Chicago Review Press, 2009); http://web.eltonjohn.com/index.jsp, accessed September 5, 2010. On Sha Na Na: http://www.shanana.com/, accessed September 5, 2010. On Badfinger: Dan Matovina, *Without You: The Tragic Story of Badfinger* (San Mateo, CA: Frances Glover, 2000).

53. On McCartney: Barry Miles, *Paul McCartney: Many Years from Now* (New York: Holt, 1998); http://www.paulmccartney.com/, accessed September 5, 2010; see additional citations under Beatles above, note 36. Howard Sounes, *Fab: The Life of Paul McCartney* (New York: Da Capo, 2010) appeared too late to be consulted for this essay. On Ringo: Alan Clayson, *Ringo Starr*, 2d ed. (Tampa, FL: Sanctuary, 2001); http://www.ringostarr.com/, accessed September 5, 2010; see additional citations under Beatles above, note 36.

54. On Stills: Zimmer, *Crosby, Stills & Nash* and *Four Way Street: The Crosby, Stills, Nash, & Young Reader*; http://www.crosbystillsnash.com/ and http://csny.com/, accessed September 5, 2010. On Sebastian: http://www.johnbsebastian.com/, accessed September 5, 2010. On ELP: Emerson, *Pictures of an Exhibitionist*; Edward Macan, *Endless Enigma: A Musical Biography of Emerson, Lake, and Palmer* (Peru, IL: Open Court, 2006); http://www.emersonlakepalmer.com/, accessed September 5, 2010. George Forrester, Martyn Hanson, and Frank Askew, *Emerson Lake and Palmer: The Show That Never Ends* (London: Helter Skelter, 2010) appeared too late to be consulted for this essay. On Rundgren: Billy James, *A Dream Goes on Forever*; http://www.tr-i.com/, accessed September 5, 2010; Paul Myers, *A Wizard, A True Star: Todd Rundgren in the Studio* (London: Jawbone, 2010) appeared too late to be consulted for this essay. On Burdon and War: Eric Burdon and J. Marshal Craig, *Don't Let Me Be Misunderstood*; http://www.wartheband.com/home.html, accessed September 5, 2010.

55. On Gentle Giant: Paul Stump, *Gentle Giant: Acquiring the Taste* (London: SAF, 2005); http://www.blazemonger.com/GG/Gentle_Giant_Home_Page, accessed September 5, 2010. On Hawkwind: Ian Abrahams, *Hawkwind: Sonic Assassins* (London: SAF, 2004); Carol Clerk, *The*

Saga of Hawkwind, 2d ed. (London: Omnibus, 2006); Robert Godwin, *The Illustrated Collector's Guide to Hawkwind* (Burlington, ON: Collector's Guide Publishing, 1995); http://www.hawk wind.com/, accessed September 5, 2010. On Supertramp: Martin Melhuish, *The Supertramp Book* (London: Omnibus, 1986); http://supertramp.com/, accessed September 5, 2010. On Focus: http://www.focustheband.com/, accessed September 5, 2010. On Kraftwerk: Tim Barr, *Kraftwerk: From Düsseldorf to the Future* (London: Ebury, 1999); Pascal Bussy, *Kraftwerk: Man, Machine, and Music,* revised ed. (London: SAF, 2004); Wolfgang Flur, *Kraftwerk: I Was a Robot* (Tampa, FL: Sanctuary, 2005); Kotsopoulos, *Krautrock.* On Tangerine Dream: Paul Stump, *Digital Gothic: A Critical Discography of Tangerine Dream* (London: SAF, 1997); http://www.tan gerinedream.org/, accessed September 5, 2010. On the Ides of March: http://www.theidesof march.com/, accessed September 5, 2010.

56. On Black Sabbath: Carol Clerk, *Diary of a Madman: Ozzy Osbourne: The Stories Behind the Songs* (New York: Da Capo, 2002); Martin Popoff, *Black Sabbath: Doom Let Loose: An Illustrated History* (Toronto: ECW, 2006); Joe McIver, *Sabbath Bloody Sabbath* (London: Omnibus, 2007); Paul Wilkinson, *Rat Salad: Black Sabbath, The Classic Years, 1969–1975* (New York: Thomas Dunne, 2007). Brian Aberback, *Black Sabbath: Pioneers of Heavy Metal* (Berkeley Heights, NJ: Enslow, 2010) and Dave Thompson, *The Wit and Wisdom of Ozzy Osbourne* (Iola, WI: Krause, 2010) appeared too late to be consulted for this essay. On Mountain: Leslie West and Corky Laing, *Nantucket Sleighride and Other Mountain On-the-Road Stories* (London: SAF, 2003). On Uriah Heep: David Ling, *Wizards and Demons: The Uriah Heep Story* (n.p.: Classic Rock Productions, 2002); http://www.uriah-heep.com/newa/index.php, September 5, 2010. On Wishbone Ash: Mark Chatterton and Gary Carter, *Blowin' Free: Thirty Years of Wishbone Ash* (Wembley, UK: Fire Fly, 2001); http://wishboneash.com/, accessed September 5, 2010. On Lindisfarne: http://www.lindisfarne.co.uk, accessed September 5, 2010. On Steeleye Span: Hinton and Wall, *Ashley Hutchings.* On Taylor: Timothy White, *James Taylor Long Ago and Far Away: His Life and His Music,* 2d ed. (London: Omnibus, 2005). On Clinton: Dave Marsh, *For the Record 5: George Clinton & P-Funkadelic* (New York: Harper Perennial, 1998); http://www.georgeclinton.com/, accessed September 5, 2010.

57. On the Doobie Brothers: Mark Bego, *The Doobie Brothers: Behind the Scenes with Today's Hottest Group* (New York: Popular Library, 1980); http://www.doobiebros.com/. On ELO: Bev Bevan, *Electric Light Orchestra Story* (New York: Putnam, 1981). On Prine: John Prine, *John Prine* (Van Nuys, CA: Alfred, 1999); http://www.johnprine.net/, accessed September 5, 2010. On Simon: Weller, *Girls Like Us;* http://www.carlysimon.com/, accessed September 5, 2010. On King: James Perone, *The Words and Music of Carole King* (Westport, CT: Praeger, 2006); Weller, *Girls Like Us;* http://www.caroleking.com/home.php, accessed September 5, 2010. On Mahavishnu Orchestra: Walter Kolosky, *Power, Passion & Beauty: The Story of the Legendary Mahavishnu Orchestra* (Cary, NC: Abstract Logix, 2006); Paul Stump, *Go Ahead: The Music of John McLaughlin* (London: SAF, 2000); http://www.johnmclaughlin.com/, accessed September 5, 2010. On Wings: Garry McGee, *Band on the Run: A History of Paul McCartney and Wings* (New York: Taylor Trade Publishing, 2003); http://www.paulmccartney.com/, accessed September 5, 2010. On ZZ Top: David Blayney, *Sharp-Dressed Men: ZZ Top Behind the Scenes from Blues to Boogie to Beards* (New York: Hyperion, 1994); Billy F. Gibbons, *Billy F. Gibbons: Rock & Roll Gearhead* (Minneapolis: MBI, 2005); http://www.zztop.com/, accessed September 5, 2010.

58. On Brown: Hoskyns, *Hotel California;* Rich Wiseman, *Jackson Browne: The Story of a Hold Out* (New York: Doubleday, 1982); http://www.jacksonbrowne.com/, accessed September 5, 2010. On the Eagles: Marc Eliot, *To the Limit: The Untold Story of the Eagles* (Boston: Little, Brown, and Company, 1998); Don Felder and Wendy Holden, *Heaven and Hell: My Life in the Eagles 1974–2001* (Hoboken, NJ: Wiley, 2009); Hoskyns, *Hotel California;* http://www.eaglesband.com/, accessed September 5, 2010. Andrew Vaughan, *The Eagles: An American Band* (New York: Sterling, 2010) appeared too late to be consulted for this essay. On Foghat: http://www.foghat.com/, accessed September 5, 2010. On Reed: Victor Bockris, *Transformer: The Lou Reed Story* (New York: Da Capo, 1997); Doggett, *Lou Reed;* Thompson, *Your Pretty Face Is Going to Hell;* http://www.loureed.com/00/index.html/, accessed September 5, 2010. On Roxy Music:

Michael Bracewell, *Re-make/Re-model: Becoming Roxy Music* (New York: Da Capo, 2008); David Buckley, *The Thrill of It All: Bryan Ferry and Roxy Music* (Chicago: Chicago Review Press, 2005); Jonathan Rigby, *Roxy Music: Both Ends Burning*, revised ed. (London: Reynolds & Hearn, 2008); Paul Stump, *Unknown Pleasures: Cultural Biography of Roxy Music* (New York: Thunder's Mouth, 1998); http://www.roxymusic.co.uk/, accessed September 5, 2010. On the IBBBB: http://www.petelevin.com/ibbbb/ibbbb01.htm, accessed September 5, 2010. On Steely Dan: http://www.steelydan.com/, accessed September 5, 2010. On Thompson: Patrick Humphries, *Richard Thompson*; http://www.richardthompson-music.com/, accessed September 5, 2010.

6

Rock and Roll Grows Up

Harry Edwin Eiss

In 1971, Don McLean gave the world an enigma, a song with lyrics that all somehow connect, but it's unclear just how. It's evident the lyrics have something to do with "the day the music died," a reference on a literal level to the infamous 1959 plane crash that killed Buddy Holly, Ritchie Valens, and J. P. Richardson, Jr. (The Big Bopper) in their prime. While refusing to give away the full meaning of the song (or more accurately, his intended meaning), Don McLean has said it is autobiographical and represents his perceptions of the decline of music from the 1950s through the 1960s, just enough to send rock enthusiasts, scholars, teachers, and people who simply browse the Internet into a growing debate over the possibilities.

Some find it an attack on the Vietnam War, similar to less obscure songs such as "For What It's Worth" (Buffalo Springfield), "Blowin' in the Wind" (Bob Dylan), "Fortunate Son" and "Have You Ever Seen the Rain" (Creedence Clearwater Revival), "Give Peace a Chance" and "Happy Christmas" (John Lennon), "Here's to the State of Richard Nixon," "Draft Dodger Rag" and "I Ain't Marchin' Anymore" (Phil Ochs), "It Better End Soon," "Chicago," "Draft Resister" (Steppenwolf), "Eve of Destruction" (Barry McGuire) "Fixin' to Die" (Country Joe and the Fish), "Front Line" (Stevie Wonder), "Dear Uncle Sam" (Loretta Lynn), "Draft Morning" (The Byrds), "Edge of Darkness" (Iron Maiden), "Question" (Moody Blues), "Peace Train" (Cat Stevens), "Ruby Don't Take Your Love to Town" (Kenny Rogers), "Running Gun Blues" (David Bowie), "Singin' in Viet Nam Talkin' Blues" (Johnny Cash), and "Where are You Now My Son" (Joan Baez).

Some think it refers to some of these same artists, Bob Dylan, the Beatles, the Byrds, and other important rock 'n' roll stars, such as Elvis. Some find references to the Apocalypse and other possible religious themes. Some suggest other political and social figures as references within the song, including the likes of Robert Kennedy, John F. Kennedy and Martin Luther King. On first blush, it might seem strange and seem at best self-indulgent to be looking for obscure and perhaps profound meanings in a rock 'n' roll song, but the times were ripe for exactly this. Indeed, serious *high art* and commercial *low art* were at the cutting edge of this postmodern world.

It is the *Pop* artists leading the way. Andy Warhol includes a "real" zipper in his reproduction of a man's jeans (suggestive of, maybe in reality, Mick Jagger's), with the bulge of a penis showing, on a cover flap "stuck" (by something that represents semen) over an album cover reproduction of a man's crotch wearing underpants, the messy crotch obviously the result of cumming, for the cover of The Rolling Stones' *Sticky Fingers* album,[1] providing a pun on "creativity" (sexual creativity and artistic creativity are a common juxtaposition), and raising questions (creating dualities to give the viewer an open space to fill) of propriety, pornography, voyeurism, and serious art, mass production (these albums are meant to be mass produced for a commercial audience) and the uniqueness of a work of serious art, and in general, the commingling of popular music (anti-art) with serious art.

This commingling of serious art and rock 'n' roll music gains even stronger sexual emphasis when the phrase "rock 'n' roll" is followed to its origin in such late 1940s R&B records as those of Wild Bill Moore, whose song "We're Gonna Rock, We're Gonna Roll" used the phrase as an obvious euphemism for having sex.[2] Furthermore, the intersections of serious art and popular music, while perhaps not firmly established, do, nevertheless, have precedents in 20th-century art, especially the impact of jazz. Stuart Davis, a frequenter of honky-tonk saloons, drew Scott Joplin in 1918, included a verse from a Duke Ellington song in *American Painting*,[3] later did two murals, *Swing Landscape*[4] and *Municipal Broadcasting Company WNYC Studio B Mural*,[5] and a work, *Report from Rockport*,[6] which H. H. Arnason says has a surface that "twists and vibrates with jagged, abstract color shapes and lines, elements that put the scene into violent and fantastic movement translating the jazz tempo of America into abstract color harmonics and dissonances."[7]

In a satisfying spiraling, *Broadway Boogie Woogie*[8] and *Victory Boogie Woogie*,[9] two later works Piet Mondrian claimed were inspired by New York's "dance halls, jazz bands, the excitement of movement and change,"[10] in turn, were the inspiration for the Bee Gees' disco music.

Matisse disciplined himself to a severe structure, a visual logic, an exploration of color, which, he writes, "must be a living harmony of tones, a harmony not unlike that of a musical composition,"[11] expressing "everything by a rhythmic, cursive line of descriptive economy."[12] We need go no farther than the title he chose for his book, *Jazz*, for assurance of the specific kind of music he embraced, where he comments, "there are wonderful things in real jazz ... the talent for improvisation, the liveliness, the being at one with the audience...."[13]

Romare Bearden, an African American raised in Harlem, was such a talent, perhaps obviously, having lived in the middle of one its centers and having been known to frequent Harlem's Savoy Ballroom, which featured bands led by such jazz greats as Duke Ellington, Cab Calloway, and Lionel Hampton, even more closely enveloped in jazz, and his mixed-media photo-collages are filled with images of jazz musicians.[14] Daniel Wheeler summarizes: "In Romare Bearden (1914–88) Harlem found its own history painter, an artist who won dominion over form by studying the Old Masters and then reinvigorated it with the jazzy rhythms pioneered in painting by Stuart Davis...."[15]

Such "beat" artists as Wallace Berman and Jay DeFeo, who frequented jazz clubs in South Los Angeles, also meshed jazz and the visual arts.[16] Larry Rivers, working in New York, and before that deciding to devote himself to painting, considered becoming a jazz musician and created such pieces as *Jazz Musician*, where an anonymous jazz player is depicted enveloped in a field of broad, fragmented brush strokes, in an attempt to convey the rhythms of jazz.[17]

While these various examples demonstrate ways in which popular music and high art found connection in the works of many artists, the mixing of high art specifically to rock 'n' roll can be said to begin with four artists: Ray Johnson, Andy Warhol, Richard Hamilton, and Sir Peter Thomas Blake, all of whom incorporated elements of rock 'n' roll in their work about 1956, the same year Elvis Presley achieved stardom. A fuller discussion of the development of the work of each of these prolific artists attests to the comingling of high art and rock 'n' roll at the time, and it demonstrates the prevalence of an attitude toward experimentation that permeated the era in which rock 'n' roll grew up — the same era that Don McLean remembered and from which McLean drew in crafting "American Pie."

Ray Johnson's experimentation with the mixing of rock 'n' roll with visual art developed out of his prolific work with collage. Most particularly, Johnson's experimentation with this connection grew from his work that influenced the Pop Art movement. However, Johnson came to that experimentation through quite a roundabout path that also aligned him with other movements and media. These additional interests and influences included performance and conceptual art early in his career, followed later in his life by involvement with the Fluxus movement and foundational roles in the use of language within the visual arts and in the Mail Art movement.

After studying from 1945 to 1948 at the famous Black Mountain College, under the guidance of the likes of Josef Albers and Robert Motherwell and alongside other avant-garde leaders ranging from John Cage to Merce Cunningham to Willem and Elaine de Kooning, Johnson moved to New York and developed an interest in using Zen and concepts of chance within his work. Once he moved to New York, Johnson first worked with abstract painting; however, by 1955, he had become so disillusioned with the abstract works of his early career that he destroyed them by burning the works in Cy Twombly's fireplace.[18] By this time, collage had become Johnson's medium of preference, and upon this medium Johnson built much of his influence throughout his career.

Though Johnson had so forcefully disavowed his work with abstraction, his initial collages grew out of that interest, as they consisted mainly of abstract works in which he made irregular designs from paper strips that he cut, painted, and distressed. Johnson called these works "moticos," and these provided a major avenue through which Johnson connected his work to popular culture. In 1955 and 1956 he created several collages by clipping the photographs of famous entertainers (including James Dean, Marilyn Monroe, Shirley Temple, and Elvis Presley) from magazines and newspapers and then changing them with ink and paint. Johnson would later cut up many of his moticos and use them to create small works consisting of layered cardboard blocks to which he would add other substances to create what he called "tessarae."[19] Johnson's moticos that later became tessarae continued his experimentation with popular culture, as he used works whose subject matter included Lucky Strike symbols, potato mashers, and "tit girls" in these forms of collages.

By the late 1950s and early 1960s, Johnson's interests would lead him to further experimentation, particularly with mail art. Johnson's mail art, which developed out of an interest in the work of Marcel Duchamp, led to what would be called the "New York Correspondence School" and would feature works that developed through Johnson's practice of mailing acquaintances and asking them to send along what he had sent to them so that it would eventually work its way back to Johnson in the form that it would take in the piece he would then exhibit. Meanwhile, by the 1960s, Johnson also became an early proponent of performance art, particularly as he staged "Nothings," which satirized the "Happenings" that Allan Kaprow and Fluxus artists staged as forms of performance art that encouraged audience participation and served as forums for improvisation.[20] Johnson juxtaposed his "Nothings" against the "Happenings" by claiming a "Nothing" to be "an attitude as opposed to a happening."[21] "Happenings" became a popular form of event, particularly as they aligned with counterculture, anti–Vietnam War, and civil rights movements. The term worked its way into popular music, as the Supremes' hit number one in 1967 with a song called "The Happening." Johnson's "Nothings" thus partook of a forum that itself was crossing the boundaries of high art and popular art.

Among all of this experimentation on Johnson's part, one of his moticos,

Elvis Presley I (Oedipus), exemplifies the combination of rock 'n' roll and visual art. The motico features a close-up of the left side of Elvis' face as he sings into a created pattern of red rectangles (perhaps a microphone), a red wash of tears streaming from his eye.[22]

Andy Warhol also experimented heavily with the association of rock 'n' roll and visual art. Perhaps most notably, Warhol included rock 'n' roll imagery and subject matter as part of his projected persona, using the teenager as his prototype. According to David Bourdon, when serious visitors from the world of art visited Warhol's studio, he would purposely display teenage fan magazines and pop records, and he would play songs such as Dion and the Belmonts' "A Teenager in Love."[23]

Andy Warhol's career continued to be intertwined with rock 'n' roll, eventually including multiple silkscreens of Mick Jagger, Prince, Aretha Franklin, Paul Anka, Deborah Harry, and John Lennon. Warhol also worked extensively in collaboration with Velvet Underground (a group he traveled with and even produced an album by, designing the cover himself, with a banana peel sticker that can be peeled off to reveal a flesh-toned banana; note the sexual connotations and the relation to the *Sticky Fingers* album).[24]

However, Andy Warhol's bringing of the popular imagery and interests of the American teenager's world into the world of serious art was not restricted to rock 'n' roll music, nor was it narrowed to the teenager's world. It included these elements, but it also extended throughout the entire world of popular culture, resulting in an energetic satire of the worlds of advertising and art (as exemplified in his famous series of Campbell soup cans and Coca-Cola bottles), while it also showed in such humorous artistic subject matter as stacks of Brillo boxes (*Brillo Boxes*, silk-screen on wood, 13 × 16 × 11½, 1964), an enthusiastic reinventing of the rich and famous, from multiple photographs of Jackie Kennedy (i.e., *Jackie*, liquitex and silk-screen on canvas, 80" × 64", 1964), and a series of Marilyn Monroe pictures (i.e., *Marilyn Monroe*, oil on canvas, 81" × 66¾", 1962), to less bright subjects (such as *Electric Chair*, silk-screen on canvas, 24" × 28") depicted in his *Death and Disaster* series.[25]

Warhol was not alone. Other "Pop" artists also found this high/low art juxtaposition a way to release exciting new metaphors and lively statements about culture, society, politics, and art itself.

These artists included Roy Lichtenstein, who juxtaposed again and again the "low, common, popular" imagery of the comic book, a subject matter already rendered two-dimensional (already removed from the "reality" it depicts) into a small, self-contained world, with the world of "high, museum art" by enlarging portions of a comic-book frame, emphasizing the medium they come from (i.e., the minute dots of a standard Ben Day dot techniques used to print comic books are enlarged, emphasized, in his paintings, as part of the subject matter), and by simply placing something not meant to be taken seriously into a context where it traditionally is meant to be taken seriously, almost reverently, thus creating a playful, ironic perspective. If we encounter a frame in a comic book where a girl is drowning that has a bubble of her thoughts that says, "I don't care! I'd rather sink than call Brad for help!" we are not surprised, think little of it. If we encounter the same subject matter on an oil canvas 68" × 68", titled *Drowning Girl*, and credited to Roy Lichtenstein, hanging in a gallery or prominent place in a wealthy establishment, we are struck by the melodramatic quality of the subject matter.[26] Either we join in the parody and laugh at the joke we are participating in, or we, in fact, are the unknowing subject of the joke.

As Susan Sontag says, such humor in contemporary art is a "mode of enjoyment, of appreciation — not judgment. Camp is generous, it wants to enjoy."[27] This is precisely the difference between postmodern (or late modern) works and early modern works, this move from condemnation, malice, cynicism, and an embracement of the nothingness of the modernist movement to the almost cartoonish world that "relishes rather than judges" the postmodern movements.[28] The embodiment of this sentiment in Lichtenstein's work demonstrates the depths to which artists had begun to go in seeing and articulating associations between high art with rock 'n' roll.

Among such artists, Sir Peter Thomas Blake, beginning with a tattoo of Elvis Presley on the leg of *Siriol, She-Devil of Naked Madness* in 1957,[29] was the first to create an extensive body of art devoted to rock 'n' roll iconography. In 1959 he began a series of prints and paintings of rock 'n' roll personalities with *Girls with Their Hero* (where several images of Elvis, a vinyl record, and adoring female fans are mixed), and he went on to include the Everly Brothers, Bo Diddley, Ricky Nelson, the Beach Boys, LaVern Baker, and the Beatles.[30]

In addition, Blake experimented with the mixing of serious art and popular art with such works as *On the Balcony* and *The First Real Target*. *On the Balcony* features a boy who holds high art in the form of Edouard Manet's *The Balcony* as well as popular art in forms such as badges and magazines. Meanwhile, in *The First Real Target*, Blake played on works by Kenneth Noland and Jasper Johns that featured targets. In this work, Blake depicts a standard archery target accompanied by, at the piece's top, the title of the piece, suggesting that the subject of Blake's painting supersedes Noland's and Johns' works, as Blake identifies what a target is. The painting offers the sense that the popular practice of using a target must precede the high art of Noland's and Johns' works; it thus suggests that high art depends on the popular for its existence. Both of these paintings from Blake remain on display in the Tate Gallery and are still considered iconic pieces of British Pop Art.

As the Pop Art movement began to take hold, others saw Blake as one of its leaders. Blake received such recognition in various forms, which included joining the Young Contemporaries exhibition in 1960 alongside such other Pop Artists as David Hockney and R. B. Kitaj; winning the 1961 John Moores junior award for his work *Self Portrait with Badges*; and receiving a featured spot in the 1962 film *Pop Goes the Easel*, which examined Pop Art. Blake's association with popular culture would increase as he became involved with the swinging London scene in 1963.

Blake's participation in the London scene also led to his most important and well-known work — the sleeve for the Beatles' album *Sgt. Pepper's Lonely Hearts Club Band*, which Blake co-designed with his wife at the time, Jann Haworth, and which became a seminal work and undoubtedly the best known work of all of Pop Art and of all of popular music.[31]

Sgt. Pepper's Lonely Hearts Club Band broke the rules of popular music. Up until this album the standard release of hit songs was the "45," a two-to-three minute song backed by a throw-away song. These singles were the driving force for all of popular music in the United States, certainly for all of rock 'n' roll music, and they were played over and over on the top radio stations. If a singer or group had a couple of hit singles (or even just one), the record companies would put together an album featuring the hit song and another ten or eleven songs randomly selected and organized with no real thematic center, with no purpose other than cashing in on the hit single. And the singers or bands went on tour to further cash in and promote their singles.

The Beatles, however, became such a huge influence they could get away with something different. For a time, they had been releasing singles without bothering to gather them into albums. They also decided to stop touring. Instead, they secluded themselves in their studio from December 6 to April 3, experimented with a number of drugs, including marijuana, cocaine, and LSD, and began creating an album that was meant to be a complete, united work.

How it all came together has since received many, many studies, and just who is responsible for the various pieces of it will forever remain guesswork. However, the initial concept seems to have come mainly from Paul McCartney. In a *Playboy* interview (Dec., 1984), he stated: "[Sgt. Pepper] was an idea I had, I think, when I was flying from L.A. to somewhere. I thought it would be nice to lose our identities, to submerge ourselves in the persona of a fake group. We would make up all the culture around it and collect all our heroes in one place. So I thought, a typical stupid-sound name for a Dr. Hook's Medicine Show and Traveling Circus kind of thing would be Sgt. Pepper's Lonely Hearts Club Band. Just a word game, really." In *Beatles in Their Own Words*, he elaborated, "After you have written that down you start to think: 'There's this Sgt. Pepper who has taught the band to play, and got them going so that at least they found one number. They're a bit of a brass band in a way, but also a rock band because they've got the San Francisco thing.'"[32]

There are other versions. According to Pete Shotton and Ringo Starr, it wasn't Paul, but Mal Evans who both coined the name Sgt. Pepper's Lonely Hearts Club Band and suggested that this fictitious group be presented as the Beatles' alter egos.[33]

John Lennon was not into it, saying "Sgt. Pepper is called the first concept album, but it doesn't go anywhere. All my contributions to the album have absolutely nothing to do with this idea of Sgt. Pepper and his band; but it works 'cause we *said* it worked."[34]

This concept of it working or being something because its creator or creators say it is actually fits it even more into the whole realm of concept art.

When Peter Blake began working on the cover, he said that "Paul explained that [the concept] was like a band you might see in a park. So the cover shot could be a photograph of them as though they were a town band finishing a concert in a park, playing on a bandstand with a municipal flowerbed next to it, with a crowd of people around them. I think my main contribution was to decide that if we made the crowd a certain way the people in it could be anybody."[35]

As it turned out, when Blake asked the Beatles to choose individuals to go into the scene, the band members chose the most well-known people they could think of. John Lennon even wanted to include Jesus, but he was vetoed here (he had already gotten himself and the group in trouble with comments about Jesus). Mahatma Gandhi also got nixed for fear of offending India.

In the end, Peter Blake explained: "All the figures which you see behind the Beatles only filled a space about two feet deep, and then there was a line of figures in front of them which were the waxworks. The actual Beatles stood on a platform about four feet deep in all with the drum in front of them, and in front of that there was a flowerbed which was pitched at an angle, maybe ten feet deep. So that from front to back the whole thing was only about fifteen feet deep."[36]

At this time, another mixture of reality and illusion was taking place — the "Paul is dead" hysteria — and this cover has been interpreted and reinterpreted by those looking for clues to that. The hand above Paul's head is supposedly a sign of death; the Beatles are supposedly standing around his freshly dug grave; the yellow hyacinth bass guitar supposedly marks his grave; the black clarinet Paul holds symbolizes death; and even the fact that Harrison's finger on the back cover is pointed to the first line of "She's Leaving Home" is thought to indicate the time of his death. Suggestions have been made that Paul is being represented by an actor named William Campbell, who had plastic surgery to look like him; the inside photo of Paul with an arm patch reading O.P.D. (Ontario Police Station) is interpreted as Officially Pronounced Dead, and the photo of Paul on the back has him facing away. On and on.[37]

Blake, along with the Beatles, had brought popular music and conceptual art together in this album sleeve. While there would never be another sleeve as major as this, Blake would also make sleeves for Pentangle's *Sweet Child*, The Who's *Face Dances* and *Live at Leeds 2*, the Band Aid single "Do They Know It's Christmas?" Paul Weller's *Stanley Road*, and the Ian Dury tribute album *Brand New Boots and Panties*.

Blake would also continue the practice of utilizing images of popular culture icons in album art. In his design for the Oasis greatest hits album *Stop the Clocks* from 2006, Blake included images of Michael Caine, Elvis, Dorothy from *The Wizard of Oz*, and the seven dwarfs from *Snow White and the Seven Dwarfs*, among others. This album art was meant to show a direct Beatles influence, particularly in echoing the artwork of *Sgt. Pepper's Lonely Hearts Club Band*.[38] In 2008, Blake also updated the album art for *Sgt. Pepper's Lonely Hearts Club Band* itself as part of a successful effort to declare Liverpool, England, as the European Capital of Culture. For this project, the update to the album art featured famous individuals from the history of Liverpool.[39]

While *Sgt. Pepper's Lonely Hearts Club Band* provided the most prominent forum for Blake to articulate associations between rock 'n' roll and high art, association with another Beatles' album, the "White Album," offered such an opportunity for Richard Hamilton. From 1952 to 1956, Hamilton was one of a British association of artists, architects, art historians, and critics, known as the Independent Group, which held seminars at London's Institute of Contemporary Art (ICA). *This Is Tomorrow*, their final exhibition, was held at the Whitechapel Art Gallery in 1956. It consisted of installations put together by twelve teams (generally, a painter, a sculptor, and an architect), each meant to explore relationships between art and the environment. Richard Hamilton, John McHale, and John Voelcker concentrated on popular culture, and included in theirs a robot from the film *Forbidden Planet*, a life-size photograph of Marilyn Monroe from the film *The Seven Year Itch*, and a jukebox that played the current Top 20 hits. He also created *Just What Is It That Makes Today's Homes so Different, so Appealing?* (1956), one of the most recognizable works of Pop Art.[40]

Like Ray Johnson, Richard Hamilton's work demonstrated a great deal of influence from Marcel Duchamp. This influence included a typographic version of Duchamp's *Green Box* in which Hamilton included Duchamp's original notes for *The Bride Stripped Bare by Her Bachelors, Even* as well as exhibition of paintings for the Hanover Gallery that paid homage to Duchamp. After Hamilton and Duchamp became friends in 1962, Hamilton served as curator for the first — and to date only — British exhibition to present Duchamp's work as a retrospective.

Duchamp's influence on Hamilton would also become apparent as Hamilton juxtaposed his work with rock 'n' roll music. While being represented by Robert Fraser in the 1960s, Hamilton created a series of prints titled *Swinging London*, which were based on the arrest of Fraser and Mick Jagger for possession of drugs. This association with the popular music scene in London also led to a friendship with Paul McCartney and ultimately to Hamilton's design for the Beatles' "White Album," which was conceived by him as a form of *conceptual art* (obviously influenced by his work with Duchamp).

Hamilton's original concept for this album cover was for it to have no "design" at all, just a white cover that has in some way been defaced, and for the albums to be consecutively numbered so as to create a limited edition of a work of art.[41] According to Pete Shotton, it was McCartney's idea to stamp each copy of the album with an individual number (as if each were a fine lithograph) and hold a lottery as a marketing gimmick, but he changed his mind thinking it would seem cheap.[42]

While *Sgt. Pepper's Lonely Hearts Club Band* is considered rightfully to be the groundbreaking *concept* album, and the *White Album* is generally thought to be a retreat, the music on the *White Album* moves more dramatically into the current *conceptual* experimentation and even *anti-music* taking place in the world of fine or high art. Certainly, John Lennon's "Revolution 9" (influenced by conceptual artist Yoko Ono) takes popular music directly into this world. And John Lennon knew what he was doing, stating: "*This* is the music of the future. You can forget all the rest of the shit we've done — this is *it! Everybody* will be making this stuff one day — you don't even have to know how to play a musical instrument to do it!"[43]

But this did not come out of nowhere. Other songs, such as "I Am the Walrus," "Happiness Is a Warm Gun," and even the seemingly inane "Hello Goodbye," are all works pushing popular music into enigmatic realms; "A Day in the Life" has the unforgettable twenty-four bar full orchestra (etc.) climax that originated from Paul knowing about similar experiments in serious conceptual music.

Offerings by the Beatles, in conjunction with Blake and Hamilton, that contributed to the experimentation of the 1950s and 1960s demonstrate just how much explosion of creative interplay between popular music and serious art forms was occurring at the time. After considering this explosion, it seems tame to suggest that Don McLean's "American Pie" might have lyrics that go beyond the straightforward (or were they?) early rock 'n' roll lyrics about that nostalgic teen world of the fifties, where the major concerns were finding a date for the Saturday night hop, sneaking a cigarette in the bathroom, getting someone to purchase some beer for a clam bake, playing *chicken* in a hotrod detailed with yellow flames, or facing the heartbreak of an unfulfilled romance.

By the time "American Pie" came out, rock 'n' roll music had grown up, and even people with no poetic or artistic sensitivity were hearing complex double entendres, symbolism, analogies, and serious commentary on the political and social issues. Consider, for example, Vice President Spiro Agnew's insistence (supported by the FCC) that "Puff the Magic Dragon," recorded by Peter, Paul, and Mary, 1962, was about smoking marijuana. Or the banning of The Byrds' "Eight Miles High," 1966[44]; the Doors' "Light My Fire," 1967[45]; the Beatles' "A Little Help from my Friends," 1967; John Denver's "Rocky Mountain High," 1973; and Jefferson Airplane's "White Rabbit," 1967, for the same reason.

In 1965 the Kinks released "A Well Respected Man," one of many they would write and perform condemning the hypocritical, shallow world of the middle and upper classes.

In the same year, Barry McGuire's "Eve of Destruction" would express frustration over the Civil Rights Movement, the Nuclear Arms Race, the Cold War, the Vietnam War, and the general social, political, and economic world of the time. The following year, it would be recorded by both The Grass Roots and Jan and Dean. Paul McCartney's "Blackbird," 1968, was also about the American Civil Rights Movement,[46] as were recordings of such folk songs as "We Shall Overcome" by Peter, Paul and Mary.

The Rolling Stones' "Street Fighting Man," 1970; the Beatles' "Revolution," 1968, and Bobby Darin's "A Simple Song of Freedom," 1969, were all commentaries on war and specifically the Vietnam War. John Lennon would become even more blunt in songs such as "'Power to the People' and 'Imagine,'" 1971.

In the same year, The Who would take rock 'n' roll into the more serious world of *opera* in their concept double album *Tommy*, which provides a musical rendition of the story of a boy who becomes psychosomatically deaf, dumb and blind when traumatized after his parents attempt to cover up the murder of his mother's lover by his father, who had been reported missing in action with the military and believed to be dead. While suffering from his psychosomatic condition, Tommy experiences abuse from his cousin Kevin and his Uncle Ernie, is exposed to hallucinogens and sex by a prostitute known as the Acid Queen, and develops a knack for playing pinball, all while his parents seek out different methods of curing him. After various attempts to treat Tommy's condition, the smashing of a mirror by his mother does the trick, and Tommy eventually becomes a messianic figure who preaches a path to enlightenment based on this "miracle cure" and the visions he had while he was deaf, dumb, and blind.

Peter Townshend is the main composer of it, and he claims to have drawn his inspiration from the teachings of Indian spiritual leader Meher Baba. In addition to several theatrical performances of it since its release, a film was made in 1975, and *Tommy* represents but one part of a pattern of experimentation that has not only accompanied, but seemingly guided Townshend, Roger Daltrey, and the Who since their formation in the mid–1960s.

In 1967, James Rado, Gerome Ragni and Galt MacDermot premiered *Hair: The American Tribal Love-Rock Musical,* which depicted a "tribe" of hippies from New York City who must deal with the ramifications of the United States' involvement in the Vietnam War. More specifically, amid the group's counterculture lifestyle, their leader, Claude, faces a decision between choosing draft resistance when he is conscripted for duty in the war or reporting for duty and thereby compromising the pacifist ideals in which he and his "tribe" believed.

Arlo Guthrie's "Alice's Restaurant Massacre," 1967, a lengthy, talking anti-war song, would become a movie in 1969.

And I've barely mentioned Bob Dylan! Go online and see how hard people are working to sort out his lyrics to such songs as "Ballad of a Thin Man," "All Along the Watchtower," "Mr. Tambourine Man," "A Hard Rain's a Gonna Fall," or even such a seemingly simple song as "Quinn the Eskimo."

Notes

1. Atlantic Records, 1974.

2. Robert G. Pielke, *You Say You Want a Revolution: Rock Music in American Culture* (Chicago: Nelson-Hall, 1986), 23.

3. 1932. See John R. Lane, *Stuart Davis: Art and Art Theory* (Brooklyn: Brooklyn Museum, 1978) for more discussion.

4. 1938, Williamsburg Housing Project, New York.

5. 1939.

6. 24" × 30", 1940, Collection of Mr. and Mrs. Milton Lowenthal, New York. Another work, *The Mellow Pad* (26" × 42", 1945–1951, in the collection of Mr. and Mrs. Milton Sowenthal, New York) has an even more frenetic visual jazz rhythm.

7. H. H. Arnason, *History of Modern Art: Painting, Sculpture, Architecture* (New York: Abrams, 1968), 425–6.

8. Oil on canvas, 50" × 50", 1942–1943, Museum of Modern Art, New York.

9. Oil on canvas, 70¼" × 70¼", 1943–1944, Mr. and Mrs. Burton Tremaine, Meriden, Connecticut.

10. Quote comes from Arnason, 408.

11. "Notes d'un peintre," *La Grande Revue* (Paris), Dec. 25, 1908, 731–45; rpt., Alfred H. Barr, Jr., *Matisse: His Art and His Public* (New York: Museum of Modern Art, 1951; rpt., "Notes of a Painter," Herschel B. Chipp, ed. *Theories of Modern Art: A Source Book* by Artists and Critics (Berkeley, CA: University of California Press, 1969), 134.

12. Sam Hunter, John Jacobus, and Daniel Wheeler, *Modern Art: Painting, Sculpture, Architecture*, 3rd ed. (New York: Prentice Hall and Harry N. Abrams, 1992), 222.

13. See Pierre Schneider, *Matisse* (New York: Rizzoli, 1984), 666.

14. See Myron Schwartzman, *Romare Bearden: His Life and Art* (New York: Harry N. Abrams, 1990).

15. Hunter, 378.

16. An early drawing of Berman depicts jazz musician Bulee "Slim" Gaillard with a hypodermic syringe in his eye and blood streaming down from the corner of his mouth. DeFeo acknowledges such influences in her painting *Doctor Jazz* (1958), a picture of a large detail of a liquor bottle with a heart in its center.

For more discussion of the "Beat" scene, refer to Thomas Albright, *Art in the San Francisco Bay Area, 1945–1980: An Illustrated History* (Berkeley, CA: University of California Press, 1985).

But Berman's jazz iconography barely touches on his life-long inclusion of popular music, including numerous works centered on rock 'n' roll. His song Tosh says that "he would play music consistently in his studio — Charlie Parker, Bach, Moroccan trance music, the Beatles, John Cage, Albert King, and Motown. I specifically remember him playing The Supremes 'Baby Love' and The Kinks 'Who's Next in Line' [sic, actually the title is 'Who'll Be the Next in Line'] over and over again," (Wallace Berman and Tosh Berman, *Wallace Berman: Support the Revolution* (Amsterdam: Institute of Contemporary Art, 1992), 76). In attempting to combine his spiritual values with everyday objects, he employed a Verifax (an old copying machine) to create collages that included strongly symbolic images, and such popular music stars as Bob Dylan, The Rolling Stones, George Harrison, and Ringo Starr. He also included images of Janis Joplin, James Brown, and the Rolling Stones in a film completed in 1966.

For more on Wallace Berman, see Colin Gardner, "The Influence of Wallace Berman on the Visual Arts," and Christopher Knight, "Instant Artifacts: The Art of Wallace Berman," both in Wallace Berman and Tosh Berman, *Support the Revolution: Wallace Berman* (Amsterdam: Institute of Contemporary Art, 1992); For more on Jay DeFeo, see David S. Rubin, *Jay Defeo — Selected Works: Past and Present* (San Francisco: San Francisco Art Institute, 1984).

17. This work is reproduced in Helen Harrison, *Larry Rivers* (New York: Harper & Row, 1984). Larry Rivers also designed the album cover for *Jack Teagarden and Trombone*, Columbia Records, 1960.

18. Ray Johnson Biography, *Ray Johnson Estate*, accessed September 10, 2012, http://www.rayjohnsonestate.com/biography/.

19. Ibid.

20. Ibid.

21. See John A. Walker, *Cross-overs: Art into Pop/Pop into Art* (New York: Methuen & Co., 1987); Marco Livingstone, *Pop-Art: A Continuing History* (New York: Harry N. Abrams, 1990); Christin J. Mamiya, *Pop-Art and Consumer Culture* (Austin, TX: University of Texas Press, 1992), 74. It is generally agreed that the discussion among the Independent Group first used the phrase, "Pop-Art." See also *Ray Johnson's Bunny* at "Ray Johnson: Father of Mail Art 1927–1995" accessed April 25, 2010, http://www.actlab.utexas.edu/emma/Gallery/galleryjohnsonpix.html, and *The Detroit Artists Monthly* Interview at Jim Pallas, untitled Web page, accessed April 25, 2010, http://www.jpallas.com/hh/rj/DAMintervw-RayJ.html.

22. Collage, ink wash, paint, photograph, mounted on board, 11" × 8¾", in the collection of William S. Wilson, New York.

23. David Bourdon, *Warhol* (New York: Harry N. Abrams, 1989), 110. He also notes that Warhol earned his living as a commercial illustrator during these partially by designing record album covers for RCA Victor and Columbia Records, p. 33; and discusses a series of drawings exhibited at the Bodley Gallery, titled *Andy Warhol: The golden slipper Show or Shoes in America*, which consisted of drawings of imaginary shoes of celebrates, including Elvis Presley, p. 51. Patrick S. Smith, *Warhol's Art and Films* (Ann Arbor, MI: UMI Research Press, 1986), pp. 20–21, highlights oil canvas entitled *Rock & Roll*, a portrayal of a woman relaxing in a chair, and smiling while listening to music.

24. See David Bourdon; Kynaston McShine, *Andy Warhol: A Retrospective* (New York: Museum of Modern Art, 1989); and Henry Geldzahler and Robert Rosenblum, *Andy Warhol: Portraits of the Seventies and Eighties* (London: Anthony d'Offay Gallery, 1993).

25. David S. Rubin's *It's Only Rock and Roll: Rock and Roll Currents in Contemporary Art* (New York: Prestel, 1995) presents 154 works by contemporary artists that incorporate rock 'n' roll elements, and offers an extended discussion of the interactions. See Lucy R. Lippard, ed., *Pop Art* (New York: Praeger, 1966) and Mario Amaya, *Pop Art ... And After* (New York: Viking, 1965) for discussions from the time period and some reproductions of the works.

26. Oil, magna, canvas, 68" × 68", Mr. And Mrs. C. B. Wright, Seattle, Washington; rpt., Amaya, *Pop Art*.

27. Livingstone. 42.

28. Ibid.

29. Oil on canvas, 29½" × 8½", 1957, Pallant House Gallery, Chichester, UK.

30. See Walker, 39–41; Livingstone; and Rubin, *It's Only Rock and Roll*.
Rubin suggests that British artist David Hockney may well have been responding to Blake's paintings in 1960–61, when Hockney, who is homosexual, painted a work in homage to pop singer Cliff Richard, entitled *Doll Boy*. Blake was certainly influential on Derek Boshier, who once shared a studio with him, and who included in his folio many commercial images, including Buddy Holly (graphite, 8" × 9¼", 1962, owned by artist) and Bill Haley (graphite, 8" × 9¼", 1962, owned by artist).

Other artists of the time employing rock 'n' roll images and personalities in their work include John Chamberlain (famous for his sculptures created by welding automobile parts together), who did a series of *Rock and Roller* paintings titled after such rock 'n' roll stars as Dion, Elvis, the Beach Boys, the Kinks, the Righteous Brothers, and the Supremes. (see: Julia Sylvester, *John Chamberlain: A Catalogue Raisonne of the Sculpture, 1954–1985* (New York: Hudson Hills, 1986)); Robert Stanley, who did a series of silkscreen prints on rock 'n' roll stars for an exhibition held at Bianchini-Brillo, New York, 1965 (see: Suzi Gablik, "Bob Stanley," *ARTnews* 64 no. 3 (May 1965), 18); and Robert Rauschenberg, who included an image of the recently overdosed Janis Joplin in Signs, a visual time capsule done in silkscreen, 1970.

From 1973 into the 1980s, Annie Leibovitz created a similar chronicling of the popular counterculture of rock 'n' roll, combining humor, social commentary, and a concern for artistic representation and questioning in her photographs for *Rolling Stone*, beginning with famous photos of John Lennon, and including later final photos of him in December 8, 1980, only hours before his death. (See: Annie Leibovitz, *Annie Leibovitz: Photographs 1970–1990* (New York: Harper Collins, 1991).

From 1967 to 1971, Archie Rand produced *The Letter Paintings*, where he juxtaposed the names of lesser known musicians (this choice seen by John Yau as a satire on Warhol's embracement of the super-stars, and brightly colored paintings of various materials; and so the ironies spiral upward, puns building on puns. (quoted in Rubin, *It's Only Rock and Roll*, 35) as a satire on Warhol's embracement of the super-stars, and brightly colored paintings of various materials; and so the ironies spiral upward, puns building on puns.

31. Anthony Barnes, "Where's Adolf? The Mystery of Sgt. Pepper Is Solved," *Belfast Telegraph*, 5 February 2007.

32. William J. Dowlding, *Beatlesongs* (New York: Fireside, 1989), 159–60.

33. Max Weinberg, with Robert Santelli, *The Big Beat: Conversations with Rock's Greatest Drummers* (New York: Hal Leonard, 1984); rpt., Dowlding, 159–60.

34. Sheff, David. "Playboy Interview with John Lennon and Yoko Ono," *Playboy* (January 1981).

35. Derek Taylor, *It Was Twenty Years Ago Today* (New York: Fireside, 1987); rpt., Dowlding, 156.

36. Ibid.

37. Neville Stannard, *The Long and Winding Road: A History of the Beatles on Record* (New York: Avon, 1984; Derek Taylor; Dowlding, 157–8).

38. Marco Zanella, "Peter Blake about Oasis' *Stop the Clocks* image," *Oasis Blues: The Italian Milan Site for Pure Beady Eye, Oasis, City, and England Fans*, 13 November 2010, accessed September 10, 2012, http://www.oasisblues.com/2010/11/peter-blake-about-oasis-stop-clocks.html.

39. Mike Chapple, "Pop Art Pioneer Marks 2008," *Liverpool Daily Post*, May 26, 2006, 3.

40. Livingstone; See also, Walker; Mamiya, 74.

41. Stannard, rpt., 220; Dowlding.

42. Pete Shotton and Nicholas Schaffner, *John Lennon: In My Life* (New York: Stein and Day, 1983); rpt., Dowlding, 220.

43. Ibid., 249.

44. See John Einarson, *Mr. Tambourine Man: The Life and Legacy of The Byrds' Gene Clark.* (San Francisco: Backbeat, 2005), 82–5; and Johnny Rogan, *The Byrds: Timeless Flight Revisited: The Sequel*, 4th ed. (London: Rogan House, 1998), 158–63.

45. Ian Inglis, "Responses to Censorship in the USA: Acquiescence, Withdrawal and Resistance," in *Shoot the Singer!: Music Censorship Today*, ed. Marie Korpe (London: Zed, 2004), 178; Michael Hicks, *Sixties Rock: Garage, Psychedelic, and Other Satisfactions* (Urbana, IL: University of Illinois Press, 1999), 83; and Peter K. Hogan, and Chris Charlesworth, ed. *The Complete Guide to the Music of the Doors* (New York: London: Omnibus, 1994), 30.

46. See Ian MacDonald, *Revolution in the Head: The Beatles' Records and the Sixties*, 2d revised ed. (London: Pimlico, 2005).

7

A Generation Lost in Space
Robert McParland

Don McLean's *American Pie* begins in memory and nostalgia: "A long, long time ago, I can still remember how that music used to make me smile." Optimism and hope fill these first words: "I knew if I had a chance" says the speaker; with his music he could set the world dancing. Forty years later, we can look back at the nostalgia embodied in that song: a reflection on music and culture, from the 1950s through the 1960s. With a broad G-chord and a tenor voice, the song seems to begin so optimistically, suggesting music that could make people "happy for awhile." Yet, a chill soon descends: "February made me shiver." There is "bad news on the doorstep" that stuns the speaker into immobility. He recalls "the day the music died." The smile is gone when we get to the girl who sang the blues, or to the man at the sacred store. The music will no longer play. There is a sense of loss. Perhaps, one begins to feel, this is a song about the loss of innocence. In the distance, one hears Irish laments and ballads. Yet, liveliness plays here, as if in resistance to the lament in the lyric. The G-C-G-D chord pattern steadily picks up energy, as the imagery spills forth all those symbols of late fifties rock 'n' roll and sixties pop. Pausing on E minor and A 7th chords, followed by another E minor and a D7th chord, the chorus welcomes the song's audience into a community of singing and sweeps into the first of its energetic and sometime lyrically cryptic verses.

"American Pie" is a celebration of community and nostalgia in the midst of an uncertain future. One is asked if he or she wrote the book of love, has faith in God above, and still believes in rock 'n' roll. Can music save the mortal soul? The singer reminds us that the coat may have been borrowed from James Dean but the voice "came from you and me." Indeed, the voice that comes from us, from community, is the one that collectively sings the chorus here: "*we* were singing." In folk song tradition, it is our voice, with McLean's voice, that sings those alliterative "dirges in the dark the day the music died." It is this collective voice that also moves together into the memorable chorus. We say "bye, bye," as in farewell, to Miss American Pie. The All-American Chevy seeks the levee, but encounters something like T.S. Eliot's wasteland: "the levee was dry." As in Eliot's poem, snippets of song seek to find a way to remedy this. Hope and a despairing blues rub together, musically and lyrically.

McLean does make people "happy for awhile." This is the folksinger's public role: for despite it all, there is an assertion against demise. The chorus may be conceived of as a rousing drinking song, in the manner of an old English or Celtic ballad. Amid the drinking whiskey and rye, the rollicking piano and rhythmic guitar belie the nostalgic, at times pessimistic, lament of the lyrics. A nostalgic sadness returns in the slower sections, where the music takes a breath: "I met a girl who sang the blues and I asked her for some happy news. She just smiled and turned away." But then there we are, back in that energetic chorus again. There is affirmation here, despite the pessimism. However lagging, idealism is not lost. The world may be going to hell but we're going to make music anyway. Join together with me, the singer seems to say, and raise a toast to the sky.

Whether consciously or not, Don McLean has structured much of his song in tercets. The song verses frequently play out in threes, as in the triple rhymes before "the day the music died" (cried, bride, inside [...] bronkin' buck, pickup truck, out of luck). The lyric ends with the Trinity ("the three men I admire most"). We encounter these threes early on, as the lyric begins on two lines of six syllables ("A long, long time ago [...]"), followed by a line of nine syllables. All of these are divisible by three. This pattern loosens on the next few lines but returns with two successive nine syllable lines: "But February made me shiver [...]" followed by the six syllable "Bad news on the doorstep" and the flowing "I" eliding into another six: "couldn't take one more step." The chorus begins with two long strums "bye ... bye" followed by "Miss American Pie": a six syllable line that concludes this rhyme of three. "Chevy" and "levee" lead us to "dry" and "whiskey and rye" and "die": a somewhat repetitious locked rhyme that seems stuck in space and time but is carried forward by a broad vocal and a tensely coiled and building musical momentum.

With a tempo shift, the verse launches into two questions (Did you...? Do you...?), ending on a third line with the long "o" in "so." The three-line structure repeats with three questions, landing on "dance real slow." Here the lyric connects "rock and roll" and the spiritual air of "mortal soul" and a slow, intimate dance that seems shattered in disappointment that is punctuated rhythmically: "Well, I know that you're in love with him." For a lament, however, the music takes off quite spiritedly and lands in the rousing chorus.

McLean's song was part myth, part history: a look back over his shoulder to a perhaps simpler time in American life. He was singing the song of "everyman" — or every woman. We remember history in a similar way. "Mr. Everyman," Carl Becker wrote in his 1931 address to the American Historical Association, responds to history as part fact, part myth. "The history he imaginatively recreates as an artificial extension of his personal experience will inevitably be an engaging blend of fact and fancy, a mythical adaptation of that which actually happened."[1] This suggests that we imagine history collaboratively, constantly redefining it. McLean's song and our interpretations of it are both involved in this kind of redefinition. The past becomes part of our collective identity in the present.

McLean is the storyteller for the collective identity of a community, much like Homer was for the Greeks, conveying here a musical "epic" of seven or more minutes. His song speaks to the culture: particularly the baby boom generation emerging with the late 1950s, the 1960s, into the early years of the 1970s. In 1977, Fred Davis wrote in the *Journal of Popular Culture*: "clearly if one can speak of a collective identity crisis, of a radical discontinuity in people's sense of who and what they are, the late sixties and early seventies came about as close to realizing that condition as can be imagined."[2] McLean's song positions a kind of community of song against this disintegration. They may sing of everything being lost and going to hell, but in doing so they affirm solidarity and promise. "McLean has brought us soundly and safely back from his nostalgic reverie," wrote Tom Nolan in *Rolling Stone* in his review of *Homeless Brother* in January 1975.[3] But wasn't the nostalgic reverie the point?

"American Pie" is a form of memorialization. It is a representational form that propagates and perpetuates memory while speaking of kinship and of community. "We were all there in one place, a whole generation lost in space" may recall Woodstock specifically, or some less definable air of solidarity. The music — itself a kind of memory for listeners, who recall a pattern and anticipate what is to come — carries this memorial, along with this reminiscence in lyrics. It romps, almost joyously, against the regretful lyric, ever circling back to the familiar chorus, returning to recollection.

In recent years, that sense of connection through memory with a collective history has been considered from various angles by Maurice Halbwachs, Pierre Nora, Dominick La Capra, David W. Blight, Geoff Ely, John Bodnar, Jay Winter and many others.[4] McLean's song may be examined through what Maurice Halbwachs has termed "collective memory," although this is not easy to pin down in a clear definition.[5] What has this to do with national memory, or individual memory? How is this related to the terms "popular memory" used by Geoff Ely, or to "cultural memory" in the writing of John Bodnar? Where might we go with these notions when we consider the artifact of a song? Pierre Nora develops the idea in his study of the collective memory of France, rethinking the French past.[6] Dominick La Capra explores holocaust trauma and memory. These models seem not to exactly fit in this case — unless one reflects upon revolution or trauma in the sixties. Yet, it is important "to look at how societies remember, their common myths, to explore public collective historical consciousness," as David W. Blight, writing on the American Civil War, says.[8] Historian Bernard Bailyn has said of memory, "It's relation to the past is an embrace ... ultimately emotional, not intellectual."[9] How does our society remember Don McLean's "American Pie" on an emotional level? How do we remember our cultural history of the 1950s to the 1970s and after through this song?

We cannot know what a songwriter has intended, only how we receive a song. Given this song, we make meaning from it. However, it is clear that historical and personal conditions have inspired "American Pie." The emotion and memory evoked by this song comes from the associations that listeners bring to it. This is clearly an elegy for something that once was and it speaks to the spirit of people who are changing, people who see a shifting of the cultural landscape. A hopeful world is vanishing, a dream has come undone. As we listen, the structures of McLean's music are brought into memory. We experience a pattern of successive events musically, as well as lyrically. This music unfolds within its folk music style, built upon a few major chords (G-C-D) and a movement amid a few minor chords (E minor, A minor). We come to expect these patterns and, if we have listened to much folk music or pop music, we respond to what Leonard Meyer calls "the general system of beliefs relevant to the style of the work."[10] Meyer, in *Music and Emotion*, offered a cognitivist view of how listeners respond to the unexpected phrase and "fit it into" what comes to be "customary or expected progressions of sound."[11] Emotions change from listener to listener and, as Meyer observes, "The difference lies in the relationship of the stimulus and the responding individual."[12]

If we are to begin to understand the cultural memory that McLean evokes, it is to the lyric, with all it allusions, that we have to look. "A long, long time ago, I can still remember" begins the introduction: a memory that shivers, newspaper in hand, recalling the passing of Buddy Holly. The first verse proper of "American Pie" begins in questions. The first — "Did you write the book of love?" — is followed immediately by four more. An E minor chord crashes down on "Well, I *know* that you're in love with him" and what follows are images of the fifties, junior high or high school: dancing in the gym, teenage bronkin' bucks, pink carnations, pickup trucks, James Dean and rock 'n' roll. The song lyric moves chronologically into the 1960s, where the world begins to unravel further. It is "Helter-skelter," "eight miles high and falling fast," "with the jester on the sidelines in a cast." The Beatles, the Byrds, and Dylan have merged in an obscure lyric, on a playing field where "the marching band refused to yield" and some revelation has come. "Do you *recall* [my emphasis] what was revealed the day the music died?"

What is it that we recall? Are we saddened by the evanescence of a dream, the loss of a more optimistic era? Has hope been punctured by the Vietnam War, the loss of the Kennedys and Martin Luther King, the tragic inversion of Woodstock hopes at Altamont? Do we, the audience, chime to disappointment here, or sound a lament for the loss of heroes, counterculture co-opted, or the greening of America gone to seed? What is the "music" that has died? The girl who sang the blues has smiled and turned away. The church bells are all broken. The Trinity has caught the last train for the coast. We are drifting with their exodus, on a verse slowing proceeding to a pause before the final chorus: "And they were singing...." Reverently, drunkenly, nostalgically we raise a toast to their disappearance. For "American Pie" always brings the listener back around to the chorus. If "the jester" has sung in "a voice that came from you and me," the folk sing-along of the chorus calls this voice forth again. And so we sing, "Bye, bye, Miss American Pie."

American Pie is clearly the work of a folksinger and a song-poet of sensibility. The markings of the folksinger's craft are all there, even for those who had not heard *Tapestry*, McLean's first recording, and for those who might miss his self-titled subsequent album, or his next offering, *Homeless Brother*. *American Pie*, the album on which McLean's "epic" appears, is richly textured and the songs thematically overlap with the title cut. It is clear that McLean has left behind the suburban houses of New Rochelle, has hopped off the Clearwater Sloop that floats on the Hudson, and has begun to explore new terrain on this album.

The front cover of *American Pie* features the singer's thumb — lifted into the foreground, thumbs up — adorned with a star with a flag's red, white and blue. The mostly red back album cover shows the artist seated with his guitar — unclipped strings flying off at curious angles, as did some of his songs.

On "Crossroads," the generation lost in space becomes personal. Some people who seek the road to set them free have become lost. The singer identifies with them. Even so, there is resolve at this intersection. In the paradox of having nothing to remember or to forget, the singer claims he has no regrets. Yet, he says that he is tangled and that he has changed. One walks those roads guided by some fate, or by choice, whatever one's plans. There is some lament and a drift to that final chord.

A similar vacancy greets us on "Empty Chairs" — in those clothes that drape and fall across them. This reminds us of the regret we hear behind the up tempo verve of "American Pie." The nostalgia of *American Pie* for the

1950s and 1960s is also met by a curious fortune teller, poised perhaps to prognosticate the future, even as "American Pie" laments the past. Could Sister Fatima, a market fortune teller, predict the future? Would her vision of tomorrow be any better than that of the good old boys of "American Pie," who are drinking whiskey and rye?

In the midst of this collection we hear the reflective "Winterwood" and the tender portrait of "Vincent." With assonance and consonance from the first line, McLean's "Vincent" musically and lyrically takes us somewhere within that biography alone cannot go. The song itself is a painting, moving to an intimate understanding of the anguish and astonishing gift of Vincent van Gogh. We are brought into contact with the artist and the troubled humaneness of the man. In McLean's plaintive tenor and rich poetic imagery, we enter a poignant portrayal of Vincent. There is deep identification with the artist in society and a striking portrait of despair and sympathy. From the G major chord that begins the song, the melancholy tones of a darkened soul are ever present. Directed by the imagery, we also observe a summer day. The painter's craft is met by the songwriter's lyric with vivid pictures of the land-scape. It all so well captures the inner world and keen subjectivity of a modern artist. We meet the loneliness of Van Gogh and are asked to consider how carefully he worked at his art with many preparations. We are left with what Vincent has given and communicated to us. We are led, as through a gallery, to the bleak and stark canvas of McLean's third verse, where empty halls echo vacancy. He evokes sympathy for Vincent, as well as for all of humanity.

Finally, drawing upon Lee Hays for the round "By the Waters of Baby-lon," Don McLean evokes community again. On the one hand, he calls upon recent folk traditions of the Weavers and sing-a-longs. On the other, this song embraces a more ancient tradition of the lament of the Jews in captivity. Again, the generation lost in space encounters its exile and, in singing, gathers, even amid lamentation, to restore hope. The lament of a generation, for the sixties of Vietnam War dragging on, is evoked again. The round is communal, but it is also cyclical, as is the return of memory. The wheel of fortune turns. We say farewell: "Bye, bye, Miss American Pie," yet the chorus comes back again.

Notes

1. Carl Becker, "Every Man His Own Historian," *American Historical Review* 37 (January 1932): 229.

2. Fred Davis, "Nostalgia, Identity, and the Current Nostalgia Wave," *Journal of Popular Culture* 11 (September 1977): 421.

3. Tom Nolan, "Review of *Homeless Brother*." *Rolling Stone*, January 16, 1975, 52.

4. Maurice Halbwachs, *On Collective Memory*, trans. and ed. Lewis A. Koser (Chicago: University of Chicago Press, 1992); Pierre Nora, *Realms of Memory*, ed. Lawrence D. Kritzman, trans. Arthur Goldhammer (New York: Columbia University Press, 1992); Dominick La Capra, *Writing History, Writing Trauma* (Baltimore: Johns Hopkins University Press, 2001); David W. Blight, *Race and Reunion: The Civil War in American Memory* (Amherst, MA: University of Massachusetts Press, 2001); Geoff Ely, "Finding the People's War: Film, British Collective Memory and World War II," *American Historical Review* 106 (June 2001): 818–38; John Bodnar, "*Saving Private Ryan* and Postwar Memory in America," *American Historical Review* 106 (2001): 805–17; Jay Winter, "Film and the Matrix of Memory," *American Historical Review* 106 (2001): 857–66.

5. Halbwachs.

6. Nora.

7. La Capra.

8. Blight, David W. "Historians and 'Memory,'" *Common Place* 2, No. 3 (April 2002), http://www.common-place.org/vol-02/no-03/author.

9. Bernard Bailyn, "Considering the Slave Trade: History and Memory," *The William and Mary Quarterly* 58 (January 2001): 250.

10. Leonard Meyer, *Music and Emotion* (Chicago: University of Chicago Press, 1957), 30.

11. Ibid, 32.

12. Ibid, 13.

8

A Tale of Two Sagas

Raymond I. Schuck

By now, we all know the words: "A long, long time ago, in a galaxy far away, Naboo was under an attack."[1]

Those are one set of the words, anyway, adapted from the film *Star Wars* and used by "Weird Al" Yankovic for his song "The Saga Begins." In their entirety, they're not as well known as Don McLean's "A long, long time ago, I can still remember how that music used to make me smile" from "American Pie," though if you take out one "long," the first two phrases of Yankovic's song have become every bit as well known as "American Pie," due to the immense popularity of the *Star Wars* film series. Meanwhile, even Don McLean has found himself singing Yankovic's parody lyrics to his original "American Pie" song, after his children played Yankovic's version enough that it stuck in his head.[2]

McLean's song "American Pie" interpellates an imagined community, by which I refer to Benedict Anderson's term for a socially constructed group of people who see themselves as members of the group.[3] McLean's imagined community is built on a nostalgic narrative, situated in intertextuality, expressing a construction of United States identity most explicitly acknowledged by the phrase "American Pie." Released 28 years later, Yankovic's song "The Saga Begins" interpellates another imagined community, also built in a nostalgic narrative, situated in intertextuality, expressing a construction of United States identity that is implicit in the mythology embedded in the story about which Yankovic tells us. For McLean, the narrative is one of rock 'n' roll; for Yankovic, the narrative is one of outer space — namely, *Star Wars*. While Yankovic explicitly names his as a saga, both songs are extended narratives of epic romantic tales of understandable heroes that embody the social memories of their respective communities.[4] This essay, then, is the tale of two sagas, with a focus on the latter and how it articulates the former, arguing that the rhetorical success of "Weird Al" Yankovic's "The Saga Begins" demonstrates the usefulness of Don McLean's "American Pie" as a template for telling epic stories based in the intertextual, nostalgic mythologies that define and bring together imagined communities.

Two Imagined Communities

To begin, let's look briefly at the imagined communities that McLean and Yankovic offer. First, McLean's song relies on a community familiar with the development of rock 'n' roll from the late 1950s through 1970. While, as readings in this volume indicate, the song may metaphorically symbolize a multiplicity of meanings, "American Pie" is ultimately still explicitly about music, particularly given that it begins with indication of music making a young man smile and ends with a statement about how "the music died."[5] The song thus hails readers to a community that recognizes the development of music from the time of the beginning of the story, when the narrator is smiling, through the time of the story's end, when the narrator feels sadness.

Along the way, the song relies on intertextual references to inform the listener that the "music" it references is rock 'n' roll music. As the lyric analyses by Joseph E. Burns and Ray Schuck that appear in this volume both demonstrate, the song is replete with references to artists, songs, and events starting around the time of the plane crash in 1959 that killed Buddy Holly and continuing through the writing and recording of "American Pie" in the early 1970s. As Burns and Schuck both demonstrate, some of these references are subtle, while others are readily apparent, and still others are open to various interpretations. A great number of the references ask the listener to recall the development of rock 'n' roll from late 1950s' songs like the Monotones' "The Book of Love" and Holly's "That'll Be the Day" through the British invasion headed by the Beatles and the Rolling Stones to the popularity of the likes of Bob Dylan and The Byrds, along with the development of mass rock music events like the Altamont Music Festival near the end of the story. Additionally, all of these references require cultural capital on the part of the listener to understand the story McLean is telling. The listener must know the intertextual references, in their varying levels of explicitness, to be hailed to remember the events to which McLean alludes, to feel the emotional reactions to these events that McLean relates throughout the song, and ultimately to identify with the community that has grown up, like the young man in the song, through the development of rock 'n' roll music from the late 1950s through the early 1970s.

These intertextual references and the accompanying emotions to which the song alludes also hail the listener into an imagined community through nostalgia. That the song's narrator's emotions go from the happiness conveyed by his smile to the sadness conveyed by the passing of the music that he loved suggests that the narrator laments that passing. Through this lament, McLean offers a sentiment of nostalgia. As other essays in this volume have indicated, with references to youth the narrator of "American Pie" remembers fondly the time before both he and rock 'n' roll grew up, invoking a kind of imagined innocence that often accompanies nostalgic memories. That the narrator sees this youthful innocence as lost in the past provides the basis for the nostalgic sadness he evokes. Identification with this nostalgic loss provides the basis for identification with the imagined community that the song hails — a community all the more imagined because of its basis in the imagined sense of innocence that McLean expresses. This community largely constitutes a generational community, most explicitly hailed, depending on one's interpretation, when McLean sings "a generation lost in space."[6] As such, the imagined community is one built around memories of growing up as a member of a particular generation in United States history (namely, the Baby Boomers), with the development of rock 'n' roll recognized as one of the most significant cultural developments, if not the most significant cultural development, associated with growing up during this time period. The rock 'n' roll artists, songs, and events constitute the major cultural texts that, as evidenced in Robert McParland's essay in this volume, fill the collective memory of the Baby Boomer generation. Indeed, the history of rock 'n' roll itself can be seen as one collective, diffuse cultural text that serves as this generational touchstone.

The naming of the song as "American Pie" explicitly links the sentiments and narrative of the song to United States national identity. As such, McLean suggests that the narrative constitutes more than just a personal nostalgic tale and that the story of rock 'n' roll that guides the personal tale also constitutes more than just the story of the development of music. Both are explicitly aligned with a story of the United States during the time period. McLean's equation of rock 'n' roll history with American history is not unfounded. Well before McLean wrote the song, cultural commentators had suggested a connection between rock 'n' roll and the American experience, and the mythology of rock 'n' roll has been explicitly linked to the development of United States history and identity.[7] McLean's imagined community is thus a national community, recognizing the importance of rock 'n' roll for defining United States American identity and spirit. The loss of the music that McLean laments, then, works within the symbolic tradition of the American jeremiad, which, as Sacvan Bercovitch explains, "offers a state-of-the-covenant address" that reminds the community of its importance to and exceptionality in the world and cautions against turning away from the "errand" — or task at hand —

that the country is supposed to fulfill.[8] "American Pie" laments not just the loss of youth, the loss of time, and the loss of the music that the narrator loves; it also laments the loss of the spirit of rock 'n' roll that the narrator equates with the likes of Buddy Holly in the late 1950s and which the narrator sees as having become lost by the beginning of the 1970s — the same spirit that has made rock 'n' roll so fundamental to United States American identity. By virtue of such a connection, the song suggests a sense of loss of United States American spirit. The mythology of United States American identity, buttressed by the mythology of rock 'n' roll, becomes the basis for the nostalgia for an idyllic past to which the song refers, and the connection of that mythology to this nostalgia makes this narrative a song about a national imagined community as well as a generational one.

In "The Saga Begins," "Weird Al" Yankovic's imagined community works along some similar lines as "American Pie," drawing on familiarity with a prominent cultural text that is embedded within both generational nostalgia to recapture youth and mythology of United States identity. In this case, the cultural text is the *Star Wars* franchise, which began in 1977, then after a 16-year hiatus, returned in 1999 with *The Phantom Menace*— the film whose plot Yankovic recounts. The understanding of the meaning of the song that is necessary to identify with the imagined community relies on understanding of the story of *Star Wars* and, particularly for the full extent of the song's humor, the significance of the film series as a cultural text.

This community, like McLean's, is hailed by intertextual references. Most fully, the song depends on listeners' knowledge of the details of the film *Star Wars Episode I: The Phantom Menace*, which is the story that the song relates. These details include recognition of references to characters like Anakin Skywalker, Qui-Gon Jinn, and Jar Jar Binks; places like Naboo, Coruscant, and Tatooine; and plot details like how Jedi Knights Qui-Gon Jinn and Obi-Wan Kenobi meet up with Queen Amidala on Naboo, how Jinn and Kenobi find Anakin on Tatooine and take him to Coruscant to meet the Jedi Council, how Yoda forbids Anakin Jedi training, and how the group returns to Naboo to fight against the Trade Federation's invasion of the planet. As someone unfamiliar with the film who reads that sentence might attest, all of those details just mentioned require cultural capital in the form of knowledge about the various specific features of the film in order to understand the song and its meaning, including the parody that constitutes the basis for the song. Beyond that film, though, the song requires cultural capital in the form of knowledge about the *Star Wars* film series. While a viewer might understand some meaning of characters like Yoda and Obi-Wan Kenobi and places like Tatooine by just watching Episode I, these individuals and places gain further meaning when one understands the parts they play in the other films in the series. Additionally, when Yankovic mentions that Anakin "may be Vader someday later"[9] and that Anakin is "probably going to marry [Queen Amidala] someday,"[10] readers are asked to recognize the significance of these details — namely that this film is depicting the origins of the main antagonist from the previous three films and that the friendship developing between Anakin and Amidala will lead to their coupling, which produces the twins Luke and Leia who are main protagonists from the first three films. All of these various references depend on the listener's recognition of them; that recognition becomes the basis for listeners taking up positions within an imagined community built around identification with Star Wars, whether as devotees of the franchise, fans of the franchise, or just individuals who have seen the films and know the main details of the films.

That imagined community, like the imagined community hailed by McLean, largely constitutes a nostalgic community. While McLean's community grew up watching the development of rock 'n' roll, members of Yankovic's community grew up watching the original three *Star Wars* films, which were released in theaters between 1977 and 1983. At the time of the release of Yankovic's song, which occurred around the same time as the release of Episode I in 1999, a significant number of individuals in this imagined community had seen the original *Star Wars* trilogy as children and now, after more than a decade and a half, were experiencing as adults an opportunity to reconnect with the series by seeing the back story for the original trilogy. Like McLean's cohort who grew up with the development of rock 'n' roll, members of Yankovic's imagined community constituted a generational community, namely of Generation X members for whom *Star Wars* had become one of the defining cultural texts of their time.[11] Unlike McLean's song, though, which offered a sense of sadness over the passing of childhood, the release of Yankovic's song, along with the actual film whose plot the song recounts, offered a different kind of emotional nostalgia. In this case, to borrow from the subtitle of the original *Star Wars* film, the film offered "a new hope." Generation X members who knew growing up that the first three films were labeled parts four, five, and six of the story and that filmmaker George Lucas had invented at least some kind of back story to come before the original trilogy could now realize their hope of seeing the first three parts of the story come to life as films, beginning with *Star Wars Episode I: The Phantom Menace.* In the case of "The Saga Begins," in conjunction with the actual Episode I film, a generation experienced not the end of an imagined childhood, like in "American Pie," but the recapturing of an imagined childhood that had been lost, or at the very least put on hold.

Finally, Yankovic's nostalgia, like McLean's, is built in mythology of American identity — namely, the mythology of the U.S. Western and the

American frontier. As director George Lucas himself has said about developing the *Star Wars* stories,

> It seemed to me that there was no longer a lot of mythology in our society — the kind of stories we tell ourselves and our children, which is the way our heritage is passed down. Westerns used to provide that, but there weren't Westerns anymore. I wanted to find a new form. So I looked around, and tried to figure out where myth comes from. It comes from the borders of society, from out there, from places of mystery — the wide Sargasso Sea. And I thought, Space. Because back then space was a source of great mystery. So I thought, O.K., let's see what we can do with all those elements. I put them all into a bag, along with a little bit of "Flash Gordon" and a few other things, and out fell "Star Wars."[12]

That link of the films to Westerns has been corroborated in analysis of the films since the original release of the first film in the series.[13] Such connections include the films' use of material elements of the West such as guns, clothing reminiscent of cowboys, and open landscapes reminiscent of the deserts of the U.S. West. The connections also include use of ideological elements such as emphasis on adventurous exploration in those open spaces and use of regeneration through violence, which suggests that an act of violence can regenerate society by ridding society of a threat to its order and/or development.[14] These elements of the U.S. West have been consistently articulated as foundational to U.S. American identity, most famously by Frederick Jackson Turner in his "Frontier Thesis" at the Columbian Exposition in 1893, in which he argued that "the existence of an area of free land, its continuous recession, and the advance of American settlement westward, explain American development."[15] Given this connection, the imagined community that Yankovic interpellates — the one built around Lucas' *Star Wars* narratives — is situated squarely within a mythology of United States identity.

The songs are thus similar: intertextual, nostalgic narratives based in mythologies of United States identity. This accounts for some of the success of Yankovic's parody. So too does catchiness. Yet, a fuller rhetorical analysis can show that Yankovic creates a world for the audience to accept. The song constitutes a compelling narrative and, as such, can be analyzed through Walter Fisher's narrative paradigm to recognize the means through which it compels its listeners to accept the world it presents.

FISHER'S NARRATIVE PARADIGM

Fisher suggests that "the narrative perspective entails an analysis of stories: discrete sequences of symbolic actions" and asserts that "the meaning and value of a story are always a matter of how it stands with or against other stories. There is no story that is not embedded in other stories."[16] According to Fisher, narratives work as rhetoric through "good reasons," which are "elements that give warrants for believing or acting in accord with the message fostered by that text."[17] Good reasons work in two ways: through narrative probability (the degree to which a narrative coheres or hangs together, making sense internally) and through narrative fidelity (the degree of truthfulness; the degrees to which it corresponds with the reader's reality or sense of reality outside the story). We can understand what Yankovic articulates through McLean by looking at the narrative fidelity and narrative probability of "The Saga Begins."

NARRATIVE FIDELITY

Narrative fidelity in "The Saga Begins" occurs primarily in three ways. First, "The Saga Begins" is true to McLean's "American Pie." The song maintains this fidelity lyrically by using parallels to "American Pie" both in its overall structure and in specific lines of text within the songs that correspond in wording. In terms of overall structure, "The Saga Begins" follows the same general lyrical meter and form as "American Pie." The verses of "The Saga Begins" maintain the same rhythmic pattern as the verses of "American Pie." Additionally, the meters of the refrains of the two songs are almost entirely identical. Along the way, the intensity of "The Saga Begins" matches that of "American Pie," as both songs become louder as they go along before quieting for the final verse and the refrain that follows. Meanwhile, at numerous points "The Saga Begins" employs specific wording, sounds, and rhyming patterns that directly borrow from "American Pie." This correlation begins with the very first words of each song, which are "A long, long time ago." In another instance, late in the song "The Saga Begins" includes the lines "And the Jedi I admire most, met up with Darth Maul, and now he's toast. I'm still here, but he's a ghost."[18] This corresponds in the song to the place in which "American Pie" includes the lines "And the three men I admire most: the father, son, and the holy ghost, they caught the last train for the coast."[19] Here, Yankovic uses the words "admire most" at the same spot as McLean while also using "toast" and "ghost" for the next two lines to rhyme with "most," where McLean used "ghost" and "coast."

Use of parallel text, sounds, and rhyming patterns is perhaps most prominent, though, in the refrain, which in both songs starts with "My, my." In "The Saga Begins" the line continues with "this here Anakin guy,"[20] while in "American Pie" the line continues with "Miss American Pie."[21] Here, we see use of "this" in the same place as the rhyming "Miss" and use of "guy" to end the line, rhyming with the original's use of "Pie." In the next line of "The

Saga Begins" Yankovic sings, "May be Vader someday later,"[22] which does not use the same sounds, but does use the same rhyming pattern with "Vader" and "later" as "American Pie," where McLean rhymes "Chevy" and "levee" in "drove my Chevy to the levee."[23] From here, "The Saga Begins" then uses words to rhyme with "ie" sound of "Pie" and "guy" for remaining lines, with "fry," "goodbye," and "Jedi"[24] where "American Pie" does the same with "dry," "rye" and "die."[25] By paralleling "American Pie" in these ways, "The Saga Begins" remains narratively faithful to "American Pie," allowing listeners to connect their experiences listening to "American Pie" to corresponding aspects of "The Saga Begins." In the process, "The Saga Begins" relies on another form of intertextuality, since listeners must recognize the allusions occurring in the parallels to "American Pie" in order to understand the connections between the songs and see "The Saga Begins" as a parody of "American Pie."

Drawing on the same themes as "American Pie" also allows "The Saga Begins" to remain faithful to experiences of listening to McLean's song. As mentioned, both songs rely on similar themes of intertextual hailing of an imagined community, nostalgic longing within that community, and U.S. mythology that has significantly defined that community. By drawing on these kinds of themes, "The Saga Begins" captures much of the same kind of feeling as "American Pie." While, as I've argued above, "The Saga Begins" offers a more hopeful narrative to the imagined community than the sense of loss in "American Pie," Yankovic's song does utilize that sense of loss. Most explicitly, among the examples just mentioned, "The Saga Begins" conveys the loss that its narrator, Obi-Wan Kenobi, feels when his mentor and the Jedi he "admired most,"[26] Qui-Gon Jin is killed. The song also conveys Anakin Skywalker's sense of loss in the refrain when it notes him saying goodbye to his mother. More generally, though, "The Saga Begins," alongside its corresponding film *Star Wars Episode I: The Phantom Menace*, tells a story that is the opening act in a narrative of loss of innocence. Namely, listeners to the song and viewers of the film — especially those from the nostalgic community — recognize that the innocent and well-meaning little boy Anakin about whom this story is told will one day turn into the menacing dark lord, Darth Vader, who is the villain of the original trilogy of films. Given that context, while "The Saga Begins" and *Star Wars Episode I: The Phantom Menace* offer hope to the imagined community who grew up with Star Wars by offering them a chance to reconnect with their own childhoods as fans of the film series, the specific narrative of the story told in the film and the song is predicated on the loss of innocence that will come in Episode I's fictional future. Yankovic especially acknowledges this prescience by indicating that Anakin "may be Vader someday later,"[27] which allows "The Saga Begins" to remain consistent with the nostalgic sense of loss of innocence featured in "American Pie."

The Star Wars textual references that allow for that nostalgia to occur also provide bases for "The Saga Begins" to remain faithful to "American Pie," since McLean's song also relies on intertextual references, in his case to the history of rock 'n' roll. That both Star Wars and rock 'n' roll have been prominently culturally tied to U.S. identity allows "The Saga Begins" to embody another level of faithfulness to "American Pie."

That "The Saga Begins" relies on listeners' knowledge of the details of *Star Wars Episode I: The Phantom Menace* as well as how those details relate to the original Star Wars trilogy demonstrates a second way in which "The Saga Begins" exhibits narrative fidelity. In this case, the song remains true to the *Star Wars* film series. This occurs largely because the song tells the story of *Star Wars Episode I: The Phantom Menace* accurately. The song follows the protagonists of the film — Obi-Wan Kenobi and Qui-Gon Jinn — as the film does, beginning with in a conflict with the Trade Federation above the planet Naboo, then heading to the surface of Naboo, heading to the planet Coruscant but getting sidetracked at Tatooine along the way, finally arriving at Coruscant, and then ending up in a battle against the Trade Federation back on Naboo. Along the way, the song introduces Jar Jar Binks, Boss Nass, Queen Amidala, Anakin Skywalker and his mother, Jabba the Hutt, and Yoda and the Jedi Council at the times and in the situations that Kenobi and Jinn encounter them in the film. Additionally, the song provides accurate specific details in retelling the story from the film, including such events as the Trade Federation attacking Naboo; Qui-Gon Jinn and Obi-Wan Kenobi meeting up with Jar Jar Binks, Boss Nass, Queen Amidala, and Anakin Skywalker; Anakin winning a pod race on Tatooine; Anakin leaving his mother to seek training as a Jedi; Yoda forbidding Anakin's training; Anakin helping win the war against the Trade Federation back at Naboo; and Darth Maul killing Qui-Gon Jinn. In these ways, "The Saga Begins" maintains a high degree of narrative fidelity with the film *Star Wars Episode I: The Phantom Menace.*

This fidelity also occurs by the song remaining consistent with the other films from the series. As mentioned, "The Saga Begins" highlights that Anakin Skywalker will become Darth Vader someday, which clearly references events that listeners know will take place to allow the previous three films in the series to occur. Foreshadowing that Anakin and Amidala will marry someday also allows "The Saga Begins" to remain consistent with what Star Wars fans expect will happen in these characters' futures. Meanwhile, the song accurately and appropriately references the Force, the Jedi, Yoda, C-3PO, and more aspects of the Star Wars universe that have already been established in previous films and other Star Wars texts, including such references as allusion to Yoda's "pointy ears"[28] and the midichlorians that provide the basis for the ability to use the Force. In the process, the song maintains fidelity to the Star Wars universe as a whole, including the particular film being recounted, the three films that have preceded this film, and the films that Star Wars fan community members know will be coming.

Finally, "The Saga Begins" maintains narrative fidelity in a third way by remaining true to the style of "Weird Al" Yankovic. This trueness to Yankovic's style occurs in three ways, starting with the fact that "The Saga Begins" is a parody of a famous song. From early on, Yankovic's career success has been built on parodies of famous songs. Yankovic's first album, 1983's *"Weird Al" Yankovic*, featured parodies of prominent popular music songs such as "Ricky" (parodying Toni Basil's "Mickey"), "I Love Rocky Road" (parodying Joan Jett and the Blackhearts' "I Love Rock 'n' Roll"), "Stop Draggin' My Car Around" (parodying Stevie Nicks and Tom Petty's "Stop Draggin' My Heart Around"), "My Bologna" (parodying The Knack's "My Sharona"), and "Another One Rides the Bus" (parodying Queen's "Another One Bites the Dust").[29] In the time between that album and the release of "The Saga Begins," Yankovic had continually maintained his career as a parodist, putting out a string of albums that centered around parodies of songs by the likes of Michael Jackson, Nirvana, Coolio, the Red Hot Chili Peppers, George Harrison, U2, New Kids on the Block, and many other artists. Indeed, Yankovic has become so associated with parodying successful artists that Nirvana lead singer Kurt Cobain reportedly once indicated that he realized Nirvana had "made it" when Yankovic parodied one of the band's songs.[30] In that instance, Yankovic turned Nirvana's breakthrough and biggest hit, "Smells Like Teen Spirit" into "Smells Like Nirvana"—a tune that parodied the image, style, and musical characteristics utilized by Nirvana. As "The Saga Begins" parodies another highly successful song—in this case "American Pie"—it remains faithful to Yankovic's public identity as an artist who consistently engages in that kind of practice.

Secondly, "The Saga Begins" adds to other patterns that have occurred throughout Yankovic's career. Namely, Yankovic has used the Star Wars franchise for a parody before. When parodying the Kinks' "Lola" on his *Dare to Be Stupid* album, Yankovic chose to change the tune to "Yoda" and sing about the character from Luke Skywalker's point of view.[31] Additionally, "The Saga Begins" continues a long line of songs in which Yankovic has used television and film texts as the basis for the parody. For example, on *"Weird Al" Yankovic in 3-D* Yankovic parodied Men Without Hats' "The Safety Dance" as "The Brady Bunch"[32]; on *Polka Party!* Yankovic parodied El Debarge's "Who's Johnny" as "Here's Johnny," invoking Ed McMahon's famous line from *The Tonight Show*[33]; on the soundtrack to his film *UHF* Yankovic parodied Dire Straits' "Money For Nothing" by using the words from the theme song to *The Beverly Hillbillies*[34]; on *Alapalooza* Yankovic parodied the Red Hot Chili Peppers' "Under the Bridge" and "Give it Away" as "Bedrock Anthem," which described the life of Fred Flintstone[35]; and on *Bad Hair Day* Yankovic parodied The Presidents of the United States' "Lump" as "Gump," based on the film and character Forrest Gump.[36] By utilizing *Star Wars Episode I: The Phantom Menace*, "The Saga Begins" remains faithful to this pattern that has significantly marked Yankovic's career.

Thirdly, use of lyrics and rhyme patterns in "The Saga Begins" that correspond with the song being parodied, while showing fidelity to McLean's original, also reflects Yankovic's career pattern of using these kinds of parallel lyrics and structures in many of his parodies. While a multitude of songs could work to exemplify this pattern, perhaps the pattern is best illustrated with reference to Yankovic's song "Eat It," which at the time of the release of "The Saga Begins" had had the highest chart-performing success of any of his singles, reaching number 12 on *Billboard*'s Hot 100 chart in 1984.[37] A parody of Michael Jackson's megahit "Beat It," the parallel lyrics of "Eat It" occur most prominently in the correspondence of the two songs' titles, which appear in the same places in the refrains of the songs. Other lines throughout the song also demonstrate this pattern, including the use of the same wording in particularly memorable phrases as well as the use of words at the ends of lines that rhyme not only internally within each song, but also in the same song position across the two songs.[38] By utilizing paralleling lyrics and rhyming patterns in "The Saga Begins," Yankovic remains faithful to the formula that has made him successful and that followers of his music recognize.

Narrative Probability

Narrative probability in "The Saga Begins" occurs most directly through the narrator of the story. Like "American Pie," "The Saga Begins" is told by character who is not the main character of the overall story, though he is the individual whose experiences we follow. For McLean, that narrator is a young man growing up witnessing the development of rock 'n' roll and the United States. For Yankovic, that narrator is Obi-Wan Kenobi, a young Jedi learning the Force through his instructor, Qui-Gon Jinn, while encountering the young boy Anakin Skywalker who will eventually become central to the development of the Empire, the Rebellion against the Empire, and the entire sequence of events that transpires along the way. By telling the story from Obi-Wan's perspective, Yankovic maintains another level of narrative fidelity with "American Pie," since it, too, relies on its narrator's perspective to tell a story that ultimately revolves around someone else. At the same time, Kenobi's perspective gives "The Saga Begins" narrative probability by providing the song with a clearly consistent perspective through which to view the story. As such, the story hangs together coherently, just as "American Pie" does, because the listener can see the events transpiring as they occur within the life of the narrator.

The narrative probability produced by having Kenobi's perspective throughout the song becomes evident as Yankovic interjects Obi-Wan's emotions, judgments, and opinions while telling the story of Anakin. Kenobi's judgments and opinions can be seen in lines such as suggesting that Kenobi "knew who would win first place" when Anakin took part in a pod race on Tatooine and later indicating that Kenobi "frankly would have liked to stay" on Coruscant when the group went back to Naboo.[39] The song also at times conveys Kenobi's emotions, such as his sadness about losing his mentor when Yankovic refers to Jinn as "the Jedi I admire most," and his sarcasm when he describes Anakin's contribution to the battle on Naboo by saying, "It wasn't long at all before little hotshot flew his plane and saved the day."[40] Consistent use of these kinds of asides and characterizations throughout the song provide further internal consistency that allows the song to hang together more fully as a narrative.

Additionally, the use of a narrator who is not the main character aligns both "American Pie" and "The Saga Begins" with texts like F. Scott Fitzgerald's *The Great Gatsby* and, thus, even more fully with U.S. identity and nostalgia. While Fitzgerald's famous novel follows developments in the life of Jay Gatsby, it tells the story through the eyes of Gatsby's temporary neighbor, Nick Carraway. As an outside observer, Nick thematically associates the nostalgia that Gatsby feels in his desire for Daisy Buchanan with the American experience, most explicitly at the end of the book when Nick connects Gatsby's desire with the feelings of Dutch sailors seeing the shores of a new world upon coming to the Americas. Nick states, "Gatsby believed in the green light, the orgiastic future that year by year recedes before us. It eluded us then, but that's no matter — tomorrow we will run faster, stretch out our arms farther.... And one fine morning — So we beat on, boats against the current, borne back ceaselessly into the past."[41] Here, Gatsby's nostalgia is tempered by Nick's sense of loss based in the fruitlessness of Gatsby's mission to reclaim the past. Like the narrator in "American Pie," Nick Carraway's narrative of Jay Gatsby tells a tale of innocence lost. So, too, does Yankovic's narrator, Obi-Wan Kenobi, who has lost his mentor with the death of Qui-Gon Jinn and who hints at the lost innocence of Anakin Skywalker that will come when Anakin becomes "Vader someday later." Meanwhile, just as Nick's narration provides coherence to the story by thematically framing Gatsby's experiences, the narrator in McLean's "American Pie" and Obi-Wan Kenobi in "The Saga Begins" allow their respective narratives to cohere by providing thematic framing to their stories. This form of thematic cohesion helps "The Saga Begins" to succeed rhetorically by maintaining narrative probability alongside its narrative fidelity.

CONCLUSION

Ultimately, Fisher suggests that "good stories function in two ways: to justify (or mystify) decisions or actions already made or performed and to determine future decisions or actions."[42] Yankovic does not seem to be explicitly making a statement other than to make a parody of a well-known song using another set of well-known intertextual references. Yet, in part, the narrative works because it implicitly does something; it constitutes a speech act that articulates more than simply offering a parody.

McLean's "American Pie" articulates a nostalgic vision of the beginnings and development of rock 'n' roll, growing up and into adulthood in the 1950s and 1960s, and an America lost in the process. Yankovic articulates nostalgia reinvigorated. The frontier notion of American identity, embodied in the exploration of outer space as represented by the *Star Wars* films, is reintroduced, alongside nostalgia for youth in the 1970s and 1980s, 22 years after the original film was released and 16 years after the narrative had been stalled. Certainly, the actual film *Star Wars: The Phantom Menace* whose plot Yankovic recounts does much more to reinvigorate the nostalgia. Yet, Yankovic's song adds a significant level to that reinvigoration by embedding the saga within another saga — that of McLean's song. McLean's song provides a nostalgic frame for articulating the reinvigoration of *Star Wars* mythology. In the process, Yankovic's parody of "American Pie" to create "The Saga Begins" illustrates the usefulness of McLean's song as a template for articulating other nostalgias, other mythologies, and other sagas. For McLean, the saga dies; for Yankovic, the saga begins. In both cases, the saga is articulated.

Notes

1. "Weird Al" Yankovic, "The Saga Begins," *Running with Scissors* Volcano 61422 32118-2, 1999.

2. Chris Knight, "Interview with 'Weird Al' Yankovic — Parody Artist and Star Wars Super-Fan," *TheForce.net*, accessed December 17, 2010, http://www.theforce.net/jedicouncil/interview/weirdal.asp.

3. Benedict Anderson, *Imagined Communities: Reflections on the Origin and Spread of Nationalism* (London: Verso, 2006).

4. For more on some of the features of sagas, as well as the connection of sagas to social memory see Jesse L. Byock, "Social Memory and the Sagas: The Case of *Egils Saga*," *Scandinavian Studies* 76 (Fall 2004): 299–316.

5. Don McLean, "American Pie," *American Pie* United Artists UAS-5535, 1971.

6. Ibid.

7 Among other sources, see Glenn C. Altschuler, *All Shook Up: How rock 'n' roll Changed America* (Oxford: Oxford University Press, 2003). Also, for a critical cultural examination of the connection of rock 'n' roll music with United States identity, including analysis of the association of that connection with the American frontier, see Lawrence Grossberg, *We Gotta Get Out of This Place: Popular Conservatism and Postmodern Culture* (New York: Routledge, 1992).

8. Sacvan Bercovitch, *The American Jeremiad* (Madison, WI: The University of Wisconsin Press, 1978), 4.

9. Yankovic, "The Saga Begins."

10. Ibid.

11. See Will Brooker, *Using the Force: Creativity, Community, and* Star Wars *Fans* (New York: Continuum, 2002) for more. In particular, Chapter 10, titled "Generations," discusses the significance of the *Star Wars* narratives to Generation X members.

12. John Seabrook, "Why Is the Force Still with Us?" *The New Yorker*, 6 January 1997, ¶ 46, accessed December 17, 2010, http://www.booknoise.net/johnseabrook/stories/culture/force/index.html.

13. For more discussion of the connection of the *Star Wars* films to Westerns, see Andrew Gordon, "*Star Wars*: A Myth for Our Time," *Literature Film Quarterly* 6 (Fall 1978): 314–26; and Lane Roth, "*Vraisemblance* and the Western Setting in Contemporary Science Fiction Film," *Literature Film Quarterly* 13 (3): 180–6.

14. See Richard Slotkin, *Gunfighter Nation: The Myth of the Frontier in Twentieth-Century America* (Norman, OK: University of Oklahoma Press, 1998).

15. Frederick Jackson Turner, "The Frontier in American History," *The University of Virginia Department of English Web site*, accessed December 18, 2010, http://xroads.virginia.edu/~HYPER/TURNER/.

16. Walter R. Fisher, "The Narrative Paradigm: An Elaboration," in *Methods of Rhetorical Criticism: A Twentieth-Century Perspective*, ed. Bernard L. Brock, Robert L. Scott, and James W. Chesbro, 3d ed. (Detroit: Wayne State University Press, 1990), 245.

17. Ibid.

18 Yankovic, "The Saga Begins."

19. McLean, "American Pie."

20. Yankovic, "The Saga Begins."

21. McLean, "American Pie."

22. Yankovic, "The Saga Begins."

23. McLean, "American Pie."

24. Yankovic, "The Saga Begins."

25. McLean, "American Pie."

26. Yankovic, "The Saga Begins."

27. Ibid.

28. Ibid.

29. "Weird Al" Yankovic, "*Weird Al" Yankovic in 3-D* Rock 'n' Roll Records BFZ-39221, 1983.

30. "'Weird Al' Yankovic Dishes on James Blunt, Discusses His Role as the Whitest, Nerdiest Rock Star Ever," Rolling Stone, 9 September 2006, accessed December 29, 2010, http://www.rollingstone.com/music/news/weird-al-yankovic-dishes-on-james-blunt-discusses-his-role-as-the-whitest-nerdiest-rock-star-ever-20060919.

31. "Weird Al" Yankovic, "Yoda," Dare to Be Stupid Rock 'n' Roll Records FZ-40033, 1985.

32. "Weird Al" Yankovic, "The Brady Bunch," "*Weird Al" Yankovic in 3-D* Rock 'n' Roll Records BFZ-39221, 1984.

33. "Weird Al" Yankovic, "Here's Johnny," *Polka Party!* Rock 'n' Roll Records PZ-40520, 1986.

34. "Weird Al" Yankovic, "Money for Nothing/Beverly Hillbillies," UHF — Original Motion Picture Soundtrack and Other Stuff Rock 'n' Roll Records ZK-45265, 1989.

35. "Weird Al" Yankovic, "Bedrock Anthem," Alapalooza Scotti Bros. 518 553-2, 1993.

36. "Weird Al" Yankovic, "Gump," Bad Hair Day Volcano 32030-2, 1996.

37. Joel Whitburn, *Joel Whitburn's Top Pop Singles 1955–1990* (Menomonee Falls, WI: Record Research, 1991), 642.

38. Yankovic, "Eat It."

39. Yankovic, "The Saga Begins."

40. Ibid.

41. F. Scott Fitzgerald, *The Great Gatsby* (New York: Charles Scribner's Sons, 1925), 180.

42. Fisher, 250.

Bibliography

ABB Merchandising Company. *Hittin' the Web with the Allman Brother Band*. Last modified February 19, 2012. http://www.allmanbrothersband.com/.

Aberback, Brian. *Black Sabbath: Pioneers of Heavy Metal*. Berkeley Heights, NJ: Enslow, 2010.

Abrahams, Ian. *Hawkwind: Sonic Assassins*. London: SAF, 2004.

Adams, Cecil. "What Is Don McLean's Song 'American Pie' All About?" *The Straight Dope*. Last modified May 15, 1993. http://www.straightdope.com/columns/read/908/what-is-don-mc leans-song-american-pie-all-about.

"Alan Lomax." *Folkstreams.net*. Accessed May 23, 2011. http://www.folkstreams.net/filmmaker, 121.

"Alan Lomax Collection." *The American Folklife Center*. Last modified June 23, 2011. http:// www.loc.gov/folklife/lomax/.

Albero, Richard, and Fred Style. "There's More to the Man Than American Pie." *Guitar Player*, July/August 1972, 19.

Albright, Thomas. *Art in the San Francisco Bay Area, 1945–1980: An Illustrated History*. Berkeley: University of California Press, 1985.

Alpert, Herb, and the Tijuana Brass. *Going Places*. A&M: 1965.

_____. *What Now My Love*. A&M, 1966.

_____. *Whipped Cream and Other Delights*. A&M, 1965.

"Altamont Music Festival." *Absolute Astronomy*. Accessed January 13, 2011. http://www.absolute astronomy.com/topics/Altamont_Music_Festival.

Altschuler, Glenn C. *All Shook Up: How Rock 'n' Roll Changed America*. Oxford: Oxford University Press, 2003.

Amaya, Mario. *Pop Art ... And After*. New York: Viking, 1965.

Amon Duul II. Accessed September 5, 2010. http://www.amonduul.de/.

Anderson, Benedict. *Imagined Communities: Reflections on the Origin and Spread of Nationalism*. London: Verso, 2006.

Apple Corps. *The Beatles*. Accessed September 5, 2010. http://www.thebeatles.com/.

"Archive (1965 Blackout)." *Blackout History Project*. Last modified June 27, 2000. http://www. blackout.gmu.edu/archive/a_1965.html.

Arnason, H. H. *History of Modern Art: Painting, Sculpture, Architecture*. New York: Abrams, 1968.

Associated Press. "Investigators Close Decades Old Altamont Killing Case." *USA Today*, May 26, 2005. http://www.usatoday.com/news/nation/2005-05-26-altamont_x.htm.

Awde, Nick. *Mellotron: The Machine and the Musicians That Revolutionised Rock*. London: Desert Heart, 2008.

Baez, Joan. *And a Voice to Sing With: A Memoir*. New York: Simon & Schuster, 2009.

Baez, Joan C., and Diamonds & Rust Productions. *Joan Baez*. Accessed September 5, 2010. http://www.joanbaez.com/.

Bailyn, Bernard. "Considering the Slave Trade: History and Memory." *The William and Mary Quarterly* 58 (January 2001): 245–52. http://www.jstor.org/stable/2674426.

Baker, Ginger. *Hellraiser: The Autobiography of the World's Greatest Drummer*. London: John Blake, 2010.

Banks, Peter, and Billy James. *Beyond and Before: The Formative Years of Yes*. Bentonville, AR: Golden Treasures, 2002.

Banks, Tony, Phil Collins, Peter Gabriel, Steve Hackett, and Mike Rutherford. *Genesis: Chapter and Verse*. New York: St. Martin's, 2007.

Barger, Al. "The Rolling Stones' Altamont Music Festival, December 6, 1969: The Anti–Woodstock — Page 4." *Blogcritics*. Last modified August 27, 2006. http://blogcritics.org/video/ articlethe-rolling-stones-altamont-music- festival/page-4/.

Barnes, Anthony. "Where's Adolf? The Mystery of Sgt. Pepper Is Solved." *Belfast Telegraph*, February 5, 2007.

Barnes, Mike. *Captain Beefheart: A Biography*. Revised ed. London: Omnibus, 2009.

Barnes, Richard. *The Who: Maximum R&B*. 5th ed. Medford, NJ: Plexus, 2004.

Barr, Alfred H., Jr. *Matisse: His Art and His Public*. New York: Museum of Modern Art, 1951.

Barr, Tim. *Kraftwerk: From Düsseldorf to the Future*. London: Ebury, 1999.

Barrera, Paul. *Once He Was: The Tim Buckley Story*. Andover, UK: Agenda, 1997.

Bartkowiak, Mathew J. *The MC5 and Social Change: A Study in Rock and Revolution*. Jefferson, NC: McFarland, 2009.

Baskins, Kevin. "Buddy Holly 'The Legend.'" *The Globe Gazette*. Accessed May 23, 2011. http: //www.globegazette.com/northiowatoday/buddyholly/pages/memories.php.

Baur, Michael. "'American Pie' and the Self-Critique of Rock 'n' Roll. In *Philosophy and the Interpretation of Pop Culture*, edited by William Irwin and Jorge J. E. Garcia, 255–73. Lanham, MD: Rowan and Littlefield, 2007.

The Beach Boys. Accessed September 5, 2010. http://www.thebeachboys.com.

The Beach Boys. "Good Vibrations." *Smiley Smile*. Brother/Capitol, 1967.

Bean, Julian P. *Joe Cocker: The Authorised Biography*. London: Virgin, 2003.

The Beatles. *Rubber Soul*. Parlophone, 1965.

_____. *Sgt. Pepper's Lonely Hearts Club Band*. Parlophone, 1967.

The Beatles Anthology. San Francisco: Chronicle, 2000.

The Beatles Discography. Accessed May 23, 2011. http://www.beatles-discography.com/appendicies/.

The Beau Brummels. Accessed September 12, 2010. http://www.beaubrummels.com/.

Beck, Jeff. *JeffBeck.com*. Accessed September 5, 2010. http://www.jeffbeck.com/.

Becker, Carl. "Every Man His Own Historian." *American Historical Review* 37 (January 1932): 221–36. http://0-www.jstor.org.maurice.bgsu.edu/stable/1838208.

Becker, Walter, and Donald Fagen. *Steely Dan*. Accessed September 5, 2010. http://www.steely dan.com/.

Beesweb—The Official Site of Richard Thompson. Accessed September 5, 2010. http://www.rich ardthompson-music.com/.

Bego, Mark. *The Doobie Brothers: Behind the Scenes with Today's Hottest Group*. New York: Popular Library, 1980.

_____. *Elton John: The Bitch Is Back*. Beverly Hills, CA: Phoenix, 2009.

_____. *Linda Ronstadt: It's So Easy: An Unauthorized Biography*. New York: Eakin, 1990.

Bennett, Graham. *Soft Machine: Out-Bloody-Rageous*. London: SAF, 2005.

Bercovitch, Sacvan. *The American Jeremiad*. Madison: University of Wisconsin Press. 1978.

Berman, Wallace, and Tosh Berman. *Wallace Berman: Support the Revolution*. Amsterdam: Institute of Contemporary Art, 1992.

Bevan, Bev. *Electric Light Orchestra Story*. New York: Putnam, 1981.

Big Brother and the Holding Company. Accessed September 5, 2010. http://www.bbhc.com/.

Blackburn, Robert, and Tariq Ali. "Power to the People." Accessed May 23, 2011. http://homepage.ntlworld.com/carousel/pob12.html.

Blake, Mark. *Comfortably Numb: The Inside Story of Pink Floyd*. New York: De Capo, 2008.

Blaney, John. *John Lennon: In His Life*. Edited by Valeria Manferto De Fabianis. Vercelli, Italy: White Star, 2010.

Blayney, David. *Sharp-Dressed Men: ZZ Top Behind the Scenes from Blues to Boogie to Beards*. New York: Hyperion, 1994.

Blight, David W. "Historians and 'Memory.'" *Common Place* 2, No. 3 (April 2002), http:// www.common-place.org/vol-02/no-03/author.

_____. *Race and Reunion: The Civil War in American Memory*. Amherst: University of Massachusetts Press, 2001.

Blood Sweat and Tears. *Blood Sweat and Tears.* Accessed September 5, 2010. http://www.blood sweatandtears.com/.

Bloom, Jerry. *Deep Purple: Stormbringers.* n.p.: Angry Penguin, 2008.

Bob Dylan. Accessed September 5, 2010. http://www.bobdylan.com/.

"Bob Dylan Biography." *Rolling Stone.* Accessed January 13, 2010. http://www.rollingstone.com/artists/bobdylan/biography.

The Bob Dylan Starting Point. Accessed May 23, 2011. http://www.schoneveld.com/bd.

Bob Dylan's Musical Roots. Accessed May 23, 2011. http://www.bobdylanroots.com.

Bockris, Victor. *Transformer: The Lou Reed Story.* New York: Da Capo, 1997.

"Bodies of Missing Trio Found Buried in Levee." *Neshoba Democrat,* August 6, 1964, http://neshobademocrat.com/main.asp?TypeID=1&ArticleID=8154&SectionID=17&SubSection ID=326&Page=2.

Bodnar, John. "*Saving Private Ryan* and Postwar Memory in America." *American Historical Review* 106 (June 2001): 805–17. http://www.jstor.org/stable/2692325.

Bonnie Bramlett. Accessed September 5, 2010. http://www.bonniebramlett.com/.

Bonzo Dog Band. Accessed September 5, 2010. http://www.neilinnes.org/bonzo.htm.

Booth, Stanley. *The True Adventures of the Rolling Stones.* Chicago: Chicago Review Press, 2000.

Bordowitz, Hank. *Bad Moon Rising: The Unauthorized History of Creedence Clearwater Revival.* Chicago: Chicago Review Press, 2007.

_____. *Dirty Little Secrets of the Record Business: Why So Much Music You Hear Sucks.* Chicago: Chicago Review Press, 2007.

_____. *Turning Points in Rock and Roll.* New York: Citadel, 2004.

Bourdon, David. *Warhol.* New York: Harry N. Abrams, 1989.

Bowienet. Accessed September 5, 2010. http://www.davidbowie.com/.

Boyd, Joe. *White Bicycles: Making Music in the 1960s.* London: Serpent's Tail, 2007.

Brabazon, Jason. *You Really Got Me: An Illustrated World Discography of the Kinks.* Rumford, RI: D. Hinman, 1994.

Bracewell, Michael. *Re-Make/Re-Model: Becoming Roxy Music.* New York: Da Capo, 2008.

Brackett, David. *The Pop, Rick and Soul Reader: Histories and Debates.* New York: Oxford University Press, 2008.

Brazier, Dave. "A Conversation with Martin Carthy." *The Telegraph* 42 (Summer 1992): 88–91, 94–6.

Brend, Mark. *Strange Sounds: Offbeat Instruments and Sonic Experiments in Pop.* San Francisco: Backbeat, 2005.

Bromell, Nick. *Tomorrow Never Knows: Rock and Psychedelics in the 1960s.* Chicago: University of Chicago Press, 2000.

Bronson, Fred. *The Billboard Book of Number One Hits.* Revised and updated 5th ed. New York: Billboard Books, 2003.

Brooker, Will. *Using the Force: Creativity, Community, and Star Wars Fans.* New York: Continuum, 2002.

Brooks, Ken. *The Adventures of Mike Bloomfield and Al Kooper with Paul Butterfield and David Clayton Thomas.* Andover, UK: Agenda, 1999.

Brown, Peter, and Steven Gaines. *The Love You Make: An Insider's Story of the Beatles.* With a new foreword by Anthony DeCurtis. New York: New American Library, 2002.

Browne, David. *Dream Brother: The Lives and Music of Jeff and Tim Buckley.* New York: Harper, 2001.

Bruford, Bill. *Bill Bruford: The Autobiography.* London: Jawbone, 2009.

Buckley, David. *Elton: The Biography.* Chicago: Chicago Review Press, 2009.

_____. *Strange Fascination: David Bowie, the Definitive Story.* Revised ed. London: Virgin, 2010.

_____. *The Thrill of It All: Bryan Ferry and Roxy Music.* Chicago: Chicago Review Press, 2005.

Buckley, Peter. *The Rough Guide to Rock.* London: Rough Guides, 2003.

"Buddy Holly." *Find a Grave.* Last modified January 1, 2001. http://www.findagrave.com/cgi-bin/fg.cgi?page=gr&GRid=492.

"Buddy Holly." *Internet Accuracy Project.* Last modified January 1, 2012. http://www.accuracy project.org/cbe-Holly,Buddy.html.

Buddy Holly Archives: Celebrating the Life and Music of Buddy Holly. Accessed February 4, 2012. http://www.buddyhollyarchives.com/.

Bugliosi, Vincent, and Curt Gentry. *Helter Skelter: The True Story of the Manson Murders*. New York: Norton, 2001.

Burdon, Eric, and J. Marshall Craig. *Don't Let Me Be Misunderstood*. New York: Thunder's Mouth, 2001.

Burks, John. "Rock and Roll's Worst Day: The Aftermath of Altamont." *Rolling Stone*. Accessed January 13, 2010. http://www.rollingstone.com/news/story/5934386/rock__rolls_worst_day.

Bussy, Pascal. *The Can Book*. London: SAF, 1989.

_____. *Kraftwerk: Man, Machine, and Music*. Revised ed. London: SAF, 2004.

Byock, Jesse L. "Social Memory and the Sagas: The Case of *Egils Saga*." *Scandinavian Studies* 76 (Fall 2004): 299–316.

The Byrds. "So You Want to Be a Rock 'n' Roll Star." *Younger Than Yesterday*. Columbia, 1967.

Callwood, Brett. *MC5: Sonically Speaking: A Tale of Revolution and Rock n Roll*. Church Stretton, UK: Independent Music Press, 2007.

_____. *The Stooges: A Journey Through the Michigan Underworld*. Church Stretton, UK: Independent Music Press, 2008.

Canned Heat. Accessed September 5, 2010. http://www.cannedheatmusic.com/.

Carlson, David. *Grit, Noise, & Revolution: The Birth of Detroit Rock 'n' Roll*. Ann Arbor: University of Michigan Press, 2005.

Carroll, Peter N. *It Seemed Like Nothing Happened: America in the 1970s*. New Brunswick, NJ: Rutgers University Press, 2000.

Carson, Annette. *Jeff Beck: Crazy Fingers*. San Francisco: Backbeat, 2001.

Case, George. *Jimmy Page: Magus, Musician, Man: An Unauthorized Biography*. New York: Hal Leonard, 2007.

Celmins, Martin. *Peter Green—Founder of Fleetwood Mac*. 2d ed. Tampa, FL: Sanctuary, 1998.

C'est Music. *Carly Simon.com*. Accessed September 5, 2010. http://www.carlysimon.com/.

Chad Stuart and Jeremy Clyde. Accessed September 5, 2010. http://www.chadandjeremy.net/.

Chang, Candy. "Fix Everything My Ass." *CandyChang.com*. Accessed February 8, 2012. http://candychang.com/fix-everything-my-ass/.

Chapple, Mike. "Pop Art Pioneer Marks 2008." *Liverpool Daily Post*, May 26, 2006, 3.

Charlesworth, Chris. *Cat Stevens*. London: Proteus, 1985.

_____. *The Complete Guide to the Music of Paul Simon and Simon and Garfunkel*. London: Omnibus, 1997.

_____. *David Bowie: The Archive*. London: Omnibus, 1987.

_____. *David Bowie: Profile*. London: Proteus, 1985.

_____. *Deep Purple: The Illustrated Biography*. London: Omnibus, 1998.

Charlesworth, Chris, and Ed Hanel. *The Who: The Complete Guide to Their Music*. 2d ed. London: Omnibus, 2004.

Chatterton, Mark, and Gary Carter. *Blowin' Free: Thirty Years of Wishbone Ash*. Wembley, UK: Fire Fly, 2001.

Chen, Jim. "Drove My Chevy to the Levee but the Levee Was Gone." *Jurisdynamics*. Last modified November 14, 2007. http://jurisdynamics.blogspot.com/2007/11/drove-my-chevy-to-levee-but-levee- was.html.

Chicago. *Chicago*. Accessed September 5, 2010. http://chicagotheband.com/.

Chipp, Herschel B. *Theories of Modern Art: A Source Book by Artists and Critics*. Berkeley: University of California Press, 1969.

Chomsky, Noam. *Rethinking Camelot: JFK, the Vietnam War, and U.S. Political Culture*. Cambridge, MA: South End, 1999.

Christopulos, Jim, and Phil Smart. *Van der Graaf Generator, The Book: A History of the Band Van der Graaf Generator 1967 to 1978*. n.p.: Phil and Jim, 2005.

CK Art Media Inc. *Carole King*. Accessed September 5, 2010. http://www.caroleking.com/home.php.

Clapton, Eric. *Clapton: The Autobiography*. New York: Broadway, 2007.

_____, and WBR. *Eric Clapton*. Accessed September 5, 2010. http://www.ericclapton.com/.

Clayson, Alan. *Back in the High Life: A Biography of Steve Winwood*. London: Sidgwick & Jackson, 1988.

_____. *Beat Merchants: The Origins, History, Impact, and Rock Legacy of 1960's British Pop Groups*. Worcestershire, UK: Blandford, 1995.

_____. *The Beatles Box.* Tampa, FL: Sanctuary, 2003.

_____. *Jimi Hendrix: As It Happened.* New Malden, UK: Chrome Dreams, 2002.

_____. *Maximum Doors: The Unauthorised Biography of the Doors.* New Malden, UK: Chrome Dreams, 2002.

_____. *Ringo Starr.* 2d ed. Tampa, FL: Sanctuary, 2001.

_____. *The Rolling Stones: The Origin of the Species: How, Why, and Where It All Began.* New Malden, UK: Chrome Dreams, 2008.

_____. *The Yardbirds: The Band That Launched Eric Clapton, Jeff Beck and Jimmy Page.* San Francisco: Backbeat, 2002.

_____, and Jacqueline Ryan. *The Troggs Files: Rock's Wild Things.* London: Helter Skelter, 2001.

Clerk, Carol. *Diary of a Madman: Ozzy Osbourne: The Stories Behind the Songs.* New York: Da Capo, 2002.

_____. *The Saga of Hawkwind.* 2d ed. London: Omnibus, 2006.

Cohen, David X. "The Why of Fry," *Futurama*, season 5, episode 8, directed by Wesley Archer and Rich Moore, aired April 6, 2003. 20th Century–Fox.

Coleman, Ray. *Lennon: The Definitive Biography.* New York: Harper, 2002.

Collins, Judy. *Singing Lessons: A Memoir of Love, Loss, Hope, and Healing.* New York: Pocket, 2007.

Collins, Maynard. *Gordon Lightfoot: If You Could Read His Mind.* Toronto: University of Toronto Press, 1988.

Conway, Steve. *ShipRocked: Life on the Waves with Radio Caroline.* Dublin: Liberties, 2009.

Cooper, Alice, with Keith Zimmerman and Kent Zimmerman. *Alice Cooper, Golf Monster: A Rock 'n' Roller's Life and 12 Steps to Becoming a Golf Addict.* New York: Three Rivers, 2007.

Cornell, Don. "The Bible Tells Me So." Coral, 1955.

Country Joe's Place. Accessed September 12, 2010. http://www.countryjoe.com/.

Courrier, Kevin. *Artificial Paradise: The Dark Side of the Beatles' Utopian Dream.* Westport, CT: Praeger, 2008.

_____. *Captain Beefheart's Trout Mask Replica.* New York: Continuum, 2007.

_____. *Dangerous Kitchen: The Subversive World of Zappa.* Toronto: ECW, 2002.

_____. *Randy Newman: American Dreams.* Toronto: ECW, 2005.

Crazy World of Arthur Brown. Accessed September 5, 2010. http://www.arthurbrownmusic.com/.

Cream. *Live Cream.* Polydor, 1970.

_____. *Live Cream Volume II.* Polydor, 1972.

_____. *Wheels of Fire.* Polydor, 1968.

Creature Music Limited. *Manfred Mann's Website.* Accessed September 5, 2010. http://www.manfredmann.co.uk/.

"The Crickets." *Utopia Artists.* Accessed January 13, 2010. http://www.utopiaartists.com/bio_crickets.htm.

Crosby, Stills and Nash. *Crosby, Stills and Nash.* Accessed September 5, 2010. http://www.crosbystillsnash.com/.

Cross, Charles. *Room Full of Mirrors: A Biography of Jimi Hendrix.* New York: Hyperion, 2006.

CSNY. *CSNY.com.* Accessed September 5, 2010. http://csny.com/.

"Cuban Missile Crisis." *John F. Kennedy Presidential Library and Museum.* Accessed January 13, 2010. http://www.jfklibrary.org/JFK/JFK-in-History/Cuban-Missile-Crisis.aspx.

Cutler, Phil. "Cutler's History." *Cutler's Record Shop.* Accessed January 13, 2010. http://www.cutlers.com/history.html.

Dalton, David. "Altamont: End of the Sixties: Or Big Mix-Up in the Middle of Nowhere?" *Gadfly Online.* Accessed January 13, 2010. http://www.gadflyonline.com/archive/NovDec99/archive-altamont.html.

Dann, Trevor. *Darker Than the Deepest Sea: The Search for Nick Drake.* New York: Da Capo, 2006.

Danton, Eric R. "Ill-Fated Altamont Is a Far More Fitting Symbol of the '60s Than Glorified Woodstock." *Hartford Courant*, August 9, 2009. http://www.courant.com/entertainment/hc-altamont.artaug09,0,5403034.story.

Davies, Dave. *Kink: An Autobiography.* New York: Hyperion, 1997.

Davies, Ray. *X-Ray: The Unauthorized Autobiography.* New York: Overlook, 2007.

Davis, Fred. "Nostalgia, Identity, and the Current Nostalgia Wave." *Journal of Popular Culture* 11 (September 1977): 414–24. doi: 10.1111/j.0022-3840.1977.00414.x.

Dearborn, Bob. *Bob Dearborn's Original Analysis of Don McLean's 1971 Classic "American Pie."* Accessed June 29, 2009. http://user.pa.net/~ejjeff/pie.html.

DeCurtis, Anthony, ed. *Rolling Stone Illustrated History of Rock and Roll: The Definitive History of the Most Important Artists and Their Music.* New York: Random House, 1992.

Deeha. "The 1969 Altamont Free Concert: The End of the Hippie CounterCulture." *Yahoo! Voices.* Last modified December 2, 2008. http://www.associatedcontent.com/article/1236057/the_1969_altamont_free_concert_the.html?cat=33.

De la Parra, Fito, with T. W. McGarry and Marlane McGarry. *Living the Blues: Canned Heat's Story of Music, Drugs, Death, Sex, and Survival.* n.p.: Canned Heat Music, 2002.

Densmore, John. *Riders on the Storm: My Life with Jim Morrison and the Doors.* New York: Dell, 1991.

Devine, Campbell. *All the Young Dudes: Mott the Hoople and Ian Hunter.* London: Cherry Red, 2007.

"Discography." *Fillmore East Preservation Society.* Accessed January 13, 2010. http://www.fillmore-east.com/discography.htm.

"Discography." *The Official Peter and Gordon Website.* Accessed September 5, 2010. http://www.peterandgordon.net/discography.htm.

DJ Allyn. "American Pie ~ Don McLean." *DJ Allyn: A Solid Wall of Sound.* Accessed January 13, 2010. http://djallyn.org/archives/133.

Dr. Hook and the Medicine Show. "The Cover of the Rolling Stone." *Sloppy Seconds.* Columbia, 1973.

Dr. Zhivago soundtrack. OST, 1965.

DrJohn.org. Accessed September 5, 2010. http://www.drjohn.org/.

Doggett, Peter. *Jimi Hendrix: The Complete Guide to His Music.* 2d ed. London: Omnibus, 2004.

_____. *Lou Reed: Growing Up in Public.* London: Omnibus, 1995.

_____. *There's a Riot Going On: Revolutionaries, Rock Stars, and the Rise and Fall of the '60s.* Edinburgh: Cannongate, 2009.

_____. *You Never Give Me Your Money: The Beatles After the Breakup.* New York: Harper, 2010.

_____, and Patrick Humphries. *The Beatles: The Music and the Myth.* London: Omnibus, 2010.

Dolenz, Mickey, and Mark Bego. *I'm a Believer: My Life of Monkees, Music, and Madness.* Revised ed. New York: Cooper Square, 2004.

Dominguez, J. "Religious Art Gallery." 2005. Accessed May 23, 2011. http://www.religion-cults.com/art.htm.

"Don McLean." *Answers.com.* Accessed January 13, 2010. http://www.answers.com/topic/don-mclean.

"Don McLean — In His Own Words." *Super Seventies Rocksite.* Accessed January 13, 2010. http://www.superseventies.com/ssdonmclean.html.

Donovan Discs. Accessed September 5, 2010. http://www.donovan.ie/.

The Doobie Brothers. *Doobie Brothers.* Accessed September 5, 2010. http://www.doobiebros.com/.

The Doors Partnership LLP. *The Doors.* Accessed September 5, 2010. http://www.thedoors.com/.

Dowlding, William J. *Beatlesongs.* New York: Fireside, 1989.

Downin, Dave. Arlo.net: The Official Arlo Guthrie Website. Last modified February 19, 2012. http://www.arlo.net/.

"Drove My Chevy to the Levee But The Levee Was Gone." *The Irreverent Buddhist.* Last modified September 3, 2005. http://freedomforall.net/drove-my-chevy-to-the-levee-but-the-levee-was-gone/.

"Drove My Chevy to the Levee T Shirt." *Zazzle.* Accessed February 8, 2012. http://www.zazzle.com/drove_my_chevy_to_the_levee_tshirt-235959397535378182.

Dunaway, David King. *How Can I Keep from Singing? The Ballad of Pete Seeger.* New York: Villard, 2008.

Durchholz, Daniel, and Gary Graff. *Neil Young: Long May You Run: The Illustrated History.* Minneapolis: Voyageur, 2010.

Dylan, Bob. *The Freewheelin' Bob Dylan.* Columbia, 1963.

Eaglesband.com. Accessed September 5, 2010. http://www.eaglesband.com/.

Echols, Alice. *Scars of Sweet Paradise: The Life and Times of Janis Joplin.* New York: Holt, 2000.

Eder, Bruce. "The Weavers." *The Vocal Group Hall of Fame Foundation.* Accessed January 13, 2010. http://www.vocalhalloffame.com/inductees/the_weavers.html.

Egan, Sean. *The Rough Guide to The Rolling Stones 1 (Rough Guide Reference).* London: Rough Guides, 2006.

Einarson, John. *Desperadoes: The Roots of Country Rock.* New York: Cooper Square, 2001.

_____. *For What It's Worth: The Story of Buffalo Springfield.* New York: Cooper Square, 2004.

_____. *Forever Changes: Arthur Lee and the Book of Love.* London: Jawbone, 2010.

_____. *Hot Burritos: The True Story of the Flying Burrito Brothers.* London: Jawbone, 2008.

_____. *Mr. Tambourine Man: The Life and Legacy of the Byrds' Gene Clark.* San Francisco: Backbeat, 2005.

Electric Prunes. Accessed September 5, 2010. http://www.electricprunes.net/.

Eliot, Marc. *Paul Simon: A Life.* Hoboken, NJ: Wiley, 2010.

_____. *To the Limit: The Untold Story of the Eagles.* Boston: Little, Brown, and Company, 1998.

Elliott, Ramblin' Jack. *The Official Website of Ramblin' Jack Elliott.* Accessed May 23, 2011. http://www.ramblinjack.com/.

Eltonjohn.com. Accessed September 5, 2010. http://web.eltonjohn.com/index.jsp.

Ely, Geoff. "Finding the People's War: Film, British Collective Memory and World War II." *American Historical Review* 106 (June 2001): 818–38. http://www.jstor.org/stable/2692326.

Emerick, Geoff, and Howard Massey. *Here, There and Everywhere: My Life Recording the Music of the Beatles.* New York: Gotham, 2007.

Emerson, Keith. *Pictures of an Exhibitionist: From the Nice to the Emerson, Lake and Palmer—The True Story of the Man Who Changed the Sound of Rock.* London: John Blake, 2004.

Emerson, Lake and Palmer. *Emerson Lake and Palmer.* Accessed September 5, 2010. http://www.emersonlakepalmer.com/.

EMI Group Limited. *John Lennon.* Accessed September 5, 2010. http://www.johnlennon.com/html/news.aspx.

Empson, William. *Seven Types of Ambiguity.* New York: New Directions, 2006.

Ennis, Philip H. *The Seventh Stream: The Emergence of Rocknroll in American Popular Music.* Hanover, NH: Wesleyan University Press, 1992.

Eric Burdon. Accessed September 5, 2010. http://ericburdon.ning.com/.

The Estate of Timothy C. Buckley III. *The Tim Buckley Archives.* Accessed September 12, 2010. http://www.timbuckley.net/.

Exile Productions Ltd. *Van Morrison Official Webpage.* Accessed September 5, 2010. http://www.vanmorrison.com/.

Fairport Convention. *Fairport Convention Official Website.* Accessed September 5, 2010. http://www.fairportconvention.com/.

Fann, James M. *Understanding "American Pie."* Last modified December 10, 2006, http://understandingamericanpie.com/.

Far Out Productions. *WAR.* Accessed September 5, 2010. http://www.wartheband.com/home.html.

Farley, Alan. *The Extraordinary World of Yes.* New York: iUniverse, 2004.

Feiffer, Jules, Tom Hayden, and Jon Wiener. *Conspiracy in the Streets: The Extraordinary Trial of the Chicago Eight.* New York: The New Press, 2006.

Felder, Don, and Wendy Holden. *Heaven and Hell: My Life in the Eagles 1974–2001.* Hoboken, NJ: Wiley, 2009.

Fenton, Craig. *Take Me to a Circus Tent: The Jefferson Airplane Flight Manual.* West Conshohocken, PA: Infinity, 2006.

Fisher, Marc. *Something in the Air: Radio, Rock, and the Revolution That Shaped a Generation.* New York: Random House, 2007.

Fisher, Walter R. "The Narrative Paradigm: An Elaboration." In *Methods of Rhetorical Criticism: A Twentieth-Century Perspective,* edited by Bernard L. Brock, Robert L. Scott, and James W. Chesbro. 3rd ed., 234–55. Detroit: Wayne State University Press, 1990.

Fitzgerald, F. Scott. *The Great Gatsby.* New York: Charles Scribner's Sons, 1925.

Fleetwood, Mick. *Fleetwood: My Life and Adventures in Fleetwood Mac.* New York: Avon, 1991.

Fleetwood Mac. Accessed September 5, 2010. http://www.fleetwoodmac.com/.

Flur, Wolfgang. *Kraftwerk: I Was a Robot.* Tampa, FL: Sanctuary, 2005.

Focus the Band. Accessed September 5, 2010. http://www.focustheband.com/.

Foghat. Accessed September 5, 2010. http://www.foghat.com/.

Fong-Torres, Ben. *The Doors.* New York: Hyperion, 2006.

_____. *Hickory Wind: The Life and Times of Gram Parsons.* New York: St. Martin's Griffin, 1998.

_____. *The Hits Just Keep On Coming: The History of Top 40 Radio.* San Francisco: Backbeat, 2001.

_____. *Not Fade Away: A Backstage Pass to 20 Years of Rock & Roll.* San Francisco: Miller Freeman, 1999.

Footman, Tim. *Leonard Cohen: Hallelujah: A New Biography.* New Malden, UK: Chrome Dreams, 2009.

Foreigner. "Jukebox Hero." *4.* Atlantic, 1981.

Fornatale, Pete. *Back to the Garden: The Story of Woodstock.* New York: Touchstone, 2009.

Forrester, George, Martyn Hanson, and Frank Askew. *Emerson Lake and Palmer: The Show That Never Ends.* London: Helter Skelter, 2010.

Freed, Judith Fisher. *The Official Alan Freed Website.* Accessed January 13, 2010. http://www.alanfreed.com.

Freeman, Scott. *Midnight Riders: The Story of the Allman Brothers Band.* Boston: Little, Brown and Company, 1996.

French, John. *Beefheart: Through the Eyes of Magic.* London: Omnibus, 2010.

Friedman, Myra. *Buried Alive: The Biography of Janis Joplin.* New York: Three Rivers, 1992.

Fripp, Robert. *King Crimson.* Accessed September 5, 2010. http://www.king-crimson.com/.

Gablik, Suzi. "Bob Stanley." *ARTnews* 64 no. 3 (May 1965), 18.

Gaines, Steven. *Heroes and Villains: The True Story of the Beach Boys.* New York: Da Capo, 1995.

Gallo, Armando. *Genesis: I Know What I Like.* 2d ed. London: Omnibus, 1987.

Geldzahler, Henry, and Robert Rosenblum. *Andy Warhol: Portraits of the Seventies and Eighties.* London: Anthony d'Offay Gallery, 1993.

Genesismusic.com. *Genesis.* Accessed September 5, 2010. http://www.genesis-music.com/.

Gentle Giant Home Page. Last modified October 18, 2011. http://www.blazemonger.com/GG/Gentle_Giant_Home_Page.

George, Nelson. *The Death of Rhythm and Blues.* Middlesex, UK: Plume, 2003.

GeorgeClinton.com. Accessed September 5, 2010. http://www.georgeclinton.com/.

GFR, Ltd. *Grand Funk Railroad.* Accessed September 5, 2010. http://www.grandfunkrailroad.com/.

Gianella, Mario. *The Beatles.* Accessed May 23, 2011. http://beatlesong.info/.

Gibbons, Billy F. *Billy F. Gibbons: Rock and Roll Gearhead.* Minneapolis: MBI, 2005.

Glatt, John. *Rage & Roll: Bill Graham and the Selling of Rock.* Secaucus, NJ: Carol, 1993.

Gleason, Ralph J. "Aquarius Wept." *Esquire.com.* Last modified August 12, 2009. http://www.esquire.com/features/altamont-1969-aquarius-wept-0870.

Godwin, Robert. *The Illustrated Collector's Guide to Hawkwind.* Burlington, ON: Collector's Guide Publishing, 1995.

Goldenberg, Michael D. "Altamont." *Mikegoldenberg.com.* Accessed January 13, 2010. http://www.mikegoldenberg.com/index.php?SCREEN=altamont.php.

Goldman, Albert Harry. *The Lives of John Lennon.* Chicago: Chicago Review Press, 2001.

Gordon, Andrew. "*Star Wars*: A Myth for Our Time." *Literature Film Quarterly* 6 (Fall 1978): 314–26.

Gould, Jonathan. *Can't Buy Me Love: The Beatles, Britain, and America.* New York: Three Rivers, 2007.

Graff, Gary, and Daniel Durcholz. *MusicHound Rock: The Essential Album Guide.* Farmington Hills, MI: Visible Ink, 1999.

Graham, Bill. *Bill Graham's Fillmore East.* Accessed January 13, 2010, http://subrealities.waitingforthe-sun.net/Pages/BeIn/HaightAshbury/Fillmore/fillmore_east_history.html.

Grand Funk Railroad. "We're an American Band." *We're an American Band.* Capitol, 1973.

Grateful Dead. Accessed September 5, 2010. http://www.dead.net/.

Grateful Dead. "Truckin'" *American Beauty.* Warner Bros., 1970.

Greene, Joshua M. *Here Comes the Sun: The Spiritual and Musical Journey of George Harrison.* Hoboken, NJ: Wiley, 2007.

Greenfield, Robert, and Bill Graham. *Bill Graham Presents: My Life Inside Rock and Out*. New York: Doubleday, 1992.

Greenwald, Matthew. *Go Where You Wanna Go: The Oral History of the Mamas and the Papas*. New York: Cooper Square, 2002.

"Grim Discovery in Mississippi." *Time*, August 14, 1964, http://www.time.com/time/magazine/article/0,9171,897227-1,00.html.

Gross, Terry. "Dion the Wanderer, Back 'In Blue.'" *National Public Radio*. Last modified January 6, 2006. http://www.npr.org/templates/story/story.php?storyId=5132750.

Grossberg, Lawrence. *We Gotta Get Out of This Place: Popular Conservatism and Postmodern Culture*. New York: Routledge, 1992.

Guralnick, Peter. *Last Train to Memphis: The Rise of Elvis Presley*. Boston: Little, Brown, and Company, 1995.

Hajdu, David. *Positively 4th Street: The Lives and Times of Joan Baez, Bob Dylan, Mimi Baez Fariña, and Richard Fariña*. New York: Picador, 2001.

Halbwachs, Maurice. *On Collective Memory*. Translated and edited by Lewis A. Koser. Chicago: University of Chicago Press, 1992.

Hanson, Martyn. *Hang on to a Dream: The Story of the Nice*. London: Helter Skelter, 2002.

Harrison, George. *I, Me, Mine*. San Francisco: Chronicle, 2002.

Harrison, Helen. *Larry Rivers*. New York: Harper & Row, 1984.

Harrisongs. *George Harrison*. Accessed September 5, 2010. http://www.georgeharrison.com/.

Havens, Richie, and Steve Davidowitz. *They Can't Hide Us Anymore*. New York: Spike, 1999.

Hawkwind. Accessed September 5, 2010. http://www.hawkwind.com/.

Heatley, Michael. *The Complete Deep Purple*. 2d ed. London: Reynolds & Hearn, 2008.

Heller, Greg, and Aliyah Silverstein. "The Day The Music Died," *Behind the Music*, season 2, episode 19, directed by Will Harper, aired February 3, 1999. Gay Rosenthal Productions.

Helm, Levon, and Stephen Davis. *This Wheel's On Fire: Levon Helm and the Story of the Band*. 2d ed. Chicago: Chicago Review Press, 2000.

"Helter Skelter (Ride)." *Academic Dictionaries and Encyclopedias*. Accessed January 13, 2010. http://dic.academic.ru/dic.nsf/enwiki/312526.

"Helter Skelter, South Shields Fairground." *South Shields Sanddancers*. Accessed January 13, 2010. http://www.southshields-sanddancers.co.uk/your_photos/kurly_med5.htm.

Hendrix, Jimi. *Band of Gypsys*. Capitol, 1970.

_____. *Experience*. Ember, 1971.

_____. *Hendrix in the West*. Polydor, 1972.

_____. *Isle of Wight*. Polydor, 1971.

Hertsgaard, Mark. *A Day in the Life: The Music and Artistry of the Beatles*. New York: Delacorte, 1995.

Hewitt, Paulo, and John Hellier. *Steve Marriott—All Too Beautiful*. London: Helter Skelter, 2004.

Heylin, Clinton. *Bob Dylan: Behind the Shades Revisited*. New York: HarperCollins, 2003.

_____. *Can You Feel the Silence? Van Morrison: A New Biography*. Chicago: Chicago Review Press, 2004.

Hibiscus Production. *The Official John Mayall Website*. Accessed September 5, 2010. http://www.johnmayall.com/.

Hicks, Michael. *Sixties Rock: Garage, Psychedelic, and Other Satisfactions*. Urbana: University of Illinois Press, 1999.

Hine, Thomas. *The Rise and Fall of the American Teenager*. New York: Harper Perennial, 2000.

Hinman, Doug. *The Kinks: All Day and All of the Night: Day by Day Concerts, Recordings, and Broadcasts, 1961–1996*. San Francisco: Backbeat, 2004.

Hinton, Brian. *Bob Dylan Complete Discography*. New York: Universe, 2006.

_____. *Celtic Crossroads: The Art of Van Morrison*. 2d ed. Tampa, FL: Sanctuary, 2000.

_____. *Joni Mitchell: Both Sides Now—The Biography*. 2d ed. Tampa, FL: Sanctuary, 2000.

_____. *Message to Love: Isle of Wight Festival 1968, 1969, 1970*. Tampa, FL: Sanctuary, 1996.

_____, and Geoff Wall. *Ashley Hutchings: The Guv'nor and the Rise of Folk Rock*. London: Helter Skelter, 2002.

Hixley, Martin, and Quinton Skinner. *(Behind the Music) The Day the Music Died*. New York: MTV, 2000.

Hjort, Christopher. *So You Want to Be a Rock 'n' Roll Star: The Byrds Day-by-Day 1965–1973*. London: Jawbone, 2008.

_____. *Strange Brew: Eric Clapton and the British Blues Boom*. London: Jawbone, 2007.

_____, and Doug Hinman. *Jeff's Book: A Chronology of Jeff Beck's Career 1965–1980: From the Yardbirds to Jazz-Rock*. Rumford, RI: Rock 'n' Roll Research, 2000.

"HMV Group plc." *Funding Universe*. Accessed January 13, 2010. http://www.fundinguniverse.com/company-histories/HMV-Group-plc-Company-History.html.

Hogan, Peter K., and Chris Charlesworth, ed. *The Complete Guide to the Music of the Doors*. New York: Omnibus, 1994.

The Hollies: The Official Hollies Website. Accessed September 5, 2010. http://www.hollies.co.uk/.

Holly, Buddy, and the Crickets. "That'll Be the Day." *The "Chirping" Crickets*. Brunswick, 1957.

Holm-Hudson, Kevin, ed. *Progressive Rock Reconsidered*. London: Routledge, 2001.

Hoskyns, Barney. *Across the Great Divide: The Band and America*. Revised ed. New York: Hal Leonard, 2006.

_____. *Glam! Bowie, Bolan and the Glitter Rock Revolution*. London: Faber & Faber, 1998.

_____. *Hotel California: The True-Life Adventures of Crosby, Stills, Nash, Young, Mitchell, Taylor, Browne, Ronstadt, Geffen, the Eagles, and Their Many Friends*. Hoboken, NJ: Wiley, 2007.

"House Unamerican Activities Committee, August 18, 1955, Pete Seeger." *Pete Seeger Appreciation Page*. Accessed January 13, 2010. http://www.peteseeger.net/HUAC.htm.

Howard, Alan. *The Don McLean Story: Killing Us Softly with His Songs*. n.p.: Starry Night Music, Inc., 2007.

_____, and Don McLean. *Don McLean Online: The Official Website of Don McLean and American Pie*. Last modified February 4, 2012. http://www.don-mclean.com/.

Hudson River Sloop Clearwater: The Next Generation of Environmental Leaders. Last modified January 31, 2012. http://www.clearwater.org/index.html.

Humphries, Patrick. *Meet on the Ledge: Fairport Convention—The Classic Years*. 2d ed. London: Virgin, 1997.

_____. *Nick Drake: The Biography*. New York: Bloomsbury, 1998.

_____. *Paul Simon*. New York: Doubleday, 1989.

_____. *Richard Thompson*. New York: Schirmer, 1997.

_____, and John Bauldie. *Oh No! Not Another Bob Dylan Book*. Brentwood, UK: Square One, 1991.

Hunter, Dave. *Guitar Effects Pedals: The Practical Handbook*. San Francisco: Backbeat, 2004.

_____. *Guitar Rigs: Classic Guitar and Amp Combinations*. San Francisco: Backbeat, 2005.

Hunter, Sam, John Jacobus, and Daniel Wheeler. *Modern Art: Painting, Sculpture, Architecture*. 3rd ed. New York: Prentice Hall and Harry N. Abrams, 1992.

"Hyde Park 1969." *Geetarz*. Accessed May 23, 2011. http://www.geetarz.org/reviews/stones/hyde-park-69.htm.

Ian, Janis. *Janis Ian*. Accessed September 12, 2010. http://www.janisian.com/.

_____. *Society's Child: My Autobiography*. New York: Tarcher, 2008.

The Ides of March. *The Ides of March Featuring Jim Peterik Official Website*. Accessed September 5, 2010. http://www.theidesofmarch.com/.

Iggy Pop. Accessed September 5, 2010. http://www.iggypop.com/.

"The Influence of the Beatles on Charles Manson." *Famous American Trials*. Accessed January 13, 2010. http://law2.umkc.edu/faculty/projects/ftrials/manson/mansonbeatles.html.

Inglis, Ian. "Response to Censorship in the USA: Acquiescence, Withdrawal and Resistance." In *Shoot the Singer! Music Censorship Today*, edited by Marie Korpe, 178–185. London: Zed, 2004.

Iron Butterfly: The Official Website. Accessed September 5, 2010. http://www.ironbutterfly.com/.

Ives, Burl. *The Burl Ives Songbook*. New York: Ballantine, 1953.

"J. P. 'Big Bopper' Richardson, Jr." *Find a Grave*. Last modified January 1, 2001. http://www.findagrave.com/cgi-bin/fg.cgi?page=gr&GRid=1705.

Jackson, John. *American Bandstand: Dick Clark and the Making of a Rock 'n' Roll Empire*. New York: Oxford University Press, 1999.

Jackson, Michael. "Beat It." *Thriller*. Epic, 1982.

Jackson Browne. Accessed September 5, 2010. http://www.jacksonbrowne.com/.

Jacqui McShee's Pentangle. Accessed September 5, 2010. http://www.jacquimcshee.co.uk/.

James, Billy. *An American Band: The Story of Grand Funk Railroad.* London: SAF, 1999.

_____. *A Dream Goes On Forever—The Continuing Story of Todd Rundgren: The Utopia Years.* Bentonville, AR: Golden Treasures, 2002.

_____. *Lunar Notes: Zoot Horn Rollo's Captain Beefheart Experience.* London: SAF, 2001.

_____. *Necessity Is: The Early Years of Frank Zappa and the Mothers of Invention.* 2d ed. London: SAF, 2002.

"Janis Joplin Biography." *Rolling Stone.* Accessed January 13, 2010. http://www.rollingstone.com/artists/janisjoplin/biography.

Jefferson Airplane Inc. *Jefferson Airplane.* Accessed September 5, 2010. http://www.jeffersonairplane.com/.

"Jerry Allison." *Ask.com.* Accessed January 13, 2010. http://www.ask.com/music/artist/Jerry-Allison/51382.

Jethrotull.com. *Jethro Tull: The Official Website.* Accessed September 5, 2010. http://www.j-tull.com/.

"Joe B. Maudlin." *BBC.* Accessed January 13, 2010. http://www.bbc.co.uk/music/artists/019209c4-4f28-474b-80d8-ca2fc52b10d0.

Joel, Billy. "The Entertainer." *Streetlife Serenade.* Columbia, 1975.

Johansen, Claes. *Procol Harum: Beyond the Pale.* London: SAF, 2000.

_____. *The Zombies: Hung Up on a Dream.* London: SAF, 2001.

John McLaughlin Official Website. Accessed September 5, 2010. http://www.johnmclaughlin.com/.

John Sebastian. Accessed September 5, 2010. http://www.johnbsebastian.com/.

Johns, Adrian. *Death of a Pirate: British Radio and the Making of the Information Age.* New York: W. W. Norton, 2010.

Jones, Davy. *Daydream Believin'.* Metairie, LA: Hercules Promotions, 2000.

Judy Collins. Accessed September 5, 2010. http://www.judycollins.com/index1.php.

Kaliss, Jeff. *I Want to Take You Higher: The Life and Times of Sly and the Family Stone.* Revised ed. San Francisco: Backbeat, 2009.

Kay, John, and John Einarson. *Magic Carpet Ride: The Autobiography of John Kay and Steppenwolf.* Kingston, ON: Quarry, 1994.

Kennedy, John F. "We Choose to Go to the Moon Speech." *The History Place Great Speeches Collection.* Accessed January 13, 2010. http://www.historyplace.com/speeches/jfk-space.htm.

Kent, Enoch. "Reviews." *Enoch Kent: Legendary Scottish-Canadian Songsmith.* Accessed January 13, 2010. http://www.enochkent.ca/reviews.htm.

Kerns, Williams. "Buddy and Maria Elena Holly Married 50 Years Ago." *Lubbock Avalanche-Journal,* August 15, 2008. http://www.lubbockonline.com/stories/081508/loc_3188469 94.shtml.

Kisseloff, Jeff. *Generation on Fire: Voices of Protest from the 1960s, an Oral History.* Lexington: University Press of Kentucky, 2007.

Kitts, Thomas M. *Ray Davies: Not Like Everybody Else.* New York: Routledge, 2007.

_____, and Michael J. Kraus, eds. *Living on a Thin Line: Crossing Aesthetic Borders with the Kinks.* Rumford, RI: Rock 'n' Roll Research, 2002.

Knight, Chris. "Interview with 'Weird Al' Yankovic — Parody Artist and Star Wars Super-Fan." *TheForce.net.* Accessed December 17, 2010. http://www.theforce.net/jedicouncil/interview/weirdal.asp.

Koch, Stephen. "KAAY: The Mighty 1090 Gave Arkansas to North America." *Arkansas Business,* 2004. http://www.arkansasbusiness.com/20/icon_essay.asp?essayID=19.

Kolosky, Walter. *Power, Passion and Beauty: The Story of the Legendary Mahavishnu Orchestra.* Cary, NC: Abstract Logix, 2006.

Kotsopoulos, Nikos. *Krautrock: Cosmic Rock and Its Legacy.* London: Black Dog, 2010.

Kugelberg, Johan, ed. *The Velvet Underground: New York Art.* New York: Rizzoli, 2009.

Kulawiec, Rich. "FAQ: The Annotated 'American Pie.'" *FAQs.org.* Accessed May 23, 2011. http://www.faqs.org/faqs/music/american-pie/.

La Capra, Dominick. *Writing History, Writing Trauma.* Baltimore: Johns Hopkins University Press, 2001.

Ladd, Jim. *Radio Waves: Life and Revolution on the FM Dial.* New York: St. Martin's Griffin, 1992.

Lane, John R. *Stuart Davis: Art and Art Theory.* Brooklyn: Brooklyn Museum, 1978.

Lawrence, Sharon. *Jimi Hendrix: The Intimate Story of a Betrayed Music Legend.* New York: Harper, 2006.

Lebans, Jim, and Bob McDonald. *The Quirks and Quarks Guide to Space: 42 Questions (and Answers) About Life, the Universe, and Everything.* Toronto: McLelland & Stewart, 2008.

Lee, Laura. *Arlo, Alice, and Anglicans: The Lives of a New England Church.* Lee, MA: Berkshire House, 2000.

Lefcowitz, Eric. *The Monkees Tale.* 2d ed. Berkeley, CA: Last Gasp of San Francisco, 1989.

Lehmer, Larry. *The Day the Music Died: The Last Tour of Buddy Holly, the Big Bopper and Ritchie Valens.* New York: Music Sales Corporation, 2003.

Leibovitz, Annie. *Annie Leibovitz: Photographs 1970–1990.* New York: Harper Collins, 1991.

Leitch, Donovan. *The Autobiography of Donovan: The Hurdy Gurdy Man.* New York: St. Martin's Griffin, 2005.

Lemke, Gayle. *The Art of the Fillmore: 1966–1971.* Secaucus, NJ: Carol, 1999.

Leng, Simon. *While My Guitar Weeps: The Music of George Harrison.* New York: Hal Leonard, 2006.

Lescure, Steve. "The Dylan Commentaries: A Guide to the Works of Bob Dylan." *Judas Magazine.* Accessed May 23, 2011. http://www.judasmagazine.com/pages.asp/net7.asp.

Levine, Lawrence W. *Black Culture and Black Consciousness: Afro-American Folk Thought from Slavery to Freedom.* New York: Oxford University Press, 1978.

Levitt, Saul. *The Ultimate American Pie Website.* Accessed March 1, 2011. http://www.missamericanpie.co.uk/index.html.

Lewis, Jo Ann. "Everybody Loves van Gogh." *Washington Post,* January 14, 1998. http://www.washingtonpost.com/wp-srv/style/museums/features/98vangogh/ 980114vangogh.htm.

Linder, Douglas O. "The Chicago Seven Conspiracy Trial." *Famous American Trials.* Accessed January 13, 2010. http://www.law.umkc.edu/faculty/projects/ftrials/Chicago7/Chicago7.html.

Lindisfarne Official Website. Accessed September 5, 2010. http://www.lindisfarne.co.uk/.

Lindsay, Mark. *Mark Lindsay: Former Lead Singer of Paul Revere and the Raiders.* Accessed September 5, 2010. http://www.marklindsay.com.

Ling, David. *Wizards and Demons: The Uriah Heep Story.* n.p.: Classic Rock Productions, 2002.

Lippard, Lucy R., ed. *Pop Art.* New York: Praeger, 1966.

Lipsitz, George. *Time Passages: Collective Memory and American Popular Culture.* Minneapolis: University of Minnesota Press, 1990.

Livingstone, Marco. *Pop-Art: A Continuing History.* New York: Harry N. Abrams, 1990.

Lodge, Tom. *The Ship That Rocked the World: How Radio Caroline Defied the Establishment, Launched the British Invasion and Made the Planet Safe for Rock and Roll.* Savage, MD: Bartleby, 2010.

"Lost in Space." *Internet Movie Database.* Accessed January 13, 2010. http://www.imdb.com/title/tt0058824/.

LouReed.com. Accessed September 5, 2010. http://www.loureed.com/00/index.html/.

Love on Earth Must Be Arthur Lee. Accessed September 5, 2010. http://www.lovearthurlee.com/.

Lovin' Spoonful. *The Lovin' Spoonful.* Accessed September 5, 2010. http://www.lovinspoonful.com/.

Lymon, Frankie, and the Teenagers. "Why Do Fools Fall in Love." Gee, 1956.

Macan, Edward. *Endless Enigma: A Musical Biography of Emerson, Lake, and Palmer.* Peru, IL: Open Court, 2006.

_____. *Rocking the Classics: English Progressive Rock and the Counterculture.* Oxford: Oxford University Press, 1997.

Macomber, Kris, Christine Mallinson, and Elizabeth Seale. "'Katrina That Bitch!' Hegemonic Representations of Women's Sexuality on Hurricane Katrina Souvenir T-Shirts." *Journal of Popular Culture* 44 (June 2011): 525–44. doi: 10.1111/j.1540-5931.2011.00847.x.

Mamiya, Christin J. *Pop-art and Consumer Culture.* Austin: University of Texas Press, 1992.

Marcus, Greil. *When That Rough God Goes Riding: Listening to Van Morrison.* New York: Public Affairs, 2010.

Markwick, Bill. "The Folk File: A Folkies Dictionary." *The Folk File.* Last modified November 8, 2008. http://www.folklib.net/folkfile/.

Marmorstein, Gary. *The Label: The Story of Columbia Records.* New York: Da Capo, 2007.

Marsh, Dave. *Before I Get Old: The Story of The Who.* Medford, NJ: Plexus, 2003.

_____. *For the Record 5: George Clinton and P-Funkadelic.* New York: Harper Perennial, 1998.

Martin, Bill. *Listening to the Future: The Time of Progressive Rock 1968–1978.* Peru, IL: Open Court, 1998.

_____. *Music of Yes: Structure and Vision in Progressive Rock.* Peru, IL: Open Court, 1996.

Mason, Nick. *Inside Out: A Personal History of Pink Floyd.* San Francisco: Chronicle, 2005.

Massingill, Randi L. *Total Control: The Monkees Michael Nesmith Story.* Carlsbad, CA: FLEXquarters, 2005.

Matheu, Robert. *CREEM: America's Only Rock 'N' Roll Magazine.* New York: Collins Living, 2007.

_____. *The Stooges: The Authorized and Illustrated Story.* New York: Abrams, 2009.

Matovina, Dan. *Without You: The Tragic Story of Badfinger.* San Mateo, CA: Frances Glover, 2000.

Maysles, Albert, and David Maysles. *Gimme Shelter.* Maysles Films, 1970.

The MC5. Accessed September 5, 2010. http://www.mc5.org/.

McDonald, Ian. *Revolution in the Head: The Beatles' Records and the Sixties.* 2d revised ed. London: Pimlico, 2005.

McDonough, Jimmy. *Shakey: Neil Young's Biography.* New York: Anchor, 2003.

McGee, Garry. *Band on the Run: A History of Paul McCartney and Wings.* New York: Taylor Trade Publishing, 2003.

McIver, Joe. *Sabbath Bloody Sabbath.* London: Omnibus, 2007.

McLean, Don. "American Pie." *American Pie.* United Artists, 1971.

_____. *American Pie.* United Artists, 1971.

McNally, Dennis. *A Long Strange Trip: The Inside History of the Grateful Dead.* New York: Broadway, 2003.

McShine, Kynaston. *Andy Warhol: A Retrospective.* New York: Museum of Modern Art, 1989.

McStravick, Summer, and John Roos. *Blues-Rock Explosion.* Mission Viejo, CA: Old Goat, 2002.

Melhuish, Martin. *The Supertramp Book.* London: Omnibus, 1986.

Mercer, Michelle. *Will You Take Me As I Am: Joni Mitchell's Blue Period.* New York: Free Press, 2009.

Mettler, Gregg. "Celebration Day," *That '70s Show,* season 5, episode 25, directed by David Trainer, aired May 14, 2003. Carsey-Werner Productions.

Meyer, David. *Twenty Thousand Roads: The Ballad of Gram Parsons and His Cosmic American Music.* New York: Villard, 2008.

Meyer, Leonard. *Music and Emotion.* Chicago: University of Chicago Press, 1957.

Michael Bloomfield Official Website. Accessed September 5, 2010. http://www.mikebloomfield.com/.

Michaels, Scott. "Buddy Holly, Ritchie Valens, and J. P. Richardson." *Find a Death.com.* Accessed May 23, 2011. http://www.findadeath.com/Deceased/h/Buddy%20Holly/buddy_holly.htm.

Miles, Barry. *Paul McCartney: Many Years from Now.* New York: Holt, 1998.

Miller, Andy. *The Kinks Are the Village Green Preservation Society.* New York: Continuum, 2003.

Miller, Frederic P., Agnes F. Vandome, and John McBrewster, eds. *Hoyt Axton.* Mauritius: Alphascript, 2010.

_____. *John Mayall.* Mauritius: Alphascript, 2010.

Mills, Peter. *Hymn to the Silence: Inside the Words and Music of Van Morrison.* New York: Continuum, 2010.

Mr. Talk. "Levee Goes Dry as 'American Pie' Tavern Loses Liquor License." *Talk of the Sound.* Last modified August 19, 2008. http://www.newrochelletalk.com/node/93.

The Monkees. *The Monkees.* Colgems, 1966.

_____. *More of the Monkees.* Colgems, 1967.

The Monotones. "Book of Love." Mascot, 1958.

Morella, Joe, and Patricia Barey. *Simon and Garfunkel: Old Friends: A Dual Biography.* Secaucus, NJ: Carol, 1991.

Morse, Tim. *Yesstories: Yes in Their Own Words.* New York: St. Martin's Griffin, 1996.

Moser, Margaret, and Bill Crawford. *Rock Stars Do the Dumbest Things.* New York: Renaissance, 1998.

MPL Communications Ltd./Paul McCartney. *Paul McCartney*. Accessed September 5, 2010. http://www.paulmccartney.com/.

Murphy, Peter. "Altamont: The Killing Field." *Hot Press*. Accessed January 13, 2010. http://www.hotpress.com/archive/392017.html.

Music of China. Accessed June 22, 2010. http://www.chinesemusic.eu/.

Myers, Paul. *A Wizard, a True Star: Todd Rundgren in the Studio*. London: Jawbone, 2010.

Nadel, Ira B. *Various Positions: A Life of Leonard Cohen*. Austin: University of Texas Press, 2007.

Nagy, Shawn. "Winter Dance Party." *Buddy Holly Online*. Accessed January 13, 2010. http://www.buddyhollyonline.com/mainwdp.html.

National Transportation Safety Board. "Civil Aeronautics Board: Aircraft Accident Report; Beech Bonanza N 3794N." Accessed January 13, 2010. http://www.ntsb.gov/Publictn/1959/CAB_2-3-1959.pdf.

Neary, John. "The Magical McCartney Mystery." *Life*, November 7, 1969, 103–6.

Neer, Richard. *FM: The Rise and Fall of Rock Radio*. New York: Villard, 2001.

Neil Young. Accessed September 5, 2010. http://www.neilyoung.com/.

Nelson, Ricky. "Garden Party." *Garden Party*. Geffen, 1990.

Nelson-Burns, Lesley. "The Liberty Song." Accessed June 22, 2010. http://www.contemplator.com/america/liberty.html.

_____. "Yankee Doodle." *Popular Songs in American History*. Accessed June 22, 2010. http://www.contemplator.com/america/ydoodle.html.

The New Lexicon Webster's Encyclopedic Dictionary of the English Language. New York: Lexicon, 1990.

The New Seekers. "What Have They Done to My Song Ma." *Keith Potger and the New Seekers*. Phillips, 1970.

New York Times, August 5, 1964.

New York Times, August 6, 1964.

Newman, Richard. *John Mayall: Blues Breaker*. Tampa, FL: Sanctuary, 1996.

Newsom, Michael. "UM Remembers Slain Civil Rights Workers." *Daily Mississippian*, June 18, 2004. www.thedmonline.com/2.2838/um-remembers-slain-civil-rights-workers-1.123056.

Nickelback. "Rockstar." *All the Right Reasons*. Rodrunner, 2005.

"Niki Sullivan." *Buddy Holly and the Crickets.com*. Accessed January 13, 2010. http://www.buddyhollyandthecrickets.com/related/sullivan.html.

Nolan, Tom. "Review of *Homeless Brother*." *Rolling Stone*, January 16, 1975, 52.

Nollan, Scott Allen. *Jethro Tull: A History of the Band 1968–2001*. Jefferson, NC: McFarland, 2001.

Noone, Peter. *Herman's Hermits*. Accessed September 5, 2010. http://www.hermanshermits.com/.

Nora, Pierre. *Realms of Memory*. Edited by Lawrence D. Kritzman. Translated by Arthur Goldhammer. New York: Columbia University Press, 1992.

Norman, Philip. *John Lennon: The Life*. New York: Ecco, 2009.

_____. *Shout! The Beatles in Their Generation*. Revised and updated ed. New York: Fireside, 2003.

"Not Fading Away: Jerry Allison." *JamBase*. Accessed January 13, 2010. http://www.jambase.com/Articles/5703/NOT-FADING-AWAY-JERRY- ALLISON.

Novak, B. J. "The Chair Model," *The Office*, season 4, episode 10, directed by Jeffrey Blitz, aired April 17, 2008. Universal.

O'Brien, Paul. "American Pie — The Analysis and Interpretation of Don McLean's Song Lyrics." *The Rare Exception: Music Rumors, Legends, and Fictions*. Accessed June 29, 2009. http://www.rareexception.com/?p=140.

"On This Date (April 6, 2004) Niki Sullivan / Buddy Holly and the Crickets." *The Music's Over: But the Celebration Lives On*. Accessed January 13, 2010. http://themusicsover.wordpress.com/2009/04/06/niki-sullivan.

Paid Inc. *Alice Cooper Official Website*. Accessed September 5, 2010. http://www.alicecooper.com/.

_____. *Deep Purple: The Official Website*. Accessed September 5, 2010. http://www.deeppurple.com/.

_____. *The Official Moody Blues Fan Community*. Accessed February 18, 2012. http://www.moodybluestoday.com.

Pallas, Jim. Untitled Web page. *JPallas.com*. Accessed April 25, 2010. http://www.jpallas.com/hh/rj/DAMintervw-RayJ.html.

Patterson, R. Gary. *Take a Walk on the Dark Side: Rock and Roll Myths, Legends, and Curses.* New York: Fireside, 2004.

Patterson, Rob. "Reason to Roam: Brooklyn-Born Ramblin' Jack Elliott Moseys through Houston with Some Friends." *Houston Press* (April 9, 1998).

Paxton, Tom. *The Honor of Your Company.* New York: Cherry Lane Music Company, 2000.

_____. *Tom Paxton.* Last modified February 12, 2012. http://www.tompaxton.com/.

Paytress, Mark. *Bolan: The Rise and Fall of a 20th Century Superstar.* London: Music Sales, 2007.

Perone, James E. *Mods, Rockers, and the Music of the British Invasion.* Westport, CT: Praeger, 2009.

_____. *The Words and Music of Carole King.* Westport, CT: Praeger, 2006.

_____. *The Words and Music of David Bowie.* Westport, CT: Praeger, 2007.

Pete Levin. Accessed September 5, 2010. http://www.petelevin.com/ibbbb/ibbbb01.htm.

"Pete Seeger: Folk Singer and Songwriter." *Notable American Unitarians.* Accessed May 23, 2011. http://www.harvardsquarelibrary.org/unitarians/seeger.html.

PetulaClark.net: The Official Web Site of Petula Clark. Last modified February 16, 2012. http://www.petulaclark.net/.

Phillips, Michelle. *California Dreamin': The True Story of the Mamas and the Papas: The Music, the Madness, the Magic That Was.* New York: Warner, 1986.

Pielke, Robert G. *You Say You Want a Revolution: Rock Music in American Culture.* Chicago: Nelson-Hall, 1986.

Pierce, Dave. *Riding on the Ether Express: A Memoir of 1960s Los Angeles, the Rise of Freeform Underground Radio, and the Legendary KPPC FM.* Lafayette, LA: Center for Louisiana Studies, 2008.

Pink Floyd. "Have a Cigar." *Wish You Were Here.* Harvest/EMI, 1975.

PinkFloyd.com. Accessed September 5, 2010. http://www.pinkfloyd.com/.

Poe, Randy. "Ramblin' Jack Elliott: An American Minstrel." *Sing Out!,* September 22, 2001.

_____. *Skydog: The Duane Allman Story.* San Francisco: Backbeat, 2008.

Popoff, Martin. *Black Sabbath: Doom Let Loose: An Illustrated History.* Toronto: ECW, 2006.

Povey, Glenn. *Echoes: The Complete History of Pink Floyd.* Chicago: Chicago Review Press, 2010.

_____. *Pink Floyd: In the Flesh: The Complete Performance History.* New York: St. Martin's Griffin, 1998.

Prine, John. *John Prine.* Van Nuys, CA: Alfred, 1999.

_____. *John Prine.* Accessed September 5, 2010. http://www.johnprine.net/.

"The Prosecution's Closing Argument." 2violent.com. Accessed January 13, 2010. http://www.2violent.com/closing_argument4.html.

"Punch Marty Balin in the Face Day." *Unremitting Failure: Pointless Expostulations on the Utter Futility of Everything.* Last modified December 6, 2007. http://futility.typepad.com/futility/2007/12/punch-marty-bal.html.

Randall Annie J. *Dusty! Queen of the Postmods.* Oxford: Oxford University Press, 2008.

Randy Newman. Accessed September 5, 2010. http://randynewman.com/.

Ray, Nicholas. *Rebel Without a Cause.* Warner Bros., 1955.

"Ray Johnson Biography." *Ray Johnson Estate.* Accessed September 10, 2012. http://www.rayjohnsonestate.com/biography.

"Ray Johnson: Father of Mail Art 1927–1995." Accessed April 25, 2010. http://www.actlab.utexas.edu/emma/Gallery/galleryjohnsonpix.html.

Rebennack, Mac, and Jack Rummel. *Under a Hoodoo Moon: The Life of the Night Tripper.* New York: St. Martin's Griffin, 1995.

Redding, Noel, and Carol Appleby. *Are You Experienced? The Inside Story of the Jimi Hendrix Experience.* New York: Da Capo, 1996.

Rees, David. *Minstrels in the Gallery: A History of Jethro Tull.* Wembley, UK: Fire Fly, 2001.

Reid, Jan. *Texas Tornado: The Times and Music of Doug Sahm.* Austin: University of Texas Press, 2010.

"Report of the President's Commission on the Assassination of President Kennedy." *National Archives.* Accessed January 13, 2010. http://www.archives.gov/research/jfk/warren-commission-report.

Revere, Paul, and the Raiders. *Paul Revere and the Raiders.* Accessed September 5, 2010. http://www.paulrevereraiders.com/.

Reynolds, Anthony. *Leonard Cohen: A Remarkable Life*. London: Omnibus, 2010.
Rich, Michael. "The Day the Music Died, February 3, 1959." *Fifties Web*. Accessed May 23, 2011. http://www.fiftiesweb.com/crash.htm.
Richie Havens Official Site. Accessed September 5, 2010. http://www.richiehavens.com/official_site/home.html.
Rick Davies Productions, Inc. *Supertramp*. Accessed September 5, 2010. http://supertramp.com/.
Rico. "In Ricky Nelson's 'Garden Party,' Who Is Mr. Hughes?" *The Straight Dope*. Last modified August 10, 2004. http://www.straightdope.com/columns/read/2173/in-ricky-nelsons-garden-party-who-is-mr-hughes.
Rigby, Jonathan. *Roxy Music: Both Ends Burning*. Revised ed. London: Reynolds & Hearn, 2008.
"Ritchie Valens." *Find a Grave*. Last modified January 1, 2001. http://www.findagrave.com/cgi-bin/fg.cgi?page=gr&GRid=1363.
Robbins, Marty. "A White Sport Coat (and a Pink Carnation)" Columbia, 1957.
Rock, Mick. *Iggy and the Stooges: Raw Power*. Bath, UK: Palazzo Editions, 2011.
Rogan, Johnny. *The Byrds: Timeless Flight Revisited: The Sequel*. 4th ed. London: Rogan House, 1998.
_____. *The Complete Guide to the Music of John Lennon*. London: Omnibus, 1997.
_____. *John Lennon: The Albums*. London: Music Sales Group, 2008.
_____. *Neil Young: Zero to Sixty*. London: Calidore, 2000.
_____. *Van Morrison: No Surrender*. New York: Random House, 2005.
Roger McGuinn Folk Den. Accessed September 5, 2010. http://www.ibiblio.org/jimmy/mcguinn/.
Rogers, Jude. "Josh Ritter: Monto Water Rats, London." *The Guardian*. Last modified September 17, 2007. http://www.guardian.co.uk/music/2007/sep/17/popandrock.folk.
The Rolling Stones. *Beggar's Banquet*. Decca, 1968.
_____. "Jumpin' Jack Flash." Decca, 1968.
_____. *Let It Bleed*. Decca, 1969.
_____. *Sticky Fingers*. Atlantic, 1974.
_____. "Sympathy for the Devil." *Beggar's Banquet*. ABKCO, 1968.
_____, and Universal Music Group. *The Rolling Stones*. Accessed September 5, 2010. http://www.rollingstones.com.
"Rolling Stones: Altamont Speedway Free Festival." *Collector's Music Reviews*. Last modified February 18, 2008. http://www.collectorsmusicreviews.com/rolling-stones/rolling-stones-altamont-speedway-free-festival-tarkl-tcd-001-12.
"Rolling Stones Photo Galleries: Hell's Angels at Altamont, December 6, 1969." *MoreThings. com*. Accessed January 13, 2010. http://www.morethings.com/music/rolling_stones/im ages/hells_angels/index.ht ml.
Rosen, Craig. *The Billboard Book of Number One Albums*. New York: Billboard Books, 1996.
Roth, Lane. "*Vraisemblance* and the Western Setting in Contemporary Science Fiction Film." *Literature Film Quarterly* 13 (3): 180–6.
Roxy Music. *Roxy Music*. Accessed September 5, 2010. http://www.roxymusic.co.uk/.
Rubin, David S. *It's Only Rock and Roll: Rock and Roll Currents in Contemporary Art*. New York: Prestel, 1995.
_____. *Jay Defeo — Selected Works: Past and Present*. San Francisco: San Francisco Art Institute, 1984.
Russo, Greg. *Cosmik Debris: The Collected History and Improvisations of Frank Zappa*. 2d ed. Floral Park, NY: Crossfire, 2003.
_____. *Flying Colours: The Jethro Tull Reference Manual (Remastered Version)*. Floral Park, NY: Crossfire, 2009.
_____. *Mannerisms: The Five Phases of Manfred Mann*. Floral Park, NY: Crossfire, 1995.
_____. *Time of the Season: The Zombies Collector's Guide*. Revised ed. Floral Park, NY: Crossfire, 2007.
_____. *Yardbirds: The Ultimate Rave-Up*. Floral Park, NY: Crossfire, 2001.
Russo, Joe. *TheRascalsArchives.com*. Accessed September 5, 2010. http://www.therascalsar chives.com/.
Safka, Melanie. *Melanie*. Accessed September 5, 2010. http://www.melaniesmusic.com/.
Samagai, Frank. *The Mellotron Book*. Vallejo, CA: Artistpro, 2002.

Sanders, Craig. "The True Story of American Pie: History in McLean's Lyrics." *Suite101.com.* Last modified April 22, 2010. http://folkmusic.suite101.com/article.cfm/the-true-story-of-american-pie-history-in-mcleans-lyrics.

Sandoval, Andrew. *The Monkees: The Day-by-Day Story of the 60s TV Pop Sensation.* San Diego: Thunder Bay, 2005.

Santana Management. *Santana.com: The Official Web Site of Carlos Santana.* Accessed September 5, 2010. http://www.santana.com/.

Santiago, Eddie. *The Lives of Sylvester Stewart and Sly Stone.* n.p.: Lulu.com, 2008.

Savage, Jon. *The Kinks: The Official Biography.* London: Faber & Faber, 1985.

Savoy Brown. Accessed September 5, 2010. http://www.savoybrown.com/.

Schaffner, Nicholas. *Beatles Forever.* New York: Fine, 1994.

_____. *The British Invasion: From the First Wave to the New Wave.* New York: McGraw-Hill, 1982.

_____. *Saucerful of Secrets: The Pink Floyd Odyssey.* 2d ed. London: Helter Skelter, 1992.

Schneider, Pierre. *Matisse.* New York: Rizzoli, 1984.

Schreiber, Brad. *Becoming Jimi Hendrix: From Southern Crossroads to Psychedelic London, The Untold Story of a Musical Genius.* New York: Da Capo, 2010.

Schwartzman, Myron. *Romare Bearden: His Life and Art.* New York: Harry N. Abrams, 1990.

Seabrook, John. "Why Is the Force Still with Us?" *The New Yorker,* January 6, 1997. http://www.booknoise.net/johnseabrook/stories/culture/force/index.html.

Seger, Bob. "Turn the Page." *Back in '72.* Paradise, 1973.

Segrave, Kerry. *Payola in the Music Industry: A History, 1880–1991.* Jefferson, NC: McFarland, 1994.

Seraphine, Danny. *Street Player: My Chicago Story.* Hoboken, NJ: Wiley, 2010.

Sha Na Na. Accessed September 5, 2010. http://www.shanana.com/.

Shapiro, Harry. *Eric Clapton: Lost in the Blues.* New York: Da Capo, 1992.

_____. *Jack Bruce: Composing Himself: The Authorized Biography.* London: Jawbone, 2010.

_____. *Jimi Hendrix: Electric Gypsy.* New York: St. Martin's, 1991.

_____. *Waiting for the Man: The Story of Drugs and Popular Music.* London: Helter Skelter, 2003.

Sheff, David. "*Playboy* Interview with John Lennon and Yoko Ono." *Playboy* (January 1981).

Sheppard, Gloria. *Brian Jones Straight from the Heart: The Rolling Stones Murder.* Johnstown, CO: High Seas, 2007.

Sherman, Dale. *The Illustrated Collector's Guide to Alice Cooper.* Burlington, ON: Collector's Guide Publishing, 2009.

Shotton, Pete, and Nicholas Schaffner. *John Lennon: In My Life.* New York: Stein and Day, 1983.

Simon & Garfunkel. Accessed September 5, 2010. http://www.simonandgarfunkel.com/news.html.

Sinclair, John. *Guitar Army: Rock and Revolution with the MC5 and the White Panther Party.* 35th anniversary ed. Port Townsend, WA: Process, 2007.

Slaven, Neil. *Electric Don Quixote: The Definitive Story of Frank Zappa.* 2d ed. London: Omnibus, 2003.

Slotkin, Richard. *Gunfighter Nation: The Myth of the Frontier in Twentieth-Century America.* Norman: University of Oklahoma Press, 1998.

Smiley, Ralph E. "The Coroner's Report." *Fifties Web.* Accessed January 13, 2010. http://www.fiftiesweb.com/coroner.htm.

Smith, Bradley. *The Billboard Guide to Progressive Music.* New York: Billboard Books, 1998.

Smith, Patrick S. *Warhol's Art and Films.* Ann Arbor, MI: UMI Research Press, 1986.

Smith, Ronald. *WCFL Chicago Top 40 Charts 1865–1976.* New York: iUniverse, Inc., 2007.

Smith, Sid. *In the Court of King Crimson.* London: Helter Skelter, 2002.

Snider, Charles. *The Strawberry Bricks Guide to Progressive Rock.* Chicago: Strawberry Brick, 2008.

Snider, Todd. "Talkin' Seattle Grunge Rock Blues." *Songs for the Daily Planet.* Yep Roc, 1994.

"Songs of the Century." *CNN.com.* Last modified March 7, 2001. http://archives.cnn.com/2001/SHOWBIZ/Music/03/07/list.top.365.songs/index.html.

Sony Music Entertainment. *Jimi Hendrix: Originality Electrified.* Accessed September 5, 2010. http://www.jimihendrix.com/us/home.

_____. *Joe Cocker*. Accessed September 5, 2010. http://www.cocker.com/us/home.

_____. *Leonard Cohen*. Accessed September 12, 2010. http://www.leonardcohen.com/.

_____. *Sly and the Family Stone*. Accessed September 5, 2010. http://www.slystonemusic.com/.

The Sound of Music soundtrack. RCA Victor, 1965.

Sounes, Howard. *Down the Highway: The Life of Bob Dylan*. New York: Grove, 2011.

_____. *Fab: The Life of Paul McCartney*. New York: Da Capo, 2010.

Spitz, Bob. *Barefoot in Babylon: The Creation of the Woodstock Music Festival 1969*. New York: W. W. Norton, 1989.

_____. *The Beatles: The Biography*. New York: Back Bay, 2006.

_____. *Dylan: A Biography*. New York: W. W. Norton, 1991.

Spitz, Marc. *Bowie: A Biography*. New York: Three Rivers, 2009.

Spitz, Robert Stephen. *The Making of Superstars: Artists and Executives of the Rock Music Business*. Garden City, NY: Anchor, 1978.

Spoon Records. *Can*. Accessed September 5, 2010. http://www.spoonrecords.com/.

Stannard, Neville. *The Long and Winding Road: A History of the Beatles on Record*. New York: Avon, 1984.

Starr, Larry, and Christopher Waterman. *American Popular Music: From Minstrelsy to MP3*. 2d ed. New York: Oxford University Press, 2007.

_____. *American Popular Music: From Minstrelsy to MTV*. New York: Oxford University Press, 2003.

Starr, Ringo. *Ringo Starr Official Site*. Accessed September 5, 2010. http://www.ringostarr.com/.

Status Quo: Quid Pro Quo. Last modified February 12, 2012. http://www.statusquo.co.uk/.

Stump, Paul. *Digital Gothic: A Critical Discography of Tangerine Dream*. London: SAF, 1997.

_____. *Gentle Giant: Acquiring the Taste*. London: SAF, 2005.

_____. *Go Ahead: The Music of John McLaughlin*. London: SAF, 2000.

_____. *The Music's All That Matters: A History of Progressive Rock*. London: Quartet, 1998.

_____. *Unknown Pleasures: Cultural Biography of Roxy Music*. New York: Thunder's Mouth, 1998.

The Supremes. *Greatest Hits*. Motown, 1967.

Sylvester, Julia. *John Chamberlain: A Catalogue Raisonne of the Sculpture, 1954–1985*. New York: Hudson Hills, 1986.

Szatmary, David. *Rockin' In Time: A Social History of Rock-and-Roll*. Englewood Cliffs, NJ: Prentice Hall, 2006.

Tamarkin, Jeff. *Got a Revolution! The Turbulent Flight of Jefferson Airplane*. New York: Atria, 2005.

Tangerine Dream. *Tangerine Dream: The Official Website*. Accessed September 5, 2010. http://www.tangerinedream.org/.

Taylor, Derek. *It Was Twenty Years Ago Today*. New York: Fireside, 1987.

The Temptations. *Greatest Hits*. Gordy, 1966.

Ten Years After. Accessed September 5, 2010. http://www.ten-years-after.com/.

"Testimony of Paul Watkins in the Charles Manson Trial." *Famous American Trials*. Accessed January 13, 2010. http://www.law.umkc.edu/faculty/projects/ftrials/manson/mansontestimony- w.html.

Thompson, Dave. *Cream: The World's First Supergroup*. London: Virgin, 2010.

_____. *David Bowie: Moonage Daydream*. Medford, NJ: Plexus, 1996.

_____. *Smoke on the Water: The Deep Purple Story*. Toronto: ECW, 2004.

_____. *Space Daze: The History and Mystery of Electronic Ambient Space Rock*. Los Angeles: Cleopatra Records, 1994.

_____. *Truth! ... Rod Stewart, Ron Wood, and the Jeff Beck Group*. London: Cherry Red, 2006.

_____. *Turn It On Again: Peter Gabriel, Phil Collins, and Genesis*. San Francisco: Backbeat, 2004.

_____. *The Wit and Wisdom of Ozzy Osbourne*. Iola, WI: Krause, 2010.

_____. *Your Pretty Face Is Going to Hell: The Dangerous Glitter of David Bowie, Iggy Pop, and Lou Reed*. San Francisco: Backbeat, 2009.

Tom Rush. Last modified February 12, 2012, http://tomrush.com/.

Touch the Moon Studio. *Peter Paul and Mary*. Accessed September 5, 2010. http://www.peterpaulandmary.com/.

Tracy, James. *Direct Action: Radical Pacifism from the Union Eight to the Chicago Seven.* Chicago: University of Chicago Press, 1996.

Triangle Media. *TheYardbirds.com.* Accessed September 5, 2010. http://www.theyardbirds.com/.

Tr-i.com. Accessed September 5, 2010. http://www.tr-i.com/.

The Troggs Official Website. Accessed September 5, 2010. http://www.my-generation.org.uk/Troggs/.

Turner, Frederick Jackson. "The Frontier in American History." *The University of Virginia Department of English Web site.* Last modified September 30, 1997, http://xroads.virginia.edu/~HYPER/TURNER/.

The Turtles — Flo and Eddie Inc. *The Turtles Featuring Flo and Eddie.* Accessed September 5, 2010. http://www.theturtles.com/.

Underwood, Lee. *Blue Melody: Tim Buckley Remembered.* San Francisco: Backbeat, 2002.

Unterberger, Richie. *Eight Miles High: Folk-Rock's Flight from Haight-Ashbury to Woodstock.* San Francisco: Backbeat, 2003.

_____. *The Rough Guide to Jimi Hendrix.* London: Rough Guides, 2009.

_____. *Turn! Turn! Turn!: The '60s Folk-Rock Revolution.* San Francisco: Backbeat, 2002.

_____. *Urban Spacemen and Wayfaring Strangers: Overlooked Innovators and Eccentric Visionaries of '60s Rock.* San Francisco: Miller Freeman, 2000.

_____. *White Light/White Heat: The Velvet Underground Day by Day.* London: Jawbone, 2009.

Uriah Heep. Accessed September 5, 2010. http://www.uriah-heep.com/newa/index.php.

Van der Graaf Generator. Accessed September 5, 2010. http://www.vandergraafgenerator.co.uk/.

Vanilla Fudge. Accessed September 12, 2010. http://www.vanillafudge.com/.

Vaughan, Andrew. *The Eagles: An American Band.* New York: Sterling, 2010.

Vellenga, Dirk, and Mick Farren. *Elvis and the Colonel.* New York: Delacorte, 1988.

Verve Music Group. *John Fogerty Centerfield.* Accessed September 5, 2010. http://www.johnfogerty.com/.

Waite, Lisa. "Rock and Roll! Using Classic Rock as a Guide to Fantasy-Theme Analysis." *Communication Teacher* 22 (January 2008): 10–3. doi: 10.1080/17404620801914491.

Wakeman, Rick. *Further Adventures of a Grumpy Old Rock Star.* London: Preface, 2010.

_____. *Grumpy Old Rockstar and Other Wondrous Stories.* London: Preface, 2009.

Waksman, Steve. *Instruments of Desire: The Electric Guitar and the Shaping of Musical Experience.* Cambridge, MA: Harvard University Press, 1999.

Wald, Elijah. *How the Beatles Destroyed Rock n Roll: An Alternative History of American Popular Music.* Oxford: Oxford University Press, 2009.

Walker, John A. *Cross-overs: Art into Pop/Pop into Art.* New York: Methuen, 1987.

Walsh, Joe. "Life's Been Good." *But Seriously Folks.* Asylum, 1978.

Watkinson, David, and Rick Wakeman. *Yes: Perpetual Change.* Medford, NJ: Plexus, 2001.

Watson, Ben. *Frank Zappa: The Complete Guide to His Music.* London: Omnibus, 2005.

_____. *Frank Zappa: The Negative Dialectics of Poodle Play.* New York: St. Martin's, 1995.

"The Weavers." *Folk Music Archives.* Accessed January 13, 2010. http://folkmusicarchives.org/weavers.htm.

Weinberg, Max, with Robert Santelli. *The Big Beat: Conversations with Rock's Greatest Drummers.* New York: Hal Leonard, 1984.

Weinstein, Norman. *Carlos Santana: A Biography.* Santa Barbara, CA: Greenwood, 2009.

"'Weird Al' Yankovic Dishes on James Blunt, Discusses His Role as the Whitest, Nerdiest Rock Star Ever." *Rolling Stone,* September 9, 2006. http://www.rollingstone.com/music/news/weird-al-yankovic-dishes-on-james-blunt-discusses-his-role-as-the-whitest-nerdiest-rock-star-ever-20060919.

Welch, Chris. *Changes: The Stories Behind Every David Bowie Song 1970–1980.* London: Carlton, 1999.

_____. *Cream: Eric Clapton, Jack Bruce, and Ginger Baker—The Legendary 60s Supergroup.* San Francisco: Backbeat, 2000.

_____. *David Bowie: We Could Be Heroes.* New York: Da Capo, 1999.

_____. *Genesis: The Complete Guide to Their Music.* London: Omnibus, 2006.

_____. *Hendrix: A Biography.* London: Omnibus, 1982.

_____. *Power and Glory: Jimmy Page and Robert Plant.* New York: Cherry Lane Music Company, 1986.

_____. *Steve Winwood: Roll with It.* New York: Perigee, 1990.

Weller, Sheila. *Girls Like Us: Carole King, Joni Mitchell, Carly Simon — and the Journey of a Generation.* New York: Washington Square.

Werner, Craig. *Up Around the Bend: The Oral History of Creedence Clearwater Revival.* New York: Harper Perennial, 1999.

West, Leslie, and Corky Laing. *Nantucket Sleighride and Other Mountain On-the-Road Stories.* London: SAF, 2003.

Whitburn, Joel. *The Billboard Book of Top 40 Hits.* New York: Billboard Books, 2000.

_____. *The Billboard Book of Top 40 Hits.* 9th ed. New York: Billboard Books, 2010.

_____. *Billboard's Top 1000 Hits of the Rock Era 1955–2005.* Menomonee Falls, WI: Record Research, 2006.

_____. *Joel Whitburn's Top Pop Singles 1955–1990.* Menomonee Falls, WI: Record Research, 1991.

_____. *Joel Whitburn's Top Pop Singles 1955–2002.* 10th ed. Menomonee Falls, WI: Record Research, 2004.

White, Timothy. *James Taylor Long Ago and Far Away: His Life and His Music.* 2d ed. London: Omnibus, 2005.

_____. *The Nearest Faraway Place: Brian Wilson, the Beach Boys, and the Southern California Experience.* New York: Henry Holt, 1996.

Whitesell, Lloyd. *The Music of Joni Mitchell.* Oxford: Oxford University Press, 2008.

Whittaker, Adrian. *An Incredible String Band Compendium.* London: Helter Skelter, 2003.

Wilentz, Sean. *Bob Dylan in America.* New York: Doubleday, 2010.

Wilkinson, Paul. *Rat Salad: Black Sabbath, The Classic Years, 1969–1975.* New York: Thomas Dunne, 2007.

Williamson, Nigel. *The Rough Guide to Bob Dylan 2 (Rough Guide Reference).* London: Rough Guides, 2006.

Winter, Jay. "Film and the Matrix of Memory." *American Historical Review* 106 (June 2001): 857–66. http://www.jstor.org/stable/2692328.

"The Winter Dance Party." *The History of Rock 'n' Roll.* Accessed May 23, 2011. http://www.history-of-rock.com/winter_dance_party.htm.

Winwood, Steve. *Steve Winwood.* Accessed September 5, 2010. http://www.stevewinwood.com/.

Wiseman, Rich. *Jackson Browne: The Story of a Hold Out.* New York: Doubleday, 1982.

Wishbone Ash, LLC. *Wishbone Ash.* Accessed September 5, 2010. http://wishboneash.com/.

Wohlin, Anna. *The Wild and Wycked World of Brian Jones: The True Story of My Love Affair with the Rolling Stone.* London: Blake, 2005.

Wolf World Inc. *John Kay and Steppenwolf.* Accessed September 5, 2012.

Wolfe, Tom. *The Electric Kool-Aid Acid Test.* New York: Picador, 2008.

Wolkin, Jan Mark. *Michael Bloomfield — If You Love These Blues: An Oral History.* San Francisco: Miller Freeman, 2000.

Woody Guthrie Links. Last modified June 15, 2001. http://www.woodyguthrie.de/links.html.

Woody Guthrie Productions, Inc. *The Official Woody Guthrie Website.* Accessed May 23, 2011. http://www.woodyguthrie.org/.

"World Press Photo of the Year: 1972." *World Press Photo.* Accessed January 13, 2010. http://www.worldpressphoto.org/index.php?option=com_photogallery&task=view&id=177&Itemid=115&bandwidth=high.

Yankovic, "Weird Al." "Bedrock Anthem." *Alapalooza.* Scotti Bros., 1993.

_____. "The Brady Bunch." *Weird Al" Yankovic in 3-D.* Rock 'n' Roll Records, 1984.

_____. "Eat It." *"Weird Al Yankovic in 3-D.* Rock 'n' Roll Records, 1984.

_____. "Gump." *Bad Hair Day.* Volcano, 1996.

_____. "Here's Johnny." *Polka Party!* Rock 'n' Roll Records, 1986.

_____. "Money for Nothing/Beverly Hillbillies." *UHF — Original Motion Picture Soundtrack and Other Stuff,* 1989.

_____. "The Saga Begins." *Running with Scissors.* Volcano, 1999.

_____. *"Weird Al" Yankovic.* Rock 'n' Roll Records, 1983.

_____. *"Weird Al" Yankovic in 3-D.* Rock 'n' Roll Records, 1984.

_____. "Yoda." *Dare to Be Stupid.* Rock 'n' Roll Records, 1985.

Yearhour Ltd. *The Who.* Accessed September 5, 2010. http://www.thewho.com.

Yes 97 LLC. *Yes.* Accessed September 5, 2010. http://www.yesworld.com/.

Young, Rusty, DBA Poco. *Poco.* Accessed September 5, 2010. http://www.poconut.org/.

Yusuf. Accessed September 5, 2010. http://catstevens.com/.

Zanella, Marco. "Peter Blake About Oasis' *Stop the Clocks* Image." *Oasis Blues: The Italian Milan Site for Pure Beady Eye, Oasis, City, and England Fans,* November 13, 2010. http://www.oasisblues.com/2010/11/peter-blake-about-oasis-stop-clocks.html.

Zappa, Frank, and Peter Occhiogrosso. *Real Frank Zappa Book.* New York: Fireside, 1990.

Zappanese. *Zappa.com.* Accessed September 5, 2010. http://www.zappa.com/flash/greasylove songs/index.html.

Zevon, Warren. "Even a Dog Can Shake Hands." *Sentimental Hygiene.* Virgin, 1987.

Zimmer, Dave. *Crosby, Stills and Nash: The Biography.* 3d ed. New York: Da Capo, 2008.

_____. *Four Way Street: The Crosby, Stills, Nash, and Young Reader.* New York: Da Capo, 2004.

Zimmerman, Keith, and Kent Zimmerman. *Sing My Way Home: Voices of the New American Roots Rock.* San Francisco: Backbeat Books, 2004.

The Zombies. *The Zombies featuring Colin Blunstone and Rod Argent.* Accessed September 5, 2010. http://thezombies.net/.

ZZ Top. *ZZ Top.* Accessed September 5, 2010. http://www.zztop.com/.

About the Contributors

Joseph E. **Burns** is a professor of communication at Southeastern Louisiana University where he teaches journalism, web design, film history and ethics courses. His research interests include the history of rock music, radio broadcasting and digital media, specifically podcasting and public journalism.

Russ **Crawford** is an associate professor of history at Ohio Northern University and author of *The Use of Sports to Promote the American Way of Life During the Cold War: Cultural Propaganda, 1946–1963*. His research interests include the history of sports, and he is researching the history of American football in France.

Harry Edwin **Eiss** is a professor at Eastern Michigan University. He has authored many publications, has served as an NEH humanist, and has received numerous teaching awards. He has also been the lead singer in numerous bands.

Richard J. **McGowan** teaches ethics and the history of ideas at Butler University. He has published in the areas of gender issues, history of ideas, and business ethics as well as popular culture.

Robert **McParland** is an associate professor and chair of English at Felician College in New Jersey. He is the author of *Charles Dickens's American Audience* (2010), *How to Write About Joseph Conrad* (2011), *Music and Literary Modernism* (2008), and essays on popular music. He is a songwriter member of American Society of Composers and Publishers (ASCAP).

William B. **Robison** is a professor of history and head of the Department of History and Political Science at Southeastern Louisiana University, and a lifelong musician. He is coeditor (with Ronald H. Fritze) of the *Historical Dictionary of Stuart England* (1996) and *Historical Dictionary of Late Medieval England* (2002); is coauthor (with Anna Sue Parrill) of *The Tudors on Film and Television* (2012); and has written numerous articles on early modern England.

Ray **Schuck**, a retired museum director, is a visiting assistant professor of history at Ohio Northern University in Ada, Ohio, where he established and teaches courses in the Public History/Museum Studies Program and serves as the university's rugby advisor and coach. He is the father of this book's co-editor.

Raymond I. **Schuck** is an assistant professor of communication in the Department of Humanities at Bowling Green State University Firelands. His research focuses on critical and rhetorical analysis of music, sports, television, film, literature, and popular entertainments. He has written and co-written essays for *American Behavioral Scientist*, *Journal of Communication Studies*, and *Western Journal of Communication*.

Index

Abbey Road 114, 115
ABC television network 24
Abrahams, Mick 115
Abraxas 116, 117
Absolutely Free 110
AC/DC 93
Acquiring the Taste 117
Ada, Ohio 1
Adams, Cecil 79–80
Adnopoz, Elliott *see* Elliott, Ramblin' Jack
The Adventures of Ozzie & Harriet 92
The Aerosol Grey Machine 113
After Bathing at Baxter's 110
After the Gold Rush 117
Aftermath 107
aging 83, 85
Agnew, Spiro 118, 145
aircraft 16, 18
airplane crash 17, 19, 20–21, 51, 53, 80–81, 104, 135, 158
Alapalooza 166
Albers, Josef 137
Ali, Tariq 61
Alice's Restaurant 110
"Alice's Restaurant Massacre" 146
"All Along the Watchtower" 146
All the Young Dudes 118
All Things Must Pass 115
"All You Need Is Love" 110
allegory 53, 56, 62, 64
Allison, Jerry 42–43
The Allman Brothers Band 40, 113, 116, 117, 118, 119
Allsup, Tommy 16, 17, 53

The Almanac Singers 71
Alpert, Herb, and the Tijuana Brass 105
Alpha Centauri 117
Altamont 18, 36–39, 43, 62, 65, 66–67, 81, 83, 84, 91, 154, 158
ambiguity 4, 12, 18, 44, 50, 52, 76, 78, 80, 97, 135–136, 158
"America" 89
America Eats Its Young 118
American Beauty 78, 116
American Civil War 89, 153
American frontier 161–162, 169
American Jeremiad 159–160
American Painting 136
American Pie (album) 15, 16, 18, 30, 40, 71, 100, 117, 118, 119, 150, 154
American Revolutionary War 88
Amon Düül II 113, 118, 120
"And Your Bird Can Sing" 106
Anderson, Benedict 157
Anderson, Ian 111, 115
The Animals 105, 110, 120
Anka, Paul 139
"Another One Bites the Dust" 166
"Another One Rides the Bus" 166
Aoxomoxoa 114
Aqualung 117
Archimedes 11
Are You Experienced 109, 110
Argent 115, 120
Argent, Zombie Rod 115
Aristotle 11

The Armory (Moorhead, Minnesota) 16
Arnason, H.H. 136
Ars Longa Vita Brevis 112
Arthur 114
As Safe as Yesterday Is 113
At Fillmore East 40, 117
"At the Hop" 57
Atom Heart Mother 116
Atomic Rooster 115
Autry, Gene 71
Avalon, Frankie 17
Axis: Bold as Love 109
Axton, Hoyt 104

Baba, Meher 146
Baby Boomers 88, 94, 152, 159
"Babylon" 18, 30, 119
Bach, Johann Sebastian 109
Bad Hair Day 167
Badfinger 114, 120
Baez, Joan 27, 104, 135
Bailyn, Bernard 153
Baker, Ginger 106, 112
Baker, Laverne 140
The Balcony 140
Balin, Marty 37
"Ballad of a Thin Man" 146
La Bamba (film) 17
The Band (musical act) 107, 111, 116, 117, 120
Band Aid 143
Band of Gypsies 116
Bare Trees 118
Barger, Ralph "Sonny" 37
Barre, Martin 111, 115
Barrett, Syd 108, 112
Basil, Toni 166
"The Battle Hymn of the Republic" 89

Baur, Michael 5, 11–12, 77–78, 85
Bayou Country 113
BBC Radio 2 49, 80
Beach Boys 105, 107, 110, 140
Bearden, Romare 137
Beat Generation 57, 60
"Beat It" 167
The Beatles 28, 30, 31, 33–34, 41, 58–59, 62, 63, 64, 65, 66, 84, 96, 103–104, 105, 106–107, 108, 110, 111, 112, 114, 115, 120, 135, 140, 141–143, 144, 145, 154, 158
The Beau Brummels 105
Beaumont, Texas 42
beauty queen 18
Beck, Jeff 111, 114, 117, 118, 120
Beck-Ola 114
Becker, Carl 152
"Bedrock Anthem" 166
Bee Gees 136
Beechcraft Bonanza 16
Beechmont Tavern 21, 78, 79
"Beeker Street" radio program 102
Beethoven, Ludwig van 87
Beggar's Banquet 26, 113
Behind the Music 94
"Being for the Benefit of Mr. Kite" 104, 108
Belafonte, Harry 104
The Belmonts *see* Dion and the Belmonts
Below the Salt 118
Benefit 116
Bercovitch, Sacvan 159–160
Berman, Wallace 137
Berry, Chuck 42, 60, 93
The Best of the Sir Douglas Quintet 106
Bethel, New York 65
The Beverly Hillbillies 166
The Bible 23, 56, 119
"The Bible Tells Me So" 23, 56
The Big Beat 24
The Big Bopper *see* Richardson, J.P.
Big Brother and the Holding Company 68, 110
Billboard 10, 15, 73, 104, 167
Bitches Brew 116
Black Mountain College 137

Black Oak Arkansas 117, 120
Black Sabbath (album) 116
Black Sabbath (musical act) 116, 117, 118, 120
Black Sabbath Vol. 4 118
"Blackbird" 145
Blackburn, Robin 61
The Blackhearts *see* Jett, Joan and the Blackhearts
The Blackout of 1965 31
Blake, Sir Peter Thomas 137, 140–143, 144
Blanchard, I.G. 90
Bless Its Pointed Little Head 114
Blight, David W. 152, 153
Blind Faith 113, 114, 120
Blonde on Blonde 107
Blood, Sweat, & Tears 111, 113, 116, 118, 120
Blood, Sweat & Tears 3 116
Blood, Sweat & Tears 4 118
Bloomfield, Michael 113, 120
"Blowin' in the Wind" 27, 135
Blowin' Your Mind 109
Blue 118
Blue Cheer 112, 120
blues rock 68, 109, 110, 111, 112, 113, 116
BMG (Bertelsman Music Group) 91
Bodnar, John 152
"The Bold Soldier" 88
"Bonnie Blue Flag" 89
Bonzo Dog Doo-Dah Band 109
"Book of Love" 22–23, 55–56, 69, 158
Bookends 113
Boone, Pat 24, 42
Born to Be 112
"Born to Be Wild" 111
Bourdon, David 139
Bowie, David 72, 109, 114–115, 116, 117, 118, 120, 135
Bowling Green State University 7
Boyd, William *see* Hopalong Cassidy
"The Brady Bunch" 166
Braham, David 89
Brain Capers 117
Brand New Boots and Panties 143
Bread 92

Bredahoff, Patty 38
The Bride Stripped Bare by Her Bachelors, Even 143
Bridge Over Troubled Waters 115
Brillo Boxes 139
Bringing It All Back Home 107
British Invasion 58–59, 105, 158
Broadway Boogie Woogie 136
Brockett, Jamie 114, 120
Broken Barricades 117
Brooklyn, New York 71
Broonzy, Bill 69
Brown, Arthur 112, 120
Brown, Savoy 109
"Brown Eyed Girl" 109
Brown v. Board of Education of Topeka, Kansas 51
Browne, Jackson 118, 120
Brubeck, Dave 108
Bruce, Jack 106
Bruegel, Pieter, the Elder 61
Buckley, Tim 106
Buffalo Springfield 63, 68, 84, 106, 110, 112, 113, 120, 135
Buffalo Springfield Again 110
Bunch, Carl 16
Burdon, Eric 110, 115, 120
"Buried Alive in the Blues" 39
Burnt Weeny Sandwich 116
Butler University 2–3
Butterfield, Paul 105
Butterworth, Mike 7
"By the Waters of Babylon" 155
Byrdmaniax 117
The Byrds 32–33, 63, 64, 84, 92, 105, 106, 112, 113, 117, 135, 145, 154, 158

Cage, John 137
Cahoots 117
Caine, Michael 143
Calloway, Cab 137
Calypso 104
Camelot (Broadway musical) 104
Camelot (reference to Kennedy presidency) 27
camp 140
Campbell, William 142
Can 113, 120
Candles in the Rain 116

Candlestick 35
Candlestick Park 62, 66
Canned Heat 110, 120
Can't Buy a Thrill 118
Captain Beefheart 110, 114, 120
Carnegie, Andrew 90
"Carol" 37
The Carpenters 117
Carroll, Lewis 15, 110
Casady, Jack 112
Cash, Johnny 135
Catch Bull at Four 118
CBS radio network 90
Chad & Jeremy 105
Chaney, James 76, 80, 81, 82, 84
Chapin, Ed 78
Chase 117, 120
Chevy 21, 54, 78–80, 82, 151
Chicago, Illinois 29, 51
Chicago (album) 116
Chicago (musical act) 116, 117, 118, 120
"Chicago" (song) 135
Chicago at Carnegie Hall 117
The Chicago Eight *see* the Chicago Seven
Chicago 5 118
The Chicago Seven 29
Chicago III 118
Chicago Transit Authority (album) 115
Chicago Transit Authority (musical act) 113, 115
Child Is the Father to the Man 111
Chunga's Revenge 116
church bells 41, 69, 154
civil rights movement 3, 5, 27, 51, 76, 80–82, 83, 84, 91, 138, 145
Clanton, Jimmy 17
Clapton, Eric 106, 109, 111, 114, 115
Clark, Petula 105
Clear Lake, Iowa 16, 53
"Clearwater" 71, 72, 154
The Cleftones 56, 84
Cleveland, Ohio 24, 57
Clifford, Clyde 102
Climbing! 116
Clinton, George 116
Close to the Edge 118
Close to You 117
Cobain, Kurt 166

Cochran, Eddie 43
Cocker, Joe 113, 116, 118, 120
Cohen, Leonard 110
Cold War 145
collective memory 152–155, 157, 159–161, 164, 168
Collins, Judy 29, 104
Columbian Exposition of 1893 162
The Comets 24, 91
"Comin' into Los Angeles" 70
communism 30
concept art 138, 142–144
The Concert for Bangladesh 117
Concord, Massachusetts 89
Constitutional Convention of 1787 89
Cooke, John 39
Coolio 166
Cooper, Alice 72, 113, 117, 118, 119
co-optation 83, 84, 154
CORE 80
Cornell, Don 23, 56
Cosmo's Factory 116
Cotchford Farm 26
counterculture 10, 29, 54–55, 62, 138, 146, 154
Country Joe and the Fish 64, 65, 84, 105, 110, 120, 135
country rock 103, 105, 112, 114, 119
"Courtesy of the Red, White, and Blue" 89
Cousin Brucie 57
"The Cover of the *Rolling Stone*" 95–96
Cowboy and Western music 71
"Cowboy Jack" 90
Cox, William Harold 82
Crazy Horse 114
The Crazy World of Arthur Brown 112
Cream 106, 110, 111, 112, 113, 114, 116, 120
Creedence Clearwater Revival 111, 113, 114, 116, 120, 135
The Crickets 16, 17, 40, 42–43
Cricklewood Green 117
Crosby, Bing 90
Crosby, David 32

Crosby, Stills, & Nash (album) 113
Crosby, Stills, & Nash (musical act) 113, 120
Crosby, Stills, Nash & Young 36, 37, 116, 120
"Crossroads" (song by Cream) 112
"Crossroads" (song by Don McLean) 119, 154
Crown of Creation 112
Cruising with Ruben & the Jets 113
Cry of Love 117
Cuban Missile Crisis 35, 80
cultural capital 158, 160–161, 164–165
culture 77–78, 85, 119, 150, 152, 153
Cunningham, Merce 137
Cutler, Sam 37

Daily Mississippian 81–82
Daltrey, Roger 146
dancing 19, 23, 24, 25, 53, 56–57, 64–65, 79, 153
Danny and the Juniors 57, 58, 84
Dante Alighieri 61
Dare to Be Stupid 166
Darin, Bobby 145
The Dave Clark Five 105
Davis, Fred 152
Davis, Miles 40, 116, 120
Davis, Spencer, Group 105, 109
Davis, Stuart 136, 137
"A Day in the Life" 108, 144
The day the music died (meaning in "American Pie") 15, 19, 20–21, 23, 26, 30, 38, 43, 53, 58, 62, 65, 67, 69, 72–73, 80–81, 84, 91, 135, 150–151, 153–154
"The Day the Music Died" (song) 20
Days of Future Passed 110
Dean, James 27, 60, 138, 150, 153
"Dear Mr. Fantasy" 109
"Dear Uncle Sam 135
Dearborn, Bob 79
Death and Disaster 139
Debarge, El 166
Deep Purple 112, 116, 117, 118, 120
Deep Purple in Rock 116

"The Defence of Fort McHenry" 89
DeFeo, Jay 137
Déja Vu 116
de Kooning, Elaine 137
de Kooning, Willem 137
Delaney and Bonnie 113, 115, 120
Democratic National Convention 29
Demons and Wizards 118
Denver, John 145
Derek and the Dominos 115, 120
Descartes, René 11
Dickenson, John 89
Diddley, Bo 140
DiMucci, Dion 16, 17, 58, 139
Dion and the Belmonts 16, 139
Dire Straits 166
Disraeli Gears 110, 111
The Divine Comedy 61
"Dixie" 89
Dixon, Lynda 7
"Do They Know It's Christmas?" 143
"Do You Believe in Magic" 56
Dr. Hook and the Medicine Show 95–96
Dr. Hook's Medicine Show and Traveling Circus 141
Dr. John 111, 118, 120
"Doctor Robert" 106
Doctor Zhivago 108
Does Humor Belong in Music? 107
Le Dome 94
Domino, Fats 24
Donahue, Tom 102
Donovan 105
"Don't Call Us, We'll Call You" 93
The Doobie Brothers 117, 118, 120
The Doors 102, 109, 114, 116, 118, 120, 145
Doremi Fasol Latido 118
double meaning 19, 20, 21, 27, 29, 31, 33, 35, 49, 51, 60, 78, 145, 158
Doug L 78
"Draft Dodger Rag" 135
"Draft Morning" 135
"Draft Resister" 135

Drake, Nick 114, 118, 120
Drowning Girl 140
drug use 26, 32–33, 38, 39, 54–55, 63, 64, 66, 94, 95, 97, 103, 106, 109, 122, 141, 144, 145
Duchamp, Marcel 138, 143–144
Dulle Griet 61
Dury, Ian 143
Dwyer, Jerry 17
Dwyer Flying Service 16, 17
Dylan, Bob 18, 27, 28, 33, 42, 43, 59–61, 63, 64, 70–71, 84, 91, 105, 107, 110, 114, 116, 120, 135, 146, 154, 158

The Eagles 105, 118
East Sussex, England 26
Eastern Michigan University 3
Easy Rider 111
Eat a Peach 118
"Eat It" 167
Edgar Winter's White Trash 118
"Edge of Darkness" 135
Edison, Thomas 90
"Eight Hours" 90
"Eight Miles High" 32, 63, 145
"Eleanor Rigby" 106
Electric Chair 139
Electric Flag 110
Electric Ladyland 112
Electric Light Orchestra 117, 120
Electric Music for the Mind and Body 110
The Electric Prunes 109
Electric Warrior 117
Electronic Arts Studios 96
Electronic Meditation 116
Elegy 117
Eliot, T.S. 151
Ellington, Duke 136, 137
Elliott, Ramblin' Jack 69–73, 77
Elvis Presley I (Oedipus) 138–139
Ely, Geoff 152
Emerson, Keith 115
Emerson, Lake, and Palmer 108, 117, 118, 120
EMI (Electrical & Music Industries, Ltd.) 91

Emmett, Daniel Decatur 89
"The Emperor's New Clothes" 94
"Empty Chairs" 119, 154
Empty Sky 114
"The End" 102
Ennis, Philip 103
"The Entertainer" 91
Entrance 115
environmental activism 72
Eric Burdon Declares War 115
Evans, Mal 142
"Eve of Destruction" 135, 145
"Even a Dog Can Shake Hands" 94, 95
The Everly Brothers 43, 140
Every Good Boy Deserves Favor 117
Everybody Knows This Is Nowhere 114
"Everybody Loves Me Baby" 119
Everybody's in Show-Biz 118
Everything as Nice as Mother Makes It 115
Exile on Main Street 118
experimentation 101, 103–119, 136–146
"Expecting to Fly" 63
Ezekiel (Old Testament book) 67

Fabian 17
Face Dances 143
Fairport Convention 112, 120
Family 113
Fann, James M. 10, 11, 79
Fargo, North Dakota 53
Farther Along 117
The Father, Son, and the Holy Ghost 41–42, 69–72, 77, 84, 85
FCC 145
Felician College 3
Fessenden, Reginald 90
The Fillmore East 40
Fillmore East 117
Fillmore East—June 1971 40
"Fire" 112
Fireball 117
The First Real Target 140
Fish Cheer 65
Fisher, Walter 162–163, 169
Fitzgerald, F. Scott 168
Five Bridges 116

Five Leaves Left 114
The Flamingos 24
"Flash Gordon" 162
Fleetwood Mac 111, 118, 120
Flintstone, Fred 167
Flowers of Evil 117
Fluxus movement 137, 138
The Flying Burrito Brothers 36, 37, 113
"Flying on the Ground Is Wrong" 63
Focus (musical act) 116, 117, 118, 120
Focus III 118
Foghat 118, 120
folk music 27, 30, 33, 34, 35, 62–63, 64, 68–73, 85, 87, 104–105, 106, 107, 110, 112, 113–114, 116, 117, 145, 150–151, 153, 154, 155
Fontana, Wayne and the Mindbenders 105
"For No One" 106
For the Roses 118
"For What It's Worth" 68, 135
Forbidden Planet 143
Foreigner 97
Forever Changes 110
"Fortunate Son" 135
Foster, Stephen 89
FOX television network 10
Foxtrot 118
Fragile 118
Franklin, Aretha 60, 139
Franklin, Benjamin 89
Fraser, Robert 144
Freak Out! 107, 108
Freddie and the Dreamers 105
free form radio 101–103, 104, 105, 108, 109, 110, 114, 118, 119
Free Your Mind ... and Your Ass Will Follow 116
Freed, Alan 24, 57, 58, 59
The Freewheelin' Bob Dylan 27, 28, 60
French and Indian War 88
Fresh Cream 106
"Friend of the Devil" 78
Fripp, Robert 119
From Genesis to Revelation 113
From Nowhere ... The Troggs 106

"Front Line" 135
frontier *see* Turner, Frederick Jackson
Fun House 117
Funkadelic 116, 118, 121
Furay, Richie 106
Futurama 10

Gandhi, Mahatma 142
"Garden Party" 92–93
Gates, David 92
Generation X 3, 161
Genesis 113, 116, 117, 118, 120
Gentle Giant 115, 117, 118, 120
Gerry and the Pacemakers 105
Get Together 110
"Getting Better All the Time" 108
Gibbons, Billy 97
Gilbert, Kevin 95
Gilbert, Ronnie 30
The Gilded Palace of Sin 113
Gimme Shelter 37, 38
Girls with Their Hero 140
"Give It Away" 166
"Give Peace a Chance" 135
Golden Gate Park 36, 66
"Good Day Sunshine" 106
"Good Morning Good Morning" 108
good ol' boys 21–22, 54–55, 58, 80, 82, 155
"Good Vibrations" 107
Goodbye 114
Goodman, Andrew 76, 81, 82, 84
Gorilla 109
Gorsevski, Ellen 7
"Got to Get You into My Life" 106
The Graduate 110–111
Graham, Bill 40
Graham, Billy 42
Grand Funk Railroad 96, 113, 120
Grand Ole Opry 90
The Grand Wazoo 118
The Grass Roots 145
The Grateful Dead (album) 109
The Grateful Dead (musical act) 36–37, 40, 72, 78, 81, 84, 95, 105, 109, 114, 116, 118, 120
"The Grave" 119

The Great Depression 90
The Great Gatsby 168
The Great Grizzly Bear Hunt 118
Green, Peter 111
Green Bay, Wisconsin 16
Green Box 143
Green River 114
Greystone Park Memorial Hospital 71
Gris-Gris 111
"Grizzly Bear" 118
"The Guitar Man" 92
Gulf Coast 9
Gumbo 118
"Gump" 167
Gump, Forrest 167
Guthrie, Arlo 29, 70, 110, 120, 146
Guthrie, Woody 59, 60, 61, 64, 69–73, 77
gymnasium 23, 56–57, 79, 153

H to He 116
Hair: The American Tribal Love-Rock Musical 113, 146
Hal Leonard, Inc. 7
Halbwachs, Maurice 152
Haley, Bill 24, 91
Hall, Vera 69
Hamilton, Richard 137, 143–144
Hammill, Peter 113
Hampton, Lionel 137
Hand Sown ... Home Grown 114
Handel, George F. 90
Hanes, Lee 18, 30
Hanover Gallery 143
"The Happening" 138
"Happiness Is a Warm Gun" 144
"Happy Xmas (War Is Over)" 135
"A Hard Rain's a Gonna Fall" 27, 146
Hardin, Tim 106
Hark! The Village Wait 116
Harlem, New York 137
Harrigan, Ned 89
Harrison, George 93, 105, 106, 108, 111, 115, 117, 121, 142, 166
Harry, Deborah 139
Harvest 118

"Have a Cigar" 93
"Have You Ever Seen the
    Rain" 135
Havens, Richie 105
The Hawks 107
Hawkwind 115–116, 117, 118,
    121
Haworth, Jann 141
Hays, Lee 30, 155
Hayward, Justin 110
"Heart and Soul" 56
Heavy 112
heavy metal 72, 111–112, 116
Hellerman, Fred 30
Hello, Dolly! 104
"Hello Goodbye" 110, 144
"Hello It's Me" 112
Hells Angels 36–38, 67, 81,
    84, 91
"Help, I'm a Rock" 107
helter skelter (carnival ride)
    32
"helter skelter" (phenome-
    non) 84, 153
"Helter Skelter" (song) 32,
    63
Hendrix, Jimi 40, 84, 109,
    110, 112, 115, 116, 117, 121
Henry the Human Fly 118
The Herd 113
"Here, There, and Every-
    where" 106
"Here's Johnny" 166
"Here's to the State of
    Richard Nixon" 135
Herman's Hermits 105
Hey Jude (album) 115
"Hey Jude" (song) 111
high art 136–140, 143, 144
Highway 61 Revisited 107
Hillman, Chris 92
hippies 10, 66, 113
historical inference 4, 50–51
Hockney, David 141
The Hollies 105
Holly, Buddy 10, 11, 15, 16,
    18, 20, 21, 22, 34, 41–42,
    43, 49, 53, 55, 70, 77,
    80–81, 84, 91, 104, 135,
    153, 158, 160
Holy Modal Rounders 105
Holy Trinity 41–42, 70, 151,
    154
Home (Delaney and Bonnie
    album) 113
Home (Procol Harum
    album) 116

Homeless Brother 152, 154
Homer 152
Honky Chateau 118
"Honky Tonk Women" 92
Hopalong Cassidy 71
Hot Rats 115
Hot Rocks 1964–71 118
House Un-American Activi-
    ties Committee 30
Howe, Julia Ward 89
Howe, Steve 117
Hudson River 154
Hudson Valley, New York
    71
Humble Pie 113, 121
Hunky Dory 117
Hunter, Meredith 38, 67,
    81, 83, 84
Hurricane Katrina 9–10, 11,
    12; slogans 9–10
Hyde Park, England 62, 67

"I Ain't Marchin' Anymore"
    135
"I Am the Walrus" 110, 144
I-Feel-Like-I'm-Fixin'-to-Die
    110
"I Feel Like I'm Fixin' to
    Die Rag" 135
*I Got Dem Ol' Kozmic Blues
    Again Mama!* 113
"I Had Too Much to Dream
    (Last Night)" 109
"I Have a Dream" speech
    27
"I Love Rock 'n' Roll" 166
"I Love Rocky Road" 166
"I Want to Tell You" 106
Ian, Janis 110
Ides of March 116, 121
Idlewild South 116
*If You Can Believe Your Eyes
    and Ears* 106
Ike Turner Band 24
Illinois State Armory
    (Springfield, Illinois) 17
"I'm Only Sleeping" 106
"Imagine" 145
imagined community 157–
    162, 164, 166, 169
In-A-Gadda-Da-Vida 113
In and Out of Focus 116
In Search of Space 117
In Search of the Lost Chord
    112
*In the Court of the Crimson
    King* 113

In the Wake of Poseidon 116
Incredible Broadside Brass
    Bed Band 118, 121
Incredible String Band 106
Indelibly Stamped 117
the Independent Group 143
"The Inferno" 61
The Inner Mounting Flame
    117
Institute of Contemporary
    Art 143
interdisciplinarity 4, 12
International Marxist Group
    61
interracial marriage 20
"Interstellar Overdrive" 108
intertextuality 10–11, 157–
    169
*Introducing the Beatles: En-
    gland's No. 1 Vocal Group*
    58
Iron Butterfly 112, 113, 121
Iron Maiden 135
Islands 117
"It Better End Soon" 135
It's a Beautiful Day (album)
    113
It's a Beautiful Day (band)
    113, 121
"It's a Long Way to the Top"
    93
It's Not Killing Me 113
"I've Been Working on the
    Railroad" 90

J. Geils Band 116, 118, 121
Jack Flash 35
Jackie 139
Jackson, Jesse 29
Jackson, Michael 166, 167
Jagger, Mick 37–38, 39, 61,
    66–67, 80, 91, 107, 136,
    139, 144
Jan and Dean 145
jazz 111, 136–137
Jazz Musician 137
jazz rock 111, 113, 115, 116
Jeff Beck Group 118
Jefferson Airplane 36, 37,
    40, 105, 106, 110, 112, 114,
    118, 121, 145
Jefferson Airplane Takes Off
    106
Jennings, Waylon 16, 53
The Jester 15, 18, 27, 28,
    33, 43, 59, 60–61, 64, 85,
    91, 154

Jesus Christ Superstar 117
Jesus the Christ 32, 61, 66, 142
Jethro Tull 111, 115, 116, 117, 118, 121
Jett, Joan and the Black-hearts 166
Joe Cocker 118
Joel, Billy 91, 92, 97
John, Elton 114, 116, 118, 120
John Barleycorn Must Die 117
John Lennon and the Plastic Ono Band 115
John Wesley Harding 110
Johns, Jasper 137, 140
Johnson, Lyndon 29
Johnson, Ray 137–139, 143
Johnson, Robert 38
Jones, Brian 26, 28
Joplin, Janis 10, 39, 68, 84, 110, 113, 117, 118, 121
Joplin, Scott 136
Jordan, Louis 57
Judas the Iscariot 66
Judeo-Christian tradition 50, 60–61, 66, 67, 70, 155
"Juke Box Hero" 97
"Jumpin' Jack Flash" 35, 37, 62, 66
Just Another Band from LA 118
Just What Is It That Makes Today's Homes So Differ-ent, So Appealing? 143

KAAY 102
Kaprow, Allan 138
Kasem, Casey 18
Kaufman, Murray *see* Murray the K and the Swingin' Soiree
Keith, Toby 89
Kennedy, Jacqueline 27, 91, 139
Kennedy, Joe 42
Kennedy, John 27, 29, 35, 42, 70, 77, 80, 84, 91, 135, 154
Kennedy, Robert 42, 70, 77, 135, 154
Key, Francis Scott 89
Kick Out the Jams 113
Killen, Edgar Ray 82
Killer 117
The King (reference in "American Pie") 15, 27–28, 33, 43, 59–61, 91

King, B.B. 60, 84
King, Carole 117, 118, 121
King, Coretta Scott 27
King, Martin Luther, Jr. 27, 28, 42, 70, 77, 84, 135, 154
King and Queen Pub 59–60
King Crimson 113, 115, 116, 117, 119, 121
The King of the Moondog-gies *see* Freed, Alan
Kingston Trio 62, 104
The Kinks 105, 112, 114, 116, 118, 121, 145, 166
Kitaj, R.B. 141
Kitts, Tom 7
KLOS 102
KMPX 102
The Knack 166
The Knickerbockers 105
Kooper, Al 111, 112
Kraftwerk 116, 121
Krautrock 113, 116
Ku Klux Klan 81–82

L.A. Woman 118
labor movement 51, 61
La Capra, Dominick 152, 153
Ladd, Jim 102
Ladies of the Canyon 116
Lake, Greg 115
Lambert, Louis 89
Landmark Hotel 39
"The Last DJ" 102
Last Exit 114
Last Time Around 112
Laws, G. Malcom 90
Layla and Other Assorted Love Songs 115
Leary, Timothy 29, 112
The Least We Can Do Is Wave to Each Other 116
Led Zeppelin 72, 113, 114, 116, 117, 121
Led Zeppelin II 115
Led Zeppelin III 116
Led Zeppelin IV 117
Ledbetter, Huddie "Lead Belly" 69, 72
Lee, Arthur 106
"The Legend of the U.S.S. *Titanic*" 114
Lengel, Lara Martin 7
Lenin, Vladimir Ilyich 29
Lennon, John 29–30, 39,

61–62, 91, 93, 106, 111, 114, 115, 118, 121, 135, 139, 142, 144, 145
Let It Be 115
Let It Bleed 26, 114
Letters from a Pennsylvania Farmer 89
levee 9, 10, 12, 21, 54, 55, 81–82, 83, 85, 151; mean-ing of 21, 54, 76, 78–80
Levee bar *see* Beechmont Tavern
Levine, Lawrence 87, 97
Levitt, Saul 11, 78–79, 84
Lexington, Massachusetts 89
"The Liberty Song" 89
Lichtenstein, Roy 139–140
Life magazine 65
"Life's Been Good" 96
"Light My Fire" 102, 109, 145
Lightfoot, Gordon 106
"Like a Rolling Stone" 59, 107
Lincoln, Abraham 84
Lindisfarne 116
Lipsitz, George 10, 11
Little Richard 24, 57
Little Rock, Arkansas 51, 102
Little Rock Nine 51
Live at Fillmore East 40
Live at Leeds 2 143
Live/Dead 114
"Live" Full House 118
Live Johnny Winter And 117
Live Peace in Toronto 114
Liverpool, England 143
Lizard 116
Lodge, John 110
"Lola" 166
Lola versus Powerman 116
Lomax, John (historian) 7
Lomax, John (musicologist) 69
London, England 59–60, 61, 141, 143, 144
The London Festival Or-chestra 110
"Lonely Teenager" 58
Long Island, New York 82
Long Island Sound 55
Long John Silver 118
Look at Yourself 117
"Look What They've Done to My Song Ma" 92

Los Angeles, California 39, 42, 43, 63, 84, 102, 137, 141
Lost in Space 35
Love (musical act) 106, 110, 121
"Love in Vain" 38
"Love Me Do" 105
"Lovely Rita" 108
The Lovin' Spoonful 56, 84, 105, 115
low art 136, 139
Low Spark of High Heeled Boys 118
Lubbock, Texas 20, 42
Lucas, George 161, 162
"Lucy in the Sky with Diamonds" 108
"Lump" 167
Lumpy Gravy 113
Luther, Martin 61
Lymon, Frankie 24–25
Lynn, Loretta 135
Lynyrd Skynyrd 93

MacDermot, Galt 146
Machine Head 118
Mad Dogs and Englishmen 116
Mad Meg see *Dulle Griet*
Madison Square Garden 92
Madman Across the Water 118
Madonna 10, 101
Maggot Brain 118
Magic Dick 116
Magical Mystery Tour 64, 110, 111
The Magician's Birthday 118
Maharishi Mahesh Yogi 96, 112
Mahavishnu Orchestra 117, 121
Mail Art 137, 138
Malcolm X 42
The Mamas and the Papas (album) 106
The Mamas and the Papas (musical act) 106
The Man Who Sold the World 116
Manassas 118
Mancini, Henry 104
Manet, Edouard 140
Manfred Mann's Earth Band 118
Mann, Manfred 105, 118, 121

Manson, Charles 31–32, 63
The Marching Band 15, 33–34, 64–65
Marilyn Monroe 139
Martin, George 106, 108
Marx, Karl 30, 61–62, 91
Mary Poppins 104
Mason, Dave 112
Mason City (Iowa) Municipal Airport 17, 53
Master of Reality 117
"Masters of War" 27
Matisse, Henri 136
Matthew (New Testament book) 61
Matthew and Son 110
Mauldin, Joe B. 42–43
Mayall, John 105
Maybe Tomorrow 114
Mayer, Roger 109
MCA Records 91
McCarthy, Harry 89
McCarthyism 30
McCartney 115
McCartney, Paul 32, 62, 65, 106, 107, 115, 117, 121, 141–143, 144, 145
McDonald, Joe see Country Joe and the Fish
McDowell, Julie 7
The MC5's 113, 121
McGuinn, Roger 32, 92
McGuire, Barry 135, 145
McHale, John 143
McLean, Don: birth 18, 19; childhood 18, 19, 20, 21, 53, 80, 82; comments on "American Pie" 15, 17, 18, 27, 36, 44, 49, 76, 78, 80, 135
McMahon, Ed 166
Meddle 117
Melanie see Safka, Melanie
Mellotron 103, 109, 110, 115
Melton, Barry 64
Memphis Slim 69, 84
Men Without Hats 166
"Mercedes Benz" 39
Mercer, William "Rosko" 102
Metallica 88
metaphor 15, 33, 42, 54, 59, 66, 72, 139, 158
Meyer, Leonard 153
"Mickey" 166
Miles, Buddy 112
Miller, Larry 102

The Mindbenders see Fontana, Wayne and the Mindbenders
Miss American Pie 21, 54, 151, 154, 155
Mississippi Burning 80
Mr. Fantasy 109
"Mr. Tambourine Man" 146
Mitchell, Joni 112, 116, 118, 121
Mitchell, Mitch 109
Moby Grape 109
Moffett, Charles 50
Mona Bone Jakon 117
Mondrian, Piet 136
"Money for Nothing" 166
The Monkees 108, 109
The Monotones 22–23, 55, 158
Monroe, Marilyn 138, 139, 143
Monster Movie 113
Montgomery, Alabama 51
Montgomery Bus Boycott 51
The Moody Blues 105, 110, 112, 113, 115, 116, 117, 118, 121, 135
Moog synthesizer 103
Moondance 116
Moondog Coronation Ball 24
Moore, Wild Bill 136
Moorhead, Minnesota 16, 17
Morgan, J.P. 90
Morrison, Van 109, 116, 118, 121
Morrison Hotel 116
Morrow, Bruce 57
Morton, Jelly Roll 69, 84
The Mothers of Invention 107, 110, 113, 115, 116, 117, 118, 122
Motherwell, Robert 137
motico 138–139
Motown 57
Mott the Hoople (album) 113
Mott the Hoople (musical act) 113, 117, 118, 121
Mountain 116, 117, 121
Moving Waves 117
Mozart, Wolfgang 87, 92
MTV 94
Mud Slide Slim and the Blue Horizon 117
Mulholland Drive 94
"The Mulligan Guard" 89

Muni, Scott 102
Municipal Broadcast Company WNYC Studio B Mural 136
Murray the K and the Swingin' Soiree 57
music: as business 87–88, 90–98, 100, 119, 141; as history 87–88, 97–98, 152; importance of 1, 53, 54, 56, 85, 88; recording 90; and religion 23; and technology 103, 105
Music from Big Pink 111
Music from Peter Gunn 104
Music of My Mind 118
musicology 69, 101, 103–104, 119
Muswell Hillbillies 118
"My Bologna" 166
My Fair Lady 104
"My Sharona" 166
myth 152–153, 157, 159–162, 164, 169

Nantucket Sleighride 117
narrative fidelity 163–167, 169
narrative paradigm 162–169
narrative probability 163, 167–169
Nazz (album) 112
Nazz (musical act) 112, 115
NBC radio network 90
NBC television network 11
Neer, Richard 102
Neil Young 111
Nelson, Rick 42, 92–93, 140
Neshoba County, Mississippi 5, 81
Neshoba Democrat 81
New Kids on the Block 166
New Morning 116
New Orleans, Louisiana 9, 21, 111
New Rochelle, New York 18, 20, 21, 55, 78, 79, 80, 82, 154
The New Seekers 92
New York Correspondence School 138
New York, New York 24, 31, 40, 55, 57, 62, 71, 72, 82, 90, 102, 136, 137–138, 146
New York Times 82
Newman, Randy 111

Newport Folk Festival 61, 107
Newport Jazz Festival 28
Newsday 82
The Nice 108, 112, 115, 116, 117, 121
Nicely Out of Tune 116
Nickelback 5, 97
Nicks, Stevie 166
"Nights in White Satin" 110
Nirvana 166
Nixon, Richard 42
Nolan, Tom 152
Noland, Kenneth 140
Nora, Pierre 152, 153
"Norwegian Wood" 105
nostalgia 93, 114, 144, 150–152, 154–155, 157–162, 164–165, 168, 169
"Nothings" 138
The Notorious Byrd Brothers 112
Nursery Crime 117

Oasis 143
O'Brien, Paul 80
Obscured by the Clouds 118
Ochs, Phil 105, 135
Octopus 118
The Office 10, 11, 12
"Oh! Susanna" 89
Ohio Northern University 1, 4, 7
Olen Barrage's Old Jolly Farm 81, 82, 84
O'List, David 112
Omaha, Nebraska 96
"Ombra Mai Fu" 90
On the Balcony 140
On the Threshold of a Dream 115
On Time 113
On Tour with Eric Clapton 115
"one hit wonder" 92
One Man Dog 118
Ono, Yoko 93, 111, 144
Ontario Police Department 143
opera houses 90
Oswald, Lee Harvey 29
"Our Father, Thou in Heaven Above" 61
Outlaw Motorcycle Gang 67

Page, Jimmy 111, 114
"Paint It Black" 107

Palmer, Carl 115
pantheism 49, 50, 56, 71
paperboy 18, 19, 20, 53, 79
Pappalardi, Felix 116
Paranoid 116
Parker, "Colonel" Tom 60
Parks, Ross 51
Parliament 116, 121
parody 3, 6, 93, 94, 95, 140, 157, 160, 162, 164, 166–167, 169
Parsley, Sage, Rosemary, and Thyme 107
Passaro, Alan 38
"Paul Is Dead" 62, 63, 65, 142–143
Pawn Hearts 117
Paxton, Tom 105
"Peace Train" 135
Pearl 117, 118
Pelham, New York 82
Pendulum 116
"Penny Lane" 110
Pentangle 112, 121, 143
People's Songs 61
Pet Sounds 107
Peter and Gordon 105
Peter, Paul, and Mary 105, 145
Peterson, Roger 17, 53
Petty, Tom 102, 166
Phallus Dei 113
Phil Spector's Gold Star Studios 43
Philadelphia, Mississippi 81, 84, 85
Phillips Collection 50
Phúc, Phan Thi Kim 41
Pickin' Up the Pieces 113
pickup truck 25, 58, 82, 153
Pictures at an Exhibition 117
"Pictures of Matchstick Men" 111
Picturesque Matchstickable Messages from the Status Quo 111
Pinder, Michael 110
The Pinder of Wakefield 28
pink carnation 25, 82, 153
Pink Floyd 93, 108, 112, 115, 116, 117, 118, 119
Pink Moon 118
Piper at the Gates of Dawn 108
Playboy magazine 141
Playboy Mansion 97

"Please, Please Me/Ask Me Why" 58
Please to See the King 117
Plessy v. Ferguson 51
Poco 113
Polka Party! 166
Pop Art 6, 136–144
Pop Goes the Easel 141
Popular Culture Association/American Culture Association 3, 7
post-punk revisionism 101
"Power to the People" 145
Powerhouse 109
pregnancy 20, 53
The Presidents of the United States 167
Presley, Elvis 28, 60, 91, 103, 104, 135, 137, 138–139, 140, 143
"Pressed Rat and Warthog" 112
Pretties for You 113
The Pretty Things 105
Prince 139
Prine, John 117
Procol Harum 108–109, 112, 115, 116, 117, 121
progressive rock 104, 107, 108, 109, 110, 111, 112, 113, 114, 115, 116, 117
"Psalm 137" 18, 30
psychedelic music 54–55, 59, 64, 66, 105, 106, 107, 108, 109, 110, 111, 112, 114
Puerto Rico 20
"Puff the Magic Dragon" 145

Queen (musical act) 166
The Queen (reference in "American Pie") 27–28, 43, 59–60, 91
Queen Elizabeth II 28
Queens, New York 56
"Question" 135
A Question of Balance 116
Quicksilver Messenger Service 112, 121
"Quinn the Eskimo" 146

racial consciousness 83–84
racism 24, 25, 32, 51, 63, 81–82, 84
radio, development of 90, 102–103, 119
Rado, James 146

Ragni, Gerome 146
The Raiders *see* Revere, Paul and the Raiders
Rainbow Bridge 117
Ram 117
Rebel Without a Cause 27, 60
Rebennack, Mac *see* Dr. John
record store 40, 68, 94, 108
Red Hot Chili Peppers 166
"Red Mole" 61–62
Redding, Noel 109
Reed, Lou 118, 121
regeneration through violence 162
religion 23, 49, 50, 56, 60–61, 66, 67, 70
Remember the Wind and the Rain 114
Renbourn, John 112
Report from Rockport 136
"The Return of the Son of Monster Magnet" 107
Revere, Paul, and the Raiders 105
"Revolution" 62, 145
"Revolution 9" 144
Revolver 106
rhyming 21, 32, 151, 163–164, 167
rhythm and blues 23–24, 25, 54, 57, 64, 78
Richards, Keith 107
Richardson, J.P. 15–16, 18, 20, 21, 34, 41–42, 43, 53, 70, 77, 80–81, 84, 91, 104, 135
"Ricky" 166
Rio Grande Mud 118
The Rise and Fall of Ziggy Stardust and the Spiders from Mars 118
Rivers, Larry 137
Riverside Ballroom (Green Bay, Wisconsin) 16
Roadwork 118
robber barons 90
Robbins, Marty 25, 57–58, 84
Rock and Roll Hall of Fame 24
Rock and Roll Is Here to Stay (album) 114
"Rock and Roll Is Here to Stay" (song) 58
"Rock Around the Clock" 91

Rock Band (video game) 96
rock 'n' roll: direction 21, 22, 23, 28, 33–34, 40, 41, 51, 52, 54–55, 57, 58–59, 62, 64–69, 72–73, 78, 82–85, 91–92, 95, 97–98, 101, 103–119, 158–160, 167, 169; origin of phrase 25, 57, 136
"Rocket 88" 24
"Rockstar" 5, 97
"Rocky Mountain High" 145
Rogers, Kenny 135
Rogers, Roy 71
Rolling Stone (magazine) 38, 95–96, 152
The Rolling Stones 26, 35, 36–38, 59, 62, 65, 66, 81, 84, 92, 93, 104, 105, 107, 110, 112–113, 114, 117, 118, 121, 136, 145, 158
romance 11, 52, 54, 56, 58, 64, 68–69, 79, 145
"Rondo" 108
Ronstadt, Linda 110, 114, 116
Rotten, Johnny 119
Rough and Ready 117
Roxy Music 118, 121
Royal Canadian Mounted Police 64–65
Rubber Soul 105, 106
"Ruby Don't Take Your Love to Town" 135
Rundgren, Todd 112, 115, 118, 121
"Running Gun Blues" 135
Runt 115
Rush, Tom 105
rye 21–22, 55, 78, 79, 82, 151, 155
Rye, New York 21, 22, 43, 55, 78

Sabine Pass, Texas 42
Sadler, Barry 84
Safe as Milk 110
"The Safety Dance" 166
Safka, Melanie 92, 112, 116, 121
"The Saga Begins" 3, 6, 7, 10, 157, 160–169
Sahm, Doug 106
Saint Dominic's Preview 118
St. Louis, Missouri 3, 4, 7
Saint Remy, France 50
Salisbury 117

A Salty Dog 115
Sanders, Craig 91, 92
San Francisco, California 37, 62, 66, 102, 142
Santana 36, 113, 115, 116, 117, 118, 121
Santana III 118
Santiago, Maria Elena *see* widowed bride
Sargasso Sea 162
Satan 18, 36, 37–38, 67, 91
A Saucerful of Secrets 112
Savannah College of Art & Design 7
Savoy Ballroom 137
Schon, Neil 118
School's Out 118
Schuck, Mary Ann 8
Schuck, Rich 7
Schwartz, Jonathan 102
Schwerner, Michael 76, 80, 81, 82, 84
Sears Point raceway 36
Seattle, Washington 94
Sebastian, John B. 115
Second Winter 114
Seeger, Pete 30, 42, 59, 61, 69–73, 77
Seger, Bob 95
Self Portrait 116
Self Portrait with Badges 141
Sentimental Journey 115
September 11, 2001, attacks 89
Sgt. Pepper's Lonely Hearts Club Band 33, 64, 103–104, 105, 107, 108, 113, 141–143, 144
The Seven Year Itch 143
Seventh Sojourn 118
The Sex Pistols 119
sexism 51
sexual revolution 96, 103
Sha Na Na 114
Shades of Deep Purple 112
The Shadows *see* Vee, Bobby and the Shadows
Shake Down 109
"Shake, Rattle and Roll" 24, 60
Shakespeare, William 66–67
The Shaming of the True 95
"She Said She Said" 106
Shea Stadium 62
sheet music 90

"She's Got It" 57
"She's Leaving Home" 108, 142
Shi Huangdi 87
Shi Jing (Book of Songs) 87
Shine On Brightly 112
Shore, Dinah 79
Shotton, Pete 142, 144
Silk Purse 116
Silverstein, Shel 95
Simon, Carly 117, 121
Simon and Garfunkel 105, 107, 110–111, 113, 115, 121
"A Simple Song of Freedom" 145
Sinatra, Frank 104
"Singin' in Viet Nam Talkin' Blues" 135
singing cowboy 71
Siriol, She-Devil of Naked Madness 140
Sister Fatima 119, 155
"Sitting on Top of the World" 112
"Skull and Roses" 118
Slick, Grace 106, 110
The Slider 118
Sly and the Family Stone 110, 114, 118, 121
Small Faces 113
"Smells Like Nirvana" 166
"Smells Like Teen Spirit" 166
Smile 110
Smiley Smile 110
Smith, Captain John 88
Smith, Ronnie 17
Snider, Todd 94
Snow White and the Seven Dwarfs 143
"So You Want to Be a Rock 'n' Roll Star" 92
sock hop 23, 57, 144
Soft Machine 111, 121
Soft Parade 114
Some Time in New York City 118
Something/Anything? 118
"A Song for Woody" 61
Song to a Seagull 112
Songs of Leonard Cohen 110
Sontag, Susan 140
The Sound of Music 104, 106, 108
Sounds of Silence 107
Soundtrack for the Film More 115

Southeastern Louisiana University 3, 4
A Space in Time 117
Space Oddity 109, 115
space race 35
Spirit 116, 121
Springfield, Dusty 105
Springfield, Illinois 17
Stage Fright 116
"Stairway to Heaven" 117
Stand 114
Stand Up 115
Standish, Miles 88
Stanley Road 143
"The Star Spangled Banner" 89
Star Wars 3, 6, 157, 160–162, 164–166, 169
Star Wars Episode I: The Phantom Menace 6, 10, 160–161, 163–169
Star Wars Episode IV: A New Hope 161–162
Starr, Ringo 107, 115, 142
The Starry Night 50
Status Quo 111
Steele, Alison 102
Steeleye Span 116, 117, 118, 121
Steely Dan 118, 121
Stephen Stills 2 117
Steppenwolf 72, 111, 121, 135
Stevens, Cat 110, 117, 118, 121, 135
Stevens, Ray 94
Sticky Fingers 117, 136, 139
Stills, Stephen 106, 115, 117, 118, 122
Stone, Sly *see* Sly and the Family Stone
The Stone Poneys (album) 110
The Stone Poneys (musical act) 110
The Stooges 113, 117, 122
"Stop Draggin' My Car Around" 166
"Stop Draggin' My Heart Around" 166
Stop the Clocks 143
The Straight Dope 18
"Strawberry Fields Forever" 110
"Stray Cat Blues" 38
"Street Fighting Man" 145
Sugarloaf 93
Sullivan, Niki 42–43

"Summer in the City" 84
The Summer of Love 35, 39
"The Sun Is Shining" 38
Sunset Sound Studios 39
Sunset Strip riot 68
Supertramp 116, 117, 122
The Supremes 138
Surf Ballroom (Clear Lake, Iowa) 16, 17, 53
Surrealistic Pillow 110
"Suspicious Minds" 28
Sweet Baby James 116
Sweet Child 143
Sweetheart of the Rodeo 112
Swing Landscape 136
swing music 57
Swinging London 144
"Sympathy for the Devil" 37, 62, 67

T. Rex see Tyrannosaurus Rex
"Talkin' Seattle Grunge Rock Blues" 94, 95
Talking Book 118
Tangerine Dream 116, 117, 122
Tapestry (Carole King album) 117, 118
Tapestry (Don McLean album) 18, 115, 117, 154
Tarkus 117
Tate Gallery 140
Tate-LaBianca murders 31–32, 63
"Taxman" 106
Taylor, James 116, 117, 118, 122
Taylor, Karen 7
"T.B. Sheets" 109
Tea for the Tillerman 117
Teaser and the Firecat 117, 118
"A Teenager in Love" 139
The Teenagers 24–25
Temple, Shirley 138
The Temptations 108
The Temptations' Greatest Hits 108
Ten Man Mop 117
Ten Years After 109, 117, 122
tercet 151
tessarae 138
That '70s Show 10–11
"That'll Be the Day" 22, 42, 55, 80, 158

Their Satanic Majesties Request 110
Them 109
There's a Riot Going On 118
They Only Come Out at Night 118
Thick as a Brick 118
Thin Lizzy 88
This Is Spinal Tap 95
This Is Tomorrow 143
"This Land Is Your Land" 72
This Was 111
Thomas, David Clayton 111
Thompson, Richard 112, 118
Thoreau, Henry David 49–50
The Thoughts of Emerlist Davjack 108
Three Friends 118
The Tijuana Brass see Alpert, Herb and the Tijuana Brass
Till, Emmett 51
"Till Tomorrow" 119
Time (magazine) 81
The Times They Are A-Changin' 61
Tin Pan Alley 90
To Our Children's Children's Children 115
Tommy 114, 145–146
"Tomorrow Never Knows" 107
The Tonight Show 166
Toulouse Street 118
touring 95–97
Townshend, Pete 114, 142, 146
Townshend Acts 89
Traffic 109, 113, 114, 117, 118, 122
Trang Bang 41
transcendentalism 49, 50
"Travelin' Man" 92
Trespass 116
Trilogy 118
The Trip 110
The Troggs 106
Troops Out movement 61–62
Trout Mask Replica 114
"Truckin'" 95
Truth 111
Tumbleweed Connection 116
Tupelo Honey 118
"Turn the Page" 95

Turner, Big Joe 24, 60
Turner, Frederick Jackson 162; "Frontier Thesis" 162, 169
Turner, Ike 24
The Turtles 105
Twelve Dreams of Dr. Sardonicus 116
200 Motels 118
Twombly, Cy 138
Tyrannosaurus Rex 112, 117, 118, 122

U2 166
UHF 166
Ummagumma 115
Uncle Meat 115
"Under My Thumb" 38, 107
"Under the Bridge" 166
Unfinished Music No. 1: Two Virgins 111
United Artists Records 15, 100, 101
University of Alaska 7
Uriah Heep 116, 117, 118, 122

Valens, Ritchie 10, 15, 16, 17, 18, 20, 21, 34, 41–42, 43, 53, 70, 77, 80–81, 84, 91, 104, 135
Vancouver, British Columbia 64
Van der Graaf Generator 113, 116, 117, 122
Van Gogh, Vincent 50, 119, 155
Vanilla Fudge 109, 122
Van Vliet, Don see Captain Beefheart
van Zandt, Steven 102
Varèse, Edgard 107
Vassoir, Jeanne 107
Vee, Bobby 43; and the Shadows 17
Vehicle 116
Velvet Underground 109, 122, 139
The Velvet Underground and Nico 109
Verve Records 108
Very 'eavy ... Very 'umble 116
VH1 94
Victory Boogie Woogie 136
Vietnam War 40–41, 52, 135, 138, 145, 146, 154, 155

Village Green Preservation Society 112
Vincebus Eruptum 112
"Vincent" 50, 119, 155
Voelcker, John 143
Volunteers 114

WABC 24, 57
Waka/Jawaka 118
Wakeman, Rick 115, 118
Walden Pond 49–50
Walsh, Joe 96
War (musical act) 115, 118, 120, 122
Warhol, Andy 109, 136, 137, 139
Warren Commission 29
Washington, George 88
Washington, D.C. 27, 50, 91
Washington Post 50
Waters, Muddy 69, 84
Watts Riots 63, 84
"We Shall Overcome" 145
Weasels Ripped My Flesh 116
The Weavers 18, 30–31, 62, 71, 155
Weir, Monica 7
"Weird Al" Yankovic 166
"Weird Al" Yankovic in 3-D 166
Weldon, Rebecca A. 7
"A Well Respected Man" 145
Weller, Paul 143
"We're an American Band" 96
"We're Gonna Rock, We're Gonna Roll" 136
We're Only in It for the Money 113
West, Leslie 116
West Side Story 104
Westerns 162
Wheeler, Daniel 137
Wheels of Fire 112
"When I'm Sixty-Four" 104, 108
"When Johnny Comes Marching Home" 89
"Where Are You Now My Son" 135

Whipped Cream & Other Delights 105
whiskey 21, 22, 43, 55, 78, 79, 82, 151, 155
"Whiskey in the Jar" 88
"White Album" 31, 63, 84, 112, 143, 144
"White Rabbit" 145
"White Room" 112
"A White Sport Coat (and a Pink Carnation)" 25, 58
Whitechapel Art Gallery 143
"Whiter Shade of Pale" 109
The Who 32, 105, 114, 117, 122, 143, 145–146
Who Am the Only One 116
"Who Are the Brain Police?" 107
"Who's Johnny" 166
Who's Next 117
"Why Do Fools Fall in Love" 25
widowed bride 20, 53
Wild Life 117
Wild Thing 106
Wildlife 117
Williamson, Sonny Boy 57
Willy and the Poor Boys 114
Wilson, Brian 107, 110
Wilson, Ellen 7
Wilson, Tom 109
Winds of Change 110
Wings 117, 121
WINS 57
Winter, Edgar 115, 118, 122
Winter, Jay 152
Winter, Johnny 114, 117, 122
Winter Dance Party 16, 17, 19, 20, 23, 53
"Winterwood" 119, 155
Winwood, Steve 109, 112, 114
Wishbone Ash 116, 122
With a Little Help from My Friends (album) 113
"With a Little Help from My Friends" (song) 108, 145
"Within You Without You" 108

The Wizard of Oz 143
WJW 24, 57
WMCA 57
WMGM 57
WNEW 102
Wohlin, Anna 26
Wolf City 118
Wonder, Stevie 118, 135
Wonderwall Music 111
Wood, Chris 112
Woodstock 35, 36, 38–39, 65–66, 81, 109, 114, 152, 154
Woody Guthrie's Blues 71
"Workin' for the MCA" 93
Workingman's Dead 116
The World Is a Ghetto 118
World War II 51, 90

"Yankee Doodle Dandy" 88
Yankovic, "Weird Al" 3, 6, 7, 10, 157–158, 160–169
The Yardbirds 105, 114
Yellow Submarine (film) 114
"Yellow Submarine" (song) 107
Yes (album) 113
Yes (musical act) 113, 115, 117–118, 122
The Yes Album 117
"Yoda" 166
Young, Jesse Colin 110
Young, Neil 106, 111, 114, 117, 118, 122
Young Contemporaries exhibition 141
The Young Rascals 106
The Youngbloods (album) 110
The Youngbloods (musical act) 110
youth culture 90

Zappa, Frank 40, 72, 107–108, 110, 113, 115, 116, 117, 118, 122
Zevon, Warren 94
The Zombies 105
ZZ Top 97, 117, 118, 122
ZZ Top's First Album 117